CYCLES OF CONFLICT, CENTURIES OF CHANGE

Edited by ELISA SERVÍN, LETICIA REINA, & JOHN TUTINO

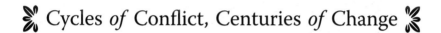 Cycles *of* Conflict, Centuries *of* Change

CRISIS, REFORM, AND REVOLUTION IN MEXICO

Duke University Press   Durham & London   2007

© 2007 Duke University Press

All rights reserved

Printed in the United States of America on acid-free paper ∞

Designed by C. H. Westmoreland

Typeset in Warnock by Keystone Typesetting, Inc.

Library of Congress Cataloging-in-Publication Data appear

on the last printed page of this book.

CONTENTS ❧

❧ Preface

Debating History to Face the Present and Imagine the Future

JOHN TUTINO ❧

This volume began with a challenge. Leticia Reina and Elisa Servín invited me to lunch, an idea, and a proposal. At the end of the eighteenth century and again at the end of the nineteenth century, Mexicans faced periods of economic boom and state-led reform. Each of those times of boom and change was celebrated, the first as enlightened, the second as liberal—the prevailing definitions of progress. Yet each of those eras of progress led to deep civil conflicts: the wars for independence, beginning in 1810, and the revolution that began in 1910. Now—it was 1998—Mexicans faced another time of celebrated progress promoted by a reforming state. This time it was globalization sanctioned by neoliberalism. And once again, amid times of boom and bust, crisis and reform, Mexicans faced deepening inequalities and political uncertainties. Could a new round of civil conflict follow? Could it possibly begin in 2010?

Elisa and Leticia invited me to join a group of scholars from Mexico, Europe, and the United States, historians and others whose works had engaged Mexico over the long term. Each would be challenged to write an essay exploring a key aspect of Mexico's history of crises, reforms, and revolutions. The goal was to probe the developments that led to the conflicts of 1810 and 1910—and to think historically about the present and the century soon to begin. There would be no search for a single approach, no pressure for a common analysis. Each participant would aim to illuminate the larger questions as she or he saw fit. The group would meet to discuss and debate understandings that would inevitably differ. The goal was a book.

The key to the project—and this volume—is the participants. The original group gathered in July 1999 at the Center for Historical Studies of the National Institute of Anthropology and History in Mexico City. Friedrich Katz, Enrique Semo, Alan Knight, François-Xavier Guerra, Antonio Annino, and I joined Leticia and Elisa. All had published key studies of Mexico's history. All were known for taking on big problems, the long term—or both. Each presented a preliminary paper. The resulting discussions focused on diverse, sometimes divergent, ways of understanding Mexico's two great revolutions. They generated the most challenging engagements I have experienced as a historian. Never have I learned so much in a few days.

At the end of the first sessions, we reached two conclusions: we needed to meet again with revised essays for continuing discussions, and we should invite new participants to address key questions none of us had explored in depth. Invitations went to Eric Van Young to bring us strength on popular communities in the eighteenth-century crisis; to Lorenzo Meyer to examine liberalism and neoliberalism, seeking continuities and changes between the late nineteenth century and the late twentieth; and to Guillermo de la Peña to analyze popular mobilizations in the late twentieth century. Our analyses and this volume are stronger for their participation.

The group gathered for a second time in June 2000 at Georgetown University. Again there were days of engagement, debate, and learning. At the end, we offered a first public presentation of our studies at a symposium hosted by the Mexican Cultural Institute in Washington, D.C. Two points became clear: we were struggling with issues of wide interest, and the debates among the participants were modest compared to the reactions of some in our audience. Placing the uncertainties of Mexico's present in the context of its conflictive past raised issues discomforting to some—and debated by all.

All the more reason, the group concluded, to push our essays to completion and to publish a volume of challenge and debate. The first result was an edition in Spanish, *Crisis, reforma y revolución: México, historias de fin de siglo*, edited by Leticia Reina and Elisa Servín, and published by Editorial Taurus and the Instituto Nacional de Antropología e Historia in 2002. That book is already provoking continuing discussions.

We also sought an English edition—addressed to the students, scholars, and politically aware others who know the importance of Mexico to the United States and the wider world. Working with Valerie Millholland of Duke University Press brought the participation of scholarly reviewers. They probed our debates and suggested ways to sharpen our analyses and strengthen our presentation. Most of the essays are revised and expanded, thanks to the reviewers' suggestions and our own continuing analyses.

(Sadly, François-Xavier Guerra passed away in the fall of 2002, as the Mexican version went to press. The loss to those who knew him—and to Mexican history—is immense. His essay is translated, but not revised—a testament to a scholar who among us, as always, was a formidable thinker.)

We offer this volume, expanded, reorganized, and revised, as *Cycles of Conflict, Centuries of Change*. It is an invitation to join and continue our discussions and debates, to ask how explorations of a long history of conflict and change can illuminate an uncertain present—and an unknown future. We aim to bring history to bear on the present in three linked ways. We begin with communities, because they have been constant, important, and too-often-ignored participants in Mexico's history, and because when Mexican political contests became revolutions, popular communities mobilized to make them revolutionary. We turn to revolutions because they marked the pivotal transformations that made Mexico a nation in 1810 and 1910. Too often, those decades of conflict have been hailed as utopian or condemned as destructive. Our essays see those conflagrations as simultaneously destructive and creative, at once arising from the popular and leading to new concentrations of power. We conclude with studies of the history of the second half of the twentieth century—histories of ideology, of popular mobilizations, and of political conflicts and accommodations. It is time to accelerate serious historical analysis of the regime, society, and culture once credited with generating the "Mexican Miracle," and recently condemned as the cause of the crisis that led to Mexico's current and uncertain democratic transition.

Our essays were generated during the Mexican presidential election season of 2000, celebrated by many as the key transition to democracy. The authors most focused on contemporary politics have added a few lines to note recent events. Enrique Semo addresses the election season of 2006, succinctly, from the perspective of the Left. Elisa Servín suggests that the uncertainties of Mexico's transition to democracy persist. Alan Knight offers his views of a changing yet enduring political landscape in a postscript. The election of 2006, the challenges to its legitimacy, and the absence of anything like a revolutionary mobilization combine to suggest that the questions we explore and debate remain open and important.

We offer this volume knowing that what happens in Mexico is pivotally and increasingly important to life in the United States. The histories of these neighboring nations, begun in conflict soon after independence, have become increasingly linked since World War II. The North American economy is deeply integrated; migrations and cultural interactions abound. States and politics, citizenship and justice, however, remain separate. Yet what happens in both polities profoundly affects every aspect of life in both nations (something that most Mexicans know, yet few in the United States grasp).

When U.S. political analysts look to Mexico, they normally ask why Mexicans don't live by "our" standards of economy and democracy. And when U.S. readers seek to learn something of Mexico's history, they often turn to works like Enrique Krauze's *Mexico: Biography of Power* (Harper Perennial, 1998) and Julia Preston and Samuel Dillon's *Opening Mexico: The Making of a Democracy* (Farrar, Straus and Giroux, 2004). Both are important works; both have taught me much. Yet both are written as if a few powerful men make Mexican history.

We seek to offer a more comprehensive perspective, exploring Mexico's complex history and political traditions. Popular communities, rural and urban, have been regular participants in the nation's history. Mexico's revolutions were conflicts with deep historical roots that mobilized every sector of society: the powerful and others seeking power; middling peoples struggling to find advantages; and diverse communities fighting for survival and better lives. The crisis of the late twentieth century mobilized peoples from every walk of Mexican life in, to date, nonrevolutionary conflicts that led to the electoral transition of 2000. A more thorough democratic transformation remains a goal that engages and challenges Mexicans: the powerful and prosperous few, those struggling to maintain lives in the middle, diverse working majorities, and expanding marginal communities. Thus we also seek a more historical, dynamic, and uncertain understanding of Mexico's present. That is the only way to prepare for the challenges ahead.

No one here thinks that history will repeat itself in any simple way. Should conflict explode precisely in 2010, none will be more surprised than the authors of this volume. Still, conflict may come in the new century. If it does, our studies suggest that it will emerge in ways we cannot now perceive. Our analyses also remain open to the possibility that Mexico's cycles of boom, crisis, and reform—leading to revolutions—have ended. The new century may begin an era in which globalization, even with periodic crises, can persist in Mexico without generating social and political conflagrations. If stability holds in the new century because globalization's neoliberal promises of shared prosperity and effective democracy become Mexican realities, celebration should follow. But what if globalization persists as it now operates, as "progress" that concentrates wealth and power among a few, while misery and insecurity proliferate among Mexico's majority, elections remain of uncertain legitimacy—and no popular mobilization challenges the powers that promote the prevailing order? Then we may pause, wonder, and worry about life in the century to come.

ACKNOWLEDGMENTS ❧

This volume emerged from a long collaboration among the editors and authors, sustained by several institutions and numerous individuals. In Mexico, the Center for Historical Studies of the National Institute of Anthropology and History was essential from the start. It hosted our first gathering in the seminar "Paradigmas y paradojas de fin de siglo: México, siglos XVIII, XIX, XX" in 1999. The early collaboration of Clara García-Ayluardo and the support of Salvador Rueda Smithers, then Center Director were indispensable.

Our second gathering came in Washington in 2000, facilitated by John Tutino's role as acting director of the Georgetown University Center for Latin American Studies and by the essential support of the Center's Mexico Project, led by John Bailey and funded by the William and Flora Hewlett Foundation. That meeting culminated in our first public presentation in "Crises, Reforms, and Revolutions: Mexico's Past, Mexico's Present, Mexico's Possibilities," a conference hosted by the Mexican Cultural Institute, thanks to the energetic collaboration of Jesús Reyes Heroles, then Mexico's ambassador to the United States.

Essential support for both gatherings came from Guadalupe Farías and Juana Inés Fernández at the Dirección de Estudios Historicos in Mexico, and from Adriana Pérez Mina and Jorge Rebolledo of Georgetown's Mexico Project.

The production of published volumes, first in Spanish, then in English, required more essential collaborators. Mónica Vega, editor for Taurus in

Mexico, brought *Crisis, reforma y revolución* to publication with remarkable efficiency. In preparing that volume, Luis Fernando Granados translated the essays by Alan Knight, John Tutino, and Eric Van Young into Spanish; Frederic Vallvé did the same for Friedrich Katz's essay. Both, now completing doctoral studies in history at Georgetown, were more than translators; they brought new clarity to the Spanish versions of our work.

Valerie Millholland, editor at Duke, encouraged us early on to consider an English version of our project. She brought our work to perceptive anonymous readers who helped us to see the way forward. John Tutino joined the founding editors to facilitate revision in English. Georgetown provided additional support, allowing us to assemble a team to translate the revised versions of the seven essays written originally in Spanish: Frederic Vallvé took on the challenge of first translations; Ben Fulwider brought his considerable skill in English editing, and John Tutino took final responsibility for the English versions—in consultation with the authors (except François-Xavier Guerra, who sadly passed away in 2002). Luis Granados returned to help convince John Tutino to write a new essay for the English volume—and to save his attempt to revise and amplify his earlier piece for another time. Emilio Coral joined the team at Georgetown to prepare the list of acronyms and the index, and to oversee the preparation of the manuscript for delivery to Duke. The four Georgetown doctoral candidates, Luis, Frederic, Ben, and Emilio, were essential to generating these volumes.

Cycles of Conflict, Centuries of Change is not a translation of *Crisis, reforma y revolución*. The preface and introduction are new, as are the book's organization and John Tutino's essay. All other essays (except Guerra's) are revised, many substantially. Our first volume focused on Mexico's turn-of-the-century crises: the revolutions of 1810 and 1910, and the question of whether another such conflagration is possible in the early twenty-first century. This book emphasizes the persistent roles of communities in Mexican history, our diverse understandings of Mexico's revolutions, the complexity of the crisis and attempted reforms of the second half of the twentieth century—and the uncertain future ahead. From our two gatherings through the production of two books, we have continued to learn—with the collaboration of many. We expect the process will continue.

ARIC: Asociaciones Rurales de Interés Colectivo (Rural Collective Interest Associations)

Barzón, El: The Spanish name for the belt linking the oxen with the plow. Also, Unión Nacional de Productores Agropecuarios, Comerciantes Industriales y Prestadores de Servicios (National Union of Agricultural Producers, Industrial Merchants, and Service Providers).

CAM: Confederación Agrarista Mexicana (Mexican Agrarianist Confederation)

CAP: Congreso Agrario Permanente (Permanent Agrarian Congress II)

CCI: Central Campesina Independiente (Independent Peasant Central)

CGOCM: Confederación General de Obreros y Campesinos de México (General Confederation of Mexican Workers and Peasants)

CIOAC: Central Independiente de Obreros Agrícolas y Campesinos (Independent Central of Agricultural Workers and Peasants)

CNA: Consejo Nacional Agropecuario (National Agricultural Council)

CNC: Confederación Nacional Campesina (National Peasant Confederation)

CNOP: Confederación Nacional de Organizaciones Populares (National Confederation of Popular Organizations)

CNPA: Coordinadora Nacional Plan de Ayala (National Coordinator Plan de Ayala; Emiliano Zapata's 1911 Agrarian Program)

CNPI: Coordinadora Nacional de Pueblos Indígenas (National Coordinator of Indigenous Communities)

CNPP: Confederación Nacional de la Pequeña Propiedad (National Confederation of Small Landowners)

CNTE: Coordinadora Nacional de Trabajadores de la Educación (National Coordinator of Education Workers)

COCEI: Coalición Obrero-Campesino-Estudiantil del Istmo (Isthmus of Tehuantepec Worker-Peasant-Student Coalition)

COMAGRO: Comercializadora Agropecuaria del Occidente (Western Agricultural Commercial Cooperative)

CONACYT: Consejo Nacional de Ciencia y Tecnología (National Council for Science and Technology)

CONAMUP: Coordinadora Nacional del Movimiento Urbano Popular (National Coordinator of the Urban Popular Movement)

CONASUPO: Compañía Nacional de Subsistencias Populares (National Company for Popular Subsistence)

COPLAMAR: Coordinación Nacional de Planeación y Apoyo a las Zonas Marginadas (National Coordinator for Planning and Support in Marginal Areas)

CORETT: Comisión para la Regularización de la Tenencia de la Tierra (Commission to Regularize Landed Property)

CPA: Congreso Permanente Agrario (Permanent Agrarian Congress I)

CPNAB: Consejo de Pueblos Nahuas del Alto Balsas, Guerrero A.C. (Council of Nahua Peoples of the Upper Balsas)

CROC: Confederación Revolucionaria de Obreros y Campesinos (Revolutionary Confederation of Workers and Peasants)

CROM: Confederacion Regional de Obreros Mexicanos (Regional Confederation of Mexican Workers)

CT: Congreso del Trabajo (Congress of Labor)

CTM: Confederación de Trabajadores de México (Confederation of Mexican Workers)

CUD: Coordinadora Única de Damnificados (Unified Coordinator of Earthquake Victims)

EPR: Ejército Popular Revolucionario (Revolutionary Popular Army)

EZLN: Ejército Zapatista de Liberación Nacional (Zapatista National Liberation Army)

FDN: Frente Democrático Nacional (National Democratic Front)

FERTIMEX: Fertilizantes Mexicanos (Mexican Fertilizers)

FOBAPROA: Fondo Bancario de Protección al Ahorro (Bank to Protect Savings Funds)

FPPM: Federación de Partidos del Pueblo Mexicano (Federation of Parties of the Mexican People)

FSTSE: Federación de Sindicatos de Trabajadores al Servicio del Estado (Federation of Unions of Workers in Service of the State)

IEPES: Instituto de Estudios Políticos, Económicos y Sociales del Partido Revolucionario Institucional (Institutional Revolutionary Party's Institute of Political, Economic, and Social Studies)

IFE: Instituto Federal Electoral (Federal Electoral Institute)

MLN: Movimiento de Liberación Nacional (National Liberation Movement)

MUP: Movimiento Urbano Popular (Urban Popular Movement)

PAN: Partido Acción Nacional (National Action Party)

PCM: Partido Comunista Mexicano (Mexican Communist Party)

PIDER: Programa Integral para el Desarrollo Rural (named by many Programa de Inversión para el Desarrollo Rural) (Integral Rural Development Program, or Rural Development Investment Program)

PP: Partido Popular (Popular Party)

PRD: Partido de la Revolución Democrática (Party of the Democratic Revolution)

PRI: Partido Revolucionario Institucional (Institutional Revolutionary Party)

PROCAMPO: Programa de Apoyos Directos al Campo (Program for Direct Support to Rural Areas)

PROGRESA: Programa de Educación y Salud (Health and Education Program)

PRONASOL: Programa Nacional de Solidaridad (National Solidarity Program)

SAM: Sistema Alimentario Mexicano (Mexican Food System)

SARH: Secretaría de Agricultura y Recursos Hidráulicos (Department of Water Resources and Agriculture)

SME: Sindicato Mexicano de Electricistas (Mexican Electricians Union)

SRA: Secretaría de la Reforma Agraria (Department of Agrarian Reform)

SUTERM: Sindicato Único de Trabajadores Electricistas de la República Mexicana (Union of Electrical Workers of the Mexican Republic)

UCEZ: Unión de Comuneros Emiliano Zapata (Union of Communities— Emiliano Zapata)

UE: Uniones de Ejidos (Ejido Unions)

UGOCM: Unión General de Obreros y Campesinos de Mexico (General Union of Mexican Workers and Peasants)

UNAM: Universidad Nacional Autónoma de México (National Autonomous University of Mexico)

UNORCA: Unión Nacional de Organizaciones Campesinas Autónomas (National Union of Autonomous Peasant Organizations)

UNS: Unión Nacional Sinarquista (National Sinarquista Union)

Introduction

Crises, Reforms, and Revolutions in Mexico, Past and Present

LETICIA REINA, ELISA SERVÍN, and JOHN TUTINO

Turn-of-the-century crises mark Mexican history. The eighteenth, nineteenth, and twentieth centuries all ended in times of promise and uncertainty. Economic boom combined with social dislocations and calls for political change. Twice, in 1810 and again in 1910, crises escalated into revolutions that defined the century to come. The silver boom and Bourbon reforms of the late eighteenth century led to a war for independence that set Mexico on a conflictive course of nation building. The export boom and authoritarian liberalism of the late nineteenth century led to the national revolution that brought Mexicans a twentieth century of authoritarian and nationalist development.

The passage from the twentieth century to the twenty-first has followed a trajectory uncomfortably reminiscent of past crises: another era of economic promise—now called "globalization"—has not ameliorated the social tragedies inherent in a development model that has plagued Mexicans since the 1970s. The 1980s and 1990s brought persistent political crises to a long-established regime, leading to the celebrated "democratic transition" of 2000. Mexico's economic course seems set by NAFTA. Integration with the globally dominant economy of the United States will continue. Will that integration bring shared prosperity to Mexicans? Does recent political change begin an enduring democratic regime that can integrate Mexico's diverse regions and peoples, promote shared welfare, and negotiate essential, yet unequal, links with the United States? If social justice remains elusive and democratic participation proves uncertain or unstable, can civil conflict, even revolution, again mark a new century in Mexico?

Studies of the crises that led to the revolutions of 1810 and 1910 are a staple of Mexican history. A few have taken longer views, analyzing comparatively the causes, course, and consequences of those two key eras of conflict.[1] Very few, however, have taken up the challenge of the history of the second half of the twentieth century.[2] The goal of this volume is to offer historically comparative perspectives on the origins and outcomes of the revolutions of the early nineteenth and twentieth centuries, and to place the unfolding history of conflict and change in contemporary Mexico in that context. Our explorations of the past are framed in an explicit consideration of the present. We aim to better understand the future emerging before us.

Studies of Mexico's revolutions, including those offered here, tend to fall into two schools. The first privileges socioeconomic factors, emphasizing how changes in national and international economic developments have shaped the organization of production and the social relations embedded in them to generate the grievances and injustices that drive revolutions. From this perspective, social demands and conflicts derive ultimately from socioeconomic processes. The sharp inequities they generate lead to revolutionary social movements that evolve and radicalize in the context of political conflicts.[3] The second school, in contrast, privileges politics. Its proponents focus on political culture, regime crises, power struggles, and breakdowns of mediation between state and society as keys to explaining revolutions. For many politically focused analysts, economic developments—often seen more positively as modernization—were not matched by parallel openings in politics, leading to implacable conflicts that generated (or allowed) the social mobilizations that drove revolutions.[4]

The studies assembled here suggest that the schools should merge. The Mexican revolutions of 1810 and 1910 developed at pivotal intersections of historic processes that linked the contested formation of a national state with the construction and consolidation—globally and locally—of capitalist production. If we are to understand Mexico's past conflicts, and if we are to have a chance of understanding the uncertain times in which we live, we must explore the interplay of socioeconomic developments, political cultures, and regime structures.[5] In addition, a comprehensive political economy must engage embedded issues of gender, ethnicity, and culture.[6] Our studies emphasize the dynamics of political economy; in the process, several raise questions of culture, ethnicity, and gender. If our accomplishments emphasize the integrated analysis of regimes, politics, and ways of production, one lesson for analyses going forward is the importance of recognizing the inseparability of culture, gender, ethnicity—and political economy.

Histories of attempts to build a Mexican state and nation in the context of accelerating capitalism emphasize three axes of conflictive change. First, many analysts focus directly on long cycles of global capitalist expansion and recession and their links to the challenges of regime building in Mexico. Others turn their attention to the attempts by liberals to legislate a society of individuals in free markets, sustained by regimes of popular sovereignty—while their opponents defended historical corporate interests and regulations asserted as being just, legitimated early on by religious sanctions, later by revolutionary proclamations. And still other scholars emphasize the conflicts and negotiations among powers promoting centralized rule, regional elites seeking shares of power, and local communities claiming autonomy—political, economic, and cultural. In history these conflicts were closely linked. Our essays engage all these questions. To clarify their dynamics, and to facilitate reading by those less grounded in studies of Mexican history, we offer an outline of the three visions of Mexican political economy and the links between them.

State making in an emerging capitalist world began during the eighteenth century, when the colonial order still ruled New Spain.[7] From the 1760s, the Spanish Bourbons pressed to strengthen state powers and to increase revenues in an Atlantic economy driven by the developing Industrial Revolution. In the regions soon to become Mexico, silver mining boomed along with commercial agriculture and textile production. Revenues increased into the first decades of the nineteenth century. After 1780, however, popular welfare faced new pressures: rising prices, falling earnings, declining access to land. Mexican elites profited, the imperial state took rising revenues, and indigenous communities rioted. The monarchical state balanced Bourbon assertions with traditional mediations of escalating conflicts to sustain the boom and prevent destabilization until 1800.

Amid European warfare, however, Napoleonic invasion broke the Spanish monarchy in 1808. Uncertain sovereignty led to escalating debates, culminating in the 1810 Hidalgo revolt that began a decade of popular insurgencies and political conflicts. In 1821, Mexico emerged as an independent nation, its silver economy in collapse, its political future unknown, its economic prospects uncertain. State creation proved long and conflictive. Ideological visions, conservative and liberal, intersected with debates over whether Mexico should try to follow Europe into industrialization (the conservative position) or build an export economy to complement European development (the liberal preference). The outcome was a long era of political instability and economic uncertainty, punctuated by

U.S. invasion and continental realignment from 1846 to 1848, French occupation from 1863 to 1867, and recurrent popular insurgencies that endured into the 1870s.

Then the Mexican state stabilized under Porfirio Díaz. Railroads allowed the economy to flourish in a new era of export development, complemented by limited industrialization. Again, elites profited and the state benefited while the populace faced declining access to land, falling incomes, and proliferating insecurities. Recession in 1907 and the succession crisis in 1910 brought regime breakdown in 1911—leading Mexico into revolution two decades before Atlantic capitalism collapsed in the Great Depression in 1930. Mexicans fought from 1911 to 1929, then consolidated a postrevolutionary regime during the Depression—a regime that brought a new era of stability and promoted a new era of capitalist development.

The postrevolutionary consolidation of the 1930s, however, generated new contradictions. Revolutionary rhetoric promised democratic participation, while postrevolutionary power holders built an authoritarian state designed to ensure stability. Demands for agrarian justice led to real land reform, whose beneficiaries were pressed to produce in support of capitalist accumulation while facing rising population pressures. A nation rebuilt in agrarian revolution began to urbanize and industrialize. Beginning in World War II, from the 1940s a regime proclaiming revolutionary nationalism linked its fortunes to the rising power of the United States.

The immediate outcome was an era of urbanization, industrial growth, and political stability, the "Mexican Miracle" of 1950 to 1970. But contradictions inherent in the miracle brought new crises. Lack of democratic participation led to student mobilization and regime repression in 1968. Economic bottlenecks saw boom growth give way to mounting debt in the early 1970s, a petroleum bonanza in the late 1970s, and unprecedented debt crisis in the 1980s. (Mexico's debt-financed oil boom helped bring petroleum prices down; Mexican revenues collapsed, and the regime faced crisis.) Amid political uncertainties and economic insecurities, social movements challenged the regime to fulfill promises rooted in its distant revolutionary and liberal pasts. Villagers in Sonora and elsewhere invaded lands they saw as rightly theirs; the state, despite its agrarian rhetoric, would not deliver. Among the throngs migrating to Mexico City, many responded to shortages of housing and services by taking possession of land and building neighborhoods without regime sanction. New unions demanded independence from a state labor sector, once in the vanguard of movements for workers' rights, but now an instrument of state control. As crisis deepened in the 1980s, calls for effective elections and political change were coupled with desperate rural poverty and difficulties feeding burgeoning populations.

Mexico's rulers—under internal and external pressures—turned to globalization and neoliberalism, culminating in the promises of NAFTA and democratization. For Mexico's majority, the social consequences, to date, have been declining incomes, widespread insecurities, the end of land reform, and accelerating migration to labor, seasonally or permanently, in the United States. While national leaders integrated Mexican farms, factories, and workers into the new North American market, persistent national restrictions on migration and citizenship kept most Mexicans in insecure poverty at home or facing lives as exploited illegal workers across the border in "El Norte." Some have responded with heightened nationalisms; others have reasserted indigenous ethnic identities in search of political rights and community autonomy. Mexico's third cycle of promise and misery has led to what sometimes seems a continuing political crisis. Yet there has been no regime collapse. For now, stability persists. History demands that we ask if breakdown may yet come and if revolutionary mobilizations may follow.

Amid centuries of conflict over state making in the context of capitalism, Mexicans have also debated—sometimes fought over—conflicting visions of society and political culture. One emerged from a colonial past, built on European and Mesoamerican antecedents. New Spain, constructed in conquest and consolidated amid disease-driven depopulation during the sixteenth century, was organized in corporate institutions.[8] Spaniards congregated in cities led by councils with rights to self-rule. The indigenous majority lived through the colonial era in communities reconstituted as *repúblicas de indios*, with rights to lands and local rule. Merchants and artisans had their guilds. Church and military—though the military remained limited until late in the colonial era—had separate judicial privileges. And relations among all were mediated by a regime that, after the early colonial reconstruction, was more judicial than administrative. The colonial order of corporate organization and state mediation endured with notable stability for three centuries.

The challenge to that order began amid late colonial boom. The Bourbons, who claimed the Spanish monarchy in the early eighteenth century and competed with the rising powers of their French kin and British foes, began in the 1760s to build a state that was less judicial and more administrative. They aimed to forge centralized powers backed by military force to promote mining and commercial production and to extract increased revenues. The reformers legitimated their programs as enlightened and rational. They were also absolutist—opposed to popular participation, to say nothing of popular sovereignty. They succeeded in promoting production and revenue increases. They also provoked a series of uprisings in the 1760s, which were crushed—and then led reformers to more careful negotiations with the powerful in New Spain, and to renewed mediations with the indigenous republics and other communities that formed the base of the colony's society and economy. Balancing enlightened assertions with corporate mediations, Bourbon reformers sustained monarchical power, Mexican boom, and imperial revenues into the early nineteenth century. But they began conflicts pitting state power against a corporate society that would persist throughout Mexico's national history.[9]

When Napoleon broke the Spanish regime in 1808, Spaniards in Europe and the Americas aimed to reconstitute sovereignty. Who would join in that reconstitution, in what ways, and toward what ends, opened debates that quickly provoked deep conflicts in Spain and New Spain. Many aimed to mobilize established corporations to act in the name of the deposed—and desired—Ferdinand VII. For them, limited participation in sovereignty would reconstitute a still corporate order. Others, led by the Cortes (Parliament) of Cádiz that wrote a liberal constitution in 1812, pressed for a new regime of state power sanctioned by popular representation grounded in individual rights—thus challenging the corporate order that defined the colonial era.[10]

Corporate and liberal visions and programs jostled each other, influencing both insurgents and royalists throughout the wars for independence. An attempt at fusion defined the short-lived empire of the ill-fated Agustín de Iturbide after 1821. But beginning with the federal constitution of 1824, Mexicans who defined themselves as liberals began to contest those, soon called conservatives, who promoted the survival of the corporate order. Liberals asserted individualism and popular sovereignty. Conservatives insisted on religiously sanctioned corporatism. Their debates, often wars, over the future of Mexico's state, society, and culture fueled an era of conflict and instability that defined the half century after independence.

After war with the United States demonstrated the weakness of the Mexican state and cost the nation vast and valuable northern territories, heightened debates led to liberal triumph in 1855. The liberal republic of the mid-nineteenth century, associated with the long rule of Benito Juárez, aimed to break the surviving corporate order. In foundational decrees included in the Constitution of 1857, liberals abolished corporate property rights and judicial privileges, made law for individual citizens, and promoted a secularizing political culture. But church corporations and indigenous communities resisted liberal legislation, often backed by a deeply religious populace. Throughout the nineteenth century, relations between state and society remained negotiations between liberal states in formation and corporate institutions under assault, but unwilling to disappear.

During the late-nineteenth-century era of authoritarian liberalism and capitalist development under Porfirio Díaz, the newly stable regime oscillated between negotiation and imposition. Díaz allowed the church, deprived of most property under Juárez, to return to the center of national cultural life. Fighting for power in the 1870s, Díaz promised "effective suffrage and no reelection," along with municipal liberty. Some indigenous communities imagined an end to land privatizations, perhaps even the return of lands lost in the Juárez era. Once in power, however, Díaz controlled elections, reelected himself repeatedly, allowed new assaults on community lands—and attempted to mediate the conflicts that inevitably followed. By mixing liberal assertions with negotiated mediations, Díaz maintained a balance of power for decades. But as stability endured and economic boom allowed him to favor elite allies, he turned from the delicate politics of consensus that had brought him to power to ever-more-brittle authoritarian impositions. After 1900, Díaz faced rising demands for democratic participation. His inability to resolve the contradictions between liberal promises of popular sovereignty and authoritarian rule, as well as conflicts between liberal individualism and communities demanding corporate land rights, helped lead to regime collapse and revolution in 1910.

That revolution was a complex affair. The most radical agrarians, led by Emiliano Zapata, and the most reactionary authoritarians, led by General Victoriano Huerta, could share corporatist visions while engaged in a conflict without quarter. Among northerners, Pancho Villa fought for a popular agenda, while Venustiano Carranza and Álvaro Obregón promoted national capitalism, sharing a broad liberalism, sometimes in concert, often in deadly conflict.[11]

Out of those conflicts, a postrevolutionary regime forged a new state built on a dominant, corporatist, incorporating party that called itself "the Revolution." The regime promoted national capitalism. The new model of state-society relations incorporated key remnants of the colonial order: mediation was privileged over participation; agrarian communities were reconstituted and granted land as state-sanctioned *ejidos*; peasants and labor, commerce and industry, were granted corporate representation— popular groups in the dominant party, business interests in the chambers sanctioned by the state. The result was an authoritarian state linked to a corporate party built by inclusion in the 1920s and 1930s. Some elements of Mexico's traditional corporate order, however, were rejected: the church was pressed from its dominant cultural-educational role, while the majority remained staunchly Catholic. The postrevolutionary consolidation appears to have been an attempt to reenergize the politics of the old regime in service of a national capitalist project while asserting revolutionary promises of corporate community rights and liberal ideals of citizenship and democratic participation. By the late twentieth century, contradictions locked into the regime forced it to grapple with the consequences of ideals never fulfilled—the promise of participatory democracy in an authoritarian regime becoming exclusionary; promises of popular welfare in a society of concentrating wealth and deepening inequities.[12]

A third historic tension has marked relations between centralizing powers and autonomist interests, regional and local. The colonial order of corporate organization and state mediation negotiated and thus sustained the central powers of the Viceroyalty in Mexico City, the regional interests of provincial Spaniards, and the limited but real autonomy of indigenous communities sanctioned as repúblicas de indios. Bourbon reformers aimed to concentrate power in the center—but the intendants they sent to provincial capitals in the 1780s solidified regional interests. The Bourbons also aimed to limit the independence—political, financial, and cultural—of indigenous communities; their reforms provoked conflicts that forced negotiations to preserve the peace essential to production. Community rights persisted.[13]

During the wars for independence, many communities, indigenous, mestizo, and Hispanic, became insurgents—some for years, others for months, many for days. All sought local autonomy.[14] Regional elites often saw independence as freedom from the powers of Mexico City. The Cádiz Constitution of 1812, promulgated while insurgencies raged in Mexico, promoted liberal individualism and promised municipal autonomy—the latter repeatedly claimed by villagers and provincials to defend their local autonomy against centralizing powers.[15] Independence came in 1821, claimed by powerful groups often based in the colonial capital and backed by an army that had fought for a decade against provincial and community autonomy. Amid attempts to build a national state in an emerging capitalist world, and while liberal visions challenged corporatist rights, Mexicans also contested centralizing power and local and regional autonomy.

During the half century after independence, economic fragmentation reinforced regionalism and localism. Communities reasserted local autonomy amid political conflicts.[16] In the late nineteenth century, railroads facilitated economic reintegration and political centralization. Provincial and municipal rights remained formalities, increasingly overruled by Porfirio Díaz's central powers. Provincial challenges to those powers helped generate the political mobilizations that led to regime breakdown and revolution in 1910. Through the ensuing decades of violence and regime reconstruction, national, provincial, and municipal rights and powers were again contested. Only in the 1930s did a regime forged in revolution find new power to rule from the center, and new means to mediate conflicts with enduring regional powers and local interests.

Yet the centralization and national integration that triumphed in Mexico in the 1930s were challenged, especially in the 1980s. The democratizing ferment of the late twentieth century included strong demands for provincial and municipal rights. The states have become increasingly important to administration and politics; municipalities clamor for new resources and autonomies. Yet a key question remains: can Mexican regions and communities claim effective autonomy in the North America of NAFTA, in which Mexico struggles as a dependent nation within an integrated regional economy? As the twenty-first century begins, diverse Mexican communities demand an array of political, social, and cultural autonomies, negotiating with—at times rebelling against—centralizing state powers and globalizing economic forces.

The essays that follow grapple with fundamental problems of state building and economic development, liberal innovations and corporate survivals, centralizing powers and autonomist demands. They offer different emphases and interpretations, rooted in different visions of Mexico's history. We have left our debates in place, even emphasized them, to facilitate analysis going forward. We hope that the juxtaposition of our differing perspectives on common questions can lead to new and more integrated understandings.

The book divides into three parts. Part I focuses on the fundamental importance of communities and their assertive participation in Mexican history from the eighteenth century through the twentieth. Part II offers comparative analyses of Mexico's revolutions, highlighting established debates, emphasizing complexities, offering new emphases—all to illuminate understandings of Mexico's present. Part III explores the history of Mexico's crisis of the late twentieth century. Focused on politics and political culture, the essays in this part engage key questions for Mexico's present—and future. The goal is to explore continuities and ruptures, similarities and differences, over the long course of Mexican history.

We begin with three essays on communities and their historical participation in Mexican political life from the eighteenth century through the twentieth. Working in a North American tradition of sociocultural history, Eric Van Young reminds us that all history is local, and that what happens in communities constitutes the basis of larger historical processes.[17] He begins with a close examination of the concept of crisis, a key to historical inquiry that is rarely explored so carefully. He then offers two case studies of communities facing conflicts. The first conflict divided Cuautitlán, just north of Mexico City, in 1785, when the colonial order of New Spain held strong. The other exploded in 1810 at Atlacomulco, farther north and west, just as the wars for independence began. Van Young details how questions of land and production, religious devotion, and local politics lay inseparably at the heart of both conflicts. And he demonstrates how the colonial regime in 1785 mediated conflict to sustain its rule, and how unmediated conflicts became confrontations that led to the regime's demise after 1810. Ultimately Van Young reminds us that politics are always relationships between communities and those who seek to rule, locally and in larger domains. National histories must focus on interactions between powers and cultural visions seeking dominance, and diverse communities that daily produce, socialize, worship, and engage in politics to create the best local lives they can.

Antonio Annino, grounded in European histories of political culture, offers a broad analysis of the role of communities in the transformation from New Spain to Mexico, focusing on their long and complex engagements with liberalism.[18] He begins by emphasizing that liberalism came to New Spain from Spain amid the wars for independence—and in service of those who aimed to preserve colonial rule. He reveals, however, that liberalism was not simply imposed on Mexican communities. Instead, they repeatedly grasped liberalism's promises of participatory citizenship to fortify their rights (including rights to community lands, which liberals preferred to privatize). Annino explains the communities' ability to negotiate liberalism to local advantage by emphasizing the long republican traditions of New Spain's indigenous peoples. He argues that the repúblicas de indios that congregated communities and organized production, worship, and political life across central and southern New Spain beginning in the sixteenth century were hybrids fusing Mesoamerican legacies and Spanish monarchical-republican traditions. Scholars have long seen those communities as places of cultural syncretism, integrating the two traditions. Annino demonstrates that they were simultaneously places of political syncretism, forging an indigenous republican tradition. He builds on that key insight to explore how the coming of liberalism and then independence to Mexico created unprecedented engagements with those centuries-old traditions. Communities adopted and adapted liberalism, often to debate and transform it. When nation building became an exercise in defining and locating sovereignty, communities presumed themselves to be key repositories, creating unprecedented and unstable contests among national, provincial, and local powers. Annino demonstrates that Mexico's founding decades of conflict were rooted in deep, active, persistent, yet changing republican traditions. The common assertion that Mexico's slow, contested development of a stable electoral polity derives from the absence of republican traditions, especially in popular communities, becomes untenable in the light of Annino's analysis. We must attend to the complexities of Mexico's long republican history, taking the republican assertions of its communities seriously, and analyzing periodic flights from republican rule in that historical perspective.[19]

Leticia Reina turns to that challenge in her exploration of the electoral participation of rural, often indigenous, communities in both the late nineteenth century and the late twentieth. Working in the dynamic Mexican tradition of anthropological histories, she joins Van Young and Annino in recognizing the deep colonial roots of indigenous republicanism.[20] She explores the creation and persistence of indigenous electoral traditions, noting the complex and changing syncretisms among local *usos y costumbres* (uses and customs) and evolving liberal institutions. Reina reminds us of the fundamental importance of ethnicity in Mexican history, and thus the necessity of attending to ethnicity in local and national analyses. She focuses on the explosion of local, often indigenous, electoral participation during the late-nineteenth-century authoritarian regime of Porfirio Díaz. While most scholars have emphasized Díaz's promotion of railroads, export development, and authoritarian rule, Reina turns her attention to the simultaneous proliferation of local electoral conflicts that allowed communities to negotiate, and sometimes resist, authoritarian impositions.

Placing Porfirian electoral mobilizations in the context of late colonial developments, Reina offers a powerful thesis of electoral paradox. Local republican assertions proliferated in response to late colonial Bourbon reforms; local electoral mobilizations accelerated to resist late-nineteenth-century authoritarian impositions. In both eras, community assertions within republican and then liberal traditions proved to be key aspects of mounting crises that would bring revolutionary mobilizations in 1810 and 1910. Yet Reina also shows that where local political assertions proved most active in the face of authoritarian challenges, subsequent revolutionary mobilizations were limited. Reina then offers a probing, if necessarily preliminary, inquiry into rural electoral participation in the crisis of the late twentieth century. Again she reports complex integrations of indigenous traditions and liberal principles now presented as democratic. She finds assertions that enabled communities to engage and shape times of uncertain change. And she wonders if a crisis of authoritarian rule accompanied by widespread local electoral mobilizations may be a sign of impending breakdown into a more revolutionary conflict—and if the regions of strongest electoral mobilization might again prove limited participants in any conflict to come.

Van Young, Annino, and Reina remind all who will take history seriously that local communities have been, and remain, the foundation of regional, national, and global histories. Those who would understand the present must take communities seriously. Too many analysts have ignored that historical truth—and faced historic surprises when communities have pressed mobilizations, revolutionary and otherwise, that forced the powerful to take note.

Part II shifts from communities to grapple with Mexico's revolutionary tradition. Debates abound. François-Xavier Guerra, perhaps the defining practitioner of the European political-cultural approach to Latin America, explores Mexican political culture from the wars for independence to the revolution.[21] He emphasizes the persistence of corporatist visions and interests, shared by the Catholic Church and indigenous communities, and their long struggles to survive the challenge of liberalism and its vision of a society of individuals. He emphasizes that the late-nineteenth-century regime of Porfirio Díaz consolidated power by pressing liberal economic programs while compromising liberal politics and individualism through deals with the church and conflictive negotiations with indigenous communities. Compromise facilitated Díaz's long rule—but left deep contradictions in Mexican political culture that generated the revolution of 1910. In Guerra's vision (a synthesis of a lifetime of work), the steadfast survival of Mexico's ancien régime with its entrenched corporatist culture led to a revolution that began with demands to implement the promises of Mexican liberalism. But a political uprising for effective suffrage quickly encountered social insurgencies, first the agrarian Zapatistas, then the religious Cristeros, who expressed and confirmed the perseverance of a social order and political culture grounded in the old regime. Guerra's vision offers a historical logic for the postrevolutionary consolidation. The new regime maintained a program of capitalist development, and the institutions and rhetoric of liberal democracy. But it organized them in a state and party that revived and modernized corporatist structures rooted in deep Mexican traditions. Corporatism and clientelism operated as essential mechanisms of mediation between the state and diverse social constituencies throughout most of the twentieth century—until late-century crisis brought a resurgence of liberalism, demands for effective democracy, and new challenges to corporatist traditions.

Alan Knight has been a leading practitioner of an Anglo-American tradition of historical political economy.[22] Here he offers a long view, exploring the political economy of Mexico from the wars for independence to the present. He focuses on the decades that led to the conflagrations of 1810 and 1910 in order to examine the late-twentieth-century decades of crisis and reform—so far without revolution. He privileges the interactions between economic infrastructures and political conflicts. Knight appropriates and refines the vision, first suggested by John Tutino in *From Insurrection to Revolution in Mexico*, that long cycles of social compression and decompression define the course of Mexican history. Knight argues that Mexico's recurrent eras of compression (in the late eighteenth, late nineteenth, and late twentieth centuries) have been marked by inflation, concentrations of wealth and power, and deepening social inequalities. He emphasizes, however, that broadly parallel socioeconomic developments engaged fundamentally different political situations in the three eras of crisis. The late colonial Bourbon monarchy and the late-nineteenth-century Díaz regime, Knight argues, had both ossified to inhibit the negotiation of deepening social difficulties. In contrast, Knight sees the late-twentieth-century regime, for all its challenges and uncertainties, as demonstrating sufficient flexibility—notably the cession of the ruling party to Vicente Fox in the elections of 2000—to suggest a regime more likely to negotiate survival than collapse into a third revolutionary conflagration.

Friedrich Katz has forged his own tradition of history, integrating international relations, political economy, and social movements.[23] He takes aim at a fundamental paradox of the revolution of 1910: how did a revolution defined by conflicts between proponents of an anti-American national capitalism and insurgents demanding popular and agrarian justice produce a regime that by the 1940s became increasingly conservative and an economic and military ally of the United States in World War II? His analysis demonstrates the essential importance of viewing national political economy in international context. He focuses on the consequences of three wars—the Spanish-American War, World War I, and World War II—on the origins and course of Mexico's revolution and the postrevolutionary consolidation. To summarize a complex vision: the Spanish-American War generated economic opportunities that helped to generate social inequities in Mexico; World War I both propelled and limited the attempts of the United States and other world powers to intervene in the conflicts that became the Mexican Revolution; and World War II created unprecedented opportunities for the leaders of Mexico's newly consolidated regime to promote capitalist development and contain popular assertions, stimulating a turn to the right in social vision, and an alliance with the United States that has deepened ever since. Katz's essay challenges those who would analyze Mexico after World War II to do so in clear context of the Cold War, the rise of the United States to continental and apparent global dominance—and the still-emerging challenges of twenty-first century conflicts.

John Tutino writes in a North American tradition of agrarian social history.[24] He too builds on and revises the analysis first offered in *From Insurrection to Revolution in Mexico*. That work emphasized the socio-economic processes that generated the grievances that fueled popular discontent, and how mounting grievances intersected with regime crises to create opportunities for insurgencies to drive the conflagrations of 1810 and 1910. Now Tutino adds a third emphasis: revolutionary capacity—the ability of rural communities to mobilize subsistence production to sustain themselves and popular insurgencies long enough to force their agendas into regional and national political and economic contests. He sees that capacity as grounded in ecological autonomy—the ability of families and communities to generate most of basic sustenance independently. His essay offers a historical overview of Mexican communities and their autonomy: their early colonial consolidation, their key roles in the revolutions of 1810 and 1910, and their historic demise in the second half of the twentieth century. He adds that the historical organization of community autonomies and their pursuit in revolutionary mobilizations were deeply patriarchal, reminding us of the importance of addressing the gender relations embedded in historical structures of production and politics.

In addition, Tutino builds on the work of Annino and Reina (and others) to suggest a historically complex relationship between ecological autonomy and the political participation of Mexican communities. Ecological autonomy and local sovereignty fused in colonial indigenous republics. They were contested and increasingly separated during the long era of liberalism, emerging capitalism, and Mexican revolutions from 1810 to 1940. Since 1950, demographic explosion, urbanization, and globalizing capitalism have ended ecological autonomy. In the wake of that watershed change, persistent and adamant popular political mobilizations have pressed the promoters of neoliberalism to allow Mexicans an expanding democratic citizenship. Meanwhile, social grievances persisted and often deepened during decades of regime crisis. Yet, as Tutino notes, there has been no turn to revolutionary mobilization. He argues that the demise of ecological autonomy has ended the revolutionary capacity of rural communities. Mexico may yet have another revolution. If it does, it will differ in fundamental and unimagined ways from Mexico's past conflagrations.

The four explorations of Mexico's history of revolutions offer diverse perspectives. Their juxtaposition leads toward common conclusions.

Analyses of revolution, and of the possibility of revolution, must attend to conflicts focused on politics and political culture. They must engage international linkages and pressures—economic, military, and diplomatic. They must deal with the complex and changing interactions of the economy, the social relations embedded in it, and the political systems that structure production and social relations and attempt to mediate their conflicts. And they must deal with changing relationships between the powerful and diverse popular communities—as the essays in Part I also emphasize.

Part III concentrates on the twentieth century, especially its final decades of crisis. Four Mexican scholars examine the conflicts and changes that have challenged, perhaps ended, the regime and development model that ruled for decades after the revolution of 1910. They explore the emerging possibilities of a new political order and new approaches to state-society relations in the twenty-first century. They wonder if another revolution is possible—or improbable. All focus on the core domain of politics. Yet each author examines, with different emphases, the international links inherent in globalization, the ideological debates provoked by neoliberalism, and the new and diverse ways that popular communities participated in decades of mounting crisis.

The decades of conflict and change sometimes celebrated, sometimes condemned, as the Mexican Revolution (1910–40) separated and linked the Porfirian era of liberal authoritarianism and the time of neoliberal development that followed—and continues. Lorenzo Meyer, a leading practitioner of historical political economy in international perspective, explores the trajectory of Mexican liberalism in the nineteenth and twentieth centuries, before and after the revolution of 1910.[25] He emphasizes that the late twentieth century brought processes broadly similar to those of the late nineteenth century: state reforms linked to a development project of international capitalism, all envisioned as liberal. The neoliberal model promoted since the 1980s recaptured key elements of the nineteenth-century vision: an idealized market, political and ideological individualism, and a reduced state—at least in affairs of the market. He notes that liberal "progress" after 1880 and neoliberal "modernization" after 1980 both brought new and deepening inequalities to Mexican society. Meyer also highlights key differences: the regime of Porfirio Díaz, however committed to liberal development, remained authoritarian and dependent on one leader, facilitating its collapse in 1911. In contrast, the regime that oversaw the shift from state-regulated capitalism to neoliberalism in the 1980s had earlier solved the problem of succession by authoritarian means—and with conflicts and uncertainties orchestrated the transition to electoral succession in 2000. Meyer joins Knight in focusing on the links between globalization, inequity, and democratization as the twenty-first century begins. He concludes by posing the essential question for Mexico's future: can democratization promote effective participation, accessible justice, and shared welfare within globalization?

Not surprisingly, the late-twentieth-century decades of authoritarian persistence, rapid globalization, and slow and contested transition to democracy brought waves of popular mobilizations that challenged and demanded change in the neoliberal model celebrated in the halls of North American governments and corporate boardrooms. Guillermo de la Peña has helped define the Mexican school of historical anthropology, adding his own sharp political emphasis.[26] Here he examines the emergence of new popular movements, urban and rural, as the postrevolutionary structure of corporate organization and mediation collapsed. He demonstrates that mobilizations both responded to and accelerated demands for effective democracy, electoral participation, economic justice, and more. De la Peña demonstrates the effectiveness of popular assertions—and their limits as nongovernmental movements that remained within the bounds of legality. Anyone who imagines that Mexico's transition to democracy was primarily an affair of leaders will encounter a far more complex and participatory world of Mexican politics in de la Peña's (and Reina's) vision. Implicitly, he raises the challenge of comparing the revolutionary mobilizations of 1810 and 1910—with their own successes, limits, and failures— with the nonrevolutionary mobilizations of the late twentieth century and the early twenty-first. Explicitly, he joins Meyer in seeking to understand how nonrevolutionary participations can generate democracy and justice and perhaps end Mexico's revolutionary tradition.

Enrique Semo provides a unique perspective on the politics of opposition in late-twentieth-century Mexico. A leading historian of the origins of capitalism in Mexico,[27] Semo has been a key participant in the politics of the Left in Mexico since the 1970s. He writes as a participant-historian, detailing developments he joined—and analyzes. He emphasizes the decision of the Left, at least the national political Left, to take the route of electoral participation, leading to important electoral triumphs, notably the consolidation of the power of the PRD in Mexico City. He contrasts the electoral emphasis of the political Left with the insurrection attempted by the Zapatistas in Chiapas in 1994, noting that both contributed to the electoral opening that removed the PRI from national power in 2000. Perhaps Semo's key contribution is his insider's understanding that the turn to electoral participation signified the Left's acceptance of processes of limited change —the end of dreams of fundamental structural transformations.

His essay, too, raises questions of comparison with the past. Political leaders of earlier times—Hidalgo, Allende, and Morelos in 1810; Madero, Carranza, and Obregón after 1910—took the risk of calling for, or allying with, popular insurgencies in search of fundamental changes. By joining popular insurrections, they helped provoke conflicts they could not control. In that context, perhaps one key to Mexico's recent past is the decision by the political Left to sometimes celebrate, but never to forge an alliance in action with, the Chiapas insurgency. Could such an alliance have led to revolutionary consequences? Or would it have destroyed the Left in an adventure doomed to failure? The historic gains and limits that flow from the decision of the national Left to forgo historical commitments to popular insurgency remain to be determined.

Finally, Elisa Servín focuses on the Mexican regime struggling to negotiate the transition from the authoritarian, corporatist, and nationalist capitalism of the postrevolutionary decades, through the crises of the late twentieth century, to a new world of globally linked democratic capitalism as the twenty-first century begins. All our authors agree that regime breakdown was a key to past revolutionary mobilizations. Some find such breakdowns and the subsequent struggles for political reconstruction to be the very essence of revolution. Others find regime collapse a key element enabling the emergence and endurance of the popular insurgencies that define revolutions. From either perspective, the question of whether the Mexican state may yet collapse—or instead is effecting a stabilizing transition to electoral democracy—remains pivotal.

Servín has pioneered the long-delayed writing of Mexican political history during the decades after World War II.[28] Her essay here builds on that work to explore the structure and operation of the postrevolutionary state, its beginnings in corporate inclusion, its shift toward exclusionary authoritarian control, its recent openness to electoral competition, and the exit of the once-dominant party from power in 2000. She focuses on how a changing regime has dealt with evolving oppositions. She explores the importance of the opposition electoral victory of 2000. She also highlights the fundamental questions that remain unresolved as an electoral polity struggles to develop from within a long authoritarian regime: notably, the renewed conflicts between the central government and regional and local interests seeking greater autonomy, and the tensions between forces advocating liberal—that is, individual and electoral—democracy and groups still promoting corporatist cultural and political practices. And while recognizing the fundamental importance of the transition to electoral competition that culminated in the victory of Vicente Fox in the 2000 presidential contest, Servín reflects on the subsequent difficulties of governance, the limits of effective democracy, and the persistence of deep injustices. She worries about the future.

As the twenty-first century begins, Mexicans face the challenge of building a new regime, hopefully one that brings democratic participation and mediation to relations between the state and diverse social groups. Can electoral democracy finally organize, negotiate, and ameliorate the social, ethnic, and regional inequities that still plague the Mexican majority? Can globalization with democratization bring a more just North American order? Or is the present vogue of electoral democracy an updated repetition of the liberal promises of Mexico's past: assertions that aim to legitimate power while limiting popular participation, seeking to prevent mobilizations yet often provoking them? Sharp and often worsening inequities remain. The question of the consolidation of electoral politics also remains —one opposition victory at the national level does not a regime make. Should electoral politics reach established maturity, can they promote the radical reversal of popular fortunes that would bring shared welfare to the Mexican majority? In a transnational economy organized by NAFTA, in which Mexicans' key roles are to provide cheap energy, inexpensive fruits and vegetables, and cheap, mobile, and insecure labor on both sides of the border, can any national political system promote social equality? And if inequity, poverty, and unsettling insecurity continue to define the lives of most Mexicans, can any regime legitimate and stabilize lives of enduring desperation?

As the twenty-first century begins, Mexico again stands at a crossroads, a time of uncertainty and change, reminiscent of the past, yet defined by a unique present and open to an unknown future. Might incomplete or failed reforms again lead to popular mobilizations that become uncontained revolutionary confrontations? Or have the cycles of revolution ended? Can profound political and social reforms lead to a society in which revolutionary traditions are a historical memory—but no longer a prospect? The future will tell.

NOTES

1 For long-term comparisons, see Friedrich Katz, ed., *Riot, Rebellion, and Revolution: Rural Social Conflict in Mexico* (Princeton: Princeton University Press, 1988); John Tutino, *From Insurrection to Revolution in Mexico: Social Bases of Agrarian Violence, 1760–1940* (Princeton: Princeton University Press, 1986); and Paul Vanderwood, "Comparing Independence with the Revolution: Causes, Concepts, and Pitfalls," in *The Independence of Mexico and the Creation of the New Nation*, ed. Jaime Rodríguez O. (Los Angeles: UCLA Latin American Center, 1989), 311–22.

2 In a key exception, Elisa Servín began the historical study of post–World War II Mexican politics in *Ruptura y oposición: El movimiento henriquista, 1945–1954* (Mexico City: Cal y Arena, 2001). Gilbert Joseph, Anne Rubenstein, and Eric Zolov, eds., *Fragments of a Golden Age* (Durham: Duke University Press, 2001), offers a collection of strong cultural studies, rarely linked to the domain of political economy.

3 Tutino, *From Insurrection to Revolution*, is a clear example of this emphasis.

4 Two studies by François-Xavier Guerra, *México del antiguo régimen a la revolución*, 2 vols. (Mexico City: Fondo de Cultura Económica, 1990), and *Modernidades e independencias: Ensayos sobre las revoluciones hispánicas* (Mexico City: Fondo de Cultura Económica, 1993), exemplify this approach.

5 For a recent examination of Mexican political economy, powerful and debated, see Stephen Haber, Armando Razo, and Noel Maurer, *The Politics of Property Rights: Political Instability, Credible Commitments, and Economic Growth in Mexico, 1876–1929* (Cambridge: Cambridge University Press, 2003).

6 This is among the many key contributions of Florencia Mallon's *Peasant and Nation: The Making of Postcolonial Mexico and Peru* (Berkeley: University of California Press, 1995).

7 This synthesis of Mexican political economy in large part reflects the essays that follow. See also Tutino, *From Insurrection to Revolution*, and Alan Knight's emerging multivolume *Mexico*, vols. 1–3 (Cambridge: Cambridge University Press, 2002, 2007).

8 Marialba Pastor, *Cuerpos socials, cuerpos sacrificiales* (Mexico City: Fondo de Cultura Económica, 2004), offers a deep synthetic analysis of the origins of corporatism in early colonial New Spain.

9 On the Bourbon reforms, see Felipe Castro Gutierréz, *Nueva ley y nuevo rey: Reformas borbónicas y rebellion popular en la Nueva España* (Zamora: El Colegio de Michoacán, 1996).

10 On the politics of Mexican independence, see Alfredo Ávila, *En nombre de la nación: La formación del gobierno representativo en México* (Mexico City: Taurus, 2002).

11 On factions in the Mexican Revolution, the classic studies are John Womack, *Zapata and the Mexican Revolution* (New York: Knopf, 1968); Alan Knight, *The Mexican Revolution*, 2 vols. (Cambridge: Cambridge University Press, 1986); and Friedrich Katz, *The Life and Times of Pancho Villa* (Stanford: Stanford University Press, 1998).

12 On regime consolidation and contradictions, see Arnaldo Córdova, *La revolución en crisis: La aventura del maximato* (Mexico City: Cal y Arena, 1995); Adolfo Gilly, *El cardenismo, una utopia mexicana* (Mexico City: Cal y Arena, 1994); and Servín, *Ruptura y oposición*.

13 For Bourbon attacks on community autonomies, economic and cultural, and the negotiations they set off, see Dorothy Tanck de Estrada, *Pueblos de indios y educación en el México colonial* (Mexico City: El Colegio de México, 1999).

14 See the detailed, culturally focused analyses in Eric Van Young, *The Other Rebellion: Popular Violence, Ideology, and the Mexican Struggle for Independence, 1810–1821* (Stanford: Stanford University Press, 2001).

15 A fine regional case study is Terry Rugeley, *Yucatán's Maya Peasantry and the Origins of the Caste War* (Austin: University of Texas Press, 1996).

16 Studies of nineteenth-century demands for community autonomy begin with Leticia Reina, *Las rebeliones campesinas en México, 1819–1906* (Mexico City: Siglo XXI, 1980).

17 For Van Young's contributions as a socioeconomic historian with a regional focus, see *Hacienda and Market in Eighteenth-Century Mexico: The Rural Economy of the Guadalajara Region, 1675–1820* (Berkeley: University of California Press, 1981). His work as a cultural historian focused on communities culminated in *The Other Rebellion*.

18 His role in promoting the larger history of liberalism and nation making in Latin America is evident in Antonio Annino and François-Xavier Guerra, eds., *Inventando la nación: Iberoamérica siglo XIX* (Mexico City: Fondo de Cultura Económica, 2003).

19 Peter Guardino, *In the Time of Liberty: Popular Political Culture in Oaxaca, 1750–1850* (Durham: Duke University Press, 2005), offers a deeply local exploration of the larger processes emphasized by Annino.

20 Reina remains, perhaps, best known for *Las rebeliones campesinas en Mexico.* In English, see her "The Sierra Gorda Peasant Rebellion, 1847–1850," in Katz, *Riot, Rebellion, and Revolution,* 269–94. Her recent contributions to ethnicity and politics emerge in Leticia Reina, ed., *Los Retos de la etnicidad en los estados-nación* (Mexico City: CIESAS, 2000).

21 See *México del antiguo régimen a la revolución* and *Modernidades e independencias.*

22 See his vast and unsurpassed analysis, *The Mexican Revolution,* in two volumes.

23 See *The Secret War in Mexico: Europe, the United States, and the Mexican Revolution* (Chicago: University of Chicago Press, 1983); *Riot, Rebellion, and Revolution*; and *The Life and Times of Pancho Villa.*

24 See *From Insurrection to Revolution.*

25 In English, Meyer is best known for *Mexico and the United States in the Oil Controversy, 1917–1942,* trans. Muriel Vasconcelos (Austin: University of Texas Press, 1972); and Hector Aguilar Camín and Lorenzo Meyer, *In the Shadow of the Mexican Revolution* (Austin: University of Texas Press, 1993).

26 See *A Legacy of Promise* (Austin: University of Texas Press, 1982).

27 See his *Historia del capitalismo en México: Los orígenes, 1521–1763* (Mexico City: Ediciones Era, 1977).

28 See Servín, *Ruptura y oposición.*

❋ PART I *Communities* ❋

Of Tempests and Teapots
Imperial Crisis and Local Conflict in Mexico at the Beginning of the Nineteenth Century

ERIC VAN YOUNG

CRISIS. *Pathology*: The point in the progress of a disease when an important development or change takes place which is decisive of recovery or death; the turning-point of a disease for better or worse; also applied to any marked or sudden variation occurring in the progress of a disease and to the phenomena accompanying it.
Figurative: A vitally important or decisive stage in the progress of anything; a turning-point; also, a state of affairs in which a decisive change for better or worse is imminent; now applied to times of difficulty, insecurity, and suspense in politics or commerce.—*Oxford English Dictionary*

The late eighteenth century and the early nineteenth have long appeared to historians a turning point in the affairs of the Western world. But even to many contemporaries of the era, whether consciously or unconsciously, a looming sense of crisis, of ineluctable change, hung over much of Europe and the Atlantic world, preoccupying both intellectuals and common people, although they may have deployed different idioms to express it.[1] Much of this anxiety and hope found religious as well as political expression, nourished decisively by the still-vital apocalypticism of the Judeo-Christian tradition. The meaning and eschatology of these beliefs often centered on the events of the French Revolution, which were to have such transcendent importance for the peoples of Ibero-America, and on the Revolution's greatest public figure, Napoleon Bonaparte.[2] In New Spain, for example, it is difficult to believe that when the great statesman and historian Lucas

Alamán sat down, many years after the events, to describe the capture of Guanajuato's Alhóndiga by Father Miguel Hidalgo's forces on September 28, 1810, Alamán did not have in mind the storming of the Bastille in Paris on July 14, 1789 (or even late medieval French jacqueries), though he did not explicitly say as much.[3] Among the notable political thinkers and artists of the age, some (among them Edmund Burke) saw in the Revolution a dark night of folly, barbarous violence, ideological excess, and the rejection of traditional political and social working arrangements, while others (among them Goethe and the romantics) saw in the Revolution, at least in its early phase, a new dawn of human potentiality. Napoleon proved a figure of lasting ambivalence in the new world and political culture created by revolutionary events. While ambitious young Creoles in Spain's New World colonies often modeled themselves on Napoleon and pursued the *cariére ouverte á talente* embodied by his trajectory in public life, others in the European orbit regarded him as an apocalyptic figure.[4] Writing less than a century after the fall of the French ancien régime and scarcely two generations after Napoleon's death, for example, Leo Tolstoy reflected the apocalyptic view of the revolutionary era in the second sentence of his novel *War and Peace* (1869). Here the great Russian novelist has Ana Pavlovna Scherer ("a distinguished lady of the court, and confidential maid-of-honour to the Empress") describing Bonaparte as "this Antichrist (upon my word, I believe he is)."[5] From his exile in St. Petersburg, the arch-conservative French thinker Joseph de Maistre similarly viewed the Revolution as a satanic revolt, emphasizing Napoleon's apocalyptic role in an approaching end-time scenario.[6] Even in England, apocalyptic religion and political crisis intertwined in the popular imagination in the years after 1789. For example, a farm woman named Joanna Southcott identified herself as the woman of Revelation 12 (and thus, incidentally, a competitor of the Virgin of Guadalupe), "clothed with the sun, and the moon under her feet, and upon her head a crown of twelve stars." Receiving revelations not only about mundane political events such as the war in France, but also concerning the coming millennial kingdom and the destruction of Satan, the sixty-four-year-old virgin Southcott convinced many of her followers in 1814 that she was pregnant with the supernaturally conceived man-child whom Revelation 12:5 foretold was "to rule all nations with a rod of iron." And so it went across the European world.[7]

"CRISIS" IN THE SPANISH REALMS

Even setting aside apocalyptic religious thinking and the strong fears and opinions evoked by the French Revolution, however, much of the Spanish

Atlantic world seemed to be undergoing some sort of fundamental transformation after the mid-eighteenth century, with all the stresses and resistances one might expect to attend such an experience. The caustic (and liberating) juices of the Enlightenment were certainly penetrating Spain and its American colonies, while international warfare, imperial competition, and economic change spurred in Spain itself a defensive stock-taking and reformist impulse most notable in the famous *tratadista* projects of Jovellanos, Campomanes, and other Spanish political figures.[8] Not only the court-centered political elite, members of the "political nation," or Spanish intellectuals articulated and shared a sense of urgency, however. After Napoleon Bonaparte took the Spanish monarchy hostage in 1808, triggering a political imbroglio within the empire, the liberal nationalist peninsular press unleashed a "political pedagogy" likely to have touched even the semiliterate populace, as the abundant pamphletry and newspapers of the post-1808 period did in New Spain.[9] Whether or not it was fully and consciously perceived as such by contemporaries, and whether or not a crisis that unfolds over several decades or even a century may still be called a crisis (issues addressed hereafter in greater detail), modern scholars have identified the "Age of Revolution" (1750–1850) as a key period for the emergence of modern Spain, the ex-Iberian dominions, and the European world more generally.[10]

Certainly from a structural perspective, the Mexican colony experienced economic, social, and political changes after the mid-eighteenth century in whose absence it is virtually impossible to imagine the advent of the movement for independence. This was indeed an "age of paradox," its internally contradictory tendencies deeply etched in chiaroscuro. As I have noted elsewhere, while baroque architectural splendors in the Churrigueresque style were gracing the low skylines of Taxco, Tepozotlán, Guanajuato, and other cities of silver and piety, travelers such as Baron von Humboldt noted the increasing numbers of beggars (the famous *léperos*) in the capital's streets, while bandits thronged countryside and urban hinterlands. Colonial commerce expanded (albeit episodically because of the Atlantic wars of the French revolutionary period), but the imperial fiscal machinery cranked up to extract ever-increasing amounts of tax revenues to pay the expenses of a state intermittently engaged in warfare. Agricultural commercialization advanced in the Mexican countryside while great subsistence crises (e.g., 1785–86, 1808–10) periodically racked a population caught in a Malthusian vice between growing numbers of the working poor and increasingly concentrated landownership. While silver production boomed, great fortunes were made, and mining entrepreneurs were ennobled for their piety, wealth, and service to the Spanish crown, the real compensation of rural labor dropped by something like 25 percent over the two generations between 1775 and independence. The Bourbon reforms in many ways modernized New Spain along absolutist lines, improving the efficiency of administration and the yield of fiscal extraction, while large sectors of the Creole elite were essentially disfranchised from the control of state and church they had gained during the preceding century from the faltering hands of the declining Habsburg monarchy. While race mixture (*mestizaje*) effectively undermined more and more in practice what had always been a rather porous system of race-based social and legal stratification, the official rhetoric of ethnic categorization became ever more rigid, detailed, and exclusionary. Finally, even as modernizing Bourbon absolutism and European thinking in art, science, and education drew Mexico more into the orbit of the Atlantic world and the Enlightenment, forms of endogenous cultural identification (e.g., Creole patriotism and neo-Aztecism) and nationalist-tinted religious sensibility (the rise of the Virgin of Guadalupe devotion) blossomed, building an ideological platform for national autonomy and state-building projects.[11]

Within the general context of the crisis of the late eighteenth century and the early nineteenth, then, and situated squarely in the center of what historians sometimes term the "Age of Revolution" (1750–1850), we may reasonably see the struggle for independence in Mexico as the resolution stage of some sort of crisis.[12] The problem with looking at this chaotic decade or two from the perspective of a global or unitary crisis, however, is that much of the historical evidence suggests that the crisis in which the colony was embroiled meant very different things to different people. For one thing, a great ideological chasm separated the political thinking of the Creole-mestizo insurgent directorate from that of popular groups, whose political ideas formed a double helix with quite traditional forms of religious sensibility. Moreover, the movement was highly fragmented—even feudalized—socially, spatially, and militarily, so that even if popular and elite rebel groups had wanted to impose ideological homogeneity on the many disparate groups and movements involved, they would have faced insuperable organizational, geographical, and technological obstacles to doing so. Finally, the modes of action and goals of popular groups, especially of the indigenous villagers in the countryside who made up as much as 60 percent of putative insurgent participants, demonstrated a notable continuity with preinsurgency rural political expression and protest rather than the emergence of new forms of consciousness, political culture, or behavior.[13]

What, then, are we to make of the conventional historiographical wisdom that the Mexican independence movement pivoted on a series of cross-class, cross-ethnic alliances represented iconographically by the universal symbol of the Virgin of Guadalupe? In other words, to employ the medical trope so common in discussions of acute transition situations in economies and polities, of whose disease-state was the crisis of independence the resolution? Part of the answer boils down to exploring how the late colonial crisis was experienced—lived on a day-to-day basis—in rural Mexico. The central explanandum of this essay is the degree to which elite visions of a colony- or empire-wide crisis mapped onto local visions of crisis, and vice versa. The question may well be raised: can local knowledge, local attitudes, and local and popular collective behavior be convincingly explained absent the assumption that "structural" (i.e., mostly economic) causes on a grand scale determined the many circumscribed episodes that went to make up much of the real struggle during the independence conflict? My response to this question would be not that the collective behavior was uninteresting, unreflective of larger histories, or random, but that we have been looking in the wrong place to explain it, and that the conventional logic of inference simply assumed facts about the determinative weight of structural factors either not in evidence, or only ambiguously so. Let me rephrase this in the terms central to this essay: while a structural crisis of great and sustained intensity may well have gripped New Spain in the last decades of the eighteenth century and the first decades of the nineteenth—a crisis in which the struggle for independence was in some way the resolution phase—that crisis was lived in the countryside in an almost hyper-localist atmosphere. Where collective political violence erupted in village Mexico, it was most often driven by local historical memory, local religious sensibility, local conflict, and local actors, and was not easily reframed in a discourse of providentialism, national or protonational political aspiration, or Enlightenment philosophical thinking.[14] Like a green wine, local political thinking might be potent, but it did not travel well.

WHAT SORT OF CONCEPT IS "CRISIS," AND HOW USEFUL IS IT AS A CATEGORY IN SOCIAL AND CULTURAL HISTORY?

Let us accept as a working assumption, then, that much of the European world, and along with it the Spanish Atlantic world more specifically, found itself in a critical conjuncture beginning sometime during the last four or five decades of the eighteenth century, if not earlier. Let us further assume that this sense of having arrived at a transformative if open-ended historical moment embraced the economic, political, social, and cultural realms, as it has in many other polities. While individuals or large groups of people may well experience stress of some sort, however, this does not necessarily translate into a *perception* of "global" crisis itself, and still less into a propensity to effect large-scale change through a political project shaped by some sort of even implicit social consensus based on shared assumptions. Let us further suppose the empire-wide crisis of the Spanish world in the late eighteenth century and the early nineteenth, therefore, to have been as much an artifact of representation—in other words, of seeing and communicating through an appropriate set of signifiers about what was socially and politically normal or pathological, moral or immoral, desirable, possible, or unattainable—as it was an effect of objectively verifiable structural conditions. The clearest response to the opportunity for positive change (or to the imperative of staving off disaster) on the part of the Spanish imperial regime was a political and economic "project" socially situated at the level of the state and elite power groupings, and largely secularized (surely this is the significance of Bourbon regalism, for example) and instrumentalist (e.g., the Bourbon reforms) in nature.

In keeping with this scenario, it is my contention that the further one descended from the commanding heights of political and economic power, the more diluted the perception of a generalized societal crisis or point of historical inflection would become. This is emphatically *not* to say that people at the margins of the "political nation" at this time were prepolitical or apolitical, since only in the most perversely narrow construction of politics could thinking about polity and public life be seen as limited to citizens focusing their attentions only on the level of imperial events, or on the fates of the subimperial units shortly to become the nation-states of Spanish America. On the other hand, it is manifestly the case that essentially cultural filters such as gender, educational attainment, language, ethnicity, social status, wealth, and closeness (both spatial and structural) to the centers of power conditioned one's view of the political horizon and the appropriate points of reference in public life. Even if common people had some diffuse sense of the "times being out of joint," therefore, they would be more prone to articulate their anxieties and hopes in familiar idioms, and to seek reequilibrating solutions by adjusting or defending familiar, small-scale frameworks rather than looking to the creation of new, large-scale ones. This is most particularly true in a colonial situation such as Mexico's at the end of the eighteenth century and was strongly conditioned by the still-prevalent multiethnic nature of late colonial society, the weakness of class structure and spatial integration, and the relative shallowness of civil society and the public sphere. In such circumstances, at least in accounting for the motives and participation of most social actors, the concept of a society-wide crisis becomes problematic as an explanation for any sort of large-scale change, which the foundation of the Mexican nation-state surely was. A pervasive crisis embodied in "objective" structural conditions thus retains some heuristic value as an etic category but, from the point of view of different social actors, looks a rather blunt instrument in terms of its emic explanatory power. To put this in another way: from the perspective of the social and cultural historian, how is a crisis actually *lived*, and what difference does it make (and how do we know)? As a way into this question, let us linger for a moment over the notional concept of crisis, since the denaturalization of such terms may lead in interesting directions.[15]

As with many terms widely in use as signifying concepts in the human sciences, and more broadly in everyday speech, "crisis" both gains and loses in expressive utility from its very connotative plasticity (and I refer to it as a concept rather than just a term or a word precisely because of this connotative breadth). Like other such connotative expressions, that of "crisis" tends to grow increasingly transparent or even to shred as one looks at it closely. Thus we speak of "critical conjunctures" (as I have done earlier) or employ the concept liberally along a wide gamut from the microsocial ("crisis of conscience") to the macrosocial ("crisis of the old order"—or again, in my own case, as in the title of my 1992 book *La crísis del orden colonial*).[16] So intuitive has its use become that some authoritative sources simply ignore its definition entirely.[17] The *International Encyclopedia of the Social Sciences*, however, includes a substantial discussion of the concept that in many general aspects parallels the essentially medical model encapsulated in the epigraph at the beginning of this essay, a discussion that is worth considering briefly.

There are a dozen elements to what the *International Encyclopedia* article designates a "procedural" definition of "crisis," but these can be synthesized to three more encompassing ones:

1. A crisis constitutes a turning point in an unfolding sequence of actions or events in which the requirement for action is high among participants because of increasing tension or anxiety among them.
2. A crisis situation produces uncertainties about courses of action, typically features inadequate information, and reduces participants' control over other actors.
3. A crisis produces an important outcome whose consequences significantly shape the future of the participants.

Cast as it was in a prevailingly social scientific (especially political science) idiom at the height of the Cold War, this definition and the discussion in which it is embedded display certain limits for the historian in terms of their usefulness.[18] For one thing, the definition is overwhelmingly developed within an international relations framework, specifically with regard to nuclear escalation or other types of direct military confrontation. While military elements were certainly not absent from the period under examination here, on either the international or local level, this seems to me the least interesting entry point into the theme of a turn-of-the-century crisis around 1800. Relatedly, the definition of the notional concept of crisis implicitly limits itself to large polities, especially nation-states in collision with one another, as opposed to smaller units or extrapolitical (say, economic) phenomena, and assumes that a crisis must be global—that is, must embrace an entire society in a homogeneously penetrating way. In glossing the literature on crisis as a concept in psychological and sociological studies, however, the article notes in passing the useful caveat that "crisis is relative; what is a crisis for one party or participant may not be for another."[19] Transposing this observation from the psychosocial register to that of a hierarchy of polities, one may suppose on the one hand that crises are not simply additive—that is, a "national" crisis is not simply an aggregate of subnational ones but instead demonstrates a structural logic and scale of its own. On the other hand (and this is the key point of the argument I will develop), a situation observed as critical by the holders of power may not be so perceived by humbler folk, or vice versa. And the idioms employed to represent a critical conjuncture, as I have suggested, as well as the living experience of it, may be quite different depending on one's structural perspective. Finally, because of its decision-oriented (probably game-theory-centered) emphasis, the *International Encyclopedia* definition is excessively voluntaristic, and ultimately more synchronic than diachronic, speaking in terms of "conditions" rather than "dynamics" over time, and providing no stage model of any kind for critical development.

In an attempt to circumvent some of the difficulties in applying a basic definition of crisis to an unfolding historical situation in which not only systemic elements but temporal dynamics are important, let me propose a stage model (see table) of how such an episode develops. The model consists of three larger phases, embracing among them six stages or identifiable "moments." In addition to the usual disclaimers about generalization, I would point out that, primitive as it may be, the model makes no assertions about the directionality of crisis outcomes—that is, whether the end-state is "better" or "worse" for the participants than the beginning-state; nor does it address the question of how long a crisis may take to unfold—a month, a year, a decade, a century—and still lay claim to the name of crisis, or the level of social organization on which a crisis may occur.[20] This is nothing more than an effort to concretize what the stages of a crisis might be, and I will not belabor the reader with discussions of what a "normal" state is, or of what constitutes disequilibrium or liminality.

CRISIS MODEL

Phase	State
Generative:	"normal" state → stress → disequilibrium →
Transition:	conflict (liminality) →
Resolution:	resolution → "normal" state (new social alignment)

Let me summarize up to this point, then. By the end of the eighteenth century there existed in much of the Western world generally, and arguably in the Spanish Atlantic world as one of its components, a widespread perception of an impending epochal turning point of some sort, whether for good or ill, a perception sometimes infused with an apocalyptic sensibility. Also occupying this cultural moment were "objective" structural conditions of rapid change and contradiction in the economic, social, and political realms. Perception of the locus of these conditions, however, as well as of the instrumentalities to accommodate, modify, or reverse them, whether through policy or collective violence, was likely to have differed much in nature depending on an individual's or group's structural perspective. How do such considerations affect our understanding of the course of the Mexican independence movement? More specifically, if Mexico's realization of political separation from Spain and its embarkation along the path of state and nation building were the resolution or realignment stage of a crisis, whose crisis was it, exactly, and how had the consciousness of such a critical conjuncture developed, if indeed it had? To put the question in terms of this essay's title: what was the relationship between the tempest (imperial crisis) and the teapot (local conflict and violence)?

To explore these questions, I will reconstruct in some detail two instances of "riot" in the Mexican countryside, both emblematic in some ways of the crisis through which the colony is thought to have passed in the late eighteenth century and the early nineteenth. The episodes share at least in part, for example, obvious roots in agrarian pressures in the latter half of the eighteenth century, ethnic conflict, and strong traces of the scapegoating of peninsular-born Spaniards by indigenous people and other rural dwellers. The earlier case (1785), at least, foreshadows the conflation of political and religious idioms so characteristic of village collective action a generation later, during the independence movement itself. But both episodes also display ambiguous, even tenuous, relationships to the formal elements of the late colonial crisis as perceived and articulated by contemporary witnesses and participants, and as described by modern scholars of the period. The major point here is that while in the aggregate there may have been a generalized crisis in late-eighteenth- and early-nineteenth-century Mexico, the etiology of crisis was also very much anchored in local history and contingency, and collective action to resolve critical stress was often limited to a local venue and aimed at local social actors. In other words, psychosocial stresses at the community level, the local knowledges that both spurred and channeled them, and the forms of localized collective action to which they gave birth did not travel well, often dissipating beyond the boundaries of small communities. Furthermore, in terms of the simple model of crisis proposed earlier, the resolution phase generally occurred locally, with the reestablishment of a local political or social equilibrium or the elimination of noxious social objects or arrangements, and not supralocally or nationally.

The first incident I will describe occurred in 1785 at Cuautitlán, a few miles northwest of Mexico City, where a long history of changes in property relations and political alignments apparently culminated in a violent dispute between indigenous and nonindigenous *vecinos* (householders) of the community over the ownership of a locally venerated religious icon. After sketching the main lines of the situation, I will narrate briefly the fate of this area in the 1810 insurgency. The second incident took place in the waning days of 1810 at the town of Atlacomulco, further to the northwest of Mexico City, at the far edge of the Toluca Valley. Here, complex old and new rivalries and conflicts within the town—some of them pitting nonindigenous individuals and factions against each other, others involving conflicts between Indians and non-Indians—combined to set the background for the lynching of four local men, two of them peninsular Spaniards, even while Father Miguel Hidalgo's army was advancing on the capital for an attack that never materialized.[21] Had the two conflicts occurred in the same locality, the 1810 incident could easily have grown out of the 1785 riot. A deconstruction of both episodes demonstrates that while broad, supralocal structural factors and events may influence small, localized collective movements, the latter are by no means easily explained as reflexive manifestations of the former but have their own history and internal logic. The method, or mode of reasoning, is by analogy. If the 1785 and 1810 episodes bear a close resemblance to each other, and the later incident occurred in conjunction with the insurgency of 1810 (of which it was in many ways a typical manifestation), then it may be true that the political sensibilities and behavior of ordinary people both before and during the short-term crisis of the independence struggle also demonstrated considerable continuity; that is, that there was much of 1810 in 1785. This would mean that crisis might actually be *lived* in a very circumscribed way, without much obvious or verifiable connection to macropolitical events or formal ideologies. Restated in terms of the preoccupations of the modern human sciences, this formulation raises the perennial questions of the relationship of structure to agency, of representation to consciousness, and of action to ideology.

CUAUTITLÁN: THE VIRGIN AND THE MICE

On the evening of December 7, 1785, a riot broke out in Cuautitlán in which the majority of the rioters were Indian vecinos of the town, and almost all the victims comfortably off Creole Spanish citizens and officeholders. Although the fragmentary accounts of participants, victims, and witnesses make the details of the incident difficult to reconstruct (not untypically for such cases), we can establish a basic narrative. The disturbance began when a venerated image of the Virgin of the Immaculate Conception was about to be brought out of the town church for a religious procession. The riot was touched off by a rumor circulating rapidly among the gathered indigenous townsmen to the effect that the body of the icon had been replaced by a new one, less holy and presumably less efficacious, under the patronage of a local non-Indian woman, doña Antonia de Medina, with the cooperation of the parish priest, Doctor don Juan Manuel Casal Bermúdez, but over the objection of members of the Indian religious confraternity (*cofradía*) that helped support the cult. Unable to calm the agitated crowd, Casal Bermúdez sent for the district's submagistrate (*teniente de justicia*), who took a long while to arrive, perhaps fearing the eruption of a violent incident already foreshadowed in a petition by the town's Indians to the viceroy some weeks previously, which sought to block the repair of the icon. As the situation became more and more tense, the priest withdrew, first to his own house, then to that of don Esteban de los Reyes, the local commander (*teniente*) of the Acordada, where he hid himself.[22] The curate's life was spared, he later testified, only through the miraculous intervention of the Virgin, when a clerk of Reyes's convinced the Indians who had invaded the house and were chopping down the door of the room in which Casal Bermúdez was hiding that the room was empty, thus allowing the priest to escape down a ladder into a patio, and thence away from the house. In the meantime, as the crowd "resolved to kill their priest and the tithe collector [also a cleric]," hunting these men through the streets with axes, sticks, and slings, the curate's residence was attacked, the windows and locks broken, and some sheets and other items stolen; the home of the tithe collector, the priest don Simón Castillo, received much rougher treatment. The riot was eventually quelled (probably the following day, by which time it would in any case almost certainly have burned itself out) with the arrival of a detachment of dragoons from the capital. As he wrote his report of the episode to the viceroy at the end of January 1786, Father Casal Bermúdez was still in refuge in the capital from his riotous parishioners.[23]

The reaction of the Cuautitlán district's indigenous inhabitants to this tampering with their venerated icon was probably not a complete surprise to Father Casal Bermúdez or other local white authorities, although they may not have anticipated the violent turn it took, and certainly had not tried to provoke it. Set against a background of often problematic priest-parishioner relations, conflicts between rural curates and their Indian flocks over matters of cult were, if not common, then at least not infrequent in the late colonial countryside, and Casal Bermúdez would almost certainly have known of other such incidents in Central Mexico.[24] In any case, the natives' resistance to what they must have regarded as a sinister conspiracy between the curate and a nonindigenous parishioner was foreshadowed just two days before the riot in a petition of December 5, 1785, directed to Viceroy Bernardo Gálvez by don Manuel Gómez, Indian *gobernador* of Cuautitlán, and two former *gobernadores.* Reviewing briefly the relationship of the Virgin to the indigenous cofradía attached to the chapel where she resided, the petition went on to stress the "singular beauty" of the icon and the "tender affection" of the villagers for an advocation of the Virgin, which had in past performed "innumerable prodigies." Doña Antonia Medina, they claimed (the petition referred to her as doña Antonia Castañeda, perhaps a mistaken [and, if so, telling] allusion to another local tithe collector, don Juan de Castañeda), had had another image of the icon made, with the connivance of curate Casal Bermúdez, to replace the original, which she wished to send elsewhere, "without reflecting that the said image belongs to no Spaniard, but to the [Indian] natives [of the pueblo]."[25] The native officials therefore requested a viceregal injunction against the removal of the figure. Furthermore, they insisted, if the body of the icon required repairs, these should be accomplished "leaving [the figure's] face intact." The viceroy dispatched an order to this effect, but it did not arrive in Cuautitlán until the day of the riot itself, December 7.

Writing to Viceroy Gálvez from Mexico City in late January, 1786, nearly two months after the violent episode, Father Casal Bermúdez claimed that the argument over the Virgin's image was only a flimsy pretext to justify the disrespectful Cuautitlán Indians' attack on him and tithe collector Castillo. Indeed, the curate's contentious account hinted at the political turbulence and complex factional alliances within the town. To begin with, directly

1. At the center of every community was a church—sometimes a focus of unity, sometimes a center of conflict among villagers, priests, and magistrates. Reprinted by permission of Archivo General de la Nación, Sección Propiedad Artística y Literaria.

contradicting the Indian gobernadores' claim, the curate insisted: "Although the origin [of the image] is not known, it is believed with ample basis that it belongs to the Spaniards of the town [*vecinos de razón*] and not to the Indians." Furthermore, while the indigenous cofradía members had only squandered their organization's resources (a typical claim of parish priests), the non-Indians (*gente de razón*) of Cuautitlán had always voluntarily contributed funds to care for the image and improve the chapel. The hair of the statuette, for example, originally of coarse vegetable fiber (*sayal*), had been replaced with human hair; and the infestation of the icon's body with mice, which gnawed at the Virgin's clothing, had prompted the attempt to replace the body, leaving the head of the icon intact.[26] Doña Antonia Medina had undertaken to have a new body made to the same dimensions as the image of the Purísima Concepción in the Franciscan convent in Mexico City, neither she nor the priest having any intention of moving the figure to a different location. Notwithstanding what had been said in the original Indian petition to the viceroy, Casal Bermúdez claimed to have suspended the replacement of the body until he could convince the parishioners of the "usefulness and convenience" of the change, something he was unable to do in the chaotic circumstances attending the events of December 7. In his account of that evening, furthermore, the priest singled out as "leader of the disturbances [*cabecilla de inquietudes*]" and one of the "principal motors" of the riot the Indian Juan Ramos, a thorn in the side of the former *alcalde mayor*, don Nicolás Martínez de Moya (the current alcalde mayor was his brother, don Miguel Martínez de Moya), along with another Indian, Vicente Marzial Atlahuitzin. In separate testimony, Ramos, self-identified as an *indio principal* of Cuautitlán, credibly claimed that he had tried to calm the crowd rather than incite it, and was eventually absolved of any complicity in the events.[27] Shortly after the episode (March 1786), and despite curate Casal Bermúdez's attempts to suspend his taking office, Ramos was elected gobernador of Indian Cuautitlán. Eventually a judicial order was addressed by the Audiencia of New Spain to the Indian vecinos of the town, reproving them mildly for their riotous behavior and enjoining them to respect their curate. In glossing this order, the *fiscal de indios* (royal attorney charged with overseeing Indian affairs) of the Audiencia noted that at the time of the attempted repairs to the Virgin's body, the indigenous inhabitants of the town had a complaint pending against Father Casal Bermúdez (one presumes for his attempt to charge Indian *cófrades* extra for burial in the chapel, although there may have been other charges, as well).[28] Even had it been spurred by the holiest of intentions, the *fiscal* wrote, curate Casal Bermúdez's action was unwise, "since the strange way of thinking of the Indians in such questions is widely known from experience." The subsequent fate of the Virgin of the Immaculate Conception, about whose condition and ownership this contention boiled up, is unknown.

It will surprise no one familiar with the later colonial Mexican countryside, or with the background of the independence struggle, that this highly charged instance of contention over a sacred symbol of community—the indigenous vecinos claiming her as their own, the Spanish vecinos as theirs —was embedded in a long-term situation of social and economic conflict with significant political overtones. Let me relate this briefly.[29] Nearly five years before the riotous episode over the mouse-infested Virgin, Viceroy Martín Mayorga had dispatched a lengthy order (dated February 23, 1781) to the alcalde mayor of Cuautitlán, don Nicolás de Moya, relating to the complex issue of the disposition of Indian lands. The viceroy categorically ordered that under no circumstances or pretext were sales, loans, pawns, or rentals of Indian lands held by right of *repartos* (parcels of communally owned farming lands occupied by virtue of birth into an indigenous village) or private inheritance to be allowed, except with prior license from the Audiencia of Mexico, the Juzgado General de Indios (General Indian Court), or the viceroy himself; local officials and notaries were strictly forbidden to authorize such transactions without prior license, on pain of fines and other penalties. The order was to apply to transactions not only between Indians, Spaniards, and *castas* (racially mixed persons neither Indian nor Spanish) but also among the Indians themselves.[30]

Preceded by similar orders issued in 1778 by Viceroy Bucareli, and in 1780 by Mayorga himself, the viceroy's order was occasioned by news of continuing "abuses" committed by and against indigenous landowners in Central Mexico, putatively resulting in the "harmful alienation" of farming lands, house lots (*solares*), and houses owned privately, communally, and by right of reparto. These alienations by indigenous villagers, carried out either voluntarily or under coercion, were effected by Indians disguising themselves as non-Indians and then going before notaries to convey property through "simple titles," many of which had been abrogated subsequently as illegal by the Juzgado de Indios.[31] The evils following from the unregulated alienation of indigenous lands, which seemed to be reaching a crescendo in the late colonial period, comprised a familiar litany. Bereft of their property, Indians turned to laziness and vagrancy; fled their villages, thus diminishing royal tribute revenues; and, with no fixed residence, in the words of the 1781 decree, lived "without obedience to the magistrates, and without subjection to their priests." Mayorga's rationale for this sweeping decree reflected the traditional view, furthermore, that indigenous people needed to be protected by the crown from the consequences of their own diminished capacities:

> And because of this disorder, which day by day increases more and more because of the tolerance of it, [there arises] the fear that the Indians will end in a most unhappy state, not having any place to live, no lands to farm on which to occupy themselves, or to help maintain themselves, or to pay their parochial fees or taxes. . . . To this is added the damage resulting from mixing with other vicious people of different races, such as mulattos, *lobos, coyotes*, and other such people, whose malice and perversity easily prompt the Indians, owing to their simplicity and ignorance, to commit robberies, murders, and other crimes, which they commit both in towns and outside them, infesting the roads, now as petty thieves, now with greater robberies, and given over with greater abandon to the incorrigible vice of drunkenness, which makes them prone to even greater licentiousness.

Detailed information on the alienation of Indian lands in the Cuautitlán district dates from nearly two years after the promulgation of Viceroy Mayorga's decree. In early November 1782, the indigenous officials of San Mateo Ixtacalco, a subject pueblo of Cuautitlán, complained to the viceregal authorities that since Mayorga's decree, the situation for modest Indian farmers in the area had, if anything, grown worse rather than improved. They pointed to declining tribute incomes, implied that the arrangements conveying indigenous lands to the use of non-Indians were generally made under duress, and asked that all such agreements be abrogated. In the ensuing inquiry, which occupied two or three years, the rental situation (not permanent alienation by sale, it should be noted) in a number of district towns came to light, along with much testimony as to how such rentals were effected. The gobernador of Teoloyucan testified that it had long been the practice for Indians to "lend" (*prestar*—surely a euphemism) their small parcels to other Indians or Spaniards for six-month periods to grow wheat, and with the interest to finance their own maize production during the remaining six months of the year.[32] Judging by the rental records, the standard parcel for rental was a *yunta* (the amount of land that a single man working with a team of oxen [*yunta de bueyes*] might plow in a day—probably about two acres), and the standard amount of rent four reales (i.e., one-half peso) per yunta. Some witnesses were less sanguine or matter-of-fact in their account of renting practices, among them the village gobernador, who noted that "the Indian owner of a piece of land that he can cultivate . . . receives nothing more than a few reales because he rents out his land, this being the reason that they [the Indians] are always sunken in poverty." The lawyer for the gobernador and Indian villagers (*común*) of the pueblo of Santa Barbara noted that the district contained many Spanish and other non-Indian vecinos, and that the Spaniards in particular, ". . . as powerful [people] and of a domineering spirit toward the Indians . . . take the land in rental and treat it as though they own it," also monopolizing local water resources so that the Indians' own plantings suffered.[33]

With radical pruning, it is possible to extract from the rather confusing thicket of data pertaining to land rentals in the area some general conclusions that throw interesting light on local politics, ethnic relations, the distribution of wealth, and the riot of 1785. What seems to have happened is that a number of local Spaniards had acquired by various means—the weight of their capital resources, the play of market forces, coercion, strategic alliances, or all of these in combination—fairly large numbers of land parcels through rental from Indian farmers. Among the chief of these local *poderosos* was the same Spaniard (whether peninsular or Creole is not stated), don Esteban de los Reyes, teniente de Acordada, in whose home the curate Casal Bermúdez was to seek refuge from the riotous crowd on December 7, 1785. In the pueblos of Cuautitlán, Santa Barbara, San Matheo, and San Sebastián, he rented cumulatively just under seventy yuntas of land in twenty-seven parcels.[34] Don Nicolás de Moya, in the early 1780s chief magistrate (alcalde mayor) of the district, rented forty yuntas from Indians in the pueblo of San Matheo, and his brother, don Miguel de Moya, at that time teniente de alcalde mayor, rented twelve yuntas in the same village.

But the Spaniards were not alone in taking on rental farming lands from humbler indigenous villagers. There were also a number of Indian gobernadores renting large numbers of parcels from villagers, most of them very small, and several Indian "commoners," as well. During the period 1782–84, altogether nearly eight hundred yuntas (worth in rentals some four hundred pesos) were being rented out yearly, mostly by indigenous farmers of apparently modest holdings, to Spaniards, Indian notables, and wealthier Indian commoners. One of the larger renters in the area, Joseph Rodríguez, of the pueblo of San Lorenzo (he may well have been an indigenous notable, but the evidence is not clear), rented out from other Indians at least sixty-one yuntas but manipulated his own ethnic status as personal necessity and advantage dictated. According to a July 1784 report by the Spanish teniente of Tultitlán, in the *subdelegación* of Tacuba, Rodríguez, "when it favors his interests, as in having community lands to farm [*tierras de repartimiento*], and not pay sales taxes, presents himself as an Indian, when it comes time to pay the Royal Tribute, he calls himself a Mestizo." Furthermore, in their complaint, the Indian officials of Santa Barbara pueblo accused alcalde mayor Moya (whose brother would succeed him in the magistracy by the time of the 1785 riot) of being far too cozy with several other large-scale nonindigenous renters, and therefore trying to block the execution of Viceroy Mayorga's 1781 decree to keep the (now) illegally rented lands in their hands. By 1785 many of the rental agreements had in fact been abrogated, and the parcels falling within the rubric of communal (i.e., neither reparto nor private) lands had been rented out again with the approval of the viceregal authorities. The major renters on this occasion were drawn from the wealthier Indian notables and officials named as large renters in the earlier lists, among them the gobernador of Santa Barbara, the present alcalde and two *principales* of San Matheo, and a *principal* of San Lorenzo. Among them these men, all described as "very Hispanized" (*extremadamente ladinos*), took 137 yuntas in rental.

To understand fully the elite impulse to dominate local landed resources in this way, it must be remembered that the economic magnet of Mexico City was in the late colonial period exerting an ever stronger pull on the Valley of Mexico, as well as outlying areas. Cuautitlán's 6,300 pesos per year in Indian tributes (1784), along with other revenues, its twenty Indian pueblos, a total district population of about fifteen thousand people, and the presence of the former Jesuit *colegio* at Tepozotlán made the local judicial district (*corregimiento*), if well administered, a moderately profitable one in the late eighteenth century.[35] As the likely involvement of the Moya brothers and their allies in commercial farming suggests, proximity to the capital's market also yielded opportunities for economic gain, while institutional structures and political alliances facilitated access to productive resources. At the end of the colonial era, the local pottery industry, at least partially in the hands of Indian producers (it is not clear how extensive non-Indian involvement was) and emphasizing the manufacture of "everyday pottery" (*loza ordinaria*) from clay deposits in the area, was still thriving, bringing in about 100,000 pesos per year around 1800.[36] Cuautitlán and its district were also important producers of pulque for the Mexico City market, an activity that attracted attempts at exploitation by local Spanish officials and sometimes violent responses by Indian producers.[37] Finally, commercial wheat production for the capital's market, mostly in the hands of local haciendas because of the industry's infrastructural and irrigation requirements, rounded out the economic picture.[38]

What had happened in the Cuautitlán area, then, is this. The possibilities for profitable commercial agriculture had burgeoned at least by the 1780s, creating a situation in which influential local Spaniards, some of them officeholders and others not, had combined forces with some indigenous notables to gain control through questionable or outright illegal rental agreements of as much cultivable land as possible, and of the labor that went with it (since effectively landless peasants would ipso factor reenter the market as sellers of their own labor). What must essentially be seen as a land-grab had probably undermined the legitimacy of some local indigenous leaders, but even more so that of alcalde mayor Moya, his allies, Spanish merchants such as Esteban de los Reyes (himself, it will be remembered, teniente of the local Acordada), and perhaps also the priest, Manuel Casal Bermúdez.[39] In the meantime, the continuing shift of cultivable land from the sector of small-scale indigenous peasants (most of the parcels illegally rented were in the range of two yuntas in size, and singly owned) into the hands of larger, more commercially oriented farmers had skewed the local distribution of wealth, creating or consolidating not only a Spanish market economy in the area but also a stratum of more prosperous, kulak-like indigenous producers. Although the interpersonal and interfactional relationships are a bit hazy, this stressful situation appears to have opened the possibility for an oppositional political entrepreneur like the Indian don Juan Ramos (such men were typically labeled "troublemakers" [*perturbadores*] by local Spanish political establishments) to move into the legitimacy vacuum, as he did by winning the office of gobernador in March 1786 despite the curate's vigorous opposition. In this situation it is hardly surprising that an ethnically tinted, classlike conflict in the sacral realm—

the violence over the Virgin of the Immaculate Conception—should echo more diffuse local political and economic contention. I would venture to interpret this episode as a struggle over a sacral vessel common to both indigenous and nonindigenous components of local society for purposes of community self-identity, gaining power, and ensuring access to the divine.

Let me now provide a sort of longish coda to the story of Cuautitlán's diminutive crisis of the 1780s. A generation or so after the events just narrated, the town and its district were poised on the brink of the independence struggle. Although there exists for this era no overview of the town's social, political, and economic configuration comparable even to the fragmentary one of the 1780s, some documentary sources hint that trends in evidence decades earlier—the drift of landed resources into the hands of local poderosos, proletarianization in the countryside, and interethnic conflict—had continued over the intervening years. On the eve of the outbreak of the insurgency, during the harvest failure of 1809, reports by colonial authorities emphasized the presence of numerous, very-small-scale subsistence producers (*pegujaleros*) and laborers (*operarios*) on the seven haciendas and ten ranchos of the Cuautitlán district itself, which fits with the skewed distribution of land we have seen a generation or so earlier. In the nearby Huehuetoca section of the district, moreover, the only hacienda was that of San José Jalpa, owned by the Marqués de San Cristóbal.[40] This estate exceeded the size of the parish itself and was rented entire to one man, who cultivated part of it as a demesne farm and subrented the rest to rancheros. Pegujaleros and landless laborers abounded here, too, while the hacienda had over the course of time appropriated much local land putatively belonging to the pueblo. Local Indian peasants, "who are so pressed by the hacendados," produced barely enough maize even in flush times to meet their domestic needs and pay their rents, which had nearly tripled since the days when the Jesuits had owned the property before its expropriation by the Spanish government in 1767 upon the Jesuits' expulsion from the Spanish realms.[41] Jumping ahead in time about a decade, we encounter shady (possibly illegal) renting practices similar to those that had set off the petition and extensive inquiry of the early 1780s. In Tepozotlán's Barrio de las Ánimas, the (unnamed) Indian gobernador had been renting communal lands to the local royalist military commander and tithe collector, Capitán don José Pérez, who had not only preempted the village's Indian residents (*hijos del pueblo*) from their traditional commons grazing and wood collecting but was also imposing huge and arbitrary fines for incursions by local indigenous farmers on the illegally rented lands.[42]

Cuautitlán itself was the theater of recurrent military conflict during the decade of the independence struggle, although (as in most other parts of

New Spain) the story is a complicated one and cannot be recounted here except in very broad strokes. In this sense, then, the area was certainly not exempt from the military and political crisis of the insurgency of 1810–21. Since it had a certain strategic and economic value, the town was invaded by insurgent forces several times, beginning as early as September 15, 1811 (if not before), with repetitions on at least three occasions: January 26, 1812; May 24, 1812; and November 24, 1813.[43] The district also saw its share of arrests and prosecutions for seditious statements, often occasioned by personal confrontations arising in the extrapolitical realm, and lubricated by copious drink.[44] The military confrontations, as well as other more diffuse forms of disturbance in the countryside, were marked by the well-nigh standard appearance of politically suspect, indifferent, or hyperloyalist priests; selectively victimized peninsular Spanish (*gachupín*) merchants, landowners, and officials; the destruction of archives and emptying of jails by rebel bands; and so forth—all hallmarks of the era. One striking feature of the insurgency was the rather circumscribed role played by the indigenous majority in country districts such as Cuautitlán. The participation was circumscribed not quantitatively, since many Indians took part in the rebellion, but spatially, in the sense that when they did become involved in resistance to the colonial regime, they did so overwhelmingly within a very localized area, and their action was focused on known local targets. Insofar as one can determine, Cuautitlán conformed to this trend, with the size of the political map of humble people inversely related to their degree of sociocultural Indianness.[45] That is to say, the more "Indian" rural people were in culture and self-identification, the less likely they were to move much beyond their villages for purposes of collective political action.

Linked to the January 1812 attack on Cuautitlán, or at least proximate to it in time, was the sacking of the nearby Hacienda de la Corregidora, an episode bearing discussion because it illustrates in some ways the distribution and character of political violence I have just hinted at. Of the eight men captured by royalist forces and credibly accused of participation in the sack of the hacienda, all were Indians, and most of them *gañanes* on the hacienda itself—that is, local indigenous agricultural laborers. The particularly ingenuous and loose-lipped young Gabriel Benito, a twenty-two-year-old laborer from La Corregidora, made some very compromising comments to the *subdelegado* of Cuautitlán himself, somehow mistaking the Spanish official for a fellow insurgent because of his unfamiliar dress. One of Gabriel's statements related to the planned capture of an official of his own pueblo of Tultepec, whom he characterized, perhaps in an echo of the sort of elite interethnic alliance hinted at in the storm over the Virgin, as an *alcahuete* (i.e., a pimp) of the subdelegado. Another of the young man's ill-advised comments suggested that at least some of the insurgents wanted to execute any remaining peninsular Spaniards in the town of Cuautitlán. The other men predictably denied any actual involvement in the insurgency itself, either distancing themselves completely from the sack of the hacienda, claiming that they had only shown up on the scene after the rebels had left, or that they had been on the estate for the legitimate motive of collecting their weekly pay. In the end the royalist authorities in Mexico City found the denials credible enough, releasing the men after they had served for some months on the capital's defensive works (the famous *zanja cuadrada*) while their cases were being investigated.[46]

The evidence about the early 1812 insurgent sack of the Hacienda La Corregidora begins to illuminate the issue of how ordinary rural people, especially indigenous villagers, lived the crisis of the independence struggle, at what level their representation of the dissolution of the colonial regime came to rest, and what elements that representation may have embraced. The ad hoc, tentative, and confused—one might even say accidental— nature of their participation hints at the way they saw the world politically, with the major locus of the Good in the community and the rest of the political geography around them increasingly fog-bound as one moved further toward the periphery.[47] While it is true that objects of resentment and violence existed (in this case the hacienda, where most of the attackers worked), it is also true that few if any rural people attacked such objects outside the local venues they knew. One might venture to say, then, that in representational terms, local irritants and victims were unique, embedded in daily existence and history, rather than the stuff of which symbols or ideological generalizations were to be made. In this situation, rebellion frequently had to be imported into a community, rather than exploding outward from it. The evidence in the Cuautitlán case seems to conform to this model, since there is little indication that local villagers operated any distance beyond the boundaries of their communities. It was rather the case, throughout much of the country for most of the insurgency years, that bands of "outsiders" of typically mixed ethnicity attempted to mobilize local populations directly or indirectly, managed to create a military stir for a period, and then moved on under royalist counterguerrilla pressure to another zone, somewhat like frogs jumping from one lily pad to the next.

ATLACOMULCO: LYNCHINGS ON ALL SAINTS' DAY

Don José Juan de Fagoaga, chief police magistrate of Mexico City and elder member of one of New Spain's most prominent silver mining families, characterized the 1810 riot at Atlacomulco, a pueblo lying to the northwest of Toluca, as "surely because of its circumstances [one] of the greatest excesses known in the unhappy history of this Kingdom."[48] Many contemporaries shared Fagoaga's view that the riot was a particularly sanguinary event. On the evening of Thursday, November 1, a riot took place there in which four Spanish citizens of the town (three of them of European birth) were killed and considerable but remarkably focused looting took place. This episode was followed by a long series of criminal investigations and arrests stretching into the next year and beyond. Most of the witnesses agreed on the material facts of the incident and the events of the following days. Don Romualdo Magdaleno Diez, a European-born Spanish merchant of the town, had been attacked in his home and brutally murdered by a mob on the evening of All Saints' Day. His American-born son was gravely wounded by members of the same mob on the same occasion and publicly executed the next day in the town plaza along with his brother-in-law. The fourth fatality in the incident was Magdaleno Diez's administrator, also a European Spaniard, killed along with his employer in the attack on the merchant's home. The house and other property of Magdaleno Diez (including a nearby hacienda) were thoroughly sacked, and his widow, daughters, and other survivors were reduced from economic comfort to a state of penury. Although a number of men from the town and a neighboring hamlet were arrested, jailed, and interrogated for some time in the capital, the existing records do not indicate that any of the accused was ever formally brought to trial or sentenced.[49]

In the Mexican countryside of the preinsurgency and insurgency periods, the Atlacomulco riot was unusual not so much in kind as in degree. Dozens of other such collective outbursts occurred in New Spain in late 1810 and the years immediately following, some as relatively isolated incidents, others interwoven with the insurgency, which served both as cause and as outcome of local uprisings. Similar in some respects to the classic European jacquerie, but on a smaller scale, the Mexican village riot of the independence period found ample precedent in a long-standing tradition of rural collective protest and violence.[50] While anomalous in some respects, the Atlacomulco incident was also in many ways typical of insurgency-era village disturbances. Among the elements in common were the date, All Saints' Day, on which a number of other village riots occurred in this and other years, so that the sacral calendar here seems particularly important for collective outbursts.[51] Other commonalities included histories of local conflict over land, hints of intravillage factionalism and personal conflicts, the role of local structures of power, and so forth. All these factors, as we have seen, were in evidence in the Cuautitlán episode of 1785 and its sequelae. Most significantly, beyond the important but manifest role of conflict over land between the central victim, don Romualdo Magdaleno Diez, and the rural people at least partly implicated in his violent death, we may also detect in the incident some deeper cultural meanings. On this level of interpretation, one sees that the central victim's persona and activities catalyzed long-building collective anxieties over the integrity of rural communities in the face of economic and social change inimical to their established values.

But while such codes and meanings may be generalizable to other analogous incidents, the concrete circumstances of the riot were rooted in the historical particularities of the pueblo itself and the surrounding countryside and were suffused with a very localized sort of political consciousness. For example, a rumor that don Romualdo's employees may at his direction have poisoned the bread being prepared in a bakery on the premises of his general store, in conjunction with another rumor (quite common in the countryside at the time) that a marauding army of *gachupines* was coming to attack the pueblo, may have helped to touch off the murders and riot. Similarly, lying behind the violence in part seems to have been a commercial rivalry between Magdaleno Diez and another local merchant, José María Reyes, as well as personal animosities between the central victim and other pueblo men, and considerable friction between Magdaleno Diez, in his role as local landowner, and the indigenous vecinos of the small neighboring hamlet of San Juan de los Jarros. These dyadic and highly specific conflictual relationships could be detailed almost indefinitely but on the whole suggest that the victimization of don Romualdo, his kinsmen, and employee was strongly overdetermined by localized histories of stress and conflict. An accumulation of circumstances came into alignment when a triggering mechanism presented itself, in other words, in this case the news that Father Miguel Hidalgo's insurgent army was passing in close proximity to the pueblo on its way to confront royalist forces near Mexico City. At best the Hidalgo rebellion was the proximate or efficient cause of the incident at Atlacomulco, but not its ultimate cause; nor did the political discourse of the insurgent leadership provide the idioms in which local rioters expressed themselves.

Although don Romualdo Magdaleno Diez was a lightning rod in the social landscape of Atlacomulco—a proxy in many ways for local Spanish power holders as a group, and to some extent a surrogate victim for them— he had nonetheless built his own particular history and was also a victim in his own right. At least one strand of his relationship to local people, his role as a landowner, can be traced in the documents of litigation over land going back more than three decades before the bloody events of November 1810. Seen in this light, Diez's relationship with the indigenous peasant

2. Beginning in 1810, some insurgents left home to fight for political sovereignty; many more stayed home to press for local concerns. Reprinted by permission of Archivo General de la Nación, Sección Propiedad Artística y Literaria.

community of Atlacomulco and its surrounding hamlets was one of virtually unrelieved antagonism over nearly two generations: of the enclosing and engrossing of land, of the manipulation of local politics and justice to favor his own economic interests, and of extrajudicial violence when formal means failed or moved too slowly to suit him. While there is no direct evidence as to when Magdaleno Diez arrived on the scene, he must have been present from at least the early or mid-1770s. After establishing himself as a merchant in Atlacomulco, he proceeded to buy up several rural properties, at least one of them from the heirs of a declining local cacique lineage. With these purchases, he almost immediately became embroiled in a protracted land conflict that was to outlive him by at least fifteen years. This extremely complicated litigation involved a number of parties at various times (as such legal actions typically did) but can be boiled down to a few basic issues that inflamed his relations with local peasant villagers and are fairly representative of his local relationships as a whole.[52] The most important issue was the population growth among indigenous village subsistence farmers in the face of increasingly intensive land use by nonnative farmers and estate owners. Direct evidence links don Romualdo Magdaleno Diez to acrid and continuing conflict with the villagers of San Juan de los Jarros, who were so closely implicated in his death and that of his kinsmen in the riotous outbreak of late 1810.[53] Furthermore, Magdaleno Diez exerted his local political influence to sway magistrates in his favor, used the local Acordada to intimidate his opponents, and generally acted as though he were a law unto himself, especially when he actually served as submagistrate (teniente de justicia) in Atlacomulco in the early 1780s.

The background and elements of Magdaleno Diez's career, however, were hardly unique to him. Long before he arrived on the scene, the people of Atlacomulco and its subordinate villages were enmeshed in protracted, occasionally violent battles over land and political power. Members of the local indigenous elite contended among themselves and with outsiders for wealth and power even as the pueblos of Atlacomulco and San Juan de los Jarros struggled against nonnative landowners for control of increasingly scarce resources. Furthermore, much the same forces building in Atlacomulco were at work in the countryside elsewhere in New Spain, although they assumed somewhat different forms in other areas of the colony. Among these were indigenous population recovery and land pressure, a growing trend toward commercialization in large-scale agriculture, increasing competition for land resources between indigenous and nonindigenous peasants, and a growing social and economic differentiation internal to peasant communities themselves. Important as these material stressors were, however, they largely served as proxies for deeper conflicts woven through them—conflicts involving the political integrity of peasant and Indian communities, ethnic confrontation between native and nonnative social sectors, and the cultural coherence of indigenous lifeways under siege by agricultural commercialization, the late Bourbon modernization project, and the expanding sphere of secularizing European colonial society.

Issues of landownership were tied closely to the general economic situation, as well as to questions of village integrity, social tension, and social control, in ways similar to those we have seen in Cuautitlán nearly two generations earlier. The general scenario for the late colonial agrarian economy in the Ixtlahuacán area, of which Atlacomulco and its district formed geographically a northwestern extension, was dominated by an accelerating expansion of commercial agriculture emphasizing irrigated wheat production for the Mexico City market. One can easily envision the progressively deepening shadow of irrigated wheat culture spreading north from the Toluca Valley from relatively early in the seventeenth century until it engulfed Atlacomulco and its more northerly margins in the early to mid-eighteenth century. One can also visualize a shift in local resource availability from a situation around 1650 in which labor was scarce and land plentiful, to one after about 1750 in which labor was relatively cheap and land and water increasingly valuable.

By the early eighteenth century, conflicts between native villagers and haciendas over water use were already common enough in the Ixtlahuacán area, to the south of Atlacomulco, and were to become equally common within thirty to forty years in the Atlacomulco area itself. This generalized conflict over land and water in the Ixtlahuacán and Atlacomulco districts was attended by outright invasions of hacienda lands by indigenous villagers, frequent incidents of violence, abusive labor practices by estate owners, and serious indications of land hunger. The situation around Atlacomulco was thus similar to that in the more northerly margins of the Toluca area. The sources on Atlacomulco also throw into especially sharp relief another factor in evidence elsewhere in the region—the initially central role of the indigenous elite in mediating economic, social, and political pressures within indigenous communities, and the lessening or disappearance of that role over time. Over the course of a century and more, the cacique families who once owned so much agricultural land in the region, often obtaining it in conflict with their own communities, either fell into decline or themselves were politically compromised through their collusive relationships with local nonnative power holders in much the same way that similar groups had been tainted in the Cuautitlán area. This process created a sort of power and legitimacy vacuum in which the mediation of competition over economic resources was difficult, interethnic social networks developed large holes, and the general tenor of local political stress grew ever sharper, more contentious, and more polarized.

It was to these conflicts that don Romualdo Magdaleno Diez fell heir when Father Miguel Hidalgo's insurgent army passed through the area on its way to its fateful encounter with royalist forces at the Monte de las Cruces in the late fall of 1810. But what was easily construed by magistrate Fagoaga and other contemporary observers of the Atlacomulco events as an effect of Father Hidalgo's rebellion was in fact a collective expression growing out of local histories that actually had little to do directly with the outbreak of the insurgency, that antedated that rebellion in some cases by many decades, and that resembled closely the classic village disturbance of the preinsurrection period. Nor is there any evidence in this or scores of other cases of local uprisings in the Mexican countryside during the decade 1810–21 that village rioters were in any sense explicitly mobilized by insurgent leaders, that they reframed their grievances with the discourse of those leaders (multivocal and often incoherent as that discourse may have

been), or that their view of the world was in any way significantly transformed by the larger events swirling around them.

CONCLUSION

That late colonial Mexican villagers, and particularly indigenous peasants,
should not have been spouting revolutionary slogans, shouting about the
rights of man, or espousing elaborated political programs for imperial
reform, political autonomy, independence from Spain, or even agrarian
reform is hardly surprising.[54] There are some interesting lessons of a positive sort to be learned, nonetheless, from the exercise of carefully unpack-
ing the two incidents we have been looking at, and in contextualizing them
in a general way. In the first place, an effort to denaturalize the concept
"crisis" leads to an interrogation of the notion that every crisis is necessarily society-wide in the sense that it is perceived by all social groups as a
critical conjuncture in the life course of a polity, most typically a nation-
state (or would-be nation-state). The question then becomes: whose crisis
is it, anyway, and where is the locus of critical stress or change? From this
point of view, at least some political crises begin to look invented, almost
conspiratorial, even during the times in which they occur, let alone in
retrospect when they are taken up as the ideological and mnemonic uphol-
stery for the framework of the state. In the second place, looking at how the
villagers of Cuautitlán and Atlacomulco behaved reinforces the view that
"agency"—that is, the capacity of historical actors to make conscious decisions to maximize their own positions, even as they find the space for that
decision making constrained by structural factors and social forces well
beyond their control or awareness—may be a highly circumscribed and
localized component of a historical situation. Agency is certainly a value-
neutral concept in any case: it does not necessarily imply a programmatic
understanding of solutions to political problems, or the forging of alliances
with similarly situated social groups, and still less, concerted action aimed
at "progressive" changes. The agential activity of historical actors in a
critical situation may well invoke a repertoire of well-established behaviors
whose meaning may be construed by observers to change when the social
and political context changes, but whose internal logic is characterized by
a high degree of continuity over long periods of time. The many similarities marking the Cuautitlán and Atlacomulco incidents seem to bear out
this conclusion, and also the common characteristics between these two
episodes and scores of other rural disturbances spanning the period 1750–
1821, and extending far into the nineteenth century, as well. Finally, the

case studies presented here begin to throw considerable doubt on the conventional historiographical wisdom about the Mexican independence movement: that independence was eventually produced by a significant cross-class and cross-ethnic alliance embracing indigenous villagers, among other groups; that there were something like common grievances shared by a significant sector of the popular insurgency within itself, and between it and the Creole and mestizo directorate of the movement(s); that there were common to these groups iconographic symbols such as the Virgin of Guadalupe; and so forth. If there was no common political vision or sensibility forged in a widely acknowledged crisis of the colonial regime, or through the putative resolution of that crisis in the construction of a new nation-state, why would one expect to see a sense of "nationality" developing during the first decades of Mexican national life?

Beginning about the last third or so of the nineteenth century, the situation had altered sufficiently so that the political and ideological horizons of rural protesters had broadened.[55] Protest movements in the Mexican countryside from about 1860 seem to display a greater propensity for the cross-class and cross-ethnic alliances and conditions claimed for the independence upheaval, but largely absent from it for reasons I have suggested here. After about 1860, such movements tended to be inscribed more firmly and consciously within coherent ideological frameworks and national projects.[56] By contrast, the discursive landscape of the late colonial period had relatively fewer commonly recognized lexical features in it, and most of them were claimed or contested by different social groups. Among these were monarchical legitimism (the Spanish king was a rebel, or he was a royalist) and the upper levels of religious belief (Holy Virgins with different advocations, for example), both associated with religious imagery. It was thus no accident, for instance, that public discourse and pamphletry of the time from *both* sides of the independence conflict could appropriate single multivocal religious images for diametrically opposed ends. This came to be the case with the Mosaic references invoked by Father José María Morelos at the Congress of Chilpancingo, as well as by Agustín de Iturbide's partisans in the shamelessly adulatory pamphlets and civic rituals celebrating his ascent to the Mexican imperial throne in 1822.[57]

Certainly, just as the concept of crisis should be denaturalized, so the existence of a more or less common discursive framework among Mexicans should be historicized rather than taken for granted across time. What is at issue here, more broadly, is the birth—or at least the significant expansion—of civil society in Mexico.[58] This may be conceived of more concretely as the growth of horizontality in political life, particularly as related to the participation of those formerly excluded in some sense from the "political nation" by the colonial doctrine of the "two republics" (*dos repúblicas*) and the concomitant development of rudimentary ideas about citizenship and nationality, including new forms of civil associations, mobilization, and criticisms of the state.[59] The temporal locus of this process must lie in the period between about 1820 and 1860, but what accounts for the change? A number of factors can be suggested tentatively.

First, the politicizing effects of the wars of independence themselves and of the following half century of political conflict (episodes generally seen in the prevailing historiography in a strictly negative light) must be accounted a good deal of importance in the creation of Mexican civil society and the forging of enduring political ideologies. Second, the effects on the country as a whole of the Mexican-American War near midcentury should not be underestimated as an ideological crucible for the forging of widely diffused idioms of Mexican nationalism. Third, the expansion of a market economy of ever greater national reach in the latter part of the century, along with the increasing movement of people and information that this entailed, would have had much the same effect as military mobilization and the forced pace of political enculturation. Finally, the possible growth of literacy during the early national period, limited as it may have been, or even barring that (or in addition to it) the increased accessibility of print media in the form of political pamphletry and newspapers, most probably acted to spread ideas among the population at large, thickening the weave of civil society while building and diffusing a common political discourse that gave it voice. Whatever the case, by some accounts it would seem that by the time the French arrived in Mexico with their ill-fated Austrian puppet emperor in the 1860s, at least some popular groups had learned the language of nationalism.[60] And by the time the Mexican Revolution had consolidated itself (ca. 1940), a popular sense of nationalism was firmly in place. Although this seems a quite leisurely process, it should be remembered that European nationalism took centuries to develop, and that political culture can appear to move at a snail's pace in comparison with the onrushing wave of political events themselves.

NOTES

1 In a suggestive essay on political crises, elites, and regime change, Alan Knight places considerable emphasis on the subjective perception among common people (what he calls the "emic" assessment, following anthropological usage) as a major desideratum for the existence of any political crisis. Knight, "Historical and Theoretical Considerations," in *Elites, Crises, and the Origins of Regimes*, ed. Mattei Dogan and John Higley (Lanham, Md.: Rowman and Littlefield, 1998), 29–45.

2 Robert M. Maniquis, Oscar Martí, and Joseph Pérez, eds., *La Revolución Francesa y el mundo ibérico* (Madrid: Turner Libros, 1989); François-Xavier Guerra, *Modernidad e independencias: Ensayos sobre las revoluciones hispánicas* (Mexico: Fondo de Cultura Económica, 1993), esp. 19–54.

3 Lucas Alamán, *Historia de Méjico*, vol. 1 (Mexico: Editorial Jus, 1968), 270.

4 Hugh M. Hamill, for example, speaks of the "mystique of Napoleon" filtering into New Spain after the turn of the century, only to turn into outraged patriotism after 1808. Hamill, ed., *Caudillos: Dictators in Spanish America* (Norman: University of Oklahoma Press, 1992), 101. It was the fashion of the age for many young men of martial inclination to have themselves portrayed with their hands in their tunics, in imitation of Napoleon; see, for example, the portrait of Simón Bolívar in Hamill, *Caudillos*, 181.

5 Leon Tolstoy, *War and Peace*, trans. Constance Garnett (New York: Modern Library, n.d.), 1.

6 Napoleon Bonaparte was mentioned with some frequency in New Spain from around 1808 so, as political factions, intellectuals, and activists in the colony struggled to situate themselves after the events of that year. One young surgeon tried for subversion in 1809, for example, was reported to have stated that Napoleon himself was coming to conquer the colony, starting at Veracruz and ending with Guadalajara. Biblioteca Pública del Estado (de Jalisco), Criminal, paquete 17, exp. 8, no fol. nos., ser. 384, 1809–11. Pamphlets vilifying Napoleon, including tirades, plays, poems, and dialogues, circulated widely in the colony between 1808 and 1810 especially. Much of this literature bore a religious shading, even if it did not explicitly characterize him as the antichrist. The boys of a church-run school in Mexico City about the same time sang an *alabanza* to the Virgin including these lines:

Through your Pure Conception,
O Serene Princess,
Free us from Napoleon
and from the French Nation.

A pro-French (and openly sacrilegious) credo circulating within New Spain, on the other hand, began:

I believe in the French Republic, one and indivisible;
Creator of equality, of liberty;
In General Bonaparte her son our only defender;
Who was conceived of [a] Virtuous Mother;
Suffered through mountains and valleys, was reviled by tyrants;
He died and was buried;
He descended to Piedmont and is now seated at the right hand
of Vienna Capital of Austria;
From when he must come to judge the Princes and Powerful Aristocrats.

For the pamphletry, alabanza, and credo, see Hugh M. Hamill Jr., *The Hidalgo Revolt: Prelude to Mexican Independence* (1960; Westport, Conn.: Greenwood, 1981), 14–16.

7 For late-eighteenth- and early-nineteenth-century millennial and apocalyptic prophecies in Europe, see Eugen Weber, *Apocalypses: Prophecies, Cults, and Millennial Beliefs through the Ages* (Cambridge: Harvard University Press, 1999), especially chapter 7, from which the references to de Maistre and Southcott are drawn. Southcott died before she could be delivered of the man-child, and a four-day vigil by her followers witnessed neither the awaited birth nor her bodily resurrection. For a broad historical treatment of messianism and millenarianism in Latin America, see Frank Graziano, *The Millennial New World* (New York: Oxford University Press, 1999).

8 On intellectual currents in eighteenth-century Spain vis-à-vis the rest of Europe, see Francisco Sánchez-Blanco Parody, *Europa y el pensamiento español del siglo XVIII* (Madrid: Alianza Editorial, 1991), especially chapter 13, which stresses Spanish political thought in the "critical conjuncture" leading up to the French Revolution; and on defensive economic and imperial reform, Richard Herr, *The Eighteenth-Century Revolution in Spain* (Princeton: Princeton University Press, 1958), and Herr's *Rural Change and Royal Finances in Spain at the End of the Old Regime* (Berkeley: University of California Press, 1989), especially chapters 1–6.

9 On the "pedagogia politica" in Spain during the French period, and the relationship between the diffusion of political writing and revolution in the Mexican colony, see Guerra, *Modernidad e independencias*, especially chapters 7–8; and Eric Van Young, *The Other Rebellion: Popular Violence, Ideology, and the Struggle for Mexican Independence, 1810–1821* (Stanford: Stanford University Press, 2001), chapter 14.

10 One modern historian has suggestively identified the year 1815, about two-thirds of the way through the period, as the beginning point of "modernity"; see Paul Johnson, *The Birth of the Modern: World Society, 1815–1830* (New York: HarperCollins, 1991).

11 On the late colonial Mexican economy, see, among many other works on the theme, Arij Ouweneel and Cristina Torales Pacheco, eds., *Empresarios, indios y estado: Perfil de la economía mexicana (siglo XVIII)* (Mexico City: Universidad Iberoamericana, 1994), especially my essay "A modo de conclusión: El siglo paradójico," 319–54, and that of Arij Ouweneel, "Raices del *chiaroscuro* en México: Algunas consideraciones acerca de esta compilación," 13–35; Richard L. Garner with Spiro E. Stafanou, *Economic Growth and Change in Bourbon Mexico* (Gainesville: University Press of Florida, 1993); and Arij Ouweneel, *Shadows over Anahuac: An Ecological Interpretation of Crisis and Development in Central Mexico, 1730–1800* (Albuquerque: University of New Mexico Press, 1996). The Bourbon reforms are discussed from several different points of view in Josefina Zoraida Vázquez, comp., *Interpretaciones del siglo XVIII mexicano: El impacto de las reformas borbónicas* (Mexico: Nueva Imagen, 1992). On intellectual trends and Creole patriotism, see David A. Brading, *The First America: The Spanish Monarchy, Creole Patriots, and the Liberal State, 1492–1867* (Cambridge: Cambridge University Press, 1991); and on the history of Guadalupan devotion, Brading's *Mexican Phoenix: Our Lady of Guadalupe, Image and Tradition* (Cambridge: Cambridge University Press, 2001).

12 For the "Age of Revolution" scenario and the issue of historical periodization more generally, see my concluding essay, "Was There an Age of Revolution in

Spanish America?" in *State and Society in Spanish America during the Age of Revolution*, ed. Victor Uribe-Urán (Wilmington, Del.: Scholarly Resources, 2001), 219–46; and also Jaime E. Rodríguez O., ed., *Mexico in the Age of Democratic Revolutions, 1750–1850* (Boulder: Lynne Rienner, 1994); and Kenneth J. Andrien and Lyman L. Johnson, eds., *The Political Economy of Spanish America in the Age of Revolution, 1750–1850* (Albuquerque: University of New Mexico Press, 1994).

13   These and other issues are discussed in Van Young, *The Other Rebellion.*

14   For a discussion of the Mexican independence movement in relation to the eighteenth-century Euro-Atlantic revolutionary tradition, see Eric Van Young, "'To Throw Off a Tyrannical Government': Atlantic Revolutionary Traditions and Popular Insurgency in Mexico, 1800–1821," in *Revolutionary Currents: Nation-Building in the Transatlantic World, 1688–1821*, ed. Michael A. Morrison and Melinda S. Zook (New York: Rowman and Littlefield, 2004).

15   See, for example, Van Young, "Was There an Age of Revolution in Spanish America?"

16   Eric Van Young, *La crisis del orden colonial: Estructura agraria y rebeliones populares en la Nueva España, 1750–1821* (Mexico: Alianza Editorial, 1992). Many other works dealing specifically with the late eighteenth century and the early nineteenth in Mexico and Spanish America tend to employ the concept "crisis" quite freely, as well; see, for example, Jaime E. Rodríguez O., *The Independence of Spanish America* (Cambridge: Cambridge University Press, 1998); John Tutino, *From Insurrection to Revolution in Mexico: Social Bases of Agrarian Violence, 1750–1940* (Princeton: Princeton University Press, 1986); and the various authors in Leslie Bethell, ed., *The Independence of Latin America* (Cambridge: Cambridge University Press, 1987), for example, John Lynch, "The Origins of Spanish American Independence," 1–48. Other scholars of the period are more circumspect, preferring terms such as "tensions" and "conflict," as does Brian Hamnett in his *Roots of Insurgency: Mexican Regions, 1750–1824* (Cambridge: Cambridge University Press, 1986).

17   See, for example, *Encyclopedia of Social History*, ed. Peter N. Stearns (New York: Garland Publishing, 1994). Among the several hundred entries in this useful work are those for "consumerism," "cultural hegemony," and "death" (not much definitional controversy with the last term, one would think), to cite but a few from the beginning of the alphabet, but none for "crisis."

18   It is no accident, for example, that much of the article's discussion bears the imprint of the strategic nuclear thinker Herman Kahn.

19   *International Encyclopedia of the Social Sciences*, ed. David L. Sills, vol. 3 (New York: Macmillan, 1968), 510–13. The concept of crisis has been employed extensively in developmental psychology, most notably in the work of Erik H. Erikson; see, for example, his essay "'Identity Crisis' in Autobiographic Perspective," in *Life History and the Historical Moment: Diverse Presentations* (New York: W. W. Norton, 1975), 17–47; and Erikson, *Identity: Youth and Crisis* (New York: W. W. Norton, 1968).

20   I have in mind here the idea of the "seventeenth-century crisis" in Europe, for example, which is said to have lasted a hundred years or more (see T. Aston, ed., *Crisis in Europe, 1560–1660* [New York: Doubleday, 1967]); or the endemic state of

crisis in which Mexico has found itself over the last thirty years or so, after the ebbing of the high tide of the "Mexican Miracle."

21 The Cuautitlán incident is treated at considerably greater length both because it is inherently interesting and because I have treated the Atlacomulco riot in detail elsewhere; see Van Young, *The Other Rebellion*, chapter 15.

22 On the Acordada, see Colin M. MacLachlan, *Criminal Justice in Eighteenth-Century Mexico: A Study of the Tribunal of the Acordada* (Berkeley: University of California Press, 1974). Since the Acordada was a rural constabulary, its officials were often chosen from among important landowners. The legal, political, and social leverage this afforded to hacendados, it is my impression, was often abused; we shall encounter another case of this in the Atlacomulco disturbances of 1810.

23 Archivo General de la Nación, México (hereafter cited as AGN), Clero regular y secular, vol. 103, expedientes 11–12, fols. 403r–436v, 1786. William B. Taylor, *Drinking, Homicide, and Rebellion in Colonial Mexican Villages* (Stanford: Stanford University Press, 1979), 137, mentions the same incident in passing, providing no source citation and slightly mistaking the occasion for the riot; while Charles Gibson, *The Aztecs under Spanish Rule: A History of the Indians of the Valley of Mexico, 1519–1810* (Stanford: Stanford University Press, 1964), 134, provides a brief account drawn from the same AGN source, cited slightly differently and adding the detail about the arrival of the dragoons.

24 See especially William B. Taylor, *Magistrates of the Sacred: Priests and Parishioners in Eighteenth-Century Mexico* (Stanford: Stanford University Press, 1996); and Van Young, *The Other Rebellion*, especially chapter 10, "Priest and Parish."

25 The indigenous petitioners also complained that, contrary to traditional practice, the curate now wanted to charge an additional four pesos for each Indian *cofrade* buried within the chapel.

26 The freedom with which the body and clothing were repaired, improved, or replaced raises the interesting question of exactly where the locus of sacrality in the figure lay. Whether the body of the Virgin was a hollow wooden structure, or an armature of sticks with stuffing, over which clothing was placed, or took some other form, is not specified. In this context, Richard Trexler has spoken of the "vacuous divine" in his paper "Dressing and Undressing the Saints in the Old World and the New," Bronowski Renaissance Symposium dedicated to the memory of Michel de Certeau, University of California, San Diego, November, 1988.

27 Ramos's own version of his blameless behavior during the events of December 7 was supported by the testimony of at least one peninsular Spanish merchant of the town, married to Doña Lorenza de Moya, possibly herself related to the former and current alcaldes mayores.

28 Gibson, *The Aztecs under Spanish Rule*, 128, notes that the patent of the Cofradía de la Purísima Concepción de Nuestra Señora de Cuauhtitlán specified that burials in the chapel be limited to Indians and exclude all other ethnic groups.

29 The details cited here are drawn from AGN, Tierras, vol. 1494, exp. 4, no pagination (but about 160 folio pages), 1783.

30 The order was to be sent all over New Spain by circular letter, and public proclamations published in Spanish and local indigenous languages in each jurisdiction, as well as in the two Indian districts (*parcialidades*) of the capital.

31 On the Juzgado de Indios, its history, jurisdiction, and functions, see Woodrow W. Borah, *Justice by Insurance: The General Indian Court of Colonial Mexico and the Legal Aides of the Half-Real* (Berkeley: University of California Press, 1983), where a number of similar cases of litigation concerning the alienation of Indian lands are cited for the late colonial period. Borah also traces metropolitan and viceregal legislation and administrative decrees relating to licensing procedures for the sale or rental of various types of Indian lands (138–39), noting that Viceroy Mayorga's 1781 decree was subsequently overturned by the Council of the Indies as too broad and incompatible with 1571 and 1572 royal decrees of Philip II as codified in the *Recopilacion de Indias* (the colonial law code). No new ordinance was put in place after the suppression of Mayorga's, though Borah notes that after 1781 greater care was exercised in obtaining such licenses.

32 The gobernador of Tepozotlán corroborated the prevalence of this arrangement, except in asserting that wheat producers provided the maize-growing owners with plow oxen, labor, and irrigation rather than cash rents.

33 For a recent treatment of similar water distribution practices in another major wheat-growing area about the same time, see Sonya Lipsett-Rivera, *To Defend Our Water with the Blood of Our Veins: The Struggle for Resources in Colonial Puebla* (Albuquerque: University of New Mexico Press, 1999).

34 Whether the twenty-seven parcels were rented from as many individuals, or what the length of the rental period was, is not specified.

35 Enrique Florescano and Isabel Gil, eds., *Descripciones económicas generales de Nueva España, 1784–1817* (Mexico: SEP/INAH, 1973), 15, 108; Gibson, *The Aztecs*, 96. Gibson notes that even by the late colonial period, despite its economic importance, Cuauhtitlán came to be "celebrated as a backward and crime-ridden town, lacking in community pride" (365); the episode of the Virgin of the Immaculate Conception, however, tends to throw some doubt on this. Nonetheless, by the twentieth century, Cuauhtitlán had come to be known as the quintessential provincial town, with all its pejorative connotations, as indicated by the popular saying "Fuera de México, todo es Cuauhtitlán" (Outside Mexico City, everything is Cuauhtitlán).

36 Gibson, *The Aztecs under Spanish Rule*, 350–51.

37 Ibid., 318–19; Taylor, *Drinking, Homicide, and Rebellion*, 33, 35, 46–50.

38 Gibson, *The Aztecs under Spanish Rule*, 329; Garner, *Economic Growth and Change*, 102–3; Ouweneel, *Shadows over Anahuac*, 87–88. Ouweneel also notes that nearly two-thirds of the commercial cultivation of maize for local and Mexico City markets was in the hands of haciendas in Tepozotlán parish around 1800 (112).

39 It is worth noting that none of these men was explicitly identified as a peninsular Spaniard.

40 This would have been Dr. José María Romero de Terreros y Trebuesto (b. 1766, d. 1815), son of Pedro Romero de Terreros, the fabulously wealthy peninsular Spanish silver magnate ennobled in 1768 as the Conde de Regla. Doris M. Ladd, *The Mexican Nobility at Independence, 1780–1826* (Austin: University of Texas Press, 1976), 208, 214.

41 AGN, Intendencias, vol. 73, exp. 5, fols. 1r–56v, 1809.

42 AGN, Criminal, vol. 110, no exp. no., fols. 1r–6r, 1818.

43 This rough chronology, reliably embracing at least the period 1810–17, is reconstructed from the career résumé (*relación de servicios*) of the local royalist military commander and sometime *subdelegado* Capitán Don José María Marín, who still occupied the same posts in August 1820. AGN, Operaciones de Guerra, vol. 16, fols. 18r–22r, 1817. The major rebel invasion of the town in September 1811 is described in great detail in AGN, Infidencias, vol. 24, exp. 14, fols. 255r–304v, Conde de Colombini to Venegas, Mexico City, September 22, 1811. June 1811 saw the discovery of a plot among several men, some of whom were identified as Indians, to mobilize (*alborotar*) the local pueblos and seize Cuautitlán for the rebels, but this was denounced prematurely, and the plan came to nought; AGN, Infidencias, vol. 24, exp. 7, fols. 194r–221v, 1811.

44 See, for example, the case of the Indian laborer on a local hacienda, Juan Paulino, arrested in March 1815 for remarking in a work-related argument with the hacienda administrator: "These *gachupín* sons-of bitches: what a consolation it will be when not a single one is left." AGN, Criminal, vol. 110, exp. 24, fols. 453r–471v, 1811.

45 See, for example, Van Young, *The Other Rebellion*, especially chapter 2, "A Social Profile." In this and other writings, I have suggested that political action by ordinary people tended to stop at the metaphorical horizon defined by the limits of community, thus defining a sort of von Thunen's ringlike arrangement in which indigenous people were likely to be found acting, even as insurgents, within a zone of relatively close proximity to their villages, people of mixed blood in the middle distance, and Spaniards furthest out of all.

46 AGN, Criminal, vol. 267, exp. 19, fols. 250r–271r, 1812. Although the judicial dockets, both civil and military, were completely overburdened for much of the period, the royalist authorities were reasonably punctilious in legal procedures pertaining to accused insurgents and did not absolve accused rebels or rioters casually.

47 To pursue this trope, they would have spied a sudden patch of clear, sunlit mountaintop in the far distance—the messianized persona of the Spanish King Ferdinand VII, "El Deseado," who represented a figure of suprapolitical legitimacy. I have written on this theme in a number of articles, and in my book *The Other Rebellion*, especially chapter 18.

48 AGN, Infidencias, vol. 24, exp. 13, fols. 246r–254v, Fagoaga to Venegas, Mexico City, July 1, 1811.

49 My reconstruction of the Atlacomulco incident is based on the following documentary sources, except where otherwise indicated: AGN, Criminal, vol. 229, no exp. no., fols. 263r–413v, 1810, and vol. 231, exp. 1, fols. 1r–59r, 1811, which contain the bulk of the statements of participants and witnesses, and the records of the judicial investigations; vol. 238, exp. 1, fols. 1r–66v, 1811, concerning accusations against José María Reyes, alleged to be one of the major perpetrators of the murders; and AGN, Infidencias, vol. 24, exp. 13, fols. 246r–254v, the report of Fagoaga to Viceroy Venegas, dated July 1, 1811. The accounts of the riot itself are inevitably fragmentary, overlapping, and contradictory; what is presented here is an abbreviated and highly synoptic account.

50 Some of the major characteristics of these rural disturbances have been analyzed insightfully in Taylor, *Drinking, Homicide, and Rebellion.*

51 On the relationship of sacral to mundane time in the creation and maintenance of community identity, see Eric Van Young, "Paisaje de ensueño con figuras y vallados: Disputa y discurso cultural en el campo mexicano de fines de la Colonia," in *Paisajes rebeldes: Una larga noche de rebelión indígena,* ed. Jane-Dale Lloyd and Laura Pérez Rosales (Mexico City: Universidad Iberoamericana, 1995), 149–79.

52 AGN, Tierras, vol. 2145, exp. 1 (332 folios not paginated consecutively), 1777–92; this case and others involving Magdaleno Diez are treated in detail in Van Young, *The Other Rebellion,* chapter 15.

53 On his conflicts with the Jarroseños, see, for example, AGN, Tierras, vol. 2140, exp. 1, 1799.

54 For a detailed discussion of the nonprogrammatic nature of village disturbances in the independence era, see Eric Van Young, "Agrarian Rebellion and Defense of Community: Meaning and Collective Violence in Late Colonial and Independence-Era Mexico," *Journal of Social History* 27 (1993): 245–69.

55 Much of the next two paragraphs is drawn from my essay "In the Gloomy Caverns of Paganism: Popular Culture, Insurgency, and Nation-Building in Mexico, 1800–1821 (–1910)," in *Beyond Kingdom, Beyond Colony: The Creation of Modern Mexico,* ed. Christon I. Archer (Wilmington, Del.: Scholarly Resources, 2003).

56 This, at any rate, is what I take to be the gist of some major works on peasant protest movements and uprisings in the late nineteenth and twentieth centuries, up to and including the revolution of 1910. See, for example, Florencia E. Mallon, "Reflection on the Ruins: Everyday Forms of State Formation in Nineteenth-Century Mexico," in *Everyday Forms of State Formation: Revolution and the Negotiation of Rule in Modern Mexico,* ed. Gilbert M. Joseph and Daniel Nugent (Durham: Duke University Press, 1994), 69–106, along with a number of other essays in the same volume; Mallon, *Peasant and Nation: The Making of Postcolonial Mexico and Peru* (Berkeley: University of California Press, 1994); Peter F. Guardino, *Peasants, Politics, and the Formation of Mexico's National State: Guerrero, 1800–1857* (Stanford: Stanford University Press, 1996); and several of the chronologically later-situated chapters in Friedrich Katz, ed., *Riot, Rebellion, and Revolution: Rural Social Conflict in Mexico* (Princeton: Princeton University Press, 1988); there is a parallel trend in recently scholarly views of Andean peasant movements. The immersion of local and peasant movements in these broader ideological and political currents is not an unproblematic view, of course, as Alan Knight's *The Mexican Revolution* (New York: Cambridge University Press, 1986) makes clear, emphasizing as it does local social and economic struggles, political factionalism, and autonomist sentiments in the etiology of rural rebellion. Benedict Anderson's *Imagined Communities: Reflections on the Origins and Spread of Nationalism* (London: Verso, 1983) treats the factors that Anderson takes to be prerequisites for the development of supralocal political identifications, but is acutely criticized for the case of Mexico by Claudio Lomnitz in *Deep Mexico, Silent Mexico* (Minneapolis: University of Minnesota Press, 2001).

57 On the adulation of Iturbide in 1821–22, for example (and even for decades

following his death), see Javier Ocampo, *Los ideas de un día: El pueblo mexicano ante la consumación de su independencia* (Mexico City: El Colegio de México, 1969); and William H. Beezley and David E. Lorey, eds., *Viva Mexico! Viva la Independencia! Celebrations of September 16* (Wilmington, Del.: Scholarly Resources, 2001).

58 For a useful discussion of the Hegelian concept of civil society as developed by Antonio Gramsci, see Walter L. Adamson, *Hegemony and Revolution: A Study of Antonio Gramsci's Political and Cultural Theory* (Berkeley: University of California Press, 1980), 215–22.

59 During colonial times the Spanish and Indian populations in New Spain were conceived in law and policy as constituting two polities—two "republics," in essence (*dos repúblicas* in Spanish)—touching at a number of points, as for economic and evangelization purposes. In practice, of course, such political and cultural delimitations were extremely porous, but the *idea* of such a boundary left an indelible imprint on the broader Mexican political culture well into republican times. On citizenship in the nineteenth century, see Fernando Escalante Gonzalbo, *Ciudadanos imaginarios: Memorial de los afanes, desventuras de la virtud y apología del vicio triunfante en la República Mexicana; Tratado de moral política* (Mexico City: El Colegio de México, 1992); and on the growth of a "public sphere" in nineteenth-century Mexico (admittedly a somewhat different matter than civil society), Carlos Forment, "Civic Practices and Associative Democracy in Early Nineteenth-Century Mexico: A Tocquevillian Perspective," Conference on Popular Political Culture in Mexico, 1800–2000, Center for U.S.-Mexican Studies, University of California, San Diego, April, 1998.

60 On this point, see Mallon, *Peasant and Nation*.

The Two-Faced Janus

The Pueblos and the Origins of Mexican Liberalism

ANTONIO ANNINO

In 1856 Mexican liberals launched a great offensive to disentail most corporate property, to privatize the rights to lands held by institutions. A series of laws defined the issues and legal procedures. The Catholic Church was the main target, but not the only one. Indigenous communities, who had kept communally organized territories since the sixteenth century, also faced the challenge of the new legal order. For liberals, indigenous communities and their territorial rights represented a "privileged world" incompatible with the principle of equality before the law.

Across the Western world, liberals struggled against corporatist old regimes. Nevertheless, the Mexican case has a unique feature that was unprecedented and, at first sight, anomalous. Mexican liberals included constitutional *ayuntamientos*—municipal councils—among the "corporations" to be disentailed, along with indigenous communities and ecclesiastical institutions. In other words, Mexico's liberals attacked an institution of liberal origin and electoral bases. How can we explain this decision, apparently without ideological foundations?

To answer, we must look at the diffusion and social implementation of the original version of liberal constitutionalism created amid the collapse of the Spanish empire, when the Cádiz Constitution of 1812 was applied in New Spain. For a long time, historians thought that the Cádiz charter was not enforced in Mexico because of the civil wars set off by the great rebellions of Hidalgo and Morelos. Yet this was not the case. Not only was the charter implemented extensively; the scope of its new concept of cit-

izenship (which included indigenous peoples) unleashed an unprecedented and unexpected phenomenon: local societies consolidated their
autonomy before the central authorities. The Republic formalized in the
Constitution of 1824 inherited this political and cultural foundation and
was never able to modify it. *Pueblo* autonomy, persistently threatened,
endured throughout the nineteenth century, asserting its power again in
the outbreak of the Mexican Revolution of 1910.

Starting with Cádiz, the development of Mexican liberalism provided
political spaces and resources to diverse social actors. Its historical operations went beyond official, cultured, and European-oriented imaginaries.
Elites always knew that this phenomenon was beyond their control, as
demonstrated by their 1856 offensive against collective corporations. Facing repeated challenges from groups using liberal citizenship for their own
purposes, men of politics often responded with pessimistic perspectives
about the country and its future. Their pessimism masked the two faces of
Janus—the two faces of Mexican liberalism: elites who sought a model for
development and political stability, and pueblos that found that constitutional and electoral *municipios* provided the resources to defend themselves
against an official liberal project ultimately opposed to their communalism.

The two-faced Janus was born in a slippery concept of citizenship, initiated in Cádiz, which was always inclusive of, and open to, indigenous
peoples. Citizenship became a constitutional breach that the pueblos used
to defend their autonomy. Thanks to research carried out during the last
twenty years, we know that collective efforts of Mesoamerican peoples
to survive the colonial period were possible thanks to intercultural ex-
changes, collective memory practices, and complex webs of material and
nonmaterial strategies that altered traumatized pre-Hispanic identities
while allowing the construction of cultural autonomy within the society of
New Spain. After the collapse of the Spanish empire, efforts at cultural
survival continued, aimed at sustaining local community autonomy within
the framework of the new liberal republic. Yet during the nineteenth century, communities had to deal with a more radical challenge: legal equality
and the political forms it sanctioned. The history of liberal citizenship in
Mexico is closely tied to this other history of communities seeking autonomy, a history little seen and difficult to study because original sources are
few and dispersed.

THE NEW CITIZENSHIP'S SLIPPAGE

The constitutional breach that the pueblos opened during the Cádiz period
brought a new stage in a centuries-long process. The application of the

Cádiz Constitution began the Mexican encounter between liberal citizenship and pueblos engaged in historical struggles to preserve autonomy. The Spanish charter was implemented in New Spain far more thoroughly than previously thought. It was a desperate attempt by the colonial authorities to counteract imperial crisis; one result was the entry of Mexican communities into modern constitutionalism. The communities engaged the constitution, often attaching local norms, opening a breach that republican governments unsuccessfully worked to close for several decades. Still, the breach was not entirely arbitrary. The Cádiz Constitution came with contradictions that facilitated the pueblos' strategies.

Perhaps most obvious was the asymmetry between the idea of sovereignty and the idea of territory. Sovereignty was conceived in the style of revolutionary France, that is, in an abstract, singular, and homogenizing way, making no concessions to the historical tradition of an empire that was always a federation of kingdoms under the one crown and thus had extremely strong traditions of territorial autonomy. Territory, however, was conceived very differently from the way it was formalized by the 1789 Revolution. The Cádiz Constitution's idea of territory was not at all similar to French geometric ideas (departments, cantons, etc.). The difference, seemingly of secondary importance, brought significant consequences. The French concept of territory implied a "rational" idea of how the new political representation should be constructed; it emphasized the necessity of numbers to consolidate the link between citizenship and sovereignty. Numbers were necessary to measure differences between active and passive citizens, between the voters and the elected, between citizens and noncitizens, between voters and intermediate electors, and so on. Each of these numerical strategies assumed that the state controlled detailed information about local societies, a process that was under way in France before the Revolution and continued throughout the nineteenth century to achieve the full nationalization of its citizens.

Despite the attempt at the end of the eighteenth century, when the first American census was taken, the Spanish empire never had this key numerical ability. Not only was this effort late; it did not move beyond traditional information practices. Each report was negotiated between regime officers and local hierarchies, indigenous and ecclesiastical. Any attempt by the state to calculate directly the demographic size of a territory or a local community would have been considered an affront to collective freedom. This social and cultural boundary was overcome in Europe, the result of continuous conflicts from the sixteenth century to the eighteenth that had significantly weakened the autonomy of peasant communities in the face of the absolutist state. At the dawn of liberalism, the case of Mexico's pueblos demonstrates the fundamental importance of counting the population to any modern project seeking to change the relationship between the state and society.

The definition of citizenship at Cádiz expressed this juncture very well. The new citizen was not defined through taxation or private property, nor was there a difference between active and passive citizenship. Abstraction in the style of the French Revolution, so powerful in asserting an equal sovereignty superior to all subjects, surrendered in Cádiz to the power of local territories and cultures. The citizen of Cádiz, and later of the Mexican Republic, was the *vecino*, the old householder of Iberian and Latin American cities. Before 1812 this character had something in common with the French pre-Revolutionary bourgeois and the British householder of the Whig era. Yet in 1812, when the liberal concept of citizenship was linked to the *vecindad* of Hispanic tradition, no means of legal identification came with the text of the constitution. There were no requisites of age or income, not even of property. Having a family was certainly important; however, above all, it was essential to have achieved community respect through "an honest way of life."[1]

The consequences of this linkage of old and new ideas of citizenship proved transcendental for Mexico's future. Once the traditional principle of social prominence ("an honest way of life") was accepted, Cádiz turned the local community into the source of political rights. And most remarkably, the makers of the constitution extended vecindad to indigenous peoples. This decision was of extraordinary significance at the time, achieved independently of the Jacobins and their postulation of universal equality. Cádiz denied all rights to blacks and *castas*, yet the entrance of Indians into the liberal world was not even questioned by the *serviles* who defended absolutism. This unanimity can be explained by noting the transformation of the Spanish ideological view of Indians that had taken place long before 1812, during the reign of Charles III, when Spanish Jansenism undermined the theological schemes of the sixteenth-century Salamanca school. By the end of the eighteenth century, the Indian was no longer imagined as spiritually "miserable." Rather, he was materially miserable. Bourbon reformers saw Indian poverty as an obstacle to production and agricultural wealth. Latin American Indians gained liberal citizenship because both Physiocrats and Jansenists had granted them, thirty years before, the status of *Homo aeconomicus*.

Rooted in the enlightened rationalism of Cádiz, the equality of citizenship granted to indigenous peoples carried potentially destabilizing consequences for the new regime. If an Indian was a citizen-vecino, then his community and his territory became a source of constitutional rights, just like nonindigenous pueblos. Thus we begin to see the extent of the constitutional breach that Mexican communities engaged and enlarged when the constitution crossed the Atlantic. The right to vote, the main attribute of sovereignty, helps us measure the original breach and its subsequent widening throughout New Spain. Cádiz made no distinction between active and passive citizens, nor did it require a roster of voters before elections. The power to determine who met the prerequisites of voting because of status as vecinos became the strategic moment in elections; if vecindad was recognized, citizenship was automatically granted. In the construction of the new political representation, the Cádiz Constitution definitely created the breach. It granted parish *juntas electorales* (electoral councils) absolute constitutional power to examine the prerequisite of citizenship and voting. The power was absolute because it could not be appealed; it lay beyond the state's jurisdiction. It is no coincidence that the parish became the fundamental electoral constituency—the basic electoral institution of Hispanic societies.

How was this voting citizenship, so far from the central state, linked to the abstract idea of sovereignty, the guarantee of the new spirit of equality in the Spanish nation? To answer, we must analyze voting and the related mechanisms. Cádiz legislators chose indirect balloting, then used in France and the United States. But Cádiz created many more levels of voting. The Spanish charter instituted four levels: vecinos, parish delegates, and *partido* (district) and provincial electors. In France and the United States there was only one level of intermediate electors, without different requirements. The Cádiz Constitution and the First Mexican Republic created complex hierarchies of voters and electors. All vecinos, literate or not, voted in parish juntas, since the first level of voting was done verbally. However, the elections in partido and provincial juntas involved secret ballots with rituals that required literacy. Finally, election to serve in the Cortes required a regular income. The number and typology of electors along the process suggest an attempt to create a hierarchy of distinct citizenships as a means of neutralizing the strength of territorial communities. It is essential to remember that until 1857, Mexican communities and pueblos retained their corporate judicial status. What we might define as the "intensity" of liberal citizenship was construed vertically throughout the electoral process, beginning in the parishes and culminating at the province level, where the most important act took place—the delegation of sovereignty to the nation's representative assembly. Nevertheless, this hierarchical conception of citizenship was countered by the horizontal citizenship of the *comunero-vecino*, whose sense of belonging to the nation was surely weaker than his sense of belonging to his pueblo, which continued to exist as an autonomous and corporative body.

Neither the writers of the Cádiz charter nor those who produced the Mexican Republican Constitution of 1824 understood fully the breach they created. Within the constitutional logic of the times, the asymmetry between sovereignty and territory had to be minimized by a boundary that never withstood the impact of Mexican society during the nineteenth century: the difference between political and administrative votes. Only elections for the Cádiz Cortes and later for Mexican federal congresses were to be political. Municipal elections were supposed to focus on local administration. The ayuntamientos were supposed to deal with "the internal government of the pueblos": street cleaning, schools, and so on. They were not supposed to have a political character. Yet that boundary never consolidated. In the few years between 1812–14 and 1820–23, the widespread diffusion of new constitutional ayuntamientos in rural areas not only made the breach obvious but expanded it to such an extent that the new citizenry became monopolized by these local institutions.

The political moment proved key. The colonial authorities in New Spain opposed Cádiz liberalism, but they saw that the charter could play a strategic role in the fight against insurgency by fulfilling old aspirations for autonomy in towns, villages, and cities. Mexico went through its first liberal experience led not by Creole elites but by the Spanish state while the colonial system collapsed. A chronological disjuncture between liberalism and independence contributed to defining the path to nationhood: the Republic did not ail from "colonial heritage"; it did not have to struggle to spread liberal constitutionalism across a society still closed by "antimodern" values. The real challenge faced by new governments was the legacy of the colonial crisis, the need to remove control over liberal citizenship from pueblos that had become constitutional municipalities before independence.

How did communities come to monopolize citizenship amid the crisis of the viceroyalty? The explanation begins with the failure of the judicial reforms attempted by Cádiz legislators. For three centuries the colonial regime concentrated local powers in the hands of *alcaldes mayores*, followed at the end of the eighteenth century by *subdelegados* and intendants, all of whom administered the so-called four "causes": military, fiscal, civil, and criminal. In 1812, Cádiz decreed that the old magistrates would keep military and fiscal powers, while new justices of the peace would administer civil and criminal justice. The liberals aimed to create a division of powers at the local level. The reform, however, did not become reality amid political crisis and revenue scarcities. Thus, when the Cortes removed the two judicial powers from the subdelegados, it created a jurisdictional vacuum that the new ayuntamientos quickly filled. The result was of transcendent and enduring importance; in a few years, a pivotal part of the state's functions lay in the hands of elected rural *cabildos*.

Meanwhile, the number of cabildos multiplied. Before Cádiz, New Spain had about a hundred. In 1821 there were almost one thousand. And in the new constitutional regime, all cabildos were equal. New ayuntamientos especially proliferated in indigenous areas. In Oaxaca alone there were around two hundred in 1821. Many old *repúblicas de indios* became ayuntamientos, demonstrating how local indigenous political cultures took control of liberal citizenship. Historically, not all pueblos had been equal; during three centuries, colonial communities were organized by the relationship between *cabeceras* (head towns) and subject pueblos. The hierarchy depended on many factors; ultimately, though, indigenous cabeceras always held powers of justice and taxation over dependent villages. The imposition of the principle of equality among the new ayuntamientos unleashed innumerable conflicts between cabeceras and subject pueblos. When the subject pueblos claimed status as municipios, they escaped tax and service obligations long owed to the caciques and *gobernadores* of the cabeceras.

Communities were neither passive nor indifferent toward liberal constitutionalism. They actively engaged the Cádiz charter: on the one hand, the character of the constitutional project was altered; on the other, many territorial hierarchies were radically transformed. The new citizenship stimulated fundamental changes within local societies, changes far from those imagined by liberal legislators. That change was negotiated locally more than imposed constitutionally confirms the significance of the process and helps us understand the dilemmas of republican governance. Indigenous pueblos, for example, followed local traditions and elected more aldermen than their populations would permit under the rules of Cádiz. Within colonial *cofradías* and councils of elders, when important decisions were made, every pueblo in the territory had to have one representative. Indigenous "proportionality" was based not on population but on the number of pueblos that participated in a common alliance or government. The weight of tradition organized everyday practices of citizenship and voting.

For example, conflict spread across the Toluca basin between 1820 and 1824 as old cabeceras opposed attempts by subject villages to become independent municipios. The head towns argued that according to the constitution, "parish" and "pueblo" defined the same territorial unit. Thus the site of the main parish church determined the only legitimate site for the municipio. The argument was groundless, yet it shows how conflicts were unleashed when citizenship linked the jurisdictional parish to the ecclesiastical parish. In addition, documents often show that each elected alderman exercised justice in his place of residence, something never foreseen by the constitutions, and neither planned nor promoted by Creole elites. What might be called the slippage of citizenship was a process entirely carried on by the pueblos. In this way, the new liberal citizenship's development produced a double rupture, involving and transforming both the old and the new orders.

It did more. Cádiz and the first Mexican republican constitution eliminated the colonial repúblicas de indios, a decision that gravely endangered the future of indigenous communities. The pueblos responded by using the liberal municipio to defend themselves against the threat of liberal equality. The ayuntamientos' control of justice relocated the pueblos within the constitutional framework, avoiding dramatic ruptures and providing a degree of legitimacy unquestioned until the Reform Laws of the 1850s. This fundamental paradox proved a defining element of the first Mexican liberalism. New liberal ayuntamientos worked tirelessly to defend communal lands, and thus to minimize the implementation of legislation seeking to divide and privatize agrarian property. In nineteenth-century Mexico, the land question lay at the heart of all dilemmas. The pueblos forged a corporate liberalism, yet the historically relevant issue was the extreme internal dynamism of the local world. The slippage of citizenship, forged by the pueblos, was reproduced repeatedly after independence. It created and sustained a breach between the new state and old communities, creating political practices unique to Mexican republicanism.

THE MONARCHICAL PACT AND REPUBLICAN NORMS

The ayuntamiento-pueblos created by the first Mexican liberal experience under Cádiz continued to define themselves as "sovereign" after 1821, as if the state did not exist. Across Mexico's territory, a common language revealed the persistence among the populace of an imaginary rooted in the constitutional tradition of Catholic monarchy. It is well known that the Hispanic concept of sovereignty belonged to the great tradition of contractual monarchism that asserted that the king's legitimacy depended on pacts with his kingdoms. The pacts stipulated reciprocal obligations based on justice, understood as the perpetual guarantee that the king would respect the kingdoms' rights and privileges. The famous formula "se acata y no se cumple" (we respect, but we do not obey), so often condemned as a symptom of pathological corruption in Spanish America during the viceregal period, in fact had a very different meaning. First, it was not invented in Latin America; it was part of Basque common law from the twelfth century, incorporated into Castilian law in the fourteenth century, and later exported to the Indies. Second, it served precisely as a warranty of the pact of reciprocal obligations: the king could not move against the kingdom's rights and privileges. If a law threatened them, judges had to suspend implementation. One implication of this tradition was that justice was always negotiable because it was practiced between two equally legitimate wills, the king's and that of his kingdoms' subjects. The extent to which these values were socialized across New Spain under the colonial ancien régime is demonstrated by the district magistrates, whose four causes, or powers, embraced the totality of life within communities. Thus the pactist base of the Catholic monarchy became an integral part of the pueblos' collective culture, so entrenched that it survived into the republican period, strengthened by the new liberal citizenship.

Pactist political culture also persisted across elite society, linked in many and complex ways with Cádiz liberalism and then with the liberalism of Mexico's first republican decades. To both Fray Servando Teresa de Mier and Lucas Alamán, the petition of the Mexico City Cabildo to organize a junta of cities in 1808 (in response to the Napoleonic capture of the Spanish crown) was the first revolutionary expression in New Spain. The peninsular merchants' plot that unseated Viceroy Iturrigaray and stopped the creation of the junta does not reduce the importance of the project. Emphasizing the principle that (after the forced abdication of Fernando VII) sovereignty reverted to the kingdoms, including New Spain, the cabildo proposed a meeting of Estates-General. In Europe's ancien régime, such estates traditionally curbed kings' authorities.[2] Yet in Mexico City, the justices of the Audiencia (High Court) who joined the merchants in blocking the call for such a gathering did so by defining the proposal as "pure liberal doctrine." The judges showed their understanding of the explosive potential of the cabildo initiative. What the ayuntamiento was asking for was effectively the territorial representation of New Spain while no king occupied the throne. Had the proposal succeeded, the balance of power would have shifted to the cabildos of New Spain (as happened in the Río de la Plata and Venezuela).

A parallel disjuncture marked the debates between Americans and *peninsulares* in the Cádiz Cortes, propelling the imperial crisis to develop through two institutional projects. The first was the constitutional transformation of the central monarchy, promoted by Spanish liberals. The second was a strengthening of territorial autonomy, in essence a move toward monarchical federalism, pressed by the Latin Americans. As early

as 1811, during a debate on the constitutional project, American representatives unsuccessfully presented to the subcommittee on overseas affairs
an imperial project built on autonomous states, led by provincial juntas
with powers to decide matters of international trade and credit. The same
year, the four American representatives on the commission in charge of
drafting the constitution argued that the charter should not be considered
ratified until provincial assemblies accepted it. Their argument emphasized the right of the "nation" to freely accept the constitution, or to modify
it, because the "national will" had its base in pacts between sovereign
territories "independent" of each other and independent of the central
authorities. This would become the cornerstone of Mexican federalism: a
"social pact," apparently recalling Rousseau; but the protagonists were not
individuals but collective entities: the territories. The municipio-pueblos
did not have to go much farther to assert their sovereignty within the same
constitution. Thus appeared, before independence, the crucible that would
dominate Mexican liberalism throughout the nineteenth century: the contest between federalism grounded in provincial states and federalism based
on municipal sovereignty.

The projects of Mexico's political insurgents also envisioned a sovereignty grounded in the territories. Lucas Alamán quotes a letter written by
José María Morelos to Ignacio López Rayón on December 7, 1812. It dealt
with the institutional question in the following terms: "I had not received
the constitutional elements until now; I have seen them and, with a few
differences, they are the same that we discussed with Sr. Hidalgo."[3] The
project asserted the exclusivity of Catholicism, with a Tribunal of Faith to
protect it, and regulations amenable to the spirit of ecclesiastical discipline. The project recognized the sovereignty of the Spanish monarchy but
also insisted that it emanated from the people, thus radicalizing the pactist
tradition. Additionally, the monarch's powers were delegated to a Supreme
American Junta, with five members appointed by provincial representatives. Once the capital city was conquered, they envisioned a Congress, to
be renewed every three years by the vote of the ayuntamientos, so that
"only the most honest people of property from the capital cities and pueblos of the respective districts should be elected." Yet the Congress would
not have legislative power in matters as important as war, the foreign debt,
and others, which fell under the jurisdiction of a Council of State formed
by senior military officers and presided over by a "National Protector"
appointed by that council. The protector would hold the power to propose
laws. The Congress would be consulted, but only the junta would have the
power to make laws.

Though the project was never implemented, it remains important to understanding crucial aspects of Mexico's march toward liberalism. It re-affirmed the principle of territorial representation via cabildos and provinces, honoring the autonomist aspirations of moderate Creoles. Yet the territories' strength was drastically limited by the fact that sovereignty, while formally still attributed to the crown, effectively resided in the army and its command structures—especially in the protector.[4]

The Apatzingan Constitution of 1814, influenced by Cádiz, brought a remarkable change in the insurgents' political vision. Morelos did not write the new insurgent charter; rather, it was the work of civilians who forced him to renounce both the post of commander in chief and the role of protector. These events foreshadowed Mexico's future difficulties finding a balance between sovereignty and territorial representation.

The unresolved contest between sovereignty and representation plagued the projects presented by the forces that confronted each other during the bloody civil war between 1810 and 1820. In 1821, Agustín de Iturbide's Plan de Iguala synthesized all the elements and incorporated all the dilemmas inherent in the Creole pactist perspective. The campaign of Iturbide's Army of the Three Guarantees was essentially a political campaign that, moving from the peripheral territories toward the capital, managed in a few months to gain the support of the new constitutional municipios. Independence came as a pact between these territorial bodies and the army, leaving aside the provincial deputations created by the Cádiz regime. Then what contemporary documents called "the Iguala system" transferred sovereignty to the army, and Iturbide became protector, the pivotal role envisioned by the first insurgent project. A close reading of the *Actas de la Junta Soberana*, appointed by Iturbide under the Treaty of Cordoba (which confirmed Mexico's independence), shows that relations among the institutions of government operated under the protectorate model, unleashing tensions that soon led to the breakdown of Iturbide's fleeting empire.[5] From the outset, Iturbide claimed power to intervene in the Junta's affairs by proposing and forcing approval of legislation, arguing that the army had sworn to uphold the government, claiming power even to modify the Cádiz Constitution—still in force after independence.

Mexico's first post-independence Constitutional Congress faced an ambiguous situation. It assembled to draft a constitution according to principles fixed by the Plan de Iguala and legitimized by the adherence of the municipios. The new regime had to be a constitutional monarchy. At the same time, to be recognized as regent, Iturbide had to pledge respect for the sovereignty of a Congress whose legitimacy came not from elections but from the Plan de Iguala. However, Iturbide as regent-protector continued to assert the right to initiate legislation before a Congress that had already claimed, upon its installation, "absolute" sovereignty. That conflict festered unresolved until mounting tensions between the two bases of the Plan de Iguala, the army and the municipios, first made the protector into an emperor and then brought about his overthrow.

It is essential to emphasize, however, that the shift from Iturbide's brief monarchy to the federal republic was not traumatic. The broad consensus that had backed the Plan de Iguala in two years became a broad consensus for the Republic. The explanation may rest on an apparent contradiction: the republican solution allowed the consolidation of the territorial bases of the old monarchical pact between the crown and its kingdoms, now reconstituted between the central government and the territories. The first federal republic was an unsuccessful attempt to institutionalize the three sovereignties in formation amid the imperial crisis: the sovereignty of the nation, of the provinces, and of the municipios.

During the first decades after independence, conflicts between federal and provincial sovereignty were constant, creating the legitimate suspicion that Mexico was in fact a confederated regime. Nonetheless, that is an incomplete understanding. Conflicts between municipal authorities and both provincial and national powers were equally important and have not received enough attention. Electoral municipalities were Mexico's foundational liberal institutions, created before independence. With Iturbide's army, the municipalities guaranteed the Plan de Iguala. In the collective imaginary, they had legitimacy far greater than the congresses and other institutions that followed. The dynamics of republican uprisings show this clearly; they were neither as "military" nor as "illegal" as analysts have long asserted. A glance at the archival evidence easily shows that the legitimacy of uprisings did not come from the army, or its units; rather, it came primarily from acts of adherence by municipalities. These were official documents drafted in public assemblies, signed by notaries following formal procedures. Thus uprisings were powerfully institutionalized actions by which some elected bodies (usually municipalities) broke pacts of subordination to a government (state or federal) and joined other corporations (the army) to reclaim sovereignty—in a way reenacting the founding Plan de Iguala. The dynamics of these uprisings, from the first proclamation, through acts of adherence, to the ultimate summoning of a constitutional congress, show that political conflicts channeled through struggles among the three different sovereignties: municipal, provincial, and national.

The Mexican Republic could not follow the trajectories of either the young North American Republic or of France's triumphant bourgeoisie. In Mexico's ancien régime republic, liberalism legitimated the struggles of actors as different as merchants, indigenous communities, and military units. No one was excluded from this legitimacy—a key to understanding the strong popular consensus in support of the Republic. It is equally evident and understandable that the Republic faced insoluble problems of governance resulting from the same process that gave birth to it: Mexico's central governments did not inherit sovereignty directly from the monarchy, as did France and the United States; instead they received it from the Spanish monarchy's legitimate heirs, that is, from territorial corporations that always felt free to sever their ties of subordination.

Those who aimed to lead faced an intense dilemma of republican governance. Without doubt, the problem of political institutions for decades dominated the culture and thinking of the ruling class. From Father Servando Teresa de Mier to Lucas Alamán, from José María Luis Mora to Lorenzo de Zavala and Melchor Ocampo, every prestigious intellectual placed the problem of governance at the core of his deliberations. At the same time, every political force gave constant attention to the normative discourse. What needs research in depth is the concept of law that continued to define political society—the monarchical, pactist tradition that remained strong within the republican regime.

An analysis of political pamphlets and the press would enlighten us further about the relationship between monarchical contractualism and republican liberalism in the understandings of the time. One example, a document dated December 18, 1835, commenting on Nicolás Bravo's plans against the government, posed the following questions:

1. Is the present administration an intended and legitimate result of the federal constitution, or merely a result of the Zavaleta Pact?
2. Did that Pact conform to the Constitution or violate it?
3. If there was violation, was it total or partial?
4. In case of infraction, then clearly there were differences: whom should we respect? Was the national will inhibited in the Constitution or in the Pact?
5. Does the Pact bind everyone to all of its parts?
6. Has it been followed by everyone in its totality?
7. Do violations of the Constitution justify uprisings and insurrections?[6]

What are the origins of this concept of sovereignty as delegated by corporate groups to a caudillo, and practiced by him in such defined and similar ways over time that among contemporaries such delegations came to operate as constitutional bases? To approach an answer, we should return to the crisis of the viceroyalty. The political differences between Juan Francisco Azcárate y Ledesma, the Creole leader of the capital's ayuntamiento in 1808, and José María Morelos, leader of the insurrection after

Hidalgo's death in 1811, were noteworthy; yet their projects derived from the shared idea that sovereignty reverted to the people upon the vacancy of the crown. The concept of a "state of natural necessity," used by both men to define the legal status of kingless New Spain, was part of the Catholic culture of natural law since the Middle Ages; it marked both the debates of the Cádiz Cortes and the declarations of juntas across the Spanish empire. We find the same concept in one of the most important documents of the insurgents: the Chilpancingo Declaration of Independence (November 6, 1813), which claimed that it assembled "due to the present circumstances in Europe, recovered the exercise of usurped sovereignty, and thus dependency on the Spanish throne is dissolved and broken forever."[7]

In 1811, during the Cádiz debates over the third article of the constitutional project, which stated that sovereignty resided "essentially in the nation"—a clear reference to Sieyés's adverb, which in 1789 transformed the States-General into a National Constituent Assembly—the Mexican deputy Guridi y Alcocer, along with other Americans, proposed to modify the article by replacing *essentially* with *radically* or *originally*, "so that it expresses that the nation will not cease to be a nation by depositing it in a person or moral corporation."[8] The two adverbs preferred by the Americans used the language of the monarchist pact. They clearly showed the Creole concept of the nation as an entity already in existence, prior to, and independent of, any government. This was far removed from the idea of a nation as created beginning with government, a notion found in José María Luis Mora, the Mexican liberals' intellectual leader in the 1830s, but a concept never shared by most members of the political class of the time.

The 1823 Plan of Veracruz was the first post-independence document that recovered the theory that a state of necessity could legitimize an uprising against the government. The plan argued that Iturbide's appointment as emperor was not valid, because it was not proclaimed by Congress. As a result, "the nation remains free and moreover, with its present emancipation, in its natural state." Therefore it is "independent, sovereign, free, and in its natural state" and thus has full right to "constitute itself" through a Congress.[9]

The American representatives at Cádiz went as far as to affirm their right to accept or reject the constitution based on the distinction between a *nation in its natural state* and a *constituted nation*. This conceptual distinction reappeared in all the main plans of the first half of the nineteenth century. After the Plan of Veracruz, we find it again in Santa Ana's 1828 Plan of Perote, in Nicolás Bravo's so-called Conciliation against the 1833 liberal Congress, in the 1834 Plan of Cuernavaca, in the San Luis de Potosí uprising of December 1845, and in the 1846 Plan of the Ciudadela.

These plans, centralist, federalist, and liberal, all show that political conflicts took place within the framework of a shared political culture.

The duality between "natural" and "constituted" explains why the implementation of a plan always required a new congress or a new constitution, despite the fact that the parliamentary class showed great continuity through the early decades of republicanism.[10] The act of *constituting* itself as the nation was never the fully sovereign action of a constituting congress. The nation already existed in its *natural state* and expressed itself through its territorial representative bodies, who granted to the constituting congress a binding political mandate: to institutionalize a new pact whose principles were already set in the plan. In the Morelia notarial archives there are writs that attest to the election of representatives for the 1824, 1841, and 1846 congresses. The formula by which the second-level electors defined the mandate of parliament went as follows:

> Therefore they grant to each one the most ample powers to constitute the Mexican nation in the way that they think best reflects the general happiness and, especially, to dictate laws for all branches of public administration under their jurisdiction, with the object of affirming the general interest by securing the bases, religion, independence and union, that must remain inalterable, as well as the popular representative Republic, as proclaimed in the first article of the August 4th plan.[11]

These three documents deal with elections for politically different constituent assemblies: the first federalist, the second centralist, and the third liberal and moderate. Monarchical pactism and republican norms were not mutually exclusive; rather, they were interdependent. This was one of the unique characteristics of the first Mexican liberalism.

LIBERAL POLITICAL SYNCRETISMS

In the first half of the nineteenth century, about 30 percent of the Mexican population was indigenous. How did liberalism engage these citizens? How did the idea of the abstract nation encounter their cultures of communal belonging? Mexican communities agreed to join the new nation. But by reinterpreting constitutions to defend their interests, communities eventually imagined alternative Mexican nations with identities grounded in updated visions of the past. Generally, these indigenous visions resorted to a process of juxtaposition of values just as they had done in viceregal times. There is not much research on the new syncretism between pueblos and liberalism; we lack even a solid chronology. It appears, though, that it evolved in cycles linked to scenarios created by national political and agrarian conjunctures. It is worth stressing that the chronologies of violent resistance and legal protests did not differ radically. Evidently, communities used both approaches simultaneously or chose one according to the needs of the moment. Among the legal approaches available under the Republic, there was, in addition to judicial litigation, a constitutional recourse that inhered in the pueblos' memories: the right to petition. Rooted in the ancient tradition of European monarchies, adopted and energized by New Spain's pueblos in the colonial compact, the right continued within modern constitutionalism, cleansed of exclusivist privileges. All Mexican constitutions explicitly honored the right of petition; the pueblos continued to use it to "represent themselves" before the new powers as they had during the colonial times.

In the 1830s and 1840s, a wave of petitions from pueblos defending their lands inundated state and federal congresses. There were so many that legislators seriously discussed how to curb the phenomenon, to no avail. A new wave of petitions came after the Reforma War and the fall of Maximilian. This enormous mass of documents is an excellent source for studying syncretism between the pueblos and liberalism. Let us turn now to one of these petitions, with the warning that it comes from 1877—meaning that, formally, it does not fall within the chronology of this study. However, precisely because it was part of the second liberalism of the mid-nineteenth-century Reforma, the document is most revealing of what liberalism became during the earlier period when communities were most active on the national political scene. Additionally, we should not forget that communities' sense of time always differed from that of official politics. And finally, the syncretism of this document expresses wonderfully a vision of the relationship between communities and liberalism rooted in cultural elements without defined chronological frontiers.

It is possible that a lawyer or an intellectual linked to the pueblos wrote the document. This is a secondary detail; since the colonial period, the pueblos' representatives were learned and often born in the city. The possibility that the author was learned and did not belong to the pueblos, however, stresses the continued and widespread use of practices and personal bonds, typical of the colonial past, during the republican era. The second piece of information that will help us read this text is the title itself: *A defense of the territorial rights of the fatherland presented by the Mexican people to the Congress of the Nation demanding the reconquest of territorial property so that it may be newly distributed among all the citizens that inhabit the Republic by agrarian laws and a general reorganization of labor, through a series of protective laws and with the funds that must be created by a Credit Bank.*[12]

BOURET Editor, México.

Tipos Mexicanos
desde la Independencia
hasta nuestros días.

EVANGELISTA ESPAÑOL *en la Plaza principal de México en* (1821

629

1. Lettered men of the city wrote petitions for villagers seeking rights and justice in the new Mexican nation. Reprinted by permission of Archivo General de la Nación, Sección Propiedad Artística y Literaria.

The document bears the signatures of the "citizens" of fifty-six ayuntamiento-pueblos from the state of Guanajuato, whose first and last names are found at the end of the text's twenty-five pages. Notably, these pueblos claimed to speak in the name of the "Mexican people" in order to demand that the Congress approve a series of measures to "reconquer territorial property" because, as the title asserts, what the petition seeks to defend are the "territorial rights of the fatherland." It is obvious that this is not merely the petition of pueblos affected by the encroachment of a hacienda onto communal lands. A lawsuit existed, as noted in the text, but it is not the central theme, which seeks national scope. For what rights and what fatherland do the Guanajuato pueblos petition? It is an indigenous Mexico that does not wish to be anti-Hispanic but seeks to use the liberal constitution to reclaim sovereignty over its territory, not to govern but to "organize correctly the property rights reconquered" after independence. The petition insists that republican governments had failed to care for these interests, "deviating from the original idea set forth by our first liberators to guarantee our glorious emancipation along with the rights and properties that have resulted from it, which without doubt focused principally on the improvement and civilization of all the inhabitants of our beautiful fatherland."

The specific measures they proposed are not important for our topic. What is most relevant is the relationship they envisioned between the land as "territory," the idea of *patria* or "nation," and the constitution. How did these pueblos justify the concept of "the Mexican people's indisputable proprietorship over the soil"? In general, pueblos and communities had defended their lands over the centuries, in lawsuits and rebellions, asserting property titles granted by the Spanish crown. In the Guanajuato petition, such references are not important. It asserted a more historical and constitutional legitimacy. The pueblos demanded the observance of individual rights to property and security, yet the point of reference was another nation: not the liberal nation but an indigenous nation, a historical nation that by its very nature had a "territorial right" that predated constitutions. The imaginary system of this indigenous nation was most complex because it attempted to link modern principles with ancient political myths and language. Clearly, the word "nation" was used in its modern sense as singular entity; indigenous peoples appear without any distinction of ethnicity or language. The indigenous nation was one of many in the age of emerging nations; it does not deny "the valuable advantage that legal procedures prescribe to enjoy the rights with which we have been endowed, equal to the men of other civilized nations, so that by reason and the law we may show to all concerned our sufferings and hardship, preparing ourselves thus to reject that hateful label by which our race has long and unfairly been degraded, demeaning our just and direct demands as the acts of uncultured savages and indomitable brutes."

The petition's discourse of the parity of nations shares with liberalism a thoroughly negative image of colonial New Spain, but with a radically different emphasis: hacienda property titles were null because they originated "in the conquest of the Americas, thus in notorious violation of the law: before that time the inhabitants enjoyed legitimate and original titles; this soil was their designated homeland, the obvious proof of their prolonged and peaceful possession cannot be challenged."

The fundamental historical element that defined the indigenous nation-homeland was therefore the legitimacy of the title to occupy the soil before the Spanish conquest. As is well known, this was one of the arguments that Francisco de Vitoria used from his chair at the University of Salamanca in the sixteenth century to deny the legitimacy of the conquest and defend that of the evangelization, in his view the only justification for the colonization of the Americas. The ideas of Bartolomé de las Casas were more radical and more recognized among indigenous peoples over the centuries.

The Guanajuato petition also evokes his memory, recalling "the detestable practice of the *encomienda*" and the Chiapas bishop's struggle to defend the "eternal principles of Catholicism." Starting with the citation of Las Casas, the text offers a synthetic yet precise survey of the principal measures that affected the indigenous nation during the colonial period, including the congregation of communities, the laws on land grants, and the titling of colonial property.

Before turning to the second historical element essential to the idea of the indigenous nation, it is worth examining the image that the petition offers of the nineteenth century, beginning with independence. Three points are key: the positive evaluation of the Cádiz Cortes's decrees on citizenship; the reference to Hidalgo's decree of December 5, 1810, on indigenous lands; and the interpretation of the events that brought independence in 1821.

> Later the Spaniards understood: many rich foreigners accepted independence to preserve their interests, joining the side of independence, thus committing treason against their fatherland. It was they who insisted that the Spanish general Iturbide should lead the Revolution, so their property would be respected. . . . This is sad to say, but it is the truth. Our authorities forgot the right to *postliminium* by which America, and within it the Mexican nation, recovered its rights with independence: thus they illegally respected property rights that were vicious and null.[13]

It is interesting to note that Iturbide is labeled "español a la colonial," that is, as white. Yet the point absolutely central to our analysis is the reference to the principle of *postliminium*. It shows that the idea of the indigenous Mexican nation has its doctrinal and thus historical foundations in the *jus gentium* (rights of peoples) of the Catholic natural law tradition, as adapted to New Spain in the sixteenth and seventeenth centuries. It is well known that the jus gentium was a conceptual and juridical structure that, from the patristic, to the Scholastic, then to the neo-Scholastic tradition, was used to decide whether a conquered domain had, before conquest, been a kingdom and thus should retain its rights. Within this framework, the postliminium recognized the right of war captives to recover their original judicial status once they were liberated.

These issues were central in the famous debate over the nature of the American Indian after the conquest. Three citations are revealing: when he debated Juan Sepúlveda in Valladolid in 1550–51, Bartolomé de las Casas denied the theory of a just war, affirming that indigenous peoples "have sufficient political life that claims of their barbarism cannot be used to wage war against them."[14] Vasco de Quiroga in *De debellandis indis* (1553) categorically affirmed that "the contrary argument cannot stand, since the lords of the Indies obtained their capitals and principalities by the Right of Peoples, they cannot be altered by the Pope or the Emperor, and even less by the aforementioned Kings of Spain."[15] It is not a coincidence, then, that Torquemada titled his sixteenth-century book *Monarquía indiana*. "As one of the conditions of Laws is to live in organized Pueblos and Republics, it is clear that the Indian nations had them, like the other People of the World."[16] In the sixteenth century, theologians appealed to jus gentium to solve the great problem of legitimate title to conquest.[17] In the middle of the nineteenth century, the author or authors of the Guanajuato pueblos' petition appealed to jus gentium to offer an alternative vision of Mexican independence and to legitimize an alternative idea of nation. Based on the principle of postliminium, with independence the Mexican indigenous nation emerged from captivity and recovered its preconquest freedom: "The inhabitants of the Americas, over whom the conquering western nations exercised sovereignty over for only three hundred years, finally proclaimed their independence, reconquered their freedom, and because of that became a country of free people, with just titles and with the right to be a patria."

Is this the patria of the ancient Mexican civilizations? Yes and no. I have stressed that the concept had a modern spirit: a population with shared characteristics based on territory. The nation of the Guanajuato petition offers a liberal face—but it maintains a mythical indigenous body: New Spain's evangelizing Catholicism. It states in modern words that "it is our right to insist and to prove that the soil of this continent belongs to us, by the same right of property and dominion enjoyed by other nations." Yet a few lines later, we find the following:

> We are sustained by faith and belief in the truth given in the Bible, Genesis, chapter 10, verse 30, that names the thirteen sons of Jectam, brother of Faleg, lineage of Sem, from whom we undoubtedly descend.... Then, soon after the confusion of tongues, their many descendants in the East Indies having multiplied, they came to populate the Western Indies, ... and we remember with noble pride the names of the seven chiefs who departed from Sennaar, ... they were the founders of the populous cities of the other continent: their immediate successors had the fortune to found in the new world the original Axoco of the Xilancas ... in Xalisco with some of the Toltecs' descendants, led by their chiefs Ehecatl and Cohuatl, the Olmecs with their chief Apopocanub taking possession toward Ecatepetl, ... toward Oaxaca the Zapotecs.

These lines, seemingly arbitrary and mythical from the perspective of a doctrinaire nineteenth-century liberal, have clear roots. They derive from the apocalyptic culture of the great Franciscan chroniclers of the sixteenth century, of Fray Toribio de Motolinía, of Jerónimo de Mendieta, and many others who linked Indians to an apocalyptic vision. According to tradition, a number of the Israelite tribes did not return from their Assyrian exile. Since no traces were found in Asia, some Franciscans explained the mysterious origins of the American Indians, then unknown, by making them the descendants of lost tribes. Another interpretation claimed that the same Amerindians were the descendants of the Jews who in 71 AD fled from the destruction of Jerusalem at the hands of Titus and Vespasianus.

The memory of these interpretations was not lost in nineteenth-century Mexico. Many convent frescoes, such as the chapel of Juan Gerson at Tecamachalco, daily reminded devout indigenous peoples of the great cycles of the syncretic imaginary of evangelization.[18] It appears that these references have a justifying role in the Guanajuato petition: to legitimize the use of jus gentium to assert the existence of a right to a territorial fatherland that preceded the liberal constitution. This would create what we would technically call a "basis of rights" that would allow indigenous petitioners to reinterpret the Mexican charter.

This document is just one among many that pueblos sent to republican governments throughout the century. We cannot forget that indigenous Mexicans were citizens with voting rights, that their pueblos retained municipal powers, and that they used those rights and powers to defend themselves against the state. The Guanajuato petition did not follow a model. It did reflect widespread practices grounded in an imaginary that generated diverse actions all grounded in a shared syncretic vision.

THE CATHOLIC QUESTION

Syncretism leads to the question of Catholicism: not the well-known issues between church and state, but the deeper and more complex dilemmas of a Mexican society that was not secularized. The documents we have analyzed clearly show that the pueblos had a vision of the world and of politics that remained deeply religious and followed the particular religious patterns consolidated in the seventeenth century and usually defined as "baroque." The pueblos sustained a Catholicism very different from that of elites. The pueblos did not separate religious and secular values. They retained many of the collective practices that enlightened reformers had worked to suppress in the later Bourbon decades, often without success. We should recall that in 1794 the Madrid Academy of History attacked devotion to Guadalupe, labeling it a "fable" and a "simple and foolish devotion." While this attack had no effect in Mexico, religious authorities

2. Popular devotion to Guadalupe, centered at her basilica near Mexico City, sometimes divided and sometimes united Mexicans searching for national unity. Reprinted by permission of Archivo General de la Nación, Sección Propiedad Artística y Literaria.

did attempt to repress the constant proliferation of local cults and miracles. In short, they attempted to contain and discipline the margins of toleration, the disordered space that had characterized baroque culture at the end of the sixteenth century.

Near the end of the imperial period, enlightened understandings changed the perception of society: over a few years, the new vision saw New Spain as full of barbarism, filthy recesses, negligence, irrationality, and spiritual libertinage. The letters of subdelegados and *intendentes*, and the bishops' obsessive pastoral letters, particularly those from Puebla and Mexico City, are astonishing if we compare them with documents from before the 1790s. Suddenly the debasement, the social degeneration, that had previously explained indigenous "laziness" was turned against society at large.

The divorce between popular devotion and the church hierarchy was never absolute. Ultimately, the fear of provoking riots was a powerful deterrent. It is also possible that the insurgency for independence, with its calls to popular devotion starting with the Virgin of Guadalupe, opened a new breach for the resurgence of "barbarisms." The 1810 civil war became a "war of images," with Guadalupe protecting the insurgents, and the Virgin of Los Remedios the royalists.

It is not difficult to imagine that the pueblos' mobilizations for or against insurgency reactivated traditional religious practices, simultaneously strengthening their political autonomy and the sacred strength of their communal territories. Yet the relationships between varied religious forms did not return to direct confrontations. In this context so crucial to the creation of Mexico's first liberalism, the Cádiz regime also played a legitimizing role. The Cádiz legislators did not promote a secularizing image of the constitution. If we examine the strategies of image and ritual the Cortes planned to broadcast their text, it is clear that they offered no new ritual or collective representation (as revolutionary France had done). The only novelty was that towns and cities had to name their main square the "Plaza de la Constitución."

There were changes: the proliferation of pamphlets, catechisms, and books against "despotism" and in favor of the constitution was remarkable. But the written discourse was detached from the visual discourse. Consequently, the change of political language did not extend beyond urban areas. If it reached the pueblos at all, it was encapsulated in local imaginaries, because of their strength and because of the legitimacy granted them by the rites of allegiance to, and publication of, the constitution. Both events were planned by the Cortes and, along with the articles about citizenship and elections, help us to comprehend how the pueblos entered the world of the first liberalism without losing their traditional religiosity. Cádiz destroyed many privileges, but it did not attack the classical idea of Catholic pactism that claimed that society was an ensemble of "natural corporations" that did not need the state to exist. Perhaps a European liberal of the time would not distinguish between corporations and privileges, but a Spanish liberal paid close attention: privileges fell within the political sphere; corporations did not. They were part of "natural" society, the same natural order we found in the plans that defined political uprisings.

The mandates of the Cortes and of the 1824 Constitutional Convention left no room for doubt: the "corporations"—that is, lawyers, physicians, artisans, university faculties, militias, administrative offices, and, of course, the pueblos—had to swear allegiance to the constitutions. Those corporate procedures persisted through the first part of the century. Different accounts show that oaths remained absolutely religious, exactly as in the past: at the center of the stage, the text of the constitution lay on a table before the Crucifix, with the Book of Gospels at its side. There were no new symbols. Yet we should not underestimate the details. Oaths were then extremely serious because they involved relations of power and collective belonging. Their forms help us understand how fundamental links were perceived and imagined. There is no doubt that the forms by which allegiance to the constitution was declared did not differ from the oaths that prevailed during three centuries of Catholic monarchy. The relationship between the nation and the constitution remained in the sphere of the sacred, never shifting to the secular sphere.

This is clearly seen if we analyze the rites of public presentation, the ceremonial framework of oaths of allegiance. These ceremonies were not identical everywhere but had much in common. Most pueblos followed the models of their patron saints' festivals. The public presentation of the constitutions was celebrated during three days of festivities, including processions of saints, *tianguis* (markets where indigenous communities exchanged products), the tolling of bells, firecrackers, cockfights, and diverse parades. In the reports that local officials and ayuntamientos sent to authorities to document their observance of instructions, we meet the world of devotion and sociability that enlightened Bourbons had branded as "paganism."[19] This rebirth or continuation of the pueblos' religious imaginary tells us that liberal constitutionalism was without doubt a great innovation for the communities, but not such an innovation that it broke the enduring world of values that still grounded collective identities in everyday life.

The Cortes at Cádiz linked the constitution to the sacred first in the oath of allegiance and then within the mass; a decree ordered every parish priest to follow the reading of the gospel with a sermon on the "excellence" of the "learned code." This was done in every pueblo. There was more: a procession of the constitutional text culminated its local proclamation. At the end of the mass, men carried on their shoulders a copy of the constitution under a canopy, as if it was the holy sacrament, parading through neighborhoods, churches, and convents. In the procession, the vecinos-citizens marched in corporations: churchmen, the subdelegado and militia officers, "respectable vecinos," and the "corporation" of indigenous notables. Then came the whole community, organized in cofradías, each carrying its patron saint's banner.[20] It is easy to imagine that the pueblos saw liberal constitutionalism as a change that remained within local codes of symbolic communication. Therefore it did not break with their collective religious cultures.

I have emphasized that these cultures were very sensitive to justice and its implementation, and that for the communities the basis for justice was a contractual relationship with the king. We must now ask to what extent the continuity of religious imaginaries, strengthened by the slippage of citizenship, perpetuated under the Republic a vision of a contractual relationship between power and the pueblo, or between the pueblos and the abstract and mysterious entity that was the new idea of the nation. The massive development of civic festivals that aimed to spread secular values across Mexico awaited the second liberalism of the Reforma. Throughout the first liberalism there was a great diffusion of civic catechisms, pamphlets, and newspapers. But we must question the impact of these materials, of all written texts, offspring of the freedom of expression, which could not engage systematically the pueblos' visual language, which was derived from an older concept of freedom inherited from the popular culture of New Spain's baroque times.

The attitudes and language of elites also reinforced links between the old and new freedoms. After all, the Republic's founding text, the *Plan de la Constitución Política de la Nación Mexicana* of May 16, 1823, proclaimed as the first duty of citizenship "to profess apostolic Roman Catholicism as the state's only religion." That premise remained in every charter until 1857. Throughout the first liberalism, the rulers themselves, regardless of political and ideological stands, promoted a continuous mixing of the political and the religious. Perhaps chronic political instability repeatedly created new opportunities for governments and their opponents to use the sacred to sanctify always-fragile power and uncertain legitimacy.[21]

We return now to the slippage of citizenship, because the means of diffusion of the first constitutionalism provide significant information. Liberalism arrived in the pueblos not as a break, not as a second conquest that would destroy collective identities. The communal bases of citizenship and voting, the control over the rules of access to the political arena that early constitutions delegated to communities, crucial in themselves, along with the failed attempts to use indirect elections to neutralize corporate bases, produced a legitimacy far from the spirit of the constitutions— because their dissemination ultimately depended on territorial rights rather than state codes. The historical problem of "distance" between norms and their implementation existed. But it should not be overly dramatized for two reasons: first, the pueblos were legally the social agents of liberalism; and second, the problem did not reflect a conflict between a secularized vision (of elites) and a nonsecularized one (of pueblos). Instead, it derived from the unsolved dilemmas of New Spain's Catholicism and the tensions between different ways of conceiving relations between state and society.

This Catholic universe, so divided between the "enlightened" and the "baroque," shared a concept of society that fused all possible tensions or conflicts, thus rendering the resolution of the most basic dilemmas more difficult. This key concept continued the trajectory of sixteenth-century Catholic natural law, as redefined by the great neo-Scholastic school at Salamanca, and exported and consolidated in the Americas by the Jesuits in the seventeenth century. The Jesuit version has points in common with the Protestant natural law of the same era, as developed by Hugo de Grotius and Samuel Pufendorf. Jesuits and Protestants shared antiregalism, the idea of sovereignty as a pact between king and kingdoms, and therefore the idea that the "absolute power" of the crowns must be curbed. It was a vision opposed to Hobbes's pessimistic naturalism. The Spanish Jesuits' natural law always theorized that a society organized in corporations is natural and unlimited, whereas a state is a limited and artificial entity unnecessary to the moral goals of individuals. Here lay the fundamental point of reference of the adverb "originally" that Guridi y Alcocer defended in Cádiz, an adverb that said everything about sovereignty and the state: the nation does not cease to be sovereign, even without a government.

Contrasting historical conjunctures meant that the Catholic natural law tradition that shaped Mexico's first liberalism could avoid the dramatic Lockean conflict between *nation* and *representation* that in the first two decades of the eighteenth century (the so-called English "parliamentary dictatorship") led the ideological way toward revolution in England's North American colonies. Thus, at the beginning of modern Spanish constitutionalism in Cádiz and then in the Mexican Republic, the encompassing view of Spanish natural law remained at its height, despite the Bourbon expulsion of the Jesuits and attempts to consolidate regalism that provoked a wave of popular rebellions in New Spain.

In this way, the slippage of liberal citizenship followed not only the model of the constitution but also the natural law tradition. It thus favored the "natural" autonomy of organized territories. This becomes even more significant when we recall that according to tradition, the city with a cabildo was a "natural" entity that did not belong to the state. Perhaps the analysis seems forced. Could social actors such as rural pueblos use an ideology rooted in "high" theology? The petition of the Guanajuato ayuntamiento-pueblos shows just that. We must remember that the pueblo memories derived from three centuries of proclamations of allegiance to the crown, in America an exclusive monopoly of the church, expressed across all levels of society. The pueblos might not know the theological foundations of the principles limiting the king's "absolute power," but they knew very well its practical effects in the courts, as so many archival studies have revealed. The pueblos' knowledge is also revealed by the many shifts of jurisdiction claimed by the slippage of liberal citizenship.

The passage from monarchical to republican allegiance was not easy. The pueblos and their municipios were born before the Republic, under a constitutional monarchy that facilitated independence under the Plan de Iguala. Despite their declarations seeking independence in 1810, neither

Hidalgo nor Morelos used the word "republic." The ayuntamiento-pueblos took advantage of the Cádiz Constitution and the civil war to take possession of their territories and to proclaim themselves "sovereign." Why would they give up their "independence" under the Republic and become subordinate to a new and supposedly absolute sovereignty simply because they voted for some distant congresses? To whom did the Republic belong? To all the citizens of the new nation, an entity as abstract as absolute sovereignty? Or to the real citizens, who through the municipios controlled territories and could support governments or cause them to fall? Where was political legitimacy located?

Throughout the early part of the century, these dilemmas were encapsulated in an ambiguous language that often asserted the sovereignty of "el pueblo" (the people) and of "los pueblos" (the communities). Constitutions, political plans, pamphlets, newspapers, and petitions constantly reproduced this dual idea of sovereignty. It is difficult to explain why the ruling class legitimized the existence of two citizenships, one national, the other local, which belonged to the municipios, the pueblos, and the communities. It is possible that those who competed for power continued to use this duality because the "sovereignty of the pueblos" retained a powerful historical legitimacy, rooted in imperial language and practice. Again we face the strength of the Catholic natural law tradition and its idea of "natural" communities entitled to inalienable rights. Finally, I should mention a long-standing linguistic fact. All the Mexican constitutions, even the revolutionary charter of 1917, assert that "sovereignty resides essentially and originally in the Nation (or in the pueblo)."

CONCLUSION

The dichotomy between "natural society" and "constituted society" is the conceptual axis of all Western natural law. In the Hispanic world, this duality became extreme for two reasons: because Catholic tradition in all its variants emphasized the thoroughly positive nature of natural society; and because the church, not the state, preached fidelity to the crown until the collapse of the empire. This notable singularity of the Hispanic world, deeply rooted in Mexico, meant that for a long time after independence, the liberal Republic had two sources of legitimacy: the pueblos and the constituent congresses, the former embodying the "natural," the latter the "constituted." The pueblos, especially the indigenous communities, interpreted liberal freedoms as recognition of ancient freedoms—of ancient rights over territory.

However, the imaginary of the pueblos lacked direct continuity with the colonial past. The "invoked" traditions did have some link to the past, but the mechanisms used in their defense did not. Liberal constitutions and practices now defined the rules of collective identity and action. Ayuntamiento elections became paramount. How and why? First, liberal codes allowed pueblos to use municipal institutions to administer the properties that sustained communal identities. Second, voting granted the pueblos a new liberal-representative matrix that redefined and sustained their contractual imaginary. Third, at least until the Porfiriato, the municipio-pueblos continued to rule local religious practices, demonstrating that the communities could maintain religious autonomy within the republican regime.

The political imaginaries of the pueblos clearly differed from those of elites. Those differences, however, did limit the historical engagement of the pueblos with liberalism. And that engagement forces us to reject many stereotypes, such as the presumed opposition between the supposedly politically modern city and backward rural areas, and the presumed divide between "center" and "periphery" that supposedly challenged the construction of a national state. The Mexican case shows that the early spread of liberalism created a double fracture between the center and the peripheries. One divided the capital from the major provincial cities; the other separated the provincial centers from the pueblos. The resulting alliances and conflicts proved complex, changing, yet enduring.

The power of the two-faced Janus, one face looking at the pueblos with their memories, the other at elites and the future, proved so strong that no government dared question it. It is thus correct to speak of Mexican "popular liberalism."[22] But that liberalism was not born, as has been argued, with the war of the Reforma. It was born with the Cádiz Constitution, before independence. From the beginning, republican governments tried to take "sovereignty" from the pueblos, as scores of municipal organic laws written by the states of the new confederation show—without success. The Laws of Reform were the most remarkable of these efforts, and to date we are unsure of the extent of their success (though the Mexican Revolution forces us to doubt their achievements). It is certain that legislators of 1856 had to recognize that popular liberalism forged during the Cádiz years was consolidated during the Republic: new constitutional ayuntamientos controlled pueblo lands, limiting the development of a society of individual property owners that the liberals envisaged.

As a result, the Reforma was even more complex than official versions suggest. The church fought to defend at all costs its independence from the new civil power of the liberal state; the pueblos did the same in their own ways. The church lost everything in a bloody civil war; the pueblos, perhaps, did not lose at all. The liberals destroyed the church, but they could not destroy the pueblos; they could not win the war without them. The Reform Laws took many judicial resources from the pueblos, yet they could not modify the dual nature of the liberal Janus: only by a pact, more or less explicit, between its two faces could liberals rule Mexico, as both Benito Juárez and Porfirio Díaz understood. The dilemma of Cádiz—the location of sovereignty—remained unresolved in Mexican society. Throughout the nineteenth century, governance required a contractual relationship between the state and the pueblos.

Without doubt, the problem of Mexican governance was worsened by civil wars and "political instability." Yet beneath those dramatic events, the silent yet persistent force of the pueblos and their ayuntamientos remained in motion. This slow and constant movement at the base of society, independent of the state, yet within its constitutional framework, was constantly at odds with the accelerated movements of elite society. The pueblos repeatedly showed their weight in the balance of forces disputing power.

Much research remains to be done before we have a clear idea of the nature and persistence of pueblo power. One point is certain: during the nineteenth century, the center of Mexican political space was located in the rural areas, not in the cities that had ruled in the colonial period. The "ruralization" of Mexican politics did not result from an assertion of hacienda power. The colonial latifundia struggled after independence: their economic power took decades to develop; their political centrality awaited the second half of the nineteenth century. The "ruralization" of politics was an abrupt, unforeseen rupture of the political space.

That key rupture was a political process, and its protagonists were pueblos and liberal ayuntamientos. Thanks to the implementation of the Cádiz Constitution and the pueblos' engagement with it, the New Spain of 1821 was very different from that of 1808, when the crisis of the monarchy began. In 1821, Bourbon New Spain no longer existed. Many leaders clearly perceived the change. Among the most eloquent witnesses was General Manuel Gómez Pedraza, who had fought the insurgents under Iturbide's command. When Gómez Pedraza published his memoirs in 1831, he related that Iturbide's original plan was a military coup in Mexico City. But, Pedraza wrote, "I made Iturbide see that his plan was unworkable, and I concluded by telling him that, in my opinion, the attempt had to begin in the periphery and move toward the center, and that taking the capital must be the last step of the enterprise." In 1808 a coup in the capital gave Spaniards control of the country; in 1821 such a scheme was not feasible, despite its military and political advantages.

We do not know the truth of Pedraza's account. Nonetheless, we do know that Mexico's independence was achieved by a campaign more political than military, moving from "the periphery toward the center." And ever since, all changes of politics and regimes, including the Mexican Revolution itself, have followed similar territorial strategies.

NOTES

1 The only official hint of what defined a citizen-vecino during the Cádiz period is found in a document issued by the Madrid Consejo de Estado dated April 28, 1820. It claims that the two million American "padres de familia"—male household heads—had the right to vote. Archivo General de Indias, Indiferente General, exp. 1523.

2 As is well known, the crisis of the Hispanic monarchy was unleashed by the royal family's illegitimate cession of the crown to Napoleon in 1808. It was illegitimate because according to all Western theories of royalty, a king could not abandon his kingdoms by his own will, because God had placed them under his protection. A dynasty could be changed only through war or marriage alliance. In view of this legitimacy crisis, the Hispanic territories were unanimous between 1808 and 1810: the king's sovereignty reverted to the kingdoms. The theory was that when the monarchy was created, the kingdoms had willingly transferred their sovereignty to the kings, and therefore, in the event of an illegitimate succession, the kingdoms had the right to reclaim it. It is also true, as most literature on the subject points out, that this idea was an integral part of the Spanish neo-Scholastic tradition. And I should add that it was not exclusively Hispanic, since many Protestant theories of royalty also shared this principle.

3 Lucas Alamán, *Historia de México desde los primeros movimientos que prepararon su independencia en el año 1808 hasta la época presente*, vol. 3 (Mexico: Imprenta de J. M. Lara, 1849–52), 509.

4 About this point see Anna Macías, *Génesis del gobierno constitucional en México: 1808–1820* (Mexico: Sepsetentas, 1973).

5 *Actas de las sesiones de la Junta Soberana Gubernativa: Cuestiones de derecho público tratadas en la Junta Provincial Gubernativa* (Mexico: Imprenta del Palacio, 1822).

6 *Unas preguntas sobre un convenio*, Colección Lafragua, 534, Mexico, 1835.

7 Macías, *Génesis del gobierno constitucional*, 129.

8 *Diario de Sesiones de las Cortes Generales y Extraordinarias* (Madrid: Imprenta de J. A. García, 1870–74), vol. 2, no. 330, p. 1714.

9 *Plan de Veracruz*, Colección Lafragua, 1525.

10 About this point see Cecilia Noriega Helio, "Los grupos parlamentarios en los congresos mexicanos, 1810 y 1857: Notas para su estudio," in *El poder y el dinero: Grupos y regiones en el siglo XIX*, ed. Beatriz Rojas (Mexico: Instituto Mora, 1994), 93–119.

11 Archivo de Notarías de Morelia, Fondo Indiferente, exp. 356.

12 This uncataloged document is found in the CONDUMEX archives. All the following quotations refer to this document.

13 This right is part of classical Greek and Roman jus gentium and refers to the condition of temporary slavery acquired through war. After recovering his freedom, the former slave had the right to recover all the rights that he had enjoyed before his captivity. About the jus gentium tradition and its evolution during modern times, see Carl Schmitt, *El Nomos de la Tierra en el Derecho de Gentes del "Jus publicum europaeum"* (1950; Madrid: Instituto de Derecho Público, 1982).

14 *Obras completas de Bartolomé de las Casas*, vol. 5 (Seville: Paulino Castañeda, 1992), 324.

15 Vasco de Quiroga, *De debellandis indis*, 1st ed. (Mexico City: UNAM, Instituto de Investigaciones Filológicas, 1988).

16 Juan de Torquemada, *Monarquía Indiana* (Mexico City: Porrúa, 1982), 3.

17 The term *jus gentium* can be traced back to classical antiquity. It was part of political vocabulary until the nineteenth century, when it was gradually substituted by the term "international law." Unlike the latter term, which attempted to formalize a systematic set of rules to regulate relations among states, the jus gentium predates the modern state and dealt with the customary relations among countless different subjects because they belonged to different poleis, that is, societies that consider each other "foreign." Because of this customary character, the jus gentium never had formal codes, but it did have a tradition of treaties that constantly redefined basic principles, especially about war and peace. One of these was written during the Middle Ages and dealt with the "just cause" that gave legitimacy to war among Christian princes or by such a prince against "infidels." Only the Roman pope had the right to decide the "just cause" of a war, and the conquest of the Americas was considered so as proved by the Alexandrian papal bulls, which legitimized it only in terms of evangelization, since the so-called New World's inhabitants were neither Christians nor "infidels." The complex problem of defining "Americans" stemmed from this and involved, among others, the Salamanca School of Theology and particularly its most prominent theologian, Francisco de Vitoria. About these issues, see Anthony Padgen, *The Fall of Natural Man* (Cambridge: Cambridge University Press, 1982).

18 About indigenous memory from the colonial period until the post-independence period, see Serge Gruzinski, *La guerra de las imágenes: De Cristóbal Colón a Blade Runner (1492–2019)* (Mexico: Fondo de Cultura Económica, 1994), and *El águila y la sibila: Frescos indios de México* (Barcelona: M. Moleiro, 1994).

19 The archival sources on this phenomenon are extensive. An excellent sample can be found in Archivo General de la Nación, ramo Historia, vols. 403 and 404.

20 Ibid.

21 This remark is found in Annick Lempérière, "¿Nación moderna o república barroca? Mexico 1823–1857," in *Imaginar la nación*, ed. François-Xavier Guerra (Münster-Hamburg: Cuadernos de Historia Latinoamericana, AHILA, 1994), 150.

22 See Guy P. Thomson, "Popular Aspects of Liberalism in Mexico, 1848–1888," *Bulletin of Latin American Research* 10, no. 3 (1991): 265–92.

❧ Local Elections and Regime Crises
The Political Culture of Indigenous Peoples

LETICIA REINA ❧

During the last quarter of the twentieth century, amid the economic dislocations of debt crises and political reforms, elections suddenly moved toward the center of Mexico's political life. Popular participation in voting escalated rapidly across the nation. The sudden importance of elections did not respond only to concerns among political and economic elites. Nor did it engage only, or even primarily, urban middle classes worried about a deteriorating way of life. Electoral participation engaged all of Mexican society. Most notably, popular communities, urban and rural, mobilized to join in elections.

The electoral participation that escalated during the 1980s began as a new dimension within the Mexican political system that had prevailed since the postrevolutionary consolidation of the 1920s and 1930s. Political analysts often assert that the electoral life of the late twentieth century was unprecedented in Mexican history. Such claims are not only wrong but produce a fundamental misunderstanding of Mexico's historical political culture. The electoral mobilization of the late twentieth century bears dramatic similarities to citizens' mobilizations that extended deep into rural communities across Mexico in both the late eighteenth century and the late nineteenth. During two previous eras of profound importance to the formation of the Mexican nation, and to the foundation and transformation of the Mexican state and political culture, Mexicans engaged in vibrant electoral contests.

A historical perspective demonstrates that Mexicans have experienced three eras of popular electoral mobilization. Each developed as a century ended; each emerged within a larger fundamental crisis of state and society. The first two eras of crisis—also times of electoral engagement— ended in traumatic and transforming revolutionary conflicts that began in 1810 and 1910. At the onset of the twenty-first century, Mexico's history poses an inescapable question: when and how will the crisis and the electoral mobilization of the late twentieth century end?

Rising waves of popular mobilization marked by burgeoning participation in local elections marked all three of Mexico's cycles of crisis. Rural and often indigenous communities demanded representation by popular candidates. And when fraud or impositions by outsiders blocked fair elections, protests escalated in all three crises. Elections, and challenges to them, have marked Mexican regime crises since the late eighteenth century. How should we explain this mobilization of citizens in a nation in which, it is repeatedly asserted, citizenship had not been consolidated?

The electoral mobilizations of the late eighteenth and late nineteenth centuries are little known to analysts of modern Mexican politics. The participation of rural, often indigenous communities in the contests of the eighteenth-century Bourbon reforms and the early-nineteenth-century political crucible that created the Mexican nation have been the subject of historical analysis for decades. In contrast, we are just beginning to study the widespread and intense participation in voting, and the conflicts that followed when votes were not respected, during the late nineteenth century and the early twentieth. After a brief sketch of popular electoral participation during the decades that led to 1810, this essay focuses on delineating the importance of popular and indigenous participation in electoral contests in the crisis that ended in the revolution of 1910—and then explores the similarities and differences of that era to the electoral mobilization of recent years.

During the colonial era, the Spanish regime recognized indigenous communities as *repúblicas de indios*—corporate entities with rights to hold land and to maintain local councils. Lands divided between those distributed among resident families for subsistence production, and others used to fund local government and religious life. Councils consisted of local governors, magistrates, and councilmen, usually elected by local elites called *principales*. By the end of the colonial era, some communities had broadened the base of local elections. Yet even where only principales participated, elections depended on the forging of a local consensus if indigenous councils were to rule with legitimacy.

In the late eighteenth century, the indigenous *repúblicas* faced new challenges. While populations grew and pressed against limited landed bases, the Bourbon regime aimed to control indigenous community revenues. Reformers saw religious festivals as wasteful expenditures; they preferred to fund teachers who would promote Spanish literacy—and to claim local revenues defined as surplus for the monarchical treasury. Across Mexico, villagers negotiated those pressures. Many assigned community lands to religious sodalities to avoid regime demands. Local councils sometimes resisted the new teachers; sometimes councils insisted on controlling teacher selection and the curriculum they taught. In the face of the Bourbon reforms, indigenous communities became key sites negotiating regime power and popular participation.

When the Spanish monarchy collapsed in the Napoleonic invasion of 1808, popular resistance produced an emerging liberalism that led to expanding electoral participation in Spain and across New Spain. The expansion of elections came simultaneously with the explosion of insurgency that began in 1810 and led to independence in 1821. Perhaps most notably, insurgency proved most intense and enduring across the Bajío—where there were few repúblicas de indios, and thus little history of popular participation in local elections and politics. Across central and southern regions, where the rural majority lived in repúblicas, uprisings were fewer and less enduring—mostly brief local *tumultos* that continued traditions of riotous resistance. After 1810, such uprisings became less numerous—but more political. Thus, while insurgency defined political and social conflicts in the Bajío and along coastal lowlands, across highlands organized by indigenous communities, local political and electoral traditions latched onto the participatory promises of the Cádiz Constitution of 1812 to produce an explosion of electoral life in cities, towns, and villages.

Electoral participation reverted to its monarchical limits with the return of Spanish absolutism in 1814. But 1820 brought both the defeat of the Bajío insurgency and a return to the Cádiz Constitution. When independence came in 1821, it came with an accelerating electoral life that culminated in the Federal Republican Constitution of 1824—and the equally republican constitutions of the several states. Municipalities and elections proliferated everywhere. Mexico became a nation amid an explosion of elections. It did not lack an electoral tradition. Subsequent decades suggest that what Mexico has lacked has been regimes and leaders ready to accept the outcome of elections, local, regional, and national, when the vote did not serve the interests of the few who aimed to rule.

Mexico's first modern crisis began in the late eighteenth century and culminated in the decade of insurgency that brought independence. The crisis included assaults on local autonomy by a reforming regime. But enduring traditions of using councils to negotiate local politics and relations with the colonial state led to negotiations of the crisis. Where communities with established councils could engage new liberal ways of voting and political participation after 1808, participation in insurgency proved limited after 1810.[1]

It is less well known that popular electoral participation began early and endured long under the Díaz regime of the late nineteenth century. For decades, expanding participation in elections—and protests of electoral frauds—helped indigenous and other rural communities negotiate with the dictator and his system. Then Mexico's second cycle of crisis and reform, marked by a rising participation in elections, culminated in another explosion of violent conflict, this time the revolution of 1910. Yet, notably, where electoral participation—even electoral conflicts—had been most widespread and intense, revolutionary insurgency again proved limited.

How should we explain this long and important history of citizens' mobilization in a country where, in theory, the concept of citizenship is new and where, according to political analysts, the population was historically apathetic toward elections? This essay attempts to answer these questions and to demystify stereotypes about the electoral behavior of the Mexican people. I pursue three perspectives. First, I look at the historical shaping of the political culture of indigenous peoples and communities during the nineteenth century—a culture that endures in and permeates, at least in essential features, today's Mexico. Second, I analyze the conflicts that resulted from electoral frauds in municipal elections between 1880 and 1910. Third, in the light of that analysis, I reconsider the results of municipal voting of the last decades of the twentieth century. The analysis demonstrates that the explosion of popular electoral participation during the late twentieth century was not unprecedented. Rather, recent decades witnessed a historical process of remunicipalization and reethnicization (or reindianization) of rural communities and their political participation. I explore the similarities and differences of the political crises of the late nineteenth century and the late twentieth, focusing on citizens' electoral participation.

Finally, I reflect on the emerging twenty-first century, pointing out elements that seem to be reappearing and suggesting that, just as in 1810 and 1910, a new cycle will soon culminate, perhaps in 2010. Despite the distance between these very different time periods, I believe that the comparison is useful and legitimate. As George Duby has stated: "Why write history if not to help our contemporaries to trust the future and to become better equipped to face day-to-day difficulties?"[2]

Modern representative systems appeared with the emergence of liberalism and the building of nation-states in the nineteenth century. Indigenous peoples were never external to this national political process. As Antonio Annino points out, elections have been a constant in the national history of Mexico; it is time to study them.[3] They may be approached from different perspectives, emphasizing different features of electoral processes. Here we focus on political culture, which Esteban Krotz defines as "the subjective sphere of political life." And within the domain of political culture, Krotz emphasizes the importance of "the entry of heterogeneous voters in the supposedly homogeneous world of modern representation."[4] How can we understand the ways that indigenous peoples and other communities with unique histories and cultures have joined in electoral processes still under construction, processes that defined representation in ways that did not recognize indigenous cultures, processes designed to express the supposed equality of all citizens?

Regardless of whether elections are considered real or fictitious, effective or fraudulent, they reveal fundamental relationships between power and society. As Silvia Gómez Tagle writes, elections are "a space for negotiation, more than an arena of struggles for political power with well-defined rules."[5] Thus we should analyze elections as gauges of discontent and as indicators of challenges to local authorities' effectiveness in representing popular and indigenous communities. We perceive local elections as struggles of rural and indigenous peoples to renew those who exercise local power, even if they do not always bring different political projects. The following questions are key: What motivated political actors to participate or not participate in local elections? In what ways did rural societies relegitimize (and sometimes delegitimize) their authorities? Mobilizations against electoral fraud were one way the people of rural municipalities expressed discontent with governmental authority. They were forms of rural and indigenous rebelliousness that aimed to resolve grievances, some old, others new. As Krotz points out, "The study of electoral conflicts lies between the theory of social movements and a new current of the theory of political culture."[6]

Historically, the Mexican people have engaged in cyclical oppositions to authoritarian rulers, periodically expressing the need to renew representatives who lost effectiveness or legitimacy. Evidence from different time periods shows "common people from the pueblos," or *macehuales* (as they were called during pre-Hispanic times), periodically acting to disavow and replace representatives who lost legitimacy and credibility. During the colonial period, abuses of authority and the concentration of land and resources in the hands of indigenous elites, whether noble caciques or commoner governors of repúblicas de indios, led to rebellions by mace-huales or common people. Periodically, with or without the consent of "principales,"[7] elders, and councils, commoners joined against caciques to replace a sclerotic power clique. Macehuales rose against "old authorities" who had become lofty and overprivileged through "ancestral rights." Over time, new rulers often became wealthy, lost legitimacy, and were also re-placed. Scholars call this the "macehualization" of community governments.[8]

In the long and contested political life of indigenous communities, elec-tions were also a form of "macehualizing" power, a key part of the pueblos' political culture. This can be observed throughout Mexico's history, albeit with regional variations and sharp differences in different historical con-texts. Repeatedly, cyclical fossilizations have occurred at the top of power structures (at the local, regional, and national levels). The resulting lack of representation has led to equally cyclical struggles by rural communities, urban peoples, and emerging groups that have destroyed the old order and installed new representatives. There are examples of this cycle before the arrival of the Spaniards. Among the Mixteca, for example, the existence of many small pre-Hispanic lordships revealed enduring resistance to power concentrations. Within Mixteca society, regular struggles replaced local and regional rulers and representatives, at times breaking political units into small, more locally responsive domains. During the colonial period there was a long, almost continuous struggle by subject pueblos demand-ing and often gaining independence from *cabeceras* (head towns). They became autonomous repúblicas de indios, often ruled by new elites that had spearheaded the separation.[9]

Over the centuries, this process combining fragmentation and the re-newal of representatives continued. Often, new rulers eventually became caciques, overprivileged and out of touch with the popular bases that brought them to power and legitimated their right to represent the com-munity before the central authorities. And often, rebellious macehuales proved ready to mobilize and replace local power holders with new repre-sentatives. This process of replacing "old authorities" is a basic feature of the Mexican political landscape, revealing enduring tensions between po-litical generations and the mechanisms that communities have used to renew groups in power. The cycles of consolidation, challenge, and re-newal persisted throughout the nineteenth and twentieth centuries.

In the nineteenth century, the macehualization of power appeared in two ways. The creation and repeated subdivision of municipalities became a new version of the fragmentation of the repúblicas de indios. Meanwhile the renewal of authorities through local elections broadened and regularized the alternation of local representatives. Throughout the nineteenth century, remunicipalization became a dynamic way to solve interethnic conflicts. In many states, pueblos separated from their municipal cabeceras to settle conflicts. In 1910, Oaxaca, an extreme case, had 516 municipalities and 630 municipal agencies. In Guerrero, many pueblos negotiated to move from one municipal head town to another. The last decade of the twentieth century saw a parallel phenomenon: more than thirty-five municipalities were created to solve old intercommunal problems, without counting towns that changed municipal allegiance.[10]

The fragmentation of political and administrative units was only one way to solve conflicts with the rulers of municipal head towns. Especially at the end of the nineteenth century, a new cycle of macehualization focused the active and widespread participation of the citizenry in elections and in struggles against electoral fraud. Pueblos repeatedly appealed to "legality," imploring rulers to respect clean elections. Communities demanded the end of electoral fraud, seeking new, more loyal, and more legitimate leaders to negotiate their needs with state and federal authorities.

Conflicts over fraudulent elections expressed three closely related issues. One was the excessive concentration of wealth and power in the hands of the authorities, separating their interests from those of the communities. The second resisted injustices committed by municipal presidents. The last was the struggle between older generations in power and emerging groups seeking access to power. The process of macehualization has not been limited to historically indigenous pueblos or rural municipalities. It has appeared during recent centuries among diverse social sectors, expressing regional and even national identities, and seeking to renew leadership on larger scales. The current internal struggles within the PRI may be understood as a movement of urban and national elites demanding macehualization (that is, effective participation and representation) inside the long-ruling authoritarian party.

The structure of power within contemporary indigenous communities emerged from the process of building the nineteenth-century liberal state. During the colonial centuries, basic elements of pre-Hispanic political and religious organization had endured and fused within the organization of local government and religious life sanctioned by the Spanish regime. Although the new national state—especially under liberal rule—worked to separate religious and political affairs, the everyday practices of indigenous communities persisted. A system with mixed political-religious attributes reemerged. A shortage of Catholic priests left many pueblos without resident pastors, helping autochthonous religious expressions emerge from the shadows to which they were condemned during the colonial period. While liberals worked to secularize formal rule, in many communities, ritual, religious, and political life remained inseparable.[11]

Ignoring the Reform Laws that asserted the separation of church and state, pueblos redefined a rationale of social reproduction that kept the two spheres united. Within communities, a complex system was created that simultaneously sustained, strengthened, and integrated the political, social, and religious spheres. It reconstructed a self-government that linked the three spheres, unifying the pueblos.[12] Such internal organization brought vitality and strength to face liberal policies that attempted to eliminate indigenous communities as legally recognized corporations. Even while pueblos lost the legal autonomy to work with or against the national state, in practical terms they consolidated self-government. They became the de facto arbiters of local rule and internal justice. Thus the social and political organization of the Indian pueblos sustained a rationale in conflict with the national institutions under construction.

The indigenous governments that consolidated in the 1800s, however rooted in pre-Hispanic and colonial traditions, and however focused on integrating political and religious affairs, took shape through municipal institutions in which liberal constitutions gave local power to the municipal president. This new official became an extremely important political player, replacing the old governor of the repúblicas de indios. The municipal president had prestige, social status, and the authority to represent his pueblo, either because he had been elected through consensus or because he led a movement that had macehualized power.[13] Often the characteristics that allowed him to lead were personality and charisma. As a result, municipal presidents tended eventually to become caciques. After starting out as ethnic representatives who mediated between the community and the state and national government, they repeatedly ended up as simply another link in the system of control. If they had gained power by making arrangements and alliances from the bottom up, in time they ruled by holding the bottom in place—in the service of higher powers. Many caudillos, midrange military officers, and political bosses emerged from indigenous communities; they began with broad social bases and created enduring patronage networks. When these locally rooted power holders became part of a regional or national political class, they often tried to modify local "political customs." Equally often, they had to use those community customs to maintain their power.[14]

Hence, while liberals worked to create secular citizens with individual identities, corporate communal political-religious cultures consolidated at the base of society. Indigenous communities and their leaders were not inevitably, or even normally, in conflict with the liberal state project. Instead, communities responded to—and negotiated with—municipal presidents, who in turn dealt with regional caciques through personal or patrimonial political loyalties.[15] Those negotiations made the municipal president pivotally important. He became the key mediator at the local level, linking local, often indigenous community politics to state and national affairs. Toward the end of the Porfiriato, escalating conflicts over elections across the Mexican countryside focused on the roles and powers of municipal presidents.

THE LOCAL ELECTIONS OF 1880–1910: THE END OF A CYCLE

Why has Mexico known historical periods when political succession is disputed through armed struggles and coups, and others when the alternation of power occurs, sometimes formally and sometimes in reality, through elections? And why, when electoral representation prevails, are there times of electoral apathy and others of active citizens' participation?

Throughout the nineteenth and twentieth centuries, the press has regularly expressed the opinion that the Mexican population was apathetic about elections, especially in small rural villages. Closer analysis reveals that the pueblos were most often indifferent toward voting for national representatives, senators, and presidents, officials whose powers and political activities seemed distant from the historical concerns of rural communities. Rural and indigenous peoples knew that their "representatives" in state and federal offices rarely represented them. Political nonparticipation prevailed less often at the local level, usually in times of relative stability when pueblos agreed to the continuation of local or municipal authorities they considered legitimate representatives. In times of conflict and change, from the eighteenth century to the twenty-first, Mexican communities have engaged in active political lives.

The local political focus of popular communities did impact regional and national political life. The reluctance to engage in politics above the community level facilitated the consolidation and the continuity of the "electing government," as brilliantly defined by Natalio Botana. Under electing governments, those in power regularly prevailed "against other electoral powers, caciques prevailed against pueblos, caciques even prevailed against other caciques."[16] At the national and regional level, a political class continued to rule through internal consensus—in other words, through implicit or explicit pacts.

In a few pivotal occasions, however, the pueblos showed a great interest and participation in elections. They often remained locally focused. Yet their mobilizations occurred primarily within the crises of the national political system that recurred at the turn of the centuries. In these conjunctures, electoral participation translated into open citizens' mobilizations stimulated by intermediaries who promoted the election of new representatives and rulers. Voters in rural and indigenous communities demanded respect for election results and challenged electoral fraud.[17] Local traditions of participation found new importance on the national stage.

Porfirio Díaz led the last military coup in nineteenth-century Mexican history. Yet he always legitimized his rule through elections. He claimed the presidency in the Tuxtepec Revolution of 1876—after he lost three elections, twice to Benito Juárez and once to Lerdo de Tejada, and after two failed military coups. Overthrowing Lerdo and refusing to recognize José María Iglesias's interim succession, Díaz used military force to become president. Then he "legalized" his military victory with an electoral "win." According to Díaz and his supporters, his first presidential term meant a return to legality, respect for the Constitution, and the beginning of national pacification.

The Porfiriato was a personal authoritarian political system that lasted until 1910. Mexico was not a democracy. But Díaz did not rule primarily through military force. The relative stability of the regime resulted from consensus among the diverse economic groups and political forces: "Political balance was achieved, for a time, because regional caudillos were displaced from their territories and social bases—that is, from the source of their real power—and integrated into centralized republican institutions located in Mexico City."[18] Political pacts were created at all levels (local, regional, and national), from the top down (and, at the beginning, from the bottom up), allowing the stabilization and consolidation of the national state.

Simultaneously, economic policies and their regional implementation followed the ideal of "order and progress." Development plans served the interests of the United States and Europe, rather than consolidating an internal market. International, national, and regional elite interests concurred in the importance of accelerated economic growth based on the construction of railways, industrial mining, and export agriculture. That political and developmental convergence stabilized the country. It created a more powerful central state and a climate of apparent tranquillity. The problem was that the modernizing project excluded the indigenous and popular classes from its economic benefits, and from its ideological projection of the social good. The majority of the people were left out of the national project.[19]

Throughout the nineteenth century, elections carried on formally as they had since their beginnings under the Cádiz Constitution.[20] Neverthe-less, they were rarely genuine; they did not offer real contests among different political parties or groups independent from the president, and they did not seek or respect the vote of the majority. In the last decades of the century, the problem became more pronounced. Díaz was the "only and great elector"; everyone knew that his candidates, and only his candi-dates, won elections. Any candidate who attempted to elicit and respect the votes of workers or artisans in electoral contests was labeled a dema-gogue, or an extremist with anarchist tendencies,[21] and was soon elimi-nated by the government machine.

The enduring ruler maintained the guise of legality. He never disavowed the Constitution and only undertook reforms when they were needed to centralize power and ensure his or his allies' reelections. In a formal sense, Porfirio Díaz was a reelected president, not a dictator who imposed his will by force. He always kept up appearances: senators and representatives met regularly, as established by the Constitution; elections for all positions, from municipal president to the Republic's president, were regularly orga-nized and carried out.

Electoral ceremonies were repeated again and again, yet, as the historian José Carlos Chiaramonte states about Argentina, they were only a farce. Chiaramonte asks: "Why this uninterrupted succession of elections, even when they seemed totally removed from an effective representative sys-tem, and thus continually repeated the opposite of what was expected from them?"[22] Rulers used the elections to assert legitimacy based on the peo-ple's will; they hoped to achieve it symbolically through electoral rituals—without effective elections.

In liberal states, even in authoritarian states claiming liberal legitimacy, voting gradually becomes the fundamental tool legitimating the class that holds ruling power. Whether elections were real or staged, they were rit-uals "of fundamental importance to the reproduction of political power, even while they became a widening space for out-of-control conflicts among different groups."[23] Public officials who did not obtain their posi-tions through effective popular representation were not obliged to heed the needs of the populace. They instead responded to pacts with patronage networks and to compromises with the power holders above them, and only secondarily with those below. Networks and alliances were created not by debating or linking alternative political projects but by making personal compromises. During periods of political flexibility, the people voted for, or "allowed" the appointment of, individuals with charisma or social status. The political class in power repeatedly gained "legal" con-tinuity in office.

At the outset of the Porfiriato, negotiation and consensus were the standards every social group used to articulate their concerns. Meanwhile, authority steadily centralized around the executive branch of government. Constitutional reforms carried out between 1891 and 1894 undercut the states' power in political matters. They also "restricted the right of pueblos to create councils," and thus to exercise local political power. Romana Falcón explains that "the job of municipal president, previously elected, was reduced to an official appointed by the *Jefes Políticos*, political bosses appointed by the President of the Republic or the State Governor."[24]

This was a fundamental change—an assault on local political life. The electoral law of February 12, 1857, at the beginning of the liberal regime Díaz claimed to continue, had created a simple if often indirect electoral system. Several election arrangements coexisted throughout the country: at the federal level, elections continued to be indirect; at the state level, municipal elections were direct, while governors and representatives were chosen indirectly. In some states, such as Oaxaca, direct elections were also used to vote for governors.[25] The Porfirian reforms threatened the basic local autonomy that municipalities had long maintained. The national assault on local autonomy led to local assertions into national political life. The regime broke established political pacts, unstated but enduring, that had allowed local autonomy in exchange for unfettered national power. Local popular mobilizations followed.

Toward the end of the nineteenth century, the Porfirian model produced its own contradictions, generating a profound economic, social, and political crisis that affected the whole society. François-Xavier Guerra has written a magnificent and exhaustive analysis of the elite crises that preceded the 1910 revolution.[26] In this essay, I explore the political crisis at the bottom of society, emphasizing how pueblos managed to express political discontent within the decrepit system. Repeatedly, they demanded truly representative municipal authorities.

From 1810 through the 1870s, while rural communities often seemed quiescent in national politics, Mexico experienced more rural rebellions than any other nation in Latin America. Then rural insurgencies decreased sharply during the Porfiriato. Yet under Díaz's rule, exploitation increased, coercive labor relations proliferated, and disguised slavery became widespread. In the face of such threats, what happened to the insurgent spirit so evident during previous decades? While the late century crisis worsened, the political consolidation of the Díaz regime blocked traditional channels of "insurgent expression." The simultaneous attack of the same regime on local political autonomy focused indigenous communities and rural people in general on new forms of struggle. The age-old defense of lands was subsumed into new struggles demonstrated in two fundamental ways: ethnicization, or the reindianization of campesinos (the assertion of rights as indigenous peoples); and *ciudadanización,* or "citizenization" (mobilizations asserting rights as citizens against fraud in the election of municipal presidents). Because of these shifts, campesino movements are difficult to see in the documents of the time. We will recover them by analyzing electoral conflicts.

The reindianization of many Mexican communities at the end of the nineteenth century was the great paradox created by the liberal state's efforts to homogenize the population. How did Indians survive concerted and persistent anti-Indian liberal policies? They showed great creativity. They responded and adapted to liberal policies in diverse, sometimes contradictory, ways. Sometimes they resisted, sometimes they acculturated, and sometimes they reaffirmed their ethnicity. There was no single movement toward a common goal.[27] What was remarkable at the end of the nineteenth century was the intolerance and blindness of those in power. Their policies radicalized indigenous movements among the Yaqui in Sonora and the Maya in Yucatán who declared their wish to become independent from Mexico. Other peoples focused on demands for land while reinforcing ethnic identities as emblems of their struggles.[28]

The other, less known, rural manifestation of the crisis at the end of the nineteenth century was the sudden citizenization of many communities. Pueblos found new political interests that led to burgeoning participation in elections. Indians and campesinos increasingly exercised their rights to vote for representatives and, above all, to mobilize and pressure leaders to respect their rights and votes as citizens. The growing electoral participation of Indians and campesinos during the years that preceded the 1910 revolution began an often-continuous campesino movement. Many of the local leaders who led in electoral struggles against aging and sclerotic local rulers before 1910 continued as pivotal actors during the decade of revolutionary conflict. The emerging political mobilization of opposition movements in rural, often indigenous communities revealed the rigidities of the aging Porfirian system—while demands for representation and styles of participation differed in diverse regions, even in neighboring municipalities.

The pueblos' escalating participation in municipal elections in the late Porfiriato is difficult to explain—if we accept the common vision of indigenous communities as homogeneous worlds isolated from national social dynamics. In fact, while indigenous pueblos had different political cultures and different social and cultural practices, they had learned to engage the national political system and to operate within its rules. There was a "constant interaction between the corporate or communal rationales and the individualist fictions of modern politics. As a result, neither stayed the same."[29] The communities' economic, social, and political links with the rest of society were mediated through indigenous *cabildos* or *ayuntamientos* (councils), and notably through municipal presidents who became key links in the political system. The election of municipal presidents happened at the intersection of two different models of representation: one local and often indigenous, the other national and in theory liberal. During the fin de siècle crisis, the selection of municipal presidents became extremely conflict ridden, revealing long-submerged conflicts between the two visions of representation, conflicts heightened by the intersection of deepening social exploitation and Porfirian political rigidities.

The relative calm of the Porfiriato ended around 1907, when recession in the United States intruded on Mexico. New and strengthened opposition groups appeared, both inside and outside the government. The emerging political crisis reached the heights of power. Thus began a new era of mobilization as diverse groups, some demanding local rights, others insisting on national participation, coalesced around the struggle for democracy.

The Indian pueblos had long protected and fortified themselves in municipal governments. In response, Díaz's dictatorial regime acted against municipal autonomy. The 1888 Civil Code abruptly stopped the creation of new municipalities. Nine years later, the Ley General de Ingresos de las Municipalidades (General Law on Municipal Income, 1897) granted the executive branch unchecked authority to allocate local revenues, and thus to shape municipal policies according to national interests.[30] Exhausted municipal coffers faced rising demands for payments to the federal treasury, minimizing the resources available for local needs. These measures inflamed old grievances.

The pueblos reacted against the new legislation by brandishing the slogan of free municipalities—a slogan Díaz had used while claiming power in 1870. They fought to keep the relative autonomy they had achieved within their jurisdictions. Elections for municipal presidents became votes not only to select and defend representative authorities; they were also used to defend communal lands, self-government, and the right to implement local justice according to customary law.

In contrast to repeated assertions that indigenous pueblos exhibit extreme traditionalism and a conservative nature, historically they have shown a great ability to change and adapt to circumstances. After independence, the government imposed the municipal system on the indigenous pueblos. In time, they not only accepted the ground rules of the Mexican state but appropriated municipal institutions to their own purposes. Early on, they used municipalities secretively to defend indigenous authorities and cultures. By the end of the nineteenth century, their banner of struggle became the defense of the free municipality. As the Chinese proverb says, "They put on the mask so often, it eventually stuck to the skin."

Throughout the nineteenth century, the pueblos participated formally in elections. "From the beginning, electoral rights were very broad; in that lay the force of local autonomies. The great problem for elites was not how to expand the number of voters, but how to channel electoral dynamics toward the center and resolve grave problems of governance."[31] As central control became a reality in the last quarter of the century, government rules blocked the election of indigenous leaders by consensus and imposed outside authorities. In 1901, "Miguel Macedo justified the appointment of municipal authorities rather than popular election, adding that thus the councils would have 'honest and intelligent men with administrative aptitude, though they lack popularity among the illiterate masses who are a majority in the villages.' "[32]

Before the Porfirian imposition, the election of local authorities formally followed rules set by outsiders, yet operated informally according to local custom. Groups of local notables acted as intermediaries,[33] political figures who acted publicly as liberal citizens, organizing local elections to confirm traditional corporate representation, linking the legal ayuntamiento to the traditional pueblos. Thus indigenous social hierarchies fit within liberal electoral systems. In municipal political documents of much of the nineteenth century, the men called citizens often did not exercise liberal citizenship. Rather, designation as a citizen was a verbal modernization that legitimized traditional roles focused on maintaining ancient community practices.[34]

The rigidity of the late Porfirian political system broke old linkages at every level: local, regional, state, and national. Once again, emerging economic groups and new political generations mobilized to demand space to share in, or at least negotiate with, power. A rising bourgeoisie, industrial and agricultural entrepreneurs from many regions, but especially from the north, began to protest against Díaz's regime and declared war against the "old sclerotic state." These citizens' mobilizations coincided with, recognized, and began to seek alliances with campesinos as well as with local and regional elites.

Thus indigenous and campesino communities longing for justice and seeking new rulers took advantage of circumstances; they abandoned (for a time and in certain regions) their traditions of elections through consensus (what we now call by "customary ways and laws"). They embraced the civic ideal and participated actively in elections as prescribed by law. They discovered that under the iron-fisted political control that characterized the

Porfiriato, voting was the only available site for political expression. This is why so many municipalities fought for and demanded clean elections in the years that preceded the Mexican Revolution.

To date, no documents allow us to understand how the indigenous communities involved in these electoral processes perceived themselves. However, if we compare late Porfirian elections with the present situation, we may surmise that the inhabitants of the pueblos did not have clear political visions of federal and state elections. They were, however, surely aware of the meaning of electing local authorities by consensus and of voting to demand candidates who truly represented them. And they knew that the goal of political alliances was to solve their most immediate problems.

Electoral conflicts and confrontations over the selection of municipal presidents, congressional representatives, governors, and other "elected" officials became points of struggle. At times they led to local violence. As the nation moved into the twentieth century, elections and the conflicts they provoked revealed contradictions and expressed discontent. François-Xavier Guerra has remarked that the old agrarian demands began to find a "modern political formulation," and because of that, Magonismo (the movement for popular rights led by the Flores Magón brothers) grew in areas of deep social tensions: "It gave a unity of belonging and a political banner."[35]

The political crisis became grave because the aging political system contradicted the economic modernity the Porfiriato had set in motion. Rapid economic development created powerful new economic interests; new and excluded groups demanded political participation. The same development increased awareness that society was no longer represented by the fossilized gerontocracy entrenched in power. Anti-reelection clubs, modernizing political parties, and citizens' mobilizations proliferated and coalesced around the struggle for democracy. Participation in elections escalated, creating pressure to ensure that voting would be carried out according to established rules. All these factors permeated Mexico's diverse regions and communities as 1910 approached.

In rural areas, confrontations polarized as municipalities faced economic difficulties, political interventions, and deepening social contradictions. Elections became the legal chance to remove old caciques, regionally and locally. Entrenched bosses did not go willingly; many elections became bloody conflicts around the turn of the century. Opposition groups, whether pueblos resisting outside bosses or young macehuales trying to remove aging local rulers, fought to prevent electoral fraud.

Instances of local conflict, sometimes violent, increased between 1880 and 1911.[36] Most responded more to political grievances and demands

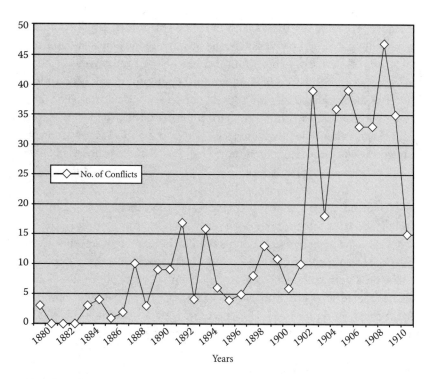

1. Local conflicts, 1880–1911.
Sources: Colección Porfirio Díaz, CPD, correspondence between
political bosses, municipal presidents, and local population with Porfirio
Díaz, Expedientes de 1880 a 1911; National Newspapers Library; *Diario
del Hogar*, 1884–1910; *El Tiempo*, 1884–1910; *El Hijo del Ahuizote*, 1885–
1903; *El Siglo XIX*, 1898; *El Imparcial*, 1899–1902, 1909–10; *El Nacional*,
1896, 1900–1901.

than to old agrarian problems. Communities began to show a greater
degree of citizens' participation at the polls, putting a new face on social
mobilizations to address old grievances. Old questions of land, taxation,
and injustice became linked inextricably with new issues of effective representation. A variety of causes and grievances fused in local conflicts—
contests often perceived differently depending on the source consulted. It
is difficult to separate economic issues from political causes. Figure 1
shows electoral conflicts along with conflicts over abuse of authority and
those against injustices by political bosses. In many conflicts, local repression struck against new regional alliances that linked communities with
opposition hacendados, merchants, and manufacturers in struggles to unseat the old rulers. Conflicts also focused, though often less directly, on the
resurgence of enduring issues of land and taxes.

Figure 1 documents the expansion of the late Porfirian political crisis across the base of society. It details the increase of local postelection conflicts, until the cycle of rising political conflict closed and revolution began in 1910. The 1888 law restricting municipal autonomy gave rise to local conflicts that escalated into the 1890s. Political and social stress then moderated, only to increase and reach new intensity during the 1903–4 presidential campaign. There was then a great deal of political propaganda and a huge mobilization demanding "no reelection." Paradoxically, the pueblos voted in favor of Porfirio Díaz as president, while they joined in confrontations to remove governors, political bosses, municipal presidents, and leaders of municipal agencies. In 1905 and 1906 there were again large mobilizations of pueblo notables and intermediaries, often linked to the economic and social contradictions within the communities, and to the federal government's imposition of outsiders in local offices.

The peak moment of electoral struggle came in 1909. Political mobilization escalated after the publication of James Creelman's interview with Porfirio Díaz, a report in which the president stated that he would allow a peaceful transition of power. The year before, the Liberal Party had led a great campaign that commentators described as unleashing the democratic spirit of the whole country. Now many pueblos and small villages saw a chance to finish off old and fossilized caciques.

After seventy years of intense agrarian struggles, at the end of the nineteenth century and into the twentieth, protests and conflicts at the base of Mexican society became notably political and electoral. A parallel situation with an almost identical rhythm marked the end of the twentieth century. Between 1880 and 1910, out of 439 conflicts reported in rural areas of the country, half resulted from accusations of corruption, injustice, and imposed reelection against local officials and political bosses. A third were postelectoral conflicts caused by fraud in local polls. Only one-fifth explicitly defended natural resources (land, water, and forests) or protested tax increases.

The regional distribution of electoral conflicts is revealing; pueblos across the central and southern areas of the country showed the most bellicose tendencies. Over half of the recorded conflicts took place in the states of Puebla, Oaxaca, Veracruz, Michoacán, Guerrero, and México. The rest were distributed among the other twenty-two states. In 2000, the same states (excluding Guerrero and adding Chiapas) had the greatest number of municipal presidents who were members of the Left opposition PRD.

It is not surprising that confrontations concentrated in the geographic center and south. Traditional caciques held strong there, often as a result of regional power bases first established by veterans of the radical military units that had fought for independence between 1810 and 1821, for the Ayutla revolution that brought the liberals to power in 1854, in the Three Year Reform War of 1858 to 1860, and in the Tuxtepec rising that put Díaz in power in 1876. Many also fought against the U.S. invasion of 1846–47 and the French occupation of 1863–67. Throughout the nineteenth century, political cadres who began as liberators gained privileges and sinecures and eventually became local or regional caciques.[37] New generations fought against these old ex-soldiers. Proliferating local political struggles developed amid sharpening class contradictions. Analysis of the late Porfirian crisis must engage its political focus and its social-agrarian links.

The struggles of indigenous pueblos and rural communities against electoral fraud resulted from two different and opposite situations, both the result of Díaz's authoritarian rule. Communities repudiated their own aging caciques and at the same time opposed the imposition of outsiders in local offices.

In resisting local leaders, pueblos argued that old caciques had become unjust, corrupt, and had allowed state and federal authorities to abuse the common people. Such leaders no longer represented the communities. In many places, municipal presidents had become bosses who perpetuated their local rule with the support of the *jefes políticos*, state officials who pressed land and labor policies promoting a savage capitalism that threaten to destroy communities. In response, communities organized to prevent the caciques' continued reelection. Pueblos led civic mobilizations defending the vote and the will of the people, backing new leaders crying out for political space. It was the struggle of a new generation, another cyclical macehualization of power. Most revealing was that, in the first decade of the twentieth century, the pueblos worked for change at the polls.

Many such conflicts erupted in the sierras of Puebla and Oaxaca, both areas of old *cacicazgos*. One of many instances took place from 1906 to 1910 in the Sierra de Ixtlán, Oaxaca. The Meixueiro family ruled as regional caciques. Guillermo Meixueiro, taking advantage of his situation as a lawyer, plotted to maintain and extend his political power and economic dominance, often, his accusers said, by forging documents. Allied with local authorities supporting him, Guillermo reelected himself against the will of the "principales"—ethnic notables he had jailed to stifle protest. He became a dominant cacique; he imposed unpopular municipal presidents in neighboring communities, carried out fraudulent land sales, collected illegal taxes, and forced villagers to labor to repair the highway to the city of Oaxaca.[38]

Guillermo Meixueiro also provoked discontent by blocking indigenous people from working for the Compañía Minera Natividad, located at the Ixtlán hacienda. At least according to the Banco Nacional de México, local people preferred to work at the mine because it offered better pay than labor on Meixueiro lands. But when workers chose the mines, the cacique's family lost labor. Guillermo used his power to deny the company access to labor, forcing it to leave the region. The Meixueiros controlled and monopolized cheap labor for their own and their allies' properties.[39] They blocked the modernization of the economy, limiting competition for labor that might raise wages. This was an extreme form of the *caciquismo* that prevailed in regions such as Oaxaca and Guerrero, situations of closed power that led pueblos to oppose a sclerotic regime.

The second type of local electoral conflict focused more outside the pueblos. In its eagerness to end pueblo political autonomy, the Porfirian government issued decrees ending the local election of municipal authorities. The imposition of authority from outside the community became the "legal" norm. Many pueblos with authorities still representing community interests refused to obey and fought to defend traditional local methods of appointing authorities (through "principales" and consensus). They demanded a return to local elections, which had traditionally allowed many pueblos to carry out a "double ritual": an election within the community first conducted according to local customs, followed by another poll that ratified the result according to external rules, legitimizing themselves within the national political system. When the Porfirian regime ended local elections, communities mobilized in protest. The will of the people could not be respected when authorities were imposed from outside.

In pueblos ruled by old caciques and others facing new impositions, the regime tampered with poll results to promote its policy of ending the enduring corporate rights of indigenous communities. Most confrontations took place in Oaxaca and Chiapas, the states with the greatest concentrations of indigenous people, where today authorities are still elected using *usos y costumbres*, literally "uses and customs," more colloquially customary laws. In the early twentieth century, they organized pueblo political life according to indigenous traditions, especially when those traditions allowed both effective local representation and channels of communication and mediation from the community to the regime, and back again. The same communities, however, demanded and exercised rights as citizens when traditional representation gave way to cacique impositions, and when the regime imposed authorities from outside. Paradoxically, pueblos expressed their political will through the vote and demands for effective citizenship precisely when the survival of the traditional community was at stake (fig. 2).

Indios Mixtecos.   OAXACA Mex.   Mixteco Indians.

8 7 1

No. 28.

2. Indigenous peoples, like this Mixtec couple from Oaxaca, maintained strong local traditions—and continuing participations in the struggles of national politics. Reprinted by permission of Archivo General de la Nación, Sección Propiedad Artística y Literaria.

Discontent with jefes políticos produced constant complaints from 1900 to 1911, while bosses controlled and restricted electoral processes. They imposed candidates and broke polling rules; they were directly responsible for fraud. Through their political machines they sold offices, nullified elections, controlled municipalities, and tyrannized the population.

A conflict in Catemaco, Veracruz, reveals how openly and cynically a jefe político could commit fraud in municipal elections. Joaquín A. Cárdenas and D. Manuel S. Miravet competed in a local election there. The population went to the polls and elected Cárdenas by 219 votes versus 147 for Miravet. A few hours later, however, the jefe político Carlos Pascual arrived with a local police captain and three patrolmen. After a chat with the municipal mayor, he summoned the poll commissioners. After looking at the records, he declared the election void. Pascual forced the local electoral commission to hand over the ballots. He forged new ballots and distributed new credentials, written in his own hand, to his supporters. He then forced the commissioners to sign the bogus ballots immediately.

Later Pascual reported the "election results" to the press, blocking the pueblo's attempt to announce the original count. This "inflamed the disposition" of the people even more. The community opposition eventually found a way to denounce these events. They reported to a newspaper that the original vote counts glued to the electoral booths had been removed by order of the jefe político, who forced the acceptance of his forged ballots. Only thus had Miravet won. Great discontent rose in the pueblo, which mobilized to denounce the fraud. Local leaders reported the incident to the newspaper *El Gorro Frigio*, sent telegrams to the governor and legislature of Veracruz, and to Porfirio Díaz, demanding that the fraudulent elections be rejected. Their efforts accomplished nothing; Miravet remained the "elected" municipal president.[40]

The widespread participation of Indians and campesinos in the elections of the first decade of the twentieth century demonstrated important developments. The pueblos had found a new way to struggle for political autonomy, and they showed their ability to change and adapt in dealing with the national political system. Yet the state remained inflexible and retained control over electoral boards, generating systematic frauds that led toward the 1910 revolution.

Then a paradox emerged that paralleled developments a century earlier during the wars for independence. The struggle of indigenous pueblos to maintain free municipalities, republican institutions less than a hundred years old, demonstrated the ability of the communities to adapt to new circumstances. Municipal institutions and elections offered local communities outlets for the strains and contradictions of the political system. The complex tensions that deepened across central and southern Mexico from the 1880s provoked powerful confrontations among social and political groups in the decade before the Mexican Revolution. The same local conflicts sometimes allowed the emergence of new local leaders and often renewed rural political life in ways that varied with local conditions. When the revolution arrived, electoral conflicts had relaxed or refocused the tensions caused by enduring agrarian grievances. This helped limit participation in revolutionary violence, which proved less intense across the indigenous south than in the rest of the country.

Instead, political and social violence increased across the north, the state of Morelos, and other regions where there were neither large-scale nor frequent local electoral conflicts during the Porfiriato. There alliances between popular communities, regional leaders, and middle sectors, all facing serious political crises, provoked the great social eruption into revolution. In the pueblos of the south, electoral conflicts had erupted into local violence before 1910. In Morelos and across the north, regional violence fueled the revolutionary decade that followed. Everywhere the cycle of electoral confrontation between society and the Porfirian state closed in 1910.

THE LOCAL ELECTIONS OF 1995–2000:
THE END OF ANOTHER CYCLE?

Do the defeat of the PRI and the victory of Vicente Fox in the presidential elections of July 2, 2000, mean that another cycle of crisis has closed? Will we be able to say in a few years that these events marked the start of a new stage in Mexico's political life? Will historical analyses in 2010 and after confirm political scientists' current view that the early twenty-first century is a time of democratic transition? Although the last decades of the twentieth century produced a serious political crisis, it also generated important reforms of the regime, and especially of electoral processes. Have these reforms brought structural changes, or are they just a "tune-up" that, like many adjustments, lasts a few years but ultimately makes the system's contradictions more pronounced? Could the current crisis end as another era of electoral participation that turns into a third political-social conflagration? Could it happen in 2010?

As happened a hundred years ago, the recent change of century took place amid a profound political crisis—a series of challenges that could destroy the political system. During the late nineteenth and late twentieth centuries, parallel mobilizations and conflicts engulfed the whole of Mexican society. During both eras of crisis, elites faced fundamental confrontations (between the bourgeoisie and the ruling class, among political groups fighting for access to power, even within the political parties). Here I examine—and compare—the histories of mobilizations and discontent at the bases of rural society during the crises around 1900, and then around 2000.

Mexico began the twenty-first century with an extremely complex social and occupational structure. Consequently, the crisis at the bottom of society developed in diverse ways (see the excellent essay by Guillermo de la Peña in this book). Here I deal only with political culture and conflicts in the municipalities. We can access political behavior and electoral conflicts in these small administrative and political units through municipal sources, which also reveal changing territorial divisions, and thus new political geographies.[41]

Within rural municipal spaces, the crisis of the last quarter of the twentieth century was fundamentally expressed once again through reindianization and citizenization. Ethnicization brought the growth, some would say the explosion, of ethnic movements, political and social. Citizenization produced a burgeoning civil society promoting the democratization of the government and its institutions. The same town or village might express itself politically in one or both ways. The political mobilization of the present era is not an exclusive political struggle; rather, it is a conjuncture of diverse conflicts and multiple ways of participation.

During the last twenty-five years of the twentieth century, Mexico went through a political awakening manifested at the polls; such electoral mobilization had not been seen since the decade before the revolution of 1910. The developing crisis faced a key moment in 1994. As Jorge Brenna Becerril emphasizes: "The August 1994 elections were framed within a legitimacy crisis created in 1988, and a crisis of political representation exacerbated in January 1994."[42] The illegitimate election of 1988 and the Zapatista insurgency of New Year's Day 1994 were symbols and symptoms of a deep crisis of regime legitimacy: a failure of representation extending from the nation's president to the municipal presidents and including every official in between. At the same time, political parties ceased to be effective and legitimate. In many regions, as Manuel Castells states, some parties lost "their deep connections with society."[43] The old and closed PRI did not serve; the opposition did not offer strong alternatives. Social movements and civil society overtook the parties with demands for representation and reform. Electoral participation increased; voting became unpredictable; party memberships and old loyalties lost effect.

Globalization and the neoliberal project promised, in theory, a new century of shared prosperity and political democracy. Why, then, did indigenous social movements proliferate during the last quarter of the twentieth century? Why did a segment of society, seemingly isolated and considered by many a burden imposed by the past, become a mobilized political force? The unprecedented globalization that began in the 1980s created its own paradox. Investment, trade, migration, and electronic communications rapidly integrated the world—but the people, the pueblos, the indigenous communities, did not become homogeneous. Instead, cultural differences sharpened. Long-enduring ethnic minorities remained, but few people in power or in the cities wanted to see them or to listen to them. The press, the mass media, and government institutions turned away from them. So did many intellectuals. Marginalized communities saw an alternative in fighting under banners of ethnic difference. They became visible by reindianizing.

This phenomenon is not exclusively Mexican. The twenty-first century began amid a global process of ethnicization, or ethnic recovery, notably in Latin America. New or reenergized ethnic political movements developed amid the collapse of old social structures and political pacts. They revealed social breakdowns at many levels. The new ethnicity, however, has emerged more powerfully than in previous times. It has become, among other things, a strategy that indigenous peoples use in struggles to demand new relationships with nations and states.[44]

Without doubt, global and local economic and political changes have produced profound reaccommodations. The new development projects of the neoliberal states have limited or eliminated many social programs of the welfare states. Some projects proved deadly for local populations and natural environments; others remained unfinished, frustrating and threatening social groups who depended on their success. Projects that succeeded and others that failed, plus the end of social programs, combined to deepen social inequality and produce extreme poverty, often leading to conflicts and confrontations over survival. People threatened by both the successes and the failures of neoliberal development learned that they could become politically visible only by emphasizing indigenous identities and demanding ethnic rights. They began to demand redress of unresolved ancestral grievances—and devastating recent assaults. The actions of diverse Indian pueblos, coordinated or not, were "rehabilitation actions not seeking gratuitous handouts, but demanding respect for the group's dignity."[45]

In Mexico, agrarian communities, indigenous and nonindigenous, faced additional challenges and opportunities brought by national political changes and educational programs. The aging, increasingly rigid, and newly challenged PRI government and the party machinery that had long dominated rural regions faced a crisis as traditional models of paternal and corporate control collapsed. Old networks of mediation broke down, facilitating the appearance of a new generation demanding participation in government institutions. Meanwhile, primary, high school, and even university education became more accessible, helping create newly educated rural elites who questioned the structures and symbols of the local and national order, notably in Oaxaca.

Thus emerged new ethnic intermediaries, the dynamic force behind ethnic reformulation. They became spokespeople in communities' relations with nongovernmental organizations, political parties, and the state.[46] NGOs, in turn, promoted and strengthened the indigenous movements. For the first time in Mexican history, indigenous peoples and their ethnic organizations became national political players (fig. 3). The clearest example is the Chiapas indigenous movement (EZLN).

The end of the twentieth century also brought widespread citizenization, a growing wave of popular participation in elections that ended a long era of political inertia—mobilizations parallel to the electoral conflicts that preceded the Mexican Revolution. For the last two decades, but particularly since the 1991 electoral reforms, Mexico has experienced a vigorous mobilization of civil society that encourages political participation through the vote. The population has shown political behavior that contradicts the apparent quiescence of previous decades, when Mexico gained a reputation as an apolitical country. From some perspectives within political science, the situation seems absurd. Roberto Gutiérrez, for example, reports "low

3. Comandanta Esther helped lead indigenous women and men into national and international politics. Photograph by Norma Suárez, San Miguel de Allende, México.

levels of information, along with a sense of pride in the political system, despite dissatisfaction with the everyday exercise of power."[47] More perceptive is José Antonio Crespo's proposal that predicts a growing political mobilization in favor of democracy.[48] In his estimation, historical eras in which people begin to mobilize around elections, to protest fraud, and to challenge old rulers emerge suddenly after long periods of apparent apathy. In recent decades, many voters did not vote for opposition parties as much as they voted against the dominant party.

In the last few years, popular citizenization, especially the mobilization of civil society in municipal elections, has made elections increasingly competitive, drawn a new map of voting patterns, and fragmented the regime's territorial power.[49] Pablo Vargas González observed this phenomenon from 1988 to 1994. Figure 4 demonstrates that the process accelerated from 1994 to 2000.

We see graphically that during the last decade of the twentieth century, the PRI gradually lost its predominance in the country's municipalities, while other parties gained municipal representation. In 1994 the PRI held 89 percent of Mexico's municipalities. During the seven years that followed, it lost 816, ruling only 54 percent in 2001. Meanwhile the center-right PAN gained 220 municipalities; by 1998 it had tripled its local powers. The center-left PRD also gained municipalities; in 1998 it held 228, although it lost some afterward.

Finally, in 2001 the PRI, PAN, and PRD held 54 percent, 13 percent, and 9 percent respectively of the country's 2,427 municipalities.[50] While the PRI

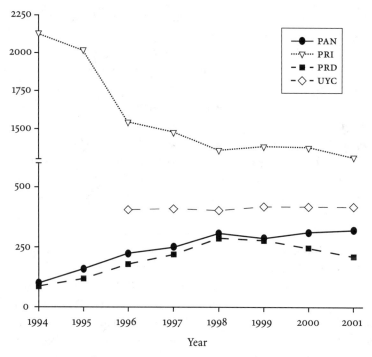

Note: UYC indicates representation by "usos y costombres," not party affiliation.

4. Municipal voting and political affiliation, 1994–2001.
Sources: Centro Nacional de Desarrollo Municipal y Sistema de Información
Nacional, Sistema Nacional de Información Municipal–CEDEMUN-SEGOB, and
XII Censo General de Población y Vivienda 2000 (Mexico City: INEGI, 2000).

continued to rule a majority of municipalities, the figure shows a down-
ward trend. The opposition parties found new strengths. Still, most of the
PRI's loss led to the growth of communities participating outside the party
system through traditional uses and customs. What does this mean? Comparing recent developments to the electoral mobilization of the late nineteenth century and the early twentieth, the historical perspective suggests
that the dynamics of citizen participation at the most recent turn of the
century imply a renewal of old local power structures more than a struggle
for democracy on the national level.

The trend toward the loss of PRI supremacy and the diversification of
rule did not mean only or simply that the population was searching for new
representation. It primarily demonstrated the crisis of a political system in
which the PRI had ruled for sixty years. People went to the polls with the
hope of electing new municipal authorities to end the PRI's monopoly of
power while also looking for alternative rulers. In the late twentieth cen-

tury, however, power was no longer an aging Porfirio Díaz and the *cien-tífico* gerontocracy, but an old hegemonic party (PRI) inserted in, and supported by, an equally sclerotic political structure.

The mobilization of civil society at the end of the twentieth century differs geographically from the historical antecedents of the 1910 revolution. In recent years, opposition to the PRI has concentrated in western and northern states, notably Jalisco, Guanajuato, Chihuahua, San Luis Potosí, and Nuevo León, plus Veracruz along the Gulf Coast and the central state of México. In Veracruz, México, and Guanajuato, the diversification of political preferences is now established; the combined, but not allied, oppositions (PRD and PAN) govern a majority of their municipalities. Yet Veracruz still has a PRI governor.

In addition to this opposition to, and fractioning of, PRI power, up to 17 percent (418) of municipalities, all in Oaxaca, do not vote for a political party but instead maintain "uses and customs." This apparently (and legally) new form of voting is in fact the state's constitutional recognition of old election practices within indigenous communities, practices that elders (principales) kept alive outside the law. Andrea Perelló notes that the government of this southern state, "by approving in 1995 reforms to its constitution, respecting traditional ways of creating municipal authorities in indigenous pueblos, . . . showed tolerance in the face of difference." She examines the reasons behind this tolerant reform and proposes three possibilities. It may be a way to contain growing ethnic political movements. It may reveal "the ability of the same state to adapt and transform itself, but only as a formula to prevent its breakdown in the face of new social demands; or perhaps the relationship between the state and indigenous people is really being reformulated by recognizing the plurality that defines Oaxaca."[51]

If we observe a map of diverse party preferences, noting the states with municipalities opposed to the preponderance of the PRI, we must pose a fundamental question: What happened to the campesino movements that focused on demands for land during the 1970s? Did they follow the same path as the campesino rebellions that defined the nineteenth century before the Porfiriato? It would seem so. In both cases, forms of struggle that focused on agrarian demands were exhausted. Old channels of communication and negotiation closed to campesinos. Agrarian demands lost effectiveness and became submerged in struggles for democracy expressed through elections, through demands for independent municipal rights, in ethnic political movements (concentrated in southern and central Mexico), and in party-based opposition.

The processes of reindianization and citizenization, at first glance opposed to each other, do not just coexist; in many communities, organizations and leaders practice both. Many of the same players also participate in the teachers' movement in southern states, particularly in Oaxaca and Chiapas. These forms of struggle are three faces of the same political problem. They converge around issues of participation and representation —electoral, ethnic, and educational—three forms of subaltern struggle within a political crisis that again coincides with the turn of the century. Is a cycle closing again?

In the last decade of the twentieth century, opposition has grown, and voting patterns have been transformed, similar to events at the end of the nineteenth century. The states with the greatest number of PRD-controlled municipalities now were those with the most electoral conflicts in the critical final years of the Porfiriato. In 2001 the states with the highest number of non-PRI municipal presidents, in descending order, were Oaxaca, Michoacán, Veracruz, Chiapas, México, and Puebla. They cover the same geographical region that dominated citizens' mobilizations a century earlier. The center-south regions of Mexico in both instances sought political changes through participatory citizenship. Paradoxically, these are the regions that have the largest populations of citizens. Notably, the most radical and belligerent episodes of the Mexican Revolution did not take place in these states. Perhaps this is explained by the stabilizing power of electoral participations, especially when they are structured by entrenched institutions and limited to local domains. During the decades before 1910, extensive electoral conflicts provided outlets for old grievances, allowed the renewal of aging structures of local power, and incorporated a new generation into the political system—limiting subsequent revolutionary mobilizations. Are parallel processes under way as the twenty-first century begins?

It is important to focus on the political moment in which Mexico now lives. Is the road to democracy clear? Or does an old political culture endure, a heavy legacy that inhibits structural change by peaceful means? In 2000, for the first time in seventy years, a candidate backed by a party out of power won the presidential elections. Still, the political map is not promising. As the twenty-first century began, nearly 43 million Mexicans lived under PRI municipal presidents. The same party held a majority of state governorships and a majority in Congress.

In the face of this situation, it is essential to remember that as long as elections are manipulated, as long as people vote for personalities rather than programs, the old political culture persists.[52] As long as client networks hold strong, voter roundups continue, and vague promises dominate campaigns, electoral participation will only inhibit the possibility of national action to forge a new, more effectively participatory, and more just social and political order. An electoral system thus constrained will only guarantee the continuity and the sclerotic rigidity of the Mexican political structure. That, in turn, will only deepen the current crisis, until another cycle finally ends. When will it close? In 2010?

FINAL THOUGHTS

Since the 1994 Zapatista uprising, Mexican society has struggled between two forces demanding change: (1) social movements, especially indigenous people's movements, that demand respect for old ways and generate new participatory values; and (2) new and increasingly active political parties that seek to become the institutional managers of a democratic electoral opening.[53] Political developments in recent years demonstrate that the indigenous movements and citizens' mobilizations have proposed new alternatives and new national projects. Meanwhile, the political parties have been worn down by internal conflicts. Their projects do not offer options leading the country in new directions; they rarely offer clear alternatives; they fight only for power.

With contradictions entrenched and crisis still shaking Mexico, how will the first decade of the twenty-first century end? Perhaps one key is to ask whether president Carlos Salinas's reforms—NAFTA, the electoral opening, the end of agrarian reform, and the political rehabilitation of the Catholic Church—are more like the liberal reforms in the mid-nineteenth century or like the reforms of the decaying Porfirian system. If they are like the liberal program, the machinery of state may be sufficiently oiled to last another fifty years. If they parallel Díaz's late and limited reforms, the machinery of state may be near a breakdown.

Much of the old political culture endures. Still, three great differences distinguish the present from the crisis of a hundred years ago. First, the new Federal Electoral Institute (IFE) works to block time-honored practices of political control; second, the media now exposes the persistence of such controls; and third, the weight of history keeps us aware of the meaning of the two previous revolutions—their violent destructions and uncertain outcomes.

The year of coincidence, 2010, looms ahead. It warns of a worsening of the current crisis. We can still learn from history. The elements of continuity and difference outlined here can be studied and analyzed. To avoid another revolutionary end, the state, the parties, and the social movements must find a new road. We must listen to the voice of every Mexican; their diversity offers the best opportunity to find a national project that includes all of us.

1 On the active political practices of late colonial pueblos, see Dorothy Tanck de Estrada, *Los pueblos de indios y la educacíon en Nueva España* (Mexico City: El Colegio de México, 1999); and Claudia Guarisco, *Los indios del valle de México y la construcción de una nueva sociabilidad política, 1770–1835* (Zinacatepec: El Colegio Mexiquense, 2003). On the tumultuous participation of indigenous communities, see William Taylor, *Drinking, Homicide, and Rebellion in Colonial Mexican Villages* (Stanford: Stanford University Press, 1979); and Eric Van Young, *The Other Rebellion* (Stanford: Stanford University Press, 2001). On Cádiz liberalism and Mexican communities, see Terry Rugeley, *Yucatán's Maya Peasantry and the Origins of the Caste War* (Austin: University of Texas Press, 1996); Alfredo Ávila, *En nombre de la nación* (Mexico City: Taurus, 2002); and Antonio Annino's essay in this volume.

2 George Duby, *Año 1000, año 2000: La huella de nuestros miedos* (Santiago de Chile: Andrés Bello, 1995), 9.

3 Antonio Annino has edited a magnificent survey of research about Latin American elections in the nineteenth century. Two of the essays deal with Mexico and analyze the origins of the phenomenon in the first two decades of the nineteenth century. In his introduction, Annino presents a new problem: "Now we should not only do a history from the bottom, we should also know how local societies lived and how they made use of their vote." See Antonio Annino, ed., *Historia de las elecciones en Iberoamérica, siglo XIX* (Buenos Aires: FCE, 1995), 7–18.

4 Esteban Krotz, ed., *El estudio de la cultura política en México: Perspectivas disciplinarias y actores politicos* (Mexico City: CNCA-CIESAS, 1993), 30. In this book, Krotz presents a fine account of recent developments in political culture and offers thought-provoking proposals to orient new research.

5 This text by Silvia Gómez Tagle is quoted in Krotz, *El estudio de la cultura política,* 15.

6 Esteban Krotz, "Antropología, elecciones y cultura política," *Nueva Antropología* 11, no. 38 (October 1990): 16.

7 The "principales" were members of the council of elders. To attain this post, they had to pass through the entire *cargo* system and serve as *mayordomo* (main caretakers) of the festival of the patron saint.

8 Hildeberto Martínez, "Organización política y administrativa," in *Tepeaca en el siglo XVI: Tenencia de la tierra y organización de un señorío* (Mexico City: CIESAS, Ediciones de la Casa Chata, 21, 1984); Francisco González Hermosillo, "Historiografía de los cabildos indios," in *Historias* 26 (April 1991): 25–53.

9 Rodolfo Pastor, *Campesinos y reformas: La Mixteca, 1700–1856* (Mexico City: El Colegio de México, 1987), 22–264.

10 "Municipios de reciente creación," Carpeta 2000, Mexico City, Sistema Nacional de Información Municipal–CEDEMUN-SEGOB, 2000. In the last four years, seven new municipalities have been created in Chiapas, one in Guerrero, and one in Quintana Roo.

11 Leticia Reina, "Raíces y fuerza de la autonomía indígena," in *Los retos de la etnicidad en los estados-nación del siglo XXI,* ed. Leticia Reina (Mexico City: CIESAS-INI–Miguel Ángel Porrúa, 2000), 245–77.

12 The database for this analysis has been extracted from Oaxaca, and the sources can be found in Reina, "Raíces y fuerza."

13 An election by consensus is achieved with the principales' unanimity, approval, and consent and is ratified in a communal assembly. Such an election is considered by "usos y costumbres" and is the opposite of a vote at the polls.

14 Fernando Escalante Gonzalbo, *Ciudadanos imaginarios* (Mexico City: El Colegio de México, 1995), 194.

15 Ibid., 189–93.

16 Annino, *Historia de las elecciones*, 16. Also see José Carlos Chiaramonte, "Vieja y nueva representación: Los procesos electorales en Buenos Aires," in Annino, *Historia de las elecciones*, 51–57.

17 Annino, *Historia de las elecciones*.

18 Salvador Rueda, "Caudillos y hacendados en el rehacer de los espacios políticos," in *La participación del Estado en la vida económica y social mexicana, 1778–1910* (Mexico City: INAH, Colección Científica, 1993), 425.

19 For an analysis of the nineteenth-century modernizing project, see "Nueva introducción (1998)" in *Las rebeliones campesinas en México (1819–1906)*, by Leticia Reina, 5th ed. (Mexico City: Siglo Veintiuno Editores, 1998).

20 Francisco González Hermosillo, "El pequeño intervencionista: Auge y crisis del modelo municipal," in *La participación del Estado*, 375–412.

21 Daniel Cosío Villegas, *Historia moderna de México*, vol. 8: *El Porfiriato: La vida política interior, parte primavera* (Mexico City: Hermes, 1970), 442–460; vol. 9: *El Porfiriato: La vida política interior, parte segunda* (1972), 27–52.

22 Chiaramonte, "Vieja y nueva representación," 20.

23 Marcela Ternavasio, "Nuevo régimen representativo," in Annino, *Historia de las elecciones*, 93.

24 Romana Falcón, "Force and the Search for Consent: The Role of the Jefaturas Políticas of Coahuila in National State Formation," in *Everyday Forms of State Formation*, ed. Gilbert M. Joseph and Daniel Nugent (Durham: Duke University Press, 1994), 107–34.

25 Daniel Cosío Villegas, *La Constitución de 1857 y sus críticos* (Mexico City: Clío, El Colegio Nacional, 1997), 112; Eduardo Castellanos Hernández, *Formas de gobierno y sistemas electorales en México, 1812–1940* (Mexico City: Centro de Investigaciones Científicas "Ing. Jorge L. Tamayo," 1996), 231; Ma. Del Carmen Salinas Sandoval, *Política y sociedad en los municipios del Estado de México (1825–1880)* (Mexico City: El Colegio Mexiquense, 1996); Marcelo Carmagnani and Alicia Hernández, "La ciudadanía orgánica mexicana, 1850–1910," in *Ciudadanía política y formación de las naciones: Perspectivas históricas de América Latina*, ed. Hilda Sábato (Mexico City: FCE–El Colegio de México–Fideicomiso Historia de las Américas, 1999), 383.

26 François-Xavier Guerra, *México: Del Antiguo Régimen a la Revolución*, vols. 1–2 (Mexico City: FCE, 1988).

27 Romana Falcón, *México, descalzo* (Mexico City: Plaza and Janés Editores, 2002).

28 Leticia Reina, "La autonomía indígena frente al Estado nacional," in *Don Porfirio presidente . . . , nunca omnipotente: Hallazgos, reflexiones y debates, 1876–*

1911, ed. Romana Falcón and Raymond Buve (Mexico City: Universidad Ibero-americana, Departamento de Historia, 1998).

29 Antonio Annino, "Cádiz y la revolución territorial de los pueblos mexicanos, 1812–1821," in Annino, *Historia de las elecciones*, 182.

30 Francisco González Hermosillo, "El pequeño intervencionista," 375–412.

31 Ibid., 13.

32 Miguel Macedo, "El municipio: Los establecimientos penales, la asistencia pública," in *México, su evolución social* (Mexico City: J. Ballescá, 1901), 1.2.665–90. Quoted by Ma. del Refugio González, "La tradición jurídica intervencionista del Estado en México," in *La participación del Estado*, 86.

33 Intermediate players are political figures, not always visible, who participate in elections as electors or as electoral civil servants, journalists, voter mobilizers, and other informal characters in the electoral process. See Chiaramonte, "Vieja y nueva representación," 51.

34 Ibid., 32.

35 Guerra, *México: Del Antiguo Régimen*, 260–62.

36 All the analysis about electoral conflicts is based on material consulted in the Colección Porfirio Díaz (hereafter cited as CPD), from 1880 to 1911. A database that included year, state, and type of conflicts was constructed. A systematic exploration of the following newspapers was also carried out in the Hemeroteca Nacional (hereafter cited as HN): *Diario del Hogar*, 1884–1910; *El Tiempo*, 1884–1910; *El Hijo del Ahuizote*, 1885–1903; *El Siglo XIX*, 1898; *El Imparcial*, 1899–1902, 1909–10; *El Nacional*, 1896, 1900–1901. The database starts in 1880, before the political crisis, to mathematically determine when the upward trend of electoral conflicts started and to see its behavior through the thirty-three years of Porfirio Díaz's regime.

37 The extensive bibliography about revolutionary movements in Puebla, Oaxaca, Veracruz, Michoacán, Guerrero, and the state of México details the conflicts with local and regional caciques.

38 The previous explanation has been achieved using the following documents: CPD, Carta de Eusebio Hernández a Porfirio Díaz acusando al licenciado Guillermo Meixueiro de perjudicar a la Sierra, ayudado por el jefe político y algunos presidentes municipales de Ixtlán, legajo XXXI, documento 014917, Oaxaca, 14 de noviembre de 1906; Carta de Pablo León, vecino de Ixtepeji, a Porfirio Díaz en la que lo pone al tanto de las amenazas del presidente municipal y de su enojo por tener comunicación con el presidente, legajo XXXII, documento 4951; Carta de Clemente Marcos, vecino de Ixtepeji, a Porfirio Díaz quejándose del control que ejerce el licenciado Guillermo Meixueiro sobre las autoridades locales y estatales; Carta de 56 "ciudadanos rancheros" de las cañadas de Yobameli y Las Palmas, quejándose de los abusos de la familia Meixueiro en la zona, ya que los obliga a pagar "partido" sobre sus cosechas, hacer tequio obligatorio y pagar "capitación."

39 CPD, Carta del gobernador de Oaxaca, Emilio Pimentel, a Porfirio Díaz explicándole el malestar de los serranos con los dueños de la mina "Natividad," legajo XXXIV, documento 019176.

40 CPD, Carta de Miguel C. Bravo, vecino del pueblo, a Porfirio Díaz quejándose de la corrupción que hay entre las autoridades y en especial del secretario

municipal, quien es pariente del jefe político, legajo XXXIII, documento 000828; HN, "Gacetilla: Atentado contra el sufragio en Catemaco" (a reproduction of the Veracruz supplement *El Gorro Frigio*, which published a letter addressed to the Honorable Legislature of the State of Veracruz), *El Monitor Republicano*, año XLIV, 15, January 18, 1894; HN, "Carta de los vecinos de Catemaco a Teodoro A. Dehesa, gobernador del estado de Veracruz, Veracruz," *El Diario del Hogar*, January 19, 1894; HN, "Gacetilla: La nulidad de elecciones en Catemaco," *El Monitor Republicano*, año XLIV, 28, February 2 and 15, 1894.

41 Danièle Dehouve, *Ensayo de geopolítica indígena: los municipios tlapanecos* (Mexico City: CIESAS, 2001).

42 Jorge E. Brenna Becerril, "Crisis de representación y nuevas formas de participación ciudadana en México," *Estudios Políticos*, cuarta época, 6 (January–March 1995): 48.

43 Manuel Castells, "Crítica de la sociedad en red," *Nexos* 266 (February 2000): 11.

44 Michiel Baud et al., *Etnicidad como estrategia en América Latina y el Caribe* (Quito: Abya-Yala, 1996); Christian Gros, "Ser diferente para ser moderno, o las paradojas de la identidad: Algunas reflexiones sobre la construcción de una nueva frontera étnica en América Latina," in Reina, *Los retos de la etnicidad*, 171–95; Pierre Beaucage, "Más allá de lo jurídico: Reflexiones sobre procesos autonómicos indígenas en América," in Reina, *Los retos de la etnicidad*, 299–321; Diego A. Iturralde Guerrero, "Demandas indígenas y reforma legal: Retos y paradojas," *Alteridades* (UAM-Iztapalapa) 7, no. 14 (1997); Rodolfo Stavenhagen, *Conflictos étnicos y Estado nacional* (Mexico City: Siglo XXI and Centro de Investigaciones Interdisciplinarias en Ciencias y Humanidades de la UNAM, 2001).

45 Guillermo de la Peña, "La cultura política entre los sectores populares de Guadalajara," *Nueva Antropología* 11, no. 38 (October 1990): 85.

46 Adriana López Monjardín, *La lucha por los ayuntamientos una utopía viable* (Mexico City: Siglo XXI, 1986); María Consuelo Mejía Piñero and Sergio Sarmiento Silva, *La lucha indígena: Un reto a la ortodoxia* (Mexico City: Siglo XXI, 1987); Luis Vázquez León, *Ser indio otra vez: La purepechización de los tarascos serranos* (Mexico City: CNCA, 1992); Luis Villoro, *Cultura y derecho de los pueblos indígenas de México* (Mexico City: Archivo General de la Nación and FCE, 1996); Jeffrey W. Rubin, *Decentering the Regime: Ethnicity, Radicalism, and Democracy in Juchitán, Mexico* (Durham: Duke University Press, 1997); Guillermo de la Peña, "Territorio y ciudadanía étnica en la nación globalizada," *Desacatos, Revista de Antropología Social*, spring 1999, 13–27; Xóchitl Leyva Solano, "De las Cañadas a Europa: Niveles, actores y discursos del nuevo movimiento zapatista (NMZ)," *Desacatos, Revista de Antropología Social*, spring 1999, 56–87; Cipriano Flores, "El sistema electoral por usos y costumbres," paper read in "Dilemas de la democracia en México," IFE-CIESAS, Mexico, February 2000; "Identidades, derechos indígenas y movimientos sociales," *Alteridades* (Departamento de Antropología de la UAM-Iztapalapa), número monográfico 10, no. 19 (January–June 2000); Natividad Gutiérrez, "El resurgimiento de la etnicidad y la condición multicultural en el Estado-nación de la era global," in Reina, *Los retos de la etnicidad*, 93–99.

47 Roberto Gutiérrez, "La cultura política en México: Teoría y análisis desde la sociología," in Krotz, *El estudio de la cultura política*, 51.

48 José Antonio Crespo, "Comportamiento electoral: Cultura política y racionalidad en los comicios de 1994," *Nueva antropología* 50 (1996): 23–47.

49 Pablo Vargas González, "Análisis de la política electoral en la era de la reforma del Estado: Acercamientos metodológicos," in *Antropología política: Enfoques contemporáneos,* ed. Héctor Tejera Gaona (Mexico City: INAH–Plaza y Valdés, 1996), 161.

50 All the data on municipal elections derive from Sistema Nacional de Información Municipal–CEDEMUN-SEGOB and *XII Censo General de Población y Vivienda 2000* (Mexico City: INEGI, 2000).

51 Andrea Perelló Reina, "El reconocimiento de los derechos indígenas: Premisa para un modelo multicultural en México; Los casos de Oaxaca y Quintana Roo" (Licenciatura thesis in Political Sciences and Public Administration, FCPYS, UNAM, Mexico City, 2000), 113–16.

52 Jorge E. Brenna Becerril, "Crisis de representación," 66.

53 Manuel Castells, "Crítica de la sociedad," 12.

❧ PART II *Revolutions* ❧

❊ Mexico from Independence to Revolution
The Mutations of Liberalism

FRANÇOIS-XAVIER GUERRA ❊

By sheer accident, the dates that mark the two great crises of contemporary Mexico, 1810 and 1910, are separated by exactly one century. Unless we hold a cyclical concept of time or a fetish for dates, this coincidence has no heuristic value. Yet, from another perspective, it is indeed interesting to view them as two pivotal moments in the development of modern politics, meaningful not only for Mexico but also for other countries of the "Latin" world. The year 1810 marks the beginning of the liberal revolution, and 1910 began the end of the search for liberal models that followed each other throughout the nineteenth century.

The development of modern politics will be the main thread that helps us to place the Mexican Revolution within the "long view" of history: to show that it belonged to a historical moment shared with other countries, yet that it was also a profoundly original moment. My approach here will be mainly political, not because I disdain social or economic determinants, but because others will deal with these issues more extensively, and because it is precisely political matters that determine the possibility of a social explosion. This is a problem common to all revolutions: are economic crises and social tensions sufficient to discharge them? The experiences of many countries during the last few decades, especially the Mexican case, show conclusively that never-ending social tensions and multifaceted economic crises do not necessarily end in revolutionary outbursts.

Any revolutionary process entails, in the first place, a breakdown of the existing political system. When I refer to a political system, I am dealing with not only an institutional structure but also an assemblage of formal and informal elements. Political stability requires, first, legitimacy, the intangible but essential feeling that makes a society believe that its rulers have the right to rule it. Second, a stable political system implies that the main political and social players are recognized and respected by the population, that channels of communication exist between the rulers and the ruled, and that the reactions, demands, and eventually grievances of the ruled will be heard. Finally, a stable system implies that negotiating mechanisms, compromises, and a sense of justice, even if it is somewhat relative, are in place. All these conditions, which may exist during certain periods, are not eternal. Players may change; some may disappear, and some may reappear. The basis for legitimacy—by whom and in what ways power is yielded—may vary, since the nation or the people, who are sovereign under modern legitimacy, may be defined in different ways. The mechanisms for the transfer of power from the sovereign to the rulers may also change, as we have recently seen in Mexico, where elections have again become the only legitimate means of this transfer. In short, the functions that are commonly ascribed to the government can be modified, gradually or suddenly.

These elements are not characteristic of one country. Rather, they characterize a wide geographic area that, following concentric circles, includes the Hispanic world, the Latin world, and the European-American world. In these regions, the evolution of political ideas and of the imagination of social groups and social actors has been quite similar, although they may be slightly out of step in time and take specific regional shapes. This explains the existence of the common cultural, political, and economic junctures so evident from a comparative perspective.

THE ORIGINS OF MODERN POLITICS IN MEXICO

If we use this perspective to examine the history of Mexico during the nineteenth century, both its similarities with other countries of the Latin area—France, Spain, and the nations of Latin America—and its particularities are evident. The similarities are due, in the first place, to the precocious adoption of the main elements of modern politics. All the countries of this area adopted at a very early stage the concept of the sovereignty of the nation, a representative system (elections based on the citizen), the separation of powers, public equality, and individual freedoms. The similarities are also clear with regard to the difficulties that they experienced in creating political systems that were stable and congruent with the new principles. Beginning with France, which led the way with the French Revolution and during the nineteenth century experienced two empires, two monarchies, three republics, and three revolutions (in 1830, 1848, and 1870–71) with their respective constitutions, almost all the countries in the Latin area experienced a great deal of governmental and constitutional instability. Despite the almost continuous existence of elections, most political changes did not stem from them; rather, they were the result of urban revolts, pronunciamientos, uprisings, and other procedures that neither political theory nor constitutional texts had envisioned. Furthermore, in some countries, these events were compounded by genuine civil wars such as the French Commune, the Spanish Carlist Wars, the Reforma and wars of foreign intervention in Mexico, the struggles between *unitarios* and *federales* in the Rio de la Plata, and the many conflicts between liberals and conservatives in Colombia and in many other areas too numerous to mention.

Mexican particularity, then, does not stem from the recurrence of such events. Rather, it stems from the existence of three great civil conflicts: the insurgency of 1810, the Reforma wars of 1858 to 1860, and the Mexican Revolution of 1910, which witnessed not only confrontations between elite factions but also the mobilization of legions of social actors with specific grievances and claims. Momentarily leaving aside the content of these grievances, we can conceptualize these phenomena as the contentious establishment of an autonomous political sphere, or less teleologically as an engagement between the social and political spheres, to a larger degree than in other European and American areas.

Mexican history is defined by the inordinate durability of many of these social actors, of their style of action, and of their demands to the extent that in many regions the microhistories of the Insurgencia or the Mexican Revolution are, from the hindsight of a century, astonishingly similar. Here we also point toward a profoundly original trait of contemporary Mexico: the central role of the mostly indigenous pueblos as permanent and essential actors in political and social life. This role hearkens back to a tenacious corporative social structure that is obvious in the countryside but also very visible in the cities, even when in the twentieth century it attempts to disguise itself in the form of modern mass organizations.

The contrast between modern political symbols and corporate social structures is a common characteristic of the Latin countries that abruptly adopted the principles of modern politics. What really makes Mexican politics of the nineteenth century sui generis is the strength of corporate actors and the imaginary nation that it hints at. As a profoundly disillusioned José María Luis Mora expressed, a great deal of Mexico's problems during the nineteenth century came from "the *corporate spirit*, broadcast by all social classes . . . which weakens or destroys the *national spirit*."[1]

It is doubtful that the national spirit existed before the corporate spirit. The opposition that Mora emphasized, however, is a key to understanding many of the problems that followed Mexico's entry into modern politics.

These problems originated, in the first place, from the sudden and abrupt nature of the passage toward modern politics throughout the Hispanic world. Unlike the French case, where the Revolution was the result of an internal evolution, the crisis of the Spanish monarchy had essentially exogenous origins: Napoleon's invasion of the Iberian Peninsula and the king's forced abdication of the throne. This unexpected and original event induced the local elites of each kingdom or province to compete for power. This led, in turn, to the dispute between Spain and Spanish America and to the rapid adoption of modern political principles across both continents. Because of this, and without ignoring the social causes that explain the scope and force of the 1810 insurrection, the crisis in New Spain was essentially a part of the global crisis of the Spanish monarchy, a crisis that stemmed from the profound imbalances that the French Revolution and its ensuing wars produced throughout the Western world. However, the social explosion that followed the political crisis common to the entire Hispanic world was unique to New Spain. In the rest of Spanish America, government juntas developed from political events undertaken by the elites of the main urban centers with a limited use of violence and without any social mobilization. It was not until later that civil wars among cities and regions progressively led to popular mobilizations, although in most instances they did not attain the characteristics of a popular revolt.

The particularity of New Spain has a political origin: the precociousness of the attempt to create its own governing junta in 1808 and the ensuing coup d'état of Don Gabriel de Yermo in September of the same year ended any possibility of a peaceful route to power by the elites of the kingdom. Repression against the "American party" provoked the conspiracies that led to the 1810 "grito de Dolores" and to its unexpected yet immense mobilization of a populace fragile from decades of difficult transformations and traumatized by immediate climate crisis. The enormous lack of legitimacy that the viceregal government had achieved since September 1808 was, in fact, what caused both the clandestine acts of the elites and the social explosion of the masses.

The corporate structure of society became obvious during the insurgency and was reinforced by it. Obviously not all groups were strengthened by the crisis. Yet two essential groups were: the pueblos and the military. The pueblos, already the basic elements of the political body of the kingdom, saw an increase in their autonomy by becoming the basis of the political and military organization of both insurgents and royalists.[2] Calleja's 1811 political and military plan ordered the pueblos to arm themselves. Soon thereafter, the pueblos of New Spain claimed the right to become constitutional municipalities under the 1812 Cádiz liberal charter. The proliferation of municipalities, the pueblos' appropriation of the judicial and fiscal attributes of the royal authorities, and the creation of militias made the pueblos essential actors within Mexico's political life for a good portion of the nineteenth century.[3]

The importance of the military was another novelty brought by the war. The militarization of a society that had been mostly civilian is an essential development of this period. The militias of the pueblos were joined by the militias of cities, haciendas, and ranchos—with bases in territory, corporate organization, or social dependence—and by new units of the regular army. All became essential players in political life throughout the nineteenth century.

Ironically, this strengthening of military and civilian corporations was matched by the adoption of political modernity, that is, of liberalism. This political mutation also resulted from the global crisis of the monarchy: from the need to implement political representation to give legitimacy to the authorities that were ruling during the king's absence; from the debates concerning sovereignty, nationhood, and citizenship that it provoked; and from the multiplication of political writings, a burgeoning popular press, widespread increases in literacy, and the birth of modern public opinion. In less than two years—from 1808 to 1810—the elites of the Hispanic world, starting with those in the Iberian Peninsula, embraced the main elements of political modernity.

The Cortes Generales of the monarchy, a congress including peninsular and American deputies (including an important contingent from New Spain), met in Cádiz and molded, in the 1812 Constitution, the main elements of modern politics. The influence and experience of the French Revolution was combined with a deeply rooted "pactist" political culture to create liberalism—a Hispanic version of political modernity.[4] All the elements of what would be modern politics in the nineteenth century were present: the sovereignty of the nation; a constitution and the separation of powers (to limit the power of rulers and the freedom of the ruled); freedom of the press; the law as an expression of the general will; the nation as an association of individual beings; individual rights; a representative system; the citizen as the basis for representation; and elections at all levels.

Beyond institutional matters, what really won the day in these experiments was an imagined individualism. The nation was envisioned as the voluntary union of the individuals that formed it. In the new conception of the collective, individualism and contractualism were inseparable. They threatened the reputation of the old corporate political body: a "republic" that was a product of history and formed by multiple bodies, the imagined consequence of the "naturally political" nature of man.

The new primacy of the individual manifested itself through an imagined and idealized society of individuals. This vision implied the destruction, or at least the weakening, of the old corporate bodies—pueblos, churches, armies. It required the building of a new "civil society" through the internalization of the new images of social relations and the development of modern sociabilities—now to be individual and contractual. Liberals began to think about society in unprecedented ways, inventing the individual and new behaviors and authorities to serve that individual. Modern sociability came with the invention of the individual, with the appreciation of contractual links, the ideal of equality, the kingdom of opinions, the sovereignty of the collective, and the ideal of a set of human relations pacified through civility.[5]

THE PROBLEMS OF THE NINETEENTH CENTURY

The precocious adoption of modern political principles and an imagined liberal nation by a society in which war had forced the strengthening of the corporate structures produced a series of permanent problems. Diverse political regimes of the nineteenth century attempted to solve these problems in ways that were disparate, and always tentative. The first problem was sovereignty. Throughout most of the nineteenth century, the idea of a nation formed by citizen-individuals coexisted with, and often conflicted with, a nation formed by bodies of all kinds. The pueblos and military units stand out. The pueblos—combining the meanings of the people and the community—might be envisioned as provinces/states, municipalities, or villages/communities. However envisioned, they remained fundamental pieces of the nation, embedded at the base of a society of imagined individuals. The existence of a unique Mexican nation, a historical community with a well-defined identity, was not questioned. Its political structure, however, was not unitarian. It was pluralistic: a conglomerate of pueblos, states, cities, and villages of varying importance but with equal rights and engaging the government through multiple pacts.

The permanent difficulties of organizing the territorial political structure of the country—the long power struggles between centralists and federalists, for example—stem from this. Although traditional history has often considered this as simply a constitutional option, the issue is much deeper, since it hearkens back to the political articulation between the states or provinces—that is, spaces under the leadership of important cities—and the nation that they constructed in 1824 through a constitutional pact. There followed the challenge of attempting to make two equally powerful ideas, the sovereignty of the nation and the sovereignty of the pueblos, compatible. This problem, which appeared in all the countries of Spanish America, did not generate a practical solution throughout most of the nineteenth century. The centralist solution was incapable of suppressing the personality and power of the provinces, and the federalist solution was unable to ensure effective global cohesion. It was not until the Porfiriato that a solution was found in political compromise, not constitutional reconstruction. It made both realities compatible—for a time.

Yet the problem of territorial political structure cannot be reduced to the relationship between the pueblos/provinces and the central authorities. It also had an equally strong municipal dimension. During the first half of the century, the relationships between municipalities and the states/provinces, on the one hand, and the pueblos/communities with their municipal *cabeceras*, on the other, were as important as their relationships with the central authorities. Municipal organization was, without a doubt, one of the most important (and still least known) problems of the nineteenth century, and municipal legislation was one of the most debated issues in congressional sessions.[6]

The second problem, very much linked to the previous one, was the question of political representation. Contrary to what constitutions and laws might make us think, elections are far from being the exclusive channel through which the will of a nation is expressed. Enduring corporate loyalties and the slow development of individualist identities among Mexicans hindered the conversion of elections into expressions of autonomous individuals acting as political citizens—as modern politics envisages. Many Mexicans did consider themselves citizens. Yet those who defined themselves as citizens, and those who saw themselves first as members of a community or other corporate body, were all immersed in dense webs of personal links that conditioned their personal actions.

Elections, although practiced regularly and at all levels throughout the century, were not the primary means of expressing public political opinion or of solving rivalries among political factions. Even if we leave aside electoral fraud, more common as the century advanced, votes were primarily either group votes, through which people expressed loyalty to a community, or deferential votes, through which the members of a group recognized their social superiors or political loyalties. Fundamental political disputes, if present, were engaged not through elections but before them during struggles to control the vote or to remove one or another party from the campaign. Consequently, elections were more of an expression of the will and ability to rule by those who governed than the means to appoint a government. This is why governments never lost power through elections. They fell through other procedures, invoking other ways that the nation could represent itself.

Most important among these were petitions—old *representaciones*—and the direct actions that often culminated in armed pronunciamientos. Both were linked to the endurance of entrenched corporate concepts of representation, concepts that meant a rejection of the modern system of representation. Although the legitimacy of state or national congresses was never questioned, political representation was never limited to them. As in the ancien régime, diverse corporate bodies continued to believe that they had a right to express their demands or grievances directly to the authorities. They assumed the right to ignore governors or their laws if they were seen as having lost their legitimacy either by abusing their powers, thus breaking the political pact, or by acting against what corporate subjects believed to be the "nation's opinion."

Since the authorities controlled elections and their outcomes, any government might be accused of illegitimacy or of "not listening to the voice of the nation." Pronunciamientos and the political plans that accompanied them were precisely how the "nation" or some of its parts expressed themselves when constitutional venues were closed.[7] A pronunciamiento is not a coup d'état, which is a purely military event. Rather, it is a long and complex consultation process with a legion of groups: military leaders and their corps, militia forces, state governors and congresses, the municipal leaders of all kinds of pueblos. Pronunciamientos were lengthy because all these groups had to meet, communicate, deliberate, and declare themselves for or against the government, usually adding new demands to those of the first leaders of the pronunciamiento.[8]

From the days of Iturbide and his 1821 Plan de Iguala—the first pronunciamiento in Mexican history—all important changes of government and constitutions were the result of pronunciamientos. Pronunciamientos were not caused by a pathological tendency to use force; they rarely led to excessive violence. Still, as the dominant means to resolve disagreements, they had harmful effects: government instability, the enduring power that accrues to armed men, the distribution of offices as sinecures and privileges. More important in the long term for building a modern society was the fact that, on the one hand, regime change by pronunciamiento increased the importance of personal connections within the social structure, while reinforcing the fiction that any armed action was an action of the "nation" or the "people." Throughout the nineteenth century, the caudillo—who ruled at the peak of a pyramid of personal connections, sustained and legitimized by the armed "voice of the nation"—remained a central character.

The third problem was the construction of a state and its corresponding civil society, the essential elements of a modern political system. The state, as theorized in the Latin world of the nineteenth century, went beyond being a more or less developed administrative apparatus. It was the embodiment of the sovereign nation. Because of its contractual origin, the nation was the source of all state power and law. Through their individualistic character, the modern state and nation opposed all estates and corporations with their particular rights. Because of this, a primary task of all modern regimes was the creation of judicial codes, not just to regulate the heterogeneous laws of the ancien régime but to unify the source of all rights. In opposition to the multiple and particular rights that history and custom had legitimized in corporate bodies, the new codes sought social unification and expressed general laws based on reason, born from the will of the nation and its embodiment, the state.[9]

This is why in the second era of liberalism there were multiple conflicts between the builders of the modern state and the corporations of the old society: the army, the pueblos, and ecclesiastical bodies, including religious brotherhoods (*cofradías*) and charitable foundations. These clashes revolved around particular corporate attributes: real or assumed wealth, properties locked into mortmain, privileges contrary to laws supposed to be general and equal for everybody. Yet beyond this, the mere existence of corporations seemed to hinder the construction of a society of individuals and the undivided loyalty that the modern idea of the nation demanded.

Modern politics also sought to create two separate spheres: the public and the private. The public was identified with the state and politics, the private with everything else. This new conception of the public created another problem: the place of religion in the new order, or, to use a more classical yet less precise vocabulary, the relationship between church and state. In fact, under the ancien régime and during the first decades of the new one, religion was one of the essential characteristics of collective identity. The political body and "the Christian republic" were two faces of a single reality. Rulers were supposed to look to both secular and spiritual realms.[10] The Catholic Church and its culture were characteristic of the Hispanic monarchy—and of the early liberalism that proclaimed in its constitutions: "In the name of God, the One and the Trinity, supreme designer and legislator of the universe,"[11] or "In the name of God Almighty, creator and supreme legislator of society,"[12] or "The religion of the Mexican nation is and will in perpetuity be Catholic, Apostolic and Roman."[13]

We must remember that the Hispanic world did not experience the religious wars that led countries such as France and England to implement a civil sovereignty independent from religion. There modern sovereignty and its embodiment, the state, inherited an understanding that allocated religion to the private sphere. When Hispanic nations legislated political modernity, the religious neutrality of the state was in violent conflict with a deeply rooted public culture in which religion was a primary dimension of community expression. As the state was invented as a purely secular institution, the church was reinvented as a separate institution—and the problem of the relationship between them appeared. This problem was much more radical than the old and new quarrels over the Patronato—the right of the state to make or approve clerical appointments. The new separation of state and church led to disputes over the secularization of the "public" sphere. This sphere now became the domain of the state, which sought to control and make secular education, matrimony, civil registries, cemeteries, public ceremonies. And to secularize the public sphere, the modern state had to demand religious tolerance in the new world of the private. It is not surprising that such unprecedented problems, challenging deeply held collective values, created deep rifts within elites and the population at large. These issues, simultaneously political and cultural (and more divisive than conflicts between centralists and federalists), led to hardening divisions between liberals and conservatives in the second half of the century.[14]

The two historical factions, or parties, had two concepts of society and two nation-building projects that went far beyond differences of institutional projects. They demanded different relationships with the legacies of the ancien régime—the material with which they aimed to build a nation. Although in practice liberals and conservatives shared many goals—the reconstruction of public administration, the restoration of strong central powers and government stability, the creation of a representative system, the exclusion of the military from politics, and the promotion of education —they disagreed on the fundamental collective values that should shape society, and thus on what attitude to take toward the multifaceted heritage of the past. Recognizing the distance between modern political principles and inherited social realities, conservatives chose to seek the support of traditional, corporate, and deeply religious sectors to rebuild the country, even if doing so meant that some modern principles had to be compromised. Liberals, on the other hand, stressed modern principles and the creation of a new nation of individuals, although that brought clashes with the corporate structure and values of their society.[15]

The political instability of a great part of the nineteenth century and the deep societal conflicts that divided political elites and mobilized, to a greater or lesser extent, regional factions and popular communities stemmed from the problems that political modernity posed for Mexico. I cannot attempt here to write a global history of the nineteenth century; I will point out, however, that these conflicts continued to grow and that none of the successive political administrations was able to stabilize the situation. Neither the first half of the century, characterized by struggles between military bosses, quarrels about the territorial political organization of the country, and the linked mobilization of the pueblos, nor the second part, in which ideological conflicts dividing liberals and conservatives, and related social mobilizations, were more significant, saw the construction of a stable political system with strong legitimacy. Although the Reforma wars and the fights against French intervention and the empire resulted in a liberal victory, the country emerged still divided by deep ideological rifts and widespread political exclusions, and with extreme regional fragmentations of political power. Meanwhile, the campaigns that reestablished liberal power left the military with unprecedented influence in political life.

The Porfiriato resolved many of these issues. It was the Mexican version of a type of regime common to several Hispanic countries in the last third of the nineteenth century. Whether in Argentina at the end of the century or in Spain during the Restoration, these regimes can be defined as "liberal and positivist" because of their ideology of "order and progress," or as "democratic and fictional" because of their political modus operandi. Their goal was to build a stable political system by achieving order, and thus to make progress possible. In their words, they wanted to stress social, economic, and civil modernization while at the same time sidestepping political modernization. I say "sidestepping" because political constitutions continued to be clearly modern. In the Mexican case, the radical liberal constitution of 1857 was kept. Immersed in the positivist ideology of the times, the new political regimes aimed to produce the synthesis between liberalism and conservatism that Auguste Compte had proposed in the 1850s. This meant that, on the one hand, modern principles and liberties had to be kept while, on the other, social cohesiveness required the removal of their disintegrating features. It was a matter of guaranteeing civil rights for everyone while at the same time restricting political rights. Only after peace, economic prosperity, and education were able to create a true civil society would it be possible to restore the effectiveness of political rights that had only been kept, in the meantime, to give legitimacy to the system.

To achieve political stability, they had to eliminate pronunciamientos and the use of armed force for political goals. The army had to be reduced and professionalized, and a system that allowed political elites to gain access to power without the help of the military had to be put in place. In Mexico, Porfirio Díaz stubbornly pursued the goal of "domesticating the warlords" by discharging irregular troops, reducing the army's strength, breaking the links between the troops and their chiefs, and creating professional officers.[16] The main caudillos disappeared from the political stage, in rare cases by means of physical elimination, often through state governorships or other sinecures, and always through the freedom to enrich themselves. The constant rule of the regime in regard to the old caudillos and newly powerful regional clans was that any use of force for political means would be immediately repressed—and would bring political disgrace and exclusion from sinecures.

To complement these strategies, regimes created systems to control and manipulate elections. They did not fear that elections could overthrow their governments, since, as mentioned previously, governments never lost elections. They controlled elections to avoid the political agitation that preceded them and the danger that the loser might promote political and social mobilizations. This was the golden age of electoral fraud and of the political bosses who organized it. What was new was not fraud per se, which had a long tradition, but the construction of cohesive and centralized systems of electoral manipulation. The numerous and disparate local or regional frauds were now unified and controlled at the national level. Thus the government could eliminate electoral uncertainties, reward its supporters, compensate its opponents, and even, as in Spain or Argentina, organize government by turns. Once the government had defined the lists of candidates to be elected, it was the job of regional and local authorities or caciques to obtain the anticipated results. This system of elections made by and from the government did not mean that it had absolute power. The selection of candidates took into account the balance of regional and local forces, and results were controlled through negotiations with the main political players, even with those excluded from power.[17]

Therefore the system acknowledged the leading political players and involved dense and constant negotiations. In the Mexican case, the enormous correspondence that Porfirio Díaz kept with all kinds of people shows his deep knowledge of local political life and the extent of his network of personal connections. The overall cohesiveness of the regime was based on a hierarchical pyramid of personal connections that ascended gradually from nameless hamlets to the president. This close web of personal ties allowed him to surmount the dilemma of centralism and federal-

ism. They were both ensured. Federalism was ensured by formally continuing the federal constitution and by allowing the freedom that state
governors enjoyed—as long as they were loyal to Díaz. Centralism was
ensured because the center—Díaz—was the judge of last resort in all political conflicts, the supreme decision maker recognized by everyone, and
alone with the capacity to act throughout the whole country.

Finally, the stability of the Porfiriato was based on compromises with a
legion of corporate players, especially the pueblos and the church, who had
been traumatized by the midcentury's radical liberalism. Modern principles such as the Laws of Reform and the 1857 Constitution were kept; yet
their implementation was postponed because Díaz was aware of the power
possessed by these players. Furthermore, both were part of the president's
and his followers' webs of personal connections. This allowed them to be
heard, present their demands, and, in many instances, obtain favorable
settlements. Such mediations rationalized the "pactist" tactics that the old
regimes had long used to deal with corporate groups. The relationships
between the authorities and important social and political players were
regulated by mutual agreements. The regime recognized the rights and
existence of the corporations; the corporations responded with loyalty to
the authorities. The result was a regime with powerful legitimacy, a regime
that combined modern principles and goals with a real structure of power
and negotiations based on traditional institutions, relationships, and political practices.

DEMOCRATIC DEMANDS AND THE CRISIS OF THE PORFIRIATO

The crisis that developed within the Porfirian regime after 1900 shared
common features with fissures in other systems of "democratic fiction" in
other Hispanic countries. Still, the Porfirian crisis developed specifically
Mexican traits, explaining why it led to a revolution beginning in 1910.

The exhaustion of these political regimes was due in large part to their
successes, not their failures—contrary to prevailing historical visions. In
fact, the regimes' opponents made up, using the assumptions of later
times, histories that highlighted their defects and, in the Mexican case,
aimed to legitimize the revolution. With the hindsight of a century, we can
offer a more balanced view of both regime successes and the problems that
remained unsolved.[18]

Mostly, these regimes achieved what they were most determined to
achieve. For several decades, they eliminated pronunciamientos, ensured
government stability, created professional armies, and forced them to obey
civil authorities. They allowed the most important players to participate in

power, in Spain and Argentina by having the different elite factions participate in turns, and in Mexico by integrating them into the president's networks of allegiance.

These regimes also established most of the elements of a modern state. They implemented new judicial codes and legal regulations, restored public administration and finances, and created relatively independent civil servants. They also widened the participation of the state in infrastructure construction, education, and social welfare, and, toward the end, labor legislation. Economically, these were years of modernization and growth, although debates about the primary causes (internal or external) and the social consequences remain lively. Culturally there were fundamental changes because, for the first time in the nineteenth century, educational reforms were implemented at all levels and promised institutions were finally created. The levels of general education that had been achieved by the end of the ancien régime were finally regained.[19] Finally, in the area of individual rights, civil rights were mostly a reality supported by a relatively independent judicial system. Only in the area of freedom of the press did the Porfiriato differ from the Spanish Restoration and fin de siècle Argentina. The almost total freedom of the press in those two nations, which extended even to political adversaries, contrasted sharply with the constant policing of opponents in Mexico. Still, the real but limited humiliations that independent journalists endured indicate that the Porfiriato did not resemble, in this area, the dictatorships of the twentieth century.

These achievements—the aspiration of nineteenth-century elites—eventually led to the weakening of these regimes. Again, all these transformations have aligned most Hispanic countries with the developed countries of Europe and North America. As in the case of these countries, modernization caused more social and geographical mobility, that is, migration toward areas that are more prosperous, notably the growing cities, and the creation of middle social strata. In Mexico, the Porfiriato led to the multiplication of rancheros, miners, workers in new industries, public and private clerical workers, schoolteachers, et cetera. All these changes weakened or destroyed the group structures of the old society and their subsequent representation, negotiation, and arbitration mechanisms. Thus one of the bases of the regime, which was precisely its ability to integrate the most important social players, vanished.

An even more important factor in the movement toward individualization promoted by these changes was the internalization of the modern political imaginary by a growing number of people. The new state-organized education, textbooks, civic ceremonies, and even the "electoral farce" were other venues through which the principles of the individual citizen, the sovereignty of the people, the division of powers, and the federalism that the government had sidestepped were expressed.

This is why, in different guises in different countries, the "new people" that social and cultural modernization had spawned demanded their effective incorporation into modern political life. In countries such as Mexico, Spain, and Argentina where "democratic fiction," with its *caciquismo* and electoral frauds, was in operation, these demands were initially political. These were the times of democratic movements and political parties.[20] These men, and increasingly women, who considered themselves citizens, wanted to be part of the genuine political people. Their petitions were mostly about the ballot: they wanted it to be universal and effective. For them, electoral truth was the basis for the other political freedoms and the first step toward being recognized and listened to.

Nonetheless, they also had social claims, since they believed that the people's rights could not be reduced solely to the political sphere. At this stage, social demands became more intense: sometimes they were concrete, such as when they demanded a variety of labor rights and measures; sometimes they were more abstract, such as revolutionary projects or the building of ideal societies. New mass organizations, new structured groups, untapped players, such as the important world of the working class, appeared. Even though time and again the new players rhetorically pledged a total rejection of the social system, they all struggled to obtain a recognized status, a space within the power systems and new pacts with the other social players and the state.

This twofold contestation of the political systems at the end of the nineteenth century already foreshadowed the two alternatives of a social or a political system of representation that, between the world wars, would often consider each other to be mutually exclusive, as if social representation and rights should lead to the replacement of formal political rights.

Within this general framework, the Mexican crisis had some specific traits that led toward the revolution. Mexican particularism was twofaced: one face was political and related to the personalist nature of the regime; the other was social and related to the grievances of the old corporate players. Unlike Argentina, Chile, or Spain, in which the political factions took turns ruling, leading to a gradual liberalization of the system, the Porfiriato alone ensured the balance of forces. In this kind of system, everything depends on the person who possesses supreme power: either he embarks on political renewal, or the issue is directed toward the selection of his successor. In this case, if no institutionalized system of succession exists, a struggle among the different factions of the regime to ensure the selection of their favorite candidate, or at least to place themselves in a strategic position after the death of the president or the caudillo, is un-avoidable.

In Mexico, the rivalries between the *reyistas* and the *científicos* filled the first decade of the century, increasing intensely as the advancing age of Porfirio Díaz made the succession issue ever more important. What could have become a mere struggle between cliques to seize the vice-presidency and, along with it, an automatic succession at the caudillo's death, as with Franco in Spain, went off course toward popular mobilization. The best-known reason was the apparent democratic liberalization that Díaz an-nounced in 1908 in his interview with James Creelman. The different factions of the regime thought that the president wanted to measure the popularity of the candidates to his succession, through a mobilization exclusive to the elites.

Yet what had started as a fictitious mobilization of "the people" gradually became a progressive grouping of diverse players into political combat formation, with the ensuing rebirth of public opinion and of modern forms of sociability. First, it involved *reyismo*, which included part of the regional elites, some of whom held power and some of whom had been recently excluded from it. It also involved part of the "new people": students, civil servants, and industrial workers. Many of the reyista clubs adopted the name "national sovereignty," showing the rebirth of modern politics by opposing in an increasingly explicit manner the will of "the nation" to the will of the president, who had until then embodied it. That this demand for "national sovereignty" was expressed through mass demonstrations, man-ifestoes, and signature collections rather than through a call for honest elections does not reduce its modern nature, though it may show the persistence of an imaginary that privileged the direct transfer of the sov-ereignty of the people.

Díaz's radical rejection of reyismo opened the door for Madero and more modern and widespread mobilization. The Maderista project that is some-times interpreted as a sentimental and romantic undertaking was ex-tremely modern. This was true both in its political organization, which included propaganda tours, political meetings, clubs and conventions to elect candidates, et cetera, and in its concept of representation. In fact, the project foresaw a twofold representation: political and social. The first was democracy envisaged, before anything else, as a nonfictitious political rep-resentation ("the effective ballot") based on individual citizens. These cit-izens, through their free vote, would send their representatives to Con-gress to defend their ideological or political options and their interests.

The other face of representation offered by Madero—the social side—was directed toward the new social players. It implied the promise of a

Triunfo de la Democracia

CLUB POLITICO
ANTI-REELECCIONISTA
J M MORELOS

MEXICO
1910

Nº II.

DEMOCRATAS EN LA RESIDENCIA
DE FRANCISCO I. MADERO.

PROP. 1911 MEXICO

H.J.GUTIERREZ FOTO

1. People backing Francisco Madero's call for democracy in 1911 honored José María Morelos, leader of the insurgency for independence in 1811. Reprinted by permission of Archivo General de la Nación, Sección Propiedad Artística y Literaria.

total right of association and freedom to unionize, which meant that the new organizations that were appearing within the new social categories were considered important players.[21] These new players would thus be able to negotiate with other social players, appeal to the government to arbitrate in conflicts with them, and make national representatives listen to their demands to obtain social laws. An additional trait of modernity is that both representations had to be independent from each other.

This two-pronged democratic promise, which did not exclude anything, allowed Madero to form a huge political and social coalition that ranged from Catholics, who wanted to modify the Reforma legislation through legal means, to the more radical liberals (their fiercest adversaries) and the new social categories (miners, office workers, industrial workers, schoolteachers) with their modern associations (fraternal and mutual societies, labor unions) and was further extended to old players such as the pueblos and the regional and local clans that were struggling to obtain local power.

The Mexican crisis acquired its revolutionary nature precisely through the mobilization of these fundamental and old players of the social and political life of the nineteenth century. The severe economic crisis at the end of the Porfiriato generated increasing social tensions in some circles, ranging from the powerful to the poor. The economic and social crisis deepened because the mechanisms of compromise and arbitration that had shaped the regime's first decades ceased to operate effectively after 1900. In fact, in the last decades of the Porfiriato, the political system became stagnant. Political posts were rarely renewed, and when they were, the incumbents belonged to more privileged social classes, more than had been the case at the outset of the regime. The pacts with the great family clans of the states and with the pueblos, that were the basis of the system's early balance, were also forgotten. Some of the pueblos were victims, again, of the process of disentailment of their lands.[22] The "modernization" of social relations brought about the growth of modern wage earners, along with pressures against ancestral customs and many traits of rural culture. Land started to be considered a means of production, and the reciprocal rights and duties that in the old society (for example, in the haciendas) had linked the rural players were forgotten. Similarly, the modern state limited local autonomy and inserted itself in new areas that had previously been out of its control.[23] Finally, the rising social tensions of the crisis substantially undermined the regulatory mechanisms of the first era of the Porfiriato.

THE MEXICAN EXCEPTION: THE REVOLUTION

Without question, all these structural causes would not have been sufficient to make the Porfiriato's crisis end with the most important revolutionary event of Mexican history. We should add to them the way in which Maderismo triumphed. Porfirio Díaz's refusal to organize free elections did not leave Madero with any options other than insurrection, although he had always feared it because of the political consequences that it would bring. Madero was a *civilista* and knew well the history of the nineteenth century and the reasons behind pronunciamientos and the social and political consequences of insurrections and civil war. Not only did they give caudillo strongmen leading roles and feudalize power, they made a democratic political life based on individual citizens and elections impossible because those who took up arms implicitly claimed to represent the people.[24]

Madero's fears were well founded. His insurrection accelerated the collapse of the political control apparatus. What had started as a division among elites ended up mobilizing the rest of society. Armed groups multiplied, but, of more importance, a type of legitimacy without an electoral basis, of the oppressed people represented by those who had taken up arms to defend them (which had been the classical mechanism to manufacture caudillos in the nineteenth century), reappeared. Thus one of the types of

2. Madero, backed most by urban reformers, struggled to rule while rural rebels demanded land and landed oligarchs fought to keep the old order. Reprinted by permission of Archivo General de la Nación, Sección Propiedad Artística y Literaria.

players that both the Porfiriato and the postrevolutionary government strove to destroy reappeared.

In addition, the insurrection liberated many players that had otherwise been moderated or controlled through the political system. The many social tensions inherent in a rapidly changing society exploded. These multiple tensions had agrarian, municipal, fiscal, labor, and cultural roots. A struggle to gain access to the local and regional power bases that the system's collapse had left vacant was also unleashed. Old and new, powerful and humble, players confronted each other in diverse combinations that can only be detected through regional history. The Porfiriato's balance between the central power and all kinds of local powers was broken, and the pendulum started to swing, as in many periods of the nineteenth century, toward the local and regional. A unified power pyramid was not established until several decades later.

All of this was merely a seedling when Madero took power, but it all came into play during his presidency. The implementation of his political program was consistent, and freedom of the press, association, and unionization were, without a doubt, more real than in any other period of Mexican history. Thanks to them, the life of associations, unions, and politics thrived extraordinarily and led in many areas to a multiplication of organizations. In some cases, these organizations stemmed spontaneously from society's bases; in others their proliferation was related to the local or regional elite's mobilization of society in the struggle to gain power.

Could representative democracy, as idealized by Madero, provide a peaceful channel for this struggle? The difficulties were weighty, since it was a matter of changing from a fictitious democracy to a real democracy. Madero's whole period as president was full of elections: federal elections as well as those to elect municipal presidents and state representatives.[25] They were the freest in the history of Mexico until recent years. Yet some well-known cases also show many irregularities that let us glimpse the reasons behind the failure of Madero's project.[26] They indeed prove that the modern people, that is autonomous individual citizens, were still a minority. Above all, these elections clearly show collective players that, even under modern disguises, continued to be mostly structured by old-type links such as personal loyalties, clientelism, and social dependence. Obviously the old practices of controlling or manipulating votes by local and regional political groups, regardless of political tendencies, were resurrected.

All these groups, because they were aware of their structure and of their modus operandi, did not trust a free ballot that might grant victory to their opponents in the areas under their own control. Soon each player started to prefer a social type of representation that they presumed to control rather than an uncertain political representation. They all believed, for different reasons, that their claims to rule were legitimate. Some, such as the notables, regardless of their political tendencies, felt legitimate because they thought that, as the heads of networks of personal links, they were the representatives of the sections of society that were under their control. Others, such as participants in armed uprisings, felt empowered by the new legitimacy of armed citizens. All of them to a greater or lesser extent in different regions used other forms of political action. Everywhere, direct actions by disenchanted revolutionaries or traumatized opponents of disorder increased.[27]

Madero's successful coalition against Díaz could not survive its ascension to power and the uncertainties of a democracy with free elections. Thus Congress nullified the many electoral victories of the recently founded National Catholic Party for political reasons and led it to its estrangement from Madero. Madero's more radical wing, *orozquismo*, chose armed rebellion, as did the *zapatistas*, which did not see elections as an answer to the grievances of their pueblos. To many old Maderistas, representative democracy was, in fact, a deception. Huerta's coup d'état, Madero's assassination, and the successive uprisings increased all the social "destructuration" phenomena. First in the conflict against Huerta and then in struggles among revolutionary factions, the weight of arms strengthened. As in similar cases in the nineteenth century, old-style personal connections and particularly loyalty to a warlord became the means to protect and access administrative or political positions. In this sense, a deep "archaicization" of social relations took place, whether we call it *caudillismo*, *personalismo*, or patronage.

These archaic political links coexisted with an advanced political discourse that became increasingly radical, both in the liberal ranks and in the anarchist or socialist ranks. In its form, discourse was always modern, since it matched the new points of reference of the intellectual elites. In essence, however, it had several meanings. In some cases it was only a simple mask to legitimize access to power; in others it was a means to mobilize men who belonged to the new social categories by offering official recognition of their organizations and part of their demands. Finally, in others it was just a translation of the ancient grievances of old social players, such as the pueblos, into modern language.

Many problems of the nineteenth century were reproduced, with twentieth century differences. When groups grounded in the old corporate spheres and organized by traditional clientelism gained power, the modern political representation of citizens became impossible. The only option that remained was to retake a long journey to at least reconstruct a stable political system. Since many of the players—such as the pueblos, the regional powers, and armed groups—were the same in the nineteenth century, it is not surprising that the solutions that were used were similar to Juárez's and Díaz's. This is how the similarities between the Porfiriato and the postrevolutionary system can be explained. They are similar, but not identical, because neither all the players nor the ideological references and discourses were the same during the two periods.

These processes nevertheless shared many common features. Regional power and factions had to be unified, as Obregón did, by signing pacts with them that recognized their power in exchange for their loyalty, even if it was at the outset negligible. Military caudillos and the legitimacy of their insurrections had to be eliminated. The crushing of the 1923 de la Huerta uprising and other minor ones subsequently had this basic purpose. Again, the state had to be restored, and a professional army had to be created.

Once more, all the modern and old players had to be integrated into a unified system of pacts and arbitration. This affected the oldest ones, the rural sectors, by first accepting,[28] and then promoting, the return to corporate forms of landholding, although they were also relatively modern, since these properties were under the tutelage of the state and did accomplish the destruction of large properties, one of the dearest goals of the Enlightenment and liberalism. After the disastrous Cristero wars, Catholics and the church were granted religious freedom on the condition that they refrain from confessional politics. The newest players, such as workers' unions, had their status recognized and were given an exclusive (and corporate) role to represent social issues. Yet not even in this case was this a matter of a real return to the old society, since the corporate construction of social representation was achieved under the tutelage of a state that caused and even guided (in order to control it better) the composition of the modern social players.

The transformation of society into a people had to continue through the development of education understood in its widest sense—through schools, museums, symbols, iconography, civil worship, and ceremonies— with characteristics that sometimes reflected, and sometimes differed from, their nineteenth-century counterparts. The state continued to base its legitimacy on the people, but now it stressed social representation instead of political representation. The political regime belonged to the people or represented the people because it organized and managed society and because all corporative organizations that ruled social space were integrated to the regime and represented it symbolically.

Finally, the problem of succession that had destroyed the Porfiriato had to be solved. This meant finding means of replacing ruling elites and, above all, inventing a method of peaceful and unquestionable succession to the presidency, the peak of the system, through which all the networks of political and social actors were articulated.

How can we define, at the end of this discussion, the Mexican Revolution? In many ways, we can define it as a new model for society and the political regime that liberals had fought for in the nineteenth century. The revolution was a retrogression toward patronage and corporative social links that was now justified through the radical language of social rights and representation. In other ways, the postrevolutionary regimes undertook many of the tasks that the liberals of the nineteenth century had left unfinished: state building, the creation of a national imaginary that integrated an indigenous heritage, and the incorporation into modern politics of many sections of the population that had not yet emerged from the old political spheres. It was accomplished, however, through old-style mechanisms. Finally, despite everything or perhaps thanks to everything, over the course of the twentieth century individualization and its reverse side, civil society, were set back in motion. And, as in many other countries of the European and American world, the model of the individual citizen, the system of representation, and the selection of leaders through free elections would eventually assert themselves. Was this a late revenge of maderismo? Certainly it was, but within a society that had little in common with the society of 1910.

1 José María Luis Mora, *Revista política de las diversas administraciones que la república mejicana ha tenido hasta 1817* (Paris, 1837), in *El Clero, la educación y la libertad* (Mexico City: Porrúa, 1949), 44 (italics in original). [*"Espíritu de cuerpo* difundido por todas las clases de la sociedad . . . que debilita o destruye el *espíritu nacional."*]

2 For these issues, see Juan Ortiz Escamilla, *Guerra y gobierno: Los pueblos y la independencia de México* (Mexico City: Instituto Mora y El Colegio de México, 1997).

3 For these issues, see some of Antonio Annino's work, for example, "Soberanías en luchas," in *De los imperios a las naciones,* ed. Antonio Annino, Luis Castro Leiva, and François-Xavier Guerra (Zaragoza, Spain: Ibercaja, Obra Cultural, 1994).

4 To these governing elements, we should, of course, add the complex heritage of the eighteenth century's European Enlightenment and American and British political models.

5 See Pilar González Bernaldo de Quirós, *Civilité et politique aux origines de la nation argentine: Les sociabilités à Buenos Aires, 1829–1862* (Paris: Publications de la Sorbonne, 1999).

6 For the state of Yucatán, see, for example, Marco Bellingeri, "De una constitución a otra: Conflicto de jurisdicciones y dispersión de poderes en Yucatán (1789–1831)," in *El liberalismo en México,* Cuadernos de Historia Latinoamericana 1, ed. Antonio Annino and Raymond Buve (Münster: Asociación de Historiadores Latinoamericanistas Europeos, 1993).

7 An excellent anthology of these political plans and their support documents is *Planes de la nación mexicana,* 5 vols. (Mexico City: Senado de la República, 1987).

8 For more details, see François-Xavier Guerra, "El pronunciamiento en México: Prácticas e imaginarios," *Trace* (Mexico City) 37 (June 2000): 15–26.

9 About these characteristics of the modern state, see Maurizio Fioravanti, *Los derechos fundamentales: Apuntes de historia de las Constituciones* (Madrid: Editorial Trotta, 1996).

10 For these issues, see Annick Lempérière, "De la república corporativa a la nación moderna: México (1821–1860)," in *Inventando la nación: Latinoamérica, siglo XIX,* ed. Antonio Annino and François-Xavier Guerra (Mexico City: Fondo de Cultura Económica, 2003).

11 Constitución de la monarquía española (1812), in Felipe Tena Ramírez, *Leyes fundamentales de México* (Mexico City: Porrúa, 1967).

12 Constitución federal de los Estados Unidos Mexicanos (1824), in Ramírez, *Leyes fundamentales de México,* 167.

13 Ibid., article 3.

14 Divisions until the Reforma war were nevertheless weaker than is commonly assumed, and in many Hispanic countries with similar problems, such as in the Río de La Plata, the liberals were the unitarian party.

15 See Charles A. Hale, *Mexican Liberalism in the Age of Mora, 1821–1853* (New Haven: Yale University Press, 1968).

16 The expression "domesticating the warlords" belongs to Francisco Bulnes.

17 Regarding these regimes, which Natalio Botana called "electing govern-ments," see, for Argentina, Botana, *El orden conservador: La política argentina entre 1880 y 1916* (Buenos Aires: Editorial Sudamericana, 1985); for Spain, Joaquín Varela Ortega, "Sobre el sistema político de la Restauración," in *Nación y estado en la España liberal*, ed. Guillermo Gortázar (Madrid: Fundación Ortega y Gasset-Noesis, 1994); and for Mexico, François-Xavier Guerra, *México: Del antiguo régi-men a la revolución*, vol. 1 (Mexico City: Fondo de Cultura Económica, 1988).

18 See, for example, for the Spanish Restauración some of the essays compiled in Gortázar, *Nación y estado en la españa liberal*.

19 The hypotheses that I have formulated about this for the Mexican case has been conclusively confirmed by Dorothy Tanck de Estrada, *Pueblos de Indios y educación en el México colonial, 1750–1821* (Mexico City: El Colegio de México, 1999).

20 Their names are different, but their goals and demands are similar: *radi-calismo* in Argentina, *partido democrático* in Chile, Maderismo in Mexico. The most remarkable exception of this movement is Spain, where the critiques of the Restauración regime did not cause a strong movement of this type, perhaps be-cause of the significance of the radical workers' movement and regionalist parties.

21 For example, see Madero's speech to the workers of Orizaba in 1910: "What you wish is that your rights should be respected, and that you should be allowed to join in powerful associations, so that you can defend your rights in a united way." Quoted in Alfonso Taracena, *La verdadera revolución mexicana: Primera etapa (1901–1911)* (Mexico City: Editorial Jus, 1965), 275.

22 The case of Morelos is well known thanks to John Womack Jr., *Zapata y la revolución mexicana* (Mexico City: Siglo Veintiuno Editores, 1969). At present we also have information about the northern Mexican case thanks to Friedrich Katz, *Pancho Villa* (Mexico City: Ediciones Era, 1998), yet there is much work to be done about other regions such as the Huasteca or Sinaloa.

23 See Alan Knight, *The Mexican Revolution* (New York: Cambridge University Press, 1986).

24 Francisco I. Madero, *La sucesión presidencial de 1910* (Mexico City: Edi-ciones de la Secretaría de Hacienda, 1960), 47.

25 Most of these elections have not been researched, especially local and state elections, but the same is true about federal elections at this level, with the remark-able exception of Jalisco, studied in Elisa Cárdenas Ayala, "Aux marges de la révolu-tion mexicaine: Le Jalisco, 1908–1913," 2 vols. (Ph.D. diss., Université de París I, 1998).

26 For legislative elections, see my essay "Las elecciones legislativas de la revo-lución mexicana, 1912," in *Anuario 96: Estudios sociales* (Puebla: El Colegio de Puebla, 1997), 109–46.

27 Besides the great rebellions, which are globally known, the press of this period is full of local news about revolts and other types of violence.

28 The tone of article 27 of the Constitution, which defines this type of property, is not enthusiastic and conveys an unwilling acceptance of an unavoidable evil. It was not until Cárdenas that this type of property acquired positive connotations.

❧ Mexico's Three Fin de Siècle Crises

ALAN KNIGHT ❧

In 1810 Mexico was shaken by a major popular rebellion that, while it did not immediately topple the old regime, posed a serious challenge and set in motion a series of conflicts that eventually led to the establishment of a radically different political regime in the following decade. The causes of that upheaval were many and complex, but they would include a growing inequality, signaled by failing real wages and rising land values; mounting social and ethnic tension (stronger in some regions than others); the diffusion of radical ideas concerning liberty and emancipation;[1] a measure of xenophobia;[2] the establishment of tougher, authoritarian rule, involving greater recourse to force;[3] the erosion of older legitimacies;[4] and the incidence of economic crises,[5] which, though cyclical and conjunctural, in turn reflected the structural inequality mentioned at the start of this blockbuster sentence. The 1810 insurgency presaged a decade of upheaval, which, when it concluded (1821), left a country weary of war, economically battered, relatively unchanged with respect to basic socioeconomic structures, but politically revolutionized.

A hundred years later, in 1910, Mexico celebrated the centenary of Hidalgo's revolt. In the wake of the celebration, the country was shaken by a major popular rebellion that, while it did not immediately topple the old regime, posed a serious challenge and set in motion a series of conflicts that eventually led to the establishment of a radically different political regime in the following decade. The causes of that upheaval were many and complex, but they would include a growing inequality, signaled by falling real wages and rising land values; mounting social and ethnic tension (stronger in some regions than others); the diffusion of radical ideas concerning liberty and emancipation;[6] a measure of xenophobia;[7] the establishment of tougher, authoritarian rule, involving greater recourse to force;[8] the erosion of older legitimacies;[9] and the incidence of economic crises,[10] which, though cyclical and conjunctural, in turn reflected the structural inequality mentioned at the start of this blockbuster sentence. The 1910 insurgency presaged a decade of upheaval, which, when it concluded (1920), left a country weary of war, economically battered, relatively unchanged with respect to basic socioeconomic structures, but politically revolutionized.

Now, while I have carefully crafted these two paragraphs so that they can be repeated verbatim, it did not require a great deal of casuistry. Nor is the comparison novel, of course.[11] John Tutino's notion of "compression" captures several of the elements I have identified in the late colonial and Porfirian periods.[12] The fact that the timing—1810, 1910—appears to obey a precise "hectohistorical" logic is, of course, largely coincidental;[13] the only rational explanation of the coincidence would be that the centennial celebrations—and the reflection on Mexico's past and present that they inspired—perhaps contributed to dissent and augmented opposition to Díaz. While this is plausible, it clearly cannot explain the 1910 revolution. So the dates are largely irrelevant; however, the similarities in terms of political-economic trends and outcome are striking and perhaps demand some fuller explanation, which this essay will try to offer.

But vaulting ambition does not stop there. A second grand historical parallel is also drawn. Let me rephrase the thumbnail portrait of the Porfiriato that I just gave. The Porfiriato was a period of prolonged political stability, in which a distinctive political regime, born amid civil war and conflict, managed to consolidate itself; initially popular (in the sense of eliciting genuine popular support while capitalizing on a widespread desire for peace and stability), the regime tended to grow more elitist with time;[14] parvenu generals were replaced by civilians and technocrats; they, in turn, encouraged foreign investment and closer integration into world markets. Old conflicts with the United States were resolved, and closer economic ties forged;[15] cross-border trade and investment surged ahead (although the regime also sought European investment by way of a counterweight). Similarly, old conflicts with the church were laid to rest, anticlericalism faded, and Catholic prelates returned to the public limelight.[16] Economic growth and capital accumulation were impressive. New transport systems knitted the country together.[17] Learned intellectuals (some boasting overseas education) justified the regime's project of development, which, they said, represented the last word in economic expertise; and a host of sycophantic foreign observers concurred: Mexico's leaders were able statesmen, who contrasted favorably with, say, the wild men of Central America.[18] For all its ostensible success, however, the economic model tended to generate greater inequality, falling real wages, and declining welfare. Peasants, in particular, lost income and access to land. Population grew, and the flow of economic migration increased. Critics denounced these social deficits (which were particularly stark in the Indian southeast);[19] they also fastened on the corruption and cronyism of the regime,[20] the lack of genuine political representation, the dominance of a narrow and remote technocratic elite,[21] official manipulation of the new mass media,[22] banking scandals,[23] and excessive deference toward the United States.[24] Cyclical crises rode on the back of growing structural inequality, resulting in sudden falls in employment and income.[25] A few radical groups launched quixotic uprisings, which were repressed.[26] Finally, a more vigorous electoral opposition emerged, confronting official candidates in gubernatorial elections and, eventually, mounting a challenge for the presidency. In 1910 this led to armed revolution and the fall of the old regime.

You may guess what comes next. Here is a thumbnail portrait of Mexico today (like all portrait painters, I reserve the right to accentuate certain features in order to capture the inner character of the sitter). Mexico has experienced a period of prolonged political stability, in which a distinctive political regime, born amid civil war and conflict, managed to consolidate itself; initially popular (in the sense of eliciting genuine popular support while capitalizing on a widespread desire for peace and stability), the regime tended to grow more elitist with time;[27] parvenu generals were replaced by civilians and technocrats; they, in turn, encouraged foreign investment and closer integration into world markets. Old conflicts with the United States were resolved, and closer economic ties forged;[28] cross-border trade and investment surged ahead (although the regime also sought European investment by way of a counterweight).[29] Similarly, old conflicts with the church were laid to rest, anticlericalism faded, and Catholic prelates returned to the public limelight.[30] Economic growth and capital accumulation were impressive. New transport systems knitted the country together.[31] Learned intellectuals (some boasting overseas education) justified the regime's project of development, which, they said, represented the last word in economic expertise; and a host of sycophantic foreign observers concurred: Mexico's leaders were able statesmen, who contrasted favorably with, say, the wild men of Central America.[32] For all its ostensible success, however, the economic model tended to generate greater inequality, failing real wages, and declining welfare. Peasants, in particular, lost income and access to land.[33] Population grew, and the flow of economic migration increased. Critics denounced these social deficits (which were particularly stark in the Indian southeast);[34] they also fastened on the corruption and cronyism of the regime, the lack of genuine political representation, the dominance of a narrow and remote technocratic elite, official manipulation of the new mass media,[35] banking scandals, and excessive deference toward the United States. Cyclical crises rode on the back of growing structural inequality, resulting in sudden falls in employment and income.[36] A few radical groups launched quixotic uprisings, which were repressed.[37] Finally, a more vigorous electoral opposition emerged, confronting official candidates in gubernatorial elections and, eventually, mounting a challenge for the presidency. I cannot, of course, repeat the punch line: in 2010 this led to armed revolution and the fall of the old regime.

This second parallel is also a familiar one. Comparisons have often been drawn between the regime of the PRI, especially in its more recent, neoliberal form, and the Porfiriato.[38] Miguel Angel Centeno concludes his excellent analysis of the Salinas administration—the "neo-Porfiriato," as he terms it—by asking (rhetorically): "As he basked in the cheers proposing his reelection and in worldwide tributes, did Salinas consider the fate of Díaz?"[39] However, such comparisons have often been casual asides—or bated polemics—rather than considered comparative analyses. I shall therefore explore both these comparisons further; in the terminology we are tending to adopt, I shall compare and contrast Mexico's three fin de siècle "conjunctures"—Bourbon, Porfirian, and PRIísta—to see if these similarities are genuine, rather than merely superficial, and to consider, briefly and tentatively, their causality and significance.

By virtue of its scope, such a comparison presents formidable problems. It is not difficult (as I have shown) to cherry-pick some apparent similarities between different "conjunctures." If we try to be more rigorous, however, we need to consider the appropriate methodology. I will approach the problem under two headings, looking first at the economic conjuncture, then the political. This is a somewhat arbitrary distinction, based, perhaps, on a belief that causal relationships tend to flow—putting it crudely—from economic infrastructure to political superstructure. This is not to say, however, that the political realm is a mere reflex. On the contrary, the relative autonomy of the political comes across fairly clearly; however, it is only a relative autonomy, and the analysis suggests that the economic conjuncture—which embodies forces beyond the control of political actors—tends to have priority.

First, we need to demonstrate the reality of the three periods of compression, circa 1760–1810, 1880–1910, and 1980–2000 (and, conversely, the decompression of intervening periods). Each was characterized by (relatively) high levels of inflation, which tended to erode real wages and incomes. The respective rates of inflation varied greatly, but the fact of inflation is clear and is linked in turn to falling real wages and enhanced inequality. In the preindustrial agrarian context, this pattern involved rising property prices; in the industrial context it can be seen in the shares of GDP accruing to labor and capital. Thus, through the eighteenth century, inflation in New Spain was less than 1 percent; however, in the last quarter of the century, it accelerated; according to a Consulado report of 1805, prices had doubled in the previous twenty-five years.[40] This occurred despite an increasingly heavy tax burden (taxes outstripped economic growth by a factor of three or four), which took specie out of Mexico and tightly limited the colony's money supply. Population growth accelerated, depressing wage levels,[41] and a combination of inefficient transport and harvest failures meant that food prices fluctuated sharply over both time and place.[42] Serious dearths occurred about every ten or twelve years, and famine about every twenty-five—most notably in 1785.[43] When food prices shot up, the colony's scant purchasing power declined in accordance with Engels's law, to the detriment of manufacturing.[44] Meanwhile, especially in regions of greater population growth and market activity, land values rose, and resources gravitated into the hands of commercial landowners.[45] By the 1800s, contemporary reports suggested that "the social order was on the verge of disintegration."[46] The imperial crisis of 1808 may have been a bolt from the blue, but it struck a debilitated colony (note that previous imperial crises, such as the War of the Spanish Succession, had been surmounted, and in large tracts of South America no popular insurrection occurred).[47] A social conflagration was not inevitable (when is it ever?), but the flammable material lay to hand, and the crisis of 1808–10 supplied the ignition. The insurgency was not, therefore, a purely conjunctural response to an extraneous crisis; it derived from structural socioeconomic circumstances. Logically, the upheaval was most intense in the Bajío—the pacemaker of the late colonial economy, where proletarianization, social control, and indigence were marked.[48] It also followed on the heels of another cyclical subsistence crisis, that of 1809–10.

After 1821, in contrast, a period of decompression ensued.[49] Partly reflecting global conditions of deflation, this also derived from Mexican circumstances (compare, say, Cuba, which remained a Spanish colony and continued to boom). Mining production and land values fell; though both gradually revived, this was a long, slow process. Margaret Chowning, who seeks to qualify the notion of a severe and prolonged fall in land values, nevertheless does not see prices of the century's first decade regained until the 1850s.[50] Oaxaca—which had lost a large chunk of the cochineal market to Guatemala—experienced "a long recession" until the 1880s.[51] Population growth remained slow, and with the collapse of the colonial nexus, tax revenues declined.[52] The "penury" of the Mexican Republic, however, implied an alleviation of the old Bourbon fiscal burden.[53] The basic infrastructure of the economy remained the same, and growth was halting.[54] But at least growth was endogenous, and no surplus was siphoned off to Spain. Given that subsistence production was crucial (Stephen Haber reckons that, as late as the 1890s, only 40 percent of the population participated in the market for manufactured goods),[55] welfare did not correlate with macroeconomic performance as it might in a thoroughly monetized market society. In addition, the fractious politics of the period gave the popular classes—the villagers of Chalco, the rioters of Mexico City—a certain leverage, which made elite exactions by means of taxes, military recruitment, or the wage nexus more risky.[56] Data on welfare are hard to find, but impressionistic accounts suggest a population that, though familiar with squalor and poverty, were nevertheless probably better off than their parents had been.[57] There were no Malthusian crises to compare to 1785; popular protest appears to have become less "defensive" (i.e., designed to ward off the exactions of church, state, and landlord) and rather more "offensive" (designed to expand village landholdings and political autonomy, especially in the new circumstances of republican or caudillo rule).[58] The presence of popular protest, therefore, is no more proof of a deterioration in welfare than its absence is proof of improvement.

This should be borne in mind when we confront the Porfiriato, the period when the "vicious" circle of political instability, governmental insolvency, and (at best) sluggish growth gave way to a "virtuous" circle of stability, solvency, and rapid *desarrollo hacia afuera*. Foreign investment grew from next to nothing to 3.4 billion pesos in 1911 (around 183 percent of GDP).[59] Exports increased tenfold and, in 1910, represented 12 percent of GDP.[60] A "traditional" Mexico, whose broad lineaments still resembled those of New Spain, now yielded to a more "modern" Mexico, closely integrated into world commodity and capital markets, hence structurally transformed (not least by railways) and more vulnerable to external shocks.[61] The process was not smooth and linear: there had been earlier revivals (and retreats), and the Porfiriato itself warrants periodization.[62] In broad terms, however, the parallel with the late colonial period is striking.[63] In particular, the last decade of the nineteenth century, and the first decade of the twentieth, are key. Growth accelerated; new legislation favored foreign investment and capital accumulation; land prices and the concentration of landownership increased;[64] landlords' profits rose;[65] inflation, hitherto low, crept upward; the price of food, in particular, rose; and real wages declined.[66] Though Malthusian crises were a thing of the past, poor harvests still undercut living standards.[67] Furthermore, the deepening of the market (and hence, inter alia, growing proletarianization), meant that Mexico's subsistence cushion was less effective at absorbing unemployment, notably in the north; and, more so than in the colony, falling real wages weakened demand and jeopardized the manufacturing sector (e.g., textiles).[68] The problems of the late Porfiriato did not, therefore, represent a carbon copy of the late colony. There was no massive dearth, as in 1785; in accordance with Mexico's (partial) transition from a "traditional" agrarian to a "modern" market economy, crises (1891, 1907) generated unemployment and hardship rather than starvation and mortality. The geographical incidence of structural change had also shifted: the Bajío, the pacemaker of colonial development and epicenter of the 1810 insurgency, was relatively quiet in 1910 (not because it was prosperous, but rather because its inhabitants had been schooled in the rigors of the market for generations);[69] while Morelos and the Mesa Central, which had spurned Hidalgo in 1810, now generated a series of popular peasant movements, of which Zapatismo was the most significant. Zapatista protest was premised on the survival of the peasant community (hence some would stress its inherent archaism), whereas northern popular protest—which nurtured the sprawling and shifting bulk of Villismo—combined such "traditional" concerns with a broader appeal to the rural and urban working class.[70] Perhaps the most crucial point, however, is that Porfirian compression involved a structural, as well as a conjunctural, shift: that is, apart from depressing wages and incomes, it also converted peasants into proletarians (or, more accurately, we could say that it pushed Mexico's rural population along the continuum that ran from free peasant to dependent proletarian status).[71] Hence status, livelihood, and self-respect were all challenged.

I could (but won't) dwell on the 1910 revolution at greater length. Despite the similarities just mentioned, the revolution differed from the insurgency of 1810 in two major respects. First, in respect of causality, it owed nothing to an external stimulus (compare the Napoleonic invasion of Spain). Skocpolian theories of international revolutionary etiology are therefore worthless.[72] The revolution was as homegrown as tequila and tortillas. Second, while the immediate outcome—as of, say, 1920—was essentially a *political* change, that is, a change in regime type, the revolution also contained the potential for *socioeconomic* change that was both formal and informal. The 1810 insurgency, too, had stimulated informal socioeconomic change (e.g., the decline of mining and commercial agricul-

1. Amid modernizing efforts, Indian and peasant ways held strong in Porfirian Mexico City. Reprinted by permission of Archivo General de la Nación, Sección Propiedad Artística y Literaria.

ture), but formal change had been essentially political. The revolution, in contrast, embodied, stimulated, and even codified a series of socioeconomic changes that, if we were old-fashioned, we might refer to as changes in class relations: protection of labor and unions; agrarian reform; and (though I would place this in third place) the regulation and curtailment of foreign interests. Over time (1920–40) this combination of formal (codified) and informal (de facto) change effected a substantial transformation of Mexico. I will address the political aspects separately; the point to make here is that this transformation involved both material improvements and a measure of popular empowerment. Real wages rose, albeit jaggedly and modestly.[73] *Sindicatos*, schools, and *ejidos* brought a genuine shift in the balance of class power or, to put it differently and more fashionably, enlarged the scope of citizenship.[74] Marshall's celebrated triad of rights—civil, political, and social—achieved at least partial recognition.[75] Meanwhile, in part because of the revolution, in part—and perhaps in greater measure—because of global economic change, the role of the state grew, and the *estado rector* came to play a substantial role in the economy, not least by buffering external shocks, such as those of 1929. During the 1930s, therefore, the Mexican economy benefited from a double buffer: the old subsistence cushion (smaller than in the past, but still significant) and the newfound ability of the state to promote social reform and (Keynesian) economic revival.[76] Meanwhile, foreign investment as a percentage of GDP fell from 183 percent in 1913 to 79 percent in 1938; growth was thus "endogenized."[77]

Like the Porfiriato, the revolutionary period (1910–1970s) was far from homogeneous and needs to be disaggregated. Disaggregation can take several forms, depending on the criteria. Since my concern is, roughly, political economy, with particular reference to welfare, two comparable macro-economic cycles can be discerned: in both, a brief period of inflation, failing real wages, and declining welfare is followed by a longer period of price stability, rising real wages, and enhanced welfare. During the armed revolution (ca. 1913–20), inflation eroded living standards (though, for obvious reasons, it did not foster capital accumulation). In the subsequent two decades, circa 1920–40, prices stabilized, real wages revived, the returns to labor probably increased (while the returns to capital declined), and redistributive social reform conspired with market trends. Mexico did not become a land flowing with milk and honey, but it became a somewhat more equal society, and certainly a more productive one.

During the 1940s, inflation accelerated, real wages fell, living standards declined, and—perhaps to a greater extent than often realized—social protest increased.[78] Meanwhile some sectors of industry (e.g., construction in the DF) boomed, the rich got richer, and graft and corruption increased. We could see this as a minicycle of compression. The important thing, however, was that this period of compression was relatively brief and—for reasons both political, economic, and international—did not give rise to a concerted protest on the lines of 1810 and 1910. War, nationalism, the constraining powers of the PRM, and the escape valve of migration all inhibited popular protest. During the early 1950s, conditions changed, and the regime took stock. Global inflation declined; the regime weathered the chastening challenge of Henriquismo; Ruiz Cortines (Mexico's most underrated president?) polished up the tarnished image of the PRI and, more important, initiated the project of *desarrollo estabilizador*, which, underpinned by a prudent fiscal policy, gave Mexico twenty years of low-inflation growth and rising real wages.[79] Population growth and political control curbed wage demands, and low unemployment could thus coexist with sustained low-inflation growth (an unusual combination in the major Latin American economies in the 1950s and 1960s).

Dating the end of this period of decompression is equivalent to dating the start of the Mexican "crisis." If, in narrowly political terms, 1968 is the conventional benchmark, in terms of political economy the salient dates are 1973, when the leap in global inflation affected an economy already prone to inflationary pressures,[80] and 1982, when inflation-with-growth gave way to inflation-with-recession, that is, the novel bugbear of stagflation.[81] After 1973, real incomes were buoyed by government policy (Echeverria's *desarrollo compartido*) and, more important, the oil boom of the late 1970s. After 1982, however, the debt crisis brought acute stagflation. Again, inflation (coupled with underemployment and unemployment) eroded real wages, the share of GDP accruing to labor declined, and inequality increased.[82] Furthermore, this period of compression endured. A painful recovery through the late 1980s and early 1990s was followed by renewed inflation and recession in 1995. The cumulative effect was that, over a period of nearly twenty years, real wages showed no increase, and inequality (already pronounced) was exacerbated.[83] Economic revival— from 1989 to 1993 and from 1996 to 1999—depended increasingly on exports, especially nontraditional exports, including the maquiladora sector. From a low of 4 percent of GDP in 1967, exports climbed to 17 percent in 1994 and 24 percent in 1995 (a year, it is true, of sharp recession).[84] But export-led growth favored certain regions and sectors over others, and healthy macroeconomic trends masked a flaccid domestic market. Parallels with the Porfirian economy were apparent: like foreign trade, foreign investment bottomed out in the 1950–70 period (17 percent of GDP in 1950, 12 percent in 1970), then steadily climbed, reaching 32 percent in 1990.[85] These parallels, of course, are approximate, not precise. Porfirian foreign investment had been channeled into infrastructure (railways), extractive industries (mines and oil), and government debt. Foreign direct investment (FDI) was therefore sunk into immobile assets. During the long period of postrevolutionary decompression (especially the years of desarrollo estabilizador), FDI was heavily concentrated in manufacturing, serving the protected domestic market. Such investment was anchored by market access as well as by fixed assets. By the 1990s, however, manufacturing investment had become more mobile (maquiladoras were less firmly "anchored"), markets moved overseas (or across the border), and FDI was eclipsed by portfolio investment, whose skittishness was exacerbated by the government's ill-judged emission of dollar-denominated bonds (the notorious *tesobonos*). Arguably, Mexico's "dependence"—its vulnerability to external shocks and stimuli—was greater in the 1990s even than it had been in the 1890s.

This superficial overview, noting some of the salient (economic) similarities linking the three fin de siècle conjunctures, is purely descriptive. It does not seek to explain causality. If we address this tricky problem, it may help to disaggregate causal factors into those (largely economic) which are exogenous and those (largely political) which are endogenous. Of course, these distinctions are rough-and-ready. Important factors—for example, changing economic fashions—reveal both exogenous and endogenous origins. Political inputs affect economic trends, while economic trends constrain political behavior. However, it is hardly surprising that, as a developing capitalist economy, Mexico should respond to general global trends while, at the same time, its political elites should enjoy at least some measure of genuine autonomy in the formation of policy.

First the cycle of compression and decompression that I have described can be plotted globally, in terms both of broad economic conjunctures and, to a lesser degree, of shared political responses. The period of the Bourbon compression was one of global inflation, following a long period of price stability (what David Hackett Fischer calls the "equilibrium of the Enlightenment," ca. 1660–1740).[86] From about the 1740s in Europe and the 1760s in Latin America, growth quickened and prices rose. However, the potential benefits were offset by intense Great Power rivalry, mercantilist restrictions on trade, increased colonial exploitation, and recurrent warfare. The Bourbon reforms thus mirrored global trends, especially in the Atlantic economy. However, the Bourbon tax take exceeded that which the British extracted from North America;[87] and, of course, the revolution of 1776 curtailed British colonial exploitation (the "Hanoverian reforms" proved short-lived),[88] while in Mexico they continued for another generation. During that generation, the incidence of warfare increased, culminating in severe dislocation of government and fresh arbitrary exactions (such as the *consolidación de vales* in 1804).[89] The 1810 insurgency thus formed part of a wider Atlantic upheaval, a "revolutionary crisis" spanning from 1789 to around 1820.[90]

Following the decompression of circa 1820–80 (Fischer's "Victorian equilibrium"),[91] Mexico experienced a rapid integration into the global economy, which, again, followed broader global trends. World trade boomed, and the export of capital reached unprecedented proportions. In particular, the so-called third world was rapidly integrated into a new global economy centered on Britain, linked by railways, steamships, and telegraphs, and embodying commodity, capital, and labor markets. Though notionally an era of laissez faire, state intervention was often crucial in advancing this process. True, Britain and its self-governing dominions combined growth, free labor, and representative government. The settler societies of the American Southern Cone offered rough parallels.[92] But in the European formal empires, from Indochina across India to West Africa, coercive state intervention was a sine qua non of development. Likewise in much of northern South America and

Mesoamerica, development premised on a positivistic logic involved coercion of labor, dispossession of peasants, and enhanced state control and taxation (taxes being required to pay for social control—army and rural police—and infrastructural investment, e.g., railway subsidies).[93] Processes of state building and capitalist penetration varied according to several criteria. One was speed. Whereas, for example, Brazil experienced an incremental deepening of the market through the nineteenth century, Mexico suffered a rapid, belated process of commercialization after 1880. Where capital-intensive mining provided the staple export (e.g., Bolivia, the Peruvian Central Sierra), upheaval tended to be less profound than in labor-intensive agrarian export economies such as Guatemala. In regions of low population density, where labor was imported on a voluntary basis (São Paulo, Buenos Aires, northern Mexico), the outcome tended to be less conflictual than in populous regions where local peasants (often Indians) had to be recruited. However, extracting Indian or peasant labor (e.g., the Peruvian and Soconusco *enganche* systems) was usually less provocative than expropriating Indian or peasant land (compare Morelos). Throughout Latin America, the decades of export-led growth generated sporadic agrarian revolts: the Rumi Maqui rebellion in southern Peru (1915–16), for example, or the 1927 Chayanta uprising in southern Bolivia.[94] Only in Mexico, however, did a full-scale social revolution ensue: an outcome that could be attributed to the speed of the process (the compression of the period of compression, as it were). However, as other analysts have noted, the same period, circa 1880–1920, witnessed major revolutions elsewhere: in Russia, China, Turkey, and Iran.[95]

This process of rapid growth and integration of the world economy came to a sudden end with World War I. Subsequent attempts to restore the prewar system—exemplified by the gold standard—were at best partially successful. Growth never recovered pre-1914 levels, and the world economy suffered from structural disarticulation until the onset of the new Bretton Woods system after 1945. Latin America's trade coefficient fell, and Latin American governments assumed a greater role in the economy. Mexico's experience was therefore a distinctively revolutionary variant on a common theme. Meanwhile, the nation in revolution during the war years (1914–18) gave way to postwar recession (1920–21) and chronic deflation during the 1930s. This short, sharp period of decompression did not, of course, benefit living standards, since, compared to earlier periods, most of the world's population was now vulnerable to market vicissitudes, dependent on wage labor (or market production), and subject to more efficient fiscal regimes.[96] The old subsistence cushion had also lost most of its stuffing. However, there were countervailing forces. In Europe, mass warfare had accelerated mass mobilization; and the quid pro quo for fighting "total war" was a measure of social reform ("homes fit for heroes"). Prudential social reform was all the more attractive, given the alarming alternative of Soviet Communism. Latin America had not significantly participated in the war (although the Mexican Revolution could be seen to have an analogous effect: "ejidos fit for heroes").[97] However, the threat from the Left was apparent, and the demonstration effect of European social reform—liberal, leftist, and fascist—carried weight. "Populism" offered a measure of reform, an enhanced state, and a commitment to a managed capitalist economy.[98] The experience of World War II rammed home these lessons, in Europe and Latin America alike. Furthermore, after 1945 the world economy entered a thirty-year phase of sustained growth that paralleled the increases from 1880 to 1914 but also saw an unusual improvement in real incomes in the industrialized core.[99] Latin America was not a prime beneficiary of this trend. However, conditions of global growth and monetary stability facilitated "populist" projects in the major countries, Mexico included. And the Cuban Revolution prompted the Alliance for Progress, the culmination of concerted, enlightened liberal capitalist reform.

Since the 1970s, of course, the pattern has again changed, both rapidly and significantly. The oil shocks of the 1970s signaled the end of the Bretton Woods era, the erosion of U.S. global economic hegemony, and a revival of inflation, inducing stagflation.[100] Both the social pacts forged in response to the two world wars and the threat of Communism began to attenuate. The Keynesian commitment to full employment gave way to monetarist experiments, and the allegedly overburdened state began to shed its responsibilities. Again, Latin America followed these trends, mutatis mutandis.[101] In Mexico and Argentina, traditionally populist parties converted to neoliberalism. Governments shrank the state and eagerly embraced the global market. Trade coefficients, as we have seen, began to climb back to their pre-1914 levels. Meanwhile, the collapse of European Communism and the discrediting of its Cuban counterpart conveniently removed both a threat and an example. Mass democracy was a good deal more tolerable when it carried no risk of lurching to the left, and it was this conjunctural consequence, rather than any innate philosophical kinship, that made possible the functional interdependence of neoliberal economics and democratic politics. It follows that the status quo may be more conjunctural than often supposed.

These broad political-economic trends seem to straddle the globe;[102] political systems can mediate their impact, but no one regime—not even the "imperial republic" of the United States—exercises central economic control. Political systems are to a large degree reactive, especially in "dependent" countries. But that does not mean that reactions are identical. Indeed, I suggest that the political counterparts to the three economic conjunctures varied and, indeed, show a growing political autonomy.

First, the Bourbon regime can be dealt with briefly. The comparison is of limited value because we are dealing with a transatlantic empire, not a sovereign state. Bourbon "politics" were quintessentially different from those of the Porfirian or PRIísta conjunctures: first, because there was scant provision for representative government (beyond the *cabildos*, which were oligarchic and extremely limited in power); second, because policy was made in Madrid, and even allowing for colonial slippage ("obedezco pero no cumplo"), it responded to Bourbon (Spanish) interests. Thus late colonial government served chiefly to raise tax revenue to pay for warfare (warfare that could be said to benefit Mexico in a roundabout way, but whose costs bore no relation to the concrete benefits received by the colony of New Spain). Bourbon Mexico therefore suffered a dual exploitation: it was milked as a colony, and its subordinate classes were milked by both Creole and peninsular officials, landlords, and merchants. Meanwhile the legitimizing authority of the church was undermined, and the crown came to rely increasingly on armed force, coupled with the new—but still corrupt—Bourbon bureaucracy. Not surprisingly, this was a recipe for social tension and protest: hence the riots of 1767, when the Jesuits were expelled, and the spate of messianic and millenarian movements that marked the late colonial era.[103] Economic compression, far from being mediated or mitigated by enlightened government, seems to have been compounded by Bourbon intransigence. The case of the intendant Juan Antonio de Riaño was emblematic: an able, enlightened naval officer, a dedicated reformer, enemy of the rent-seeking Guanajuato guilds, he imposed strict discipline on the once-fractious city, boasting that "the numerous masses which until the present were restive and insubordinate are now docile and obedient. If my predecessor did not believe himself safe without armed guards, I walk through the most obscure places without other defence than my cane of office and hat."[104] Eighteen years later, Riaño died along with his fellow gachupínes in the bloody siege of the Alhóndiga, the austere neoclassical granary built by Riaño as a symbol of Bourbon efficiency and rationalism.

A century later, a loosely comparable conjuncture occurred. We have seen that the Porfirian period of compression resembled the late Bourbon in important respects. One might have expected, however, a more effective political response. After all, Mexico was no longer a colony: it was not required to remit bullion to a European metropolis; policy was made in Mexico City, not Madrid; the Constitution provided for free speech and representative government. Indeed, the Díaz government had once enjoyed a measure of popularity.[105] And while the president's forte was the conciliation and manipulation of provincial caciques, his regime, at least in some respects, displayed a capacity for broader mediation and modest paternalism.[106] By 1910, however, the scenario was very different, such that Díaz's ouster was generally applauded.[107] In part, popular discontent stemmed from the inexorable economic trends already mentioned. But the Díaz regime showed scant ability to mediate or mitigate those trends. The regime's failure can be seen in both structural and contingent terms—that is to say, some failings were inevitable, some gratuitous.[108] For example, the regime showed little will or ability to protect peasant landholding: peasants blocked commercial farming; they did not represent a powerful political constituency; they were sometimes benighted Indians and usually illiterate clods in huaraches and baggy white trousers. Economic self-interest, coupled with racist ideology, and relatively unrestrained by political considerations, ensured that peasant interests would largely go by the board. A classic instance was the replacement of the shrewd veteran Manuel Alarcón by the effete "dukeling" Pablo Escandón in Morelos; or the story of Tamazunchale, where Díaz himself could not resist the inexorable forces of agrarian compression.[109] The state's attitude toward the urban working class offers an interesting contrast: the workers were more literate, urban, and "civilized";[110] their concentration made them potentially dangerous, but also potentially useful. Thus we find some Porfirian *políticos* mediating in industrial disputes, fostering mutualist societies, and winning working-class support; Díaz himself made a halfhearted attempt in his mediation of the textile dispute of 1906–7.[111] This clearly presaged the "populist" labor policy of the revolutionary regime of the 1920s. It also paralleled other Latin American cases: the political "incorporation" of the urban working class (in part a response to the new "social question" of the 1890s and the first decade of the twentieth century) greatly anticipated any comparable "incorporation" of the peasantry.[112]

Unfortunately for the Porfirian regime, however, it was the majority peasantry, not the minority urban working class, who took up arms in 1910 and afterward. The revolution starkly displayed the illegitimacy of the regime, and hence its failure to mediate and mitigate the profound social tensions of the conjuncture. That does not mean, however, that social revolution was inevitable in 1910. Many of the same tensions were present in other Latin American countries and regions (although it could certainly be argued that they were more acute in Mexico).[113] The revolution also occurred because of contingent or individual failings—failings that were made possible by the arbitrary, authoritarian, and personalist quality of the

2. Northern revolutionaries, men of an expansive commercial Mexico, drove key victories from 1911 to 1916. Reprinted by permission of Archivo General de la Nación, Sección Propiedad Artística y Literaria.

regime. Thus Díaz spurned the institutionalizing efforts of the Unión Liberal in the 1890s, conceded the vice-presidency only to fill it with an unpopular cipher, exiled Bernardo Reyes and refused to cut a deal with Francisco Madero (until it was too late). State caciques took their cue from the *gran cacique* and similarly perpetuated their own power, blocking the opposition, rewarding their friends, and punishing their enemies.[114] Elites, sluggishly circulating, were insulated from opinion and lacked the intelligence (in both senses of the word) to attempt policies of conciliation, especially in the countryside.

One of the key consequences and great achievements of the revolution, in contrast, was to bring the majority rural population into politics and to make the new mobile revolutionary elites sensitive to public opinion. This did not, of course, imply a functioning liberal democracy. But it meant that policy had a top-down–bottom-up dialectical quality,[115] and that politicians had to appeal to the populace—in their speeches, policies, symbols, dress, and political campaigns. The contrast with the políticos of the Porfiriato—not to mention the Bourbon intendant Riaño—was stark. This new political populism also set Mexico apart from much of Latin America, especially "Indo-America."[116] Populism was made possible, in part, by the economic conjuncture, that is, by the period of decompression that, in

Mexico, derived from the domestic impact of the revolution and the disarticulation of the international economy initiated by World War I and greatly exacerbated by the Depression. The results between 1910 and the 1960s were weaker integration in the global economy, greater economic introversion, the "endogenization" of growth, and greater state intervention and dirigisme. From the point of view of economic efficiency, this project carried progressively heavier costs. Mexican industry grew behind high tariff walls, companies were cosseted and subsidized (e.g., by cheap fuel), and favored workers won featherbedded security. But even if aggregate output was thereby depressed (and consumers were ripped off), the system embodied elements of stability, reciprocity, and manageability. Especially during the low-inflation 1950s and 1960s, the Mexican economy experienced its "miracle." Workers moderated their wage demands, and social conflict was contained (compare Argentina). Mexican public opinion continued to trust in the promises of the revolution, even if individual politicians were seen as crooks.[117] Radical challenges to the regime were few and localized, especially before 1968. Low-inflation growth, high employment, and the opportunities for migration, both domestic and international, made possible a kind of tacit social pact.[118]

The Pax PRIísta was unique within Latin America. It did not obey global trends (although global trends may well have been favorable to its maintenance). After all, many of the ingredients of the Mexican economy were replicated in Brazil or Argentina. Brazil (like Mexico) experienced an "economic miracle" but suffered regime instability. Argentina suffered regime instability and experienced no miracle (on the contrary: decline). Growth with stability was not a Mexican monopoly: Costa Rica and Colombia offer possible parallels. But the form of the stability was different in each case, suggesting, again, the relative autonomy of the political, as well as the importance of specific national trajectories (i.e., national "path dependence"). Mexico's stability depended on a monopoly of national power by the PRI; a degree of elite consensus, cohesion, and circulation; controlled doses of "populist" patronage; a manipulated labor movement (linked to a growing labor surplus); and the escape valve of international migration. The unusual conjuncture of the mid-twentieth century—especially from 1945 to 1973—favored the maintenance of this system. The "social pact" arising from the revolution thus depended on a set of specific circumstances, in which (I would suggest) macroeconomic conditions and political institutions counted for a good deal more than, say, revolutionary ideology. Indeed, the greatest stability and fastest growth occurred at a time (1940–73) when the regime was progressively shedding its revolutionary credentials.

The regime did not, however, make a virtue of this reneging on its revolutionary past. As numerous observers pointed out, it coupled cautious, conservative, capital-friendly policies with familiar revolutionary rhetoric. (It also strutted its radical stuff on the international stage, notably with Echeverría). But the shocks and reassessments of the 1970s and 1980s produced dramatic changes in both rhetoric and practice. The new neoliberal policies of the latest fin de siècle—privatization, free trade, NAFTA, the end of the ejido—were not sheepishly smuggled into the political arena; rather, they were trumpeted to the skies by articulate políticos, high-powered technocrats, and gushing foreign admirers. And they were not significantly discussed, debated, or amended in public forums. The neoliberalism of the 1990s, like the positivism of the 1890s, was the *nouvelle vogue*, scientifically valid, opposed only by fools or knaves. There was no alternative. The neoliberals were partly right: the opposition offered no macroeconomic counterproject, and Mexico merely did—with greater enthusiasm and expedition, perhaps—what governments throughout Latin America were doing.[119]

The drawing of parallels with the Porfiriato was not confined to Mexico's literati. The vox populi, recycling old fin de siècle epithets, saw the Salinas government as, in some measure, *científico* or gachupín.[120] And dissidents within the ruling party chafed at the long hegemony of the "technocrats" and the quasi dynasties that, in some notable cases, they represented.[121] (Recall that the PNR/PRM/PRI ran the country for twice as long as the Porfirians did.) It is not surprising that, given the renewed socioeconomic compression after 1982, and the partial ossification of the political regime, protest—both peaceful and violent—should have increased. What is perhaps more remarkable is the long survival of the PRI in a world where dominant parties have, for over a decade, been falling like ninepins.[122] The PRI's survival depended in part on the failings—personal and programmatic—of the opposition, and in part on the party's still formidable access to resources (e.g., patronage and the mass media). Thus, though diminished in strength and support, the PRI managed to cling to national (executive) power until 2000, while electoral democracy made genuine advances. In one sense, (neoliberal) democracy even promoted the PRI's survival, albeit in attenuated form, by offering alibis for failure: first, by stressing the limitations of government; second, by diffusing authority and responsibility (between executive and legislature, president and party, states and the Federation); and third, by giving the opposition enough rope to hang itself (e.g., Cuauhtémoc Cárdenas in the DF). We may well be witnessing the endgame of the PRI, but endgames, played by shrewd and experienced players, can last a long time.

As yet, therefore, there is no sign of the PRI losing power amid revolutionary upheaval, as its Porfirian and Bourbon predecessors did. The three periods of fin de siècle compression do display common features in terms of both socioeconomic deterioration and political alienation. But today's deterioration does not, in the main, involve the kind of structural transformation—of peasants into proletarians—that the Porfiriato promoted; that transformation has largely been accomplished. Mexico today resembles the Bajío of 1910, schooled in the rigors of the market for generations. Nor, of course, are today's "gachupínes" practitioners of colonial rule.[123] It is also possible that if the supposed new economic syndrome—that is, sustained, recession-free, low-inflation growth, premised on the huge productivity gains of information technology—proves a reality, then Mexico, hooked up to the locomotive of the U.S. economy, will be hauled into twenty-first-century prosperity. But of that I would be skeptical.

If, as seems more (historically) plausible, economic cycles and shocks continue, then the capacity of the Mexican government to manage these challenges will be continually tested, in a context of competitive elections. Again, this represents a clear departure from the previous two conjunctures, when electoral pluralism was scant (ca. 1900) or nonexistent (ca. 1800). Furthermore, the dominant party, for all its failings, has proved adaptable and resourceful. It has reinvented itself in several forms (Callismo, Cardenismo, Alemanismo, Salinismo) and has constructed new networks of patronage, for elites and masses alike, in response to changing circumstances (CROM, CTM, CNC, CNOP, PRONASOL, CONACYT, IEPES). Permitting electoral pluralism may have been to an extent unavoidable;[124] but inasmuch as it represents a calculated risk, it may serve either to prolong the PRI's hold on (national) power or to ensure a peaceful and democratic transition to a new government and, indeed, a new regime. Authoritarian regimes can retire gracefully from the scene (e.g., the Franquista *dictablanda*). If the PRI, accepting electoral defeat (whether in 2000, or 2006, or whenever), eventually takes this course, it will have avoided the violent denouement of its Porfirian and Bourbon predecessors. If, in contrast, it spurns the decision of the electorate, it runs the risk of emulating them.

This guarded conclusion—written in early 2000, before the presidential election—can now be briefly updated. I chose not to rewrite my original conclusion with the benefit of hindsight for two reasons: first, because we—historians, social scientists, pundits—should try to stick by our judgments, rather than update them in light of every new event; and second, because, for all its momentous character, the election of July 2000 must be seen as part of a longer process, whose denouement is still far in the future.

It is clear, however, that the definitive victory of the opposition in a fair and free national election, following a vigorous electoral campaign, advances the process of democratization and reinforces the Spanish parallel. The initial signs, too, are that the PRI will not only honor the opposition victory but gear itself up for future electoral competition (see notes 123 and 124). The new "rules of the game" thus look fairly secure; perhaps democracy has become "the only game in town." Of course, several imponderables remain: the performance of a politically piebald Fox administration, the conduct of a refurbished but angry PRI, and any number of possible external shocks (such as a U.S. recession).

So far, however, the PRI has avoided the egregious political mistakes of previous regimes—Bourbon and Porfirian—that outstayed their welcome and, for want of sensitivity and statecraft, provoked political dissidence during times of mounting social tension (compression). Tension and compression are palpably evident in neoliberal Mexico today, even if they seem to assume more diffuse and anomic forms than the social protest of 1810 and 1910: crime, narco-violence, and vigilantism now consort with civic protest, neo-Zapatismo, and the "new social movements." But political flexibility—and what could be more flexible than to yield power to the opposition after seventy-one years?—is also more apparent. Bourbon and Porfirian intransigence contrast with the pragmatism—a cynical, calculating, self-interested pragmatism, perhaps—with which the regime of the PRI has conducted its affairs, right to the last. Indeed, as future historians look back to this fin de siècle conjuncture (from a future in which the PRI has either recovered the presidency, or resigned itself to decades of fruitless opposition, or collapsed in a heap of waning factions), they may be tempted to cite, perhaps by way of epitaph, Malcolm's judgment on the Thane of Cawdor: "Nothing in his life became him like the leaving it."[125]

POSTSCRIPT

One of the perils of contemporary history is that events rapidly overtake analyses. I wrote this essay in early 2000 and added a brief update (without changing the preceding text) in spring 2001, following Vicente Fox's victory in the July 2000 presidential elections. A sexenio later, events have certainly overtaken analysis and, in response to editorial prompting, I offer a—definitely and absolutely—final comment. (I don't think Borges ever wrote a story about a historical account that was eternally updated at odd intervals, but he might have.) It would be wrong to rewrite my earlier text since, as historians should know as well as any, documents are products of their time and it would be disingenuous to allow hindsight to color analysis, conferring a kind of spurious prescience. Also, while history is not a sure guide to the future (nothing is), the purpose of our analyses was, in part, to see how the history of the past fin de siècle crises might shed light on those of the present (or future). For such an exercise to be transparent and legitimate, it cannot involve retrospective rewriting.

The last six years have not wanted for shocks and crises: 9/11 at the outset; the disputed presidential election and subsequent PRD protest in the summer of 2006. Neither had the effect of derailing the current economic model: NAFTA is a fact of life; migrant remittances have increased; Mexican "dependency" on the United States has been enhanced. The ramifications of 9/11 slowed economic growth; but the Iraq war and its consequences boosted oil prices, to Mexico's temporary advantage. Thus, while President Fox presided over a somewhat sluggish economy (which did not measure up to his high-flown campaign promises), there was no repeat of the crises and recessions of 1982, 1986, or 1995. Absent the PRI (at least from the presidential residence at Los Pinos), the economy chugged along and the sky did not fall in. On the political front, the country flirted with crisis in 2006, but nothing on the scale of 1810 or 1910 occurred. The PRD, if not defrauded in the poll, was certainly disadvantaged in the campaign which preceded it. Official patronage, media bias, big money, and U.S.-style negative campaigning all weighed against it. Still, it contributed some palpable errors of its own. Considerations of equity aside, López Obrador's defeat was probably detrimental to Mexico's emergent democracy, since it denied the left its opportunity to benefit from the new politics of *alternancia*; it also cast a shadow over the IFE, the Federal Electoral Institute, which played a key role in the creation of the new politics. Nevertheless, despite some apocalyptic predictions, representative democracy survived, in rather tarnished form. Democracy has—so far—weathered a potentially serious crisis; Mexicans rejected extreme measures; and, from a comparative perspective, tarnished democracies are ten-a-penny. British Prime Minister Blair struts his stuff on the basis of a 35 percent plurality of the vote, slightly less than Mexico's new President Felipe Calderón received last summer.

The other great casualty of 2006 was the PRI, which came in third in the Presidential election and saw its congressional presence drop (which the PRD did not). The PRI has therefore lost two successive elections with a declining vote (2000: 36 percent; 2006: 22 percent). Of the three possible outcomes I have suggested above—recovering the presidency, resigning itself to decades of fruitless opposition, or collapsing into a heap of warring factions—the first currently looks least likely. During the 2006 campaign season, the PRI saw some damaging splits, defections, and backstabbings (of Montiel by Madrazo; of Madrazo by La Maestra).[126] But so long as Mexican national politics remain a three-horse race, and if the PRI can choose better candidates in more decorous fashion, its cause may not be doomed.

If the PRI is wrestling with the dilemmas of opposition (something the PRD has done since birth), the PAN has had to learn how to govern. By general consensus, the Fox administration was indecisive and ineffectual: hence the protests that blocked the proposed new international airport at Atenco; the failure to implement tax and energy reform; the attempted *desafuero* which would have prevented López Obrador from even running for president; the comings and goings of cabinet secretaries; the allegations of uxorious excess and influence. The endemic problems of poverty, education, crime, and violence were scarcely addressed. Indeed, there was evidence that, as the new party of government, the PAN was picking up some bad old ways of the PRI: discretionary use of federal funds, collusion with the monopolistic media, even a descent into violent factionalism (for example, in the long-conflictive southern state of Guerrero).

With all three parties under a cloud, the election was noticeable for its negativism. Again, however, this did not denote terminal crisis, but a world-weary skepticism, which is the hallmark of many contemporary democracies. Indeed, in Mexico as elsewhere, the limited range of policies and projects on offer is likely to breed a measure of indifference, even cynicism. Mexico is not Venezuela and, despite some loose allegations during the election campaign, López Obrador is not Hugo Chávez (even if some of his post-electoral protest seemed to acquire Chavista tendencies, much to his own disadvantage). Nor, in my final and tentative judgment, is 2007 analogous to 1807 (the eve of the great imperial crisis) or 1907 (the year of the strike and repression at Rio Blanco). If, following a remarkable hectohistorical sequence, 2010 follows 1910 and 1810 in being a year of dramatic upheaval (which I think is unlikely), we can at least be sure of one thing: that the causes and character of such a putative upheaval will be very different from those of the past. And we can probably guess, on the basis of history, that any future crisis will also be unpredictable and unforeseen— less part of an inexorable sequence than one of those "surprises [which] life throws up."[127]

NOTES

1 For an analysis of the impact of the Enlightenment that avoids the old simplicities, see William B. Taylor, *Magistrates of the Sacred: Priests and Parishioners in Eighteenth-Century Mexico* (Stanford, Calif.: Stanford University Press, 1996), 23.

2 Peter F. Guardino, *Peasants, Politics, and the Formation of Mexico's National State: Guerrero, 1800–1857* (Stanford, Calif.: Stanford University Press, 1996), 49, 51, 57–58, 61–63.

3 D. A. Brading, *Miners and Merchants in Bourbon Mexico, 1763–1810* (Cambridge: Cambridge University Press, 1971), 26–27, 43, 235.

4 Taylor, *Magistrates of the Sacred*, 25–26, discusses the delegitimization of the colonial order with particular reference to the secular clergy.

5 Enrique Florescano, *Precios del maíz y crisis agrícolas en México (1708–1810)* (Mexico City: El Colegio de México, 1969), esp. chap. 10.

6 The PLM is usually given particular credit for disseminating radical, including anarchist, ideas; but more moderate (but extensive) movements, such as Maderismo, also embodied some—by Porfirian standards—radical democratic notions.

7 The scale of xenophobia is debatable; I would argue that hostility to "imperialist" exploiters (e.g., North Americans) was rather less than some historians have suggested; on the other hand, popular antipathy to Spaniards and Chinese was real, often virulent, and associated with revolutionary mobilization after 1910.

8 Note the creation of a smaller but more professional, well-equipped army and the formation of the rural police (*rurales*).

9 For example, of landlords and provincial caciques. Alan Knight, *The Mexican Revolution*, 2 vols. (Cambridge: Cambridge University Press, 1986), 1.85–86, 167–68.

10 Also open to debate. The 1907 crisis obviously had an impact on late Porfirian politics; how far it stimulated the revolution is hard to say. See Knight, *The Mexican Revolution*, 1:64, 94, 130.

11 Paul J. Vanderwood, "Comparing Mexican Independence with the Revolution: Causes, Concepts and Pitfalls," in *The Independence of Mexico and the Creation of the New Nation*, ed. Jaime E. Rodríguez O. (Los Angeles: University of California, UCLA Latin American Center, 1989), 311–22.

12 John Tutino, *From Insurrection to Revolution in Mexico: Social Bases of Agrarian Violence, 1750–1940* (Princeton, N.J.: Princeton University Press, 1986), 61–68, describes the syndrome; the terms "compression" and "decompression" are introduced by way of chapter headings (215–77), whence I have purloined them. Obviously, Tutino is not responsible for how I use them. I stress this because my use is somewhat cavalier: given that the three periods of "compression" under analysis are—as I argue—rather different, the lower common denominators are quite general: I would pick out (1) inflation, (2) declining real incomes (for at least a large slice of the population), and (3) greater inequality. Another political variable could perhaps be added: (4) an antipopular, quasi-scientific elite project.

13 David Hackett Fischer, *Historian Fallacies: Toward a Logic of Historical Thought* (New York: Harper and Row, 1970), 145.

14 Peter Smith, *Labyrinths of Power: Political Recruitment in Twentieth-Century Mexico* (Princeton: Princeton University Press, 1979), 137–41, 161.

15 Daniel Cosío Villegas, *Estados Unidos contra Porfirio Díaz* (Mexico City: Hermes, 1956).

16 Karl Schmitt, "The Díaz Conciliation Policy on State and Local Levels, 1878–1911," *Hispanic American Historical Review* 40 (1960): 182–204.

17 Sandra Kuntz Ficker and Paolo Riguzzi, eds., *Ferrocarriles y vida económica en México (1850–1950)* (Mexico City: El Colegio Mexiquense, 1996).

18 Such as that "unspeakable carrion," José Santos Zelaya, whose administration

was "a blot upon the history of Nicaragua": the words of assistant secretary of state Huntington Wilson and secretary of state Philander C. Knox, quoted in Lars Schoultz, *Beneath the United States: A History of U.S. Policy towards Latin America* (Cambridge: Harvard University Press, 1998), 208; compare the contemporary encomiums for Díaz (237–38).

19 J. K. Turner, *Barbarous Mexico* (Chicago: C. H. Kerr, 1912).

20 Knight, *The Mexican Revolution*, 1.20–21, 30–31, 34.

21 The celebrated *científicos*. Daniel Cosío Villegas, *Historia moderna de México: El Porfiriato, la vida política interior*, vol. 2 (Mexico City: Hermes, 1972), 751–55, 840–62.

22 Ibid., 525.

23 Friedrich Katz, *The Life and Times of Pancho Villa* (Stanford, Calif.: Stanford University Press, 1998), 50–52.

24 A criticism that has strongly influenced later historians, for example, Ramón E. Ruiz, *The People of Sonora and Yankee Capitalists* (Tucson: University of Arizona Press, 1989).

25 Notably in 1907–8. Rodney D. Anderson, *Outcasts in Their Own Land: Mexican Industrial Workers, 1906–1911* (DeKalb: Northern Illinois University Press, 1976), 199–200.

26 On the PLM revolts of 1906 and 1908, see Anderson, *Outcasts in Their Own Land*, 120–21, 203–4.

27 Hence Smith, in *Labyrinths of Power*, suggests that "it may not be going too far to conclude . . . that institutionalization of the Mexican regime has reinstated the social requisites for rule that prevailed under the late Porfiriato" (103).

28 NAFTA thus culminated a long period of political détente and economic integration.

29 Salinas's commitment to NAFTA was supposedly cemented by his perception that significant European investment was unlikely to be forthcoming. However, NAFTA is now complemented by a trade agreement between Mexico and the European Union.

30 These prelates, of course, now include the pope himself. Overt Catholic and clerical participation in politics seems to have reached a new high during the 2000 election campaign.

31 Roads, rather than railways: a phenomenon whose impact—economic, political, and cultural—deserves further study.

32 The Salinas administration was particularly adept at eliciting (some would say buying) favorable foreign ("expert") comment. See Jesús Velasco, "Selling Ideas, Buying Influence: Mexico and American Think Tanks in the Promotion of NAFTA," in *Bridging the Border: Transforming Mexico-U.S. Relations*, ed. Rodolfo A. de La Garza and Jesús Velasco (Lanham, Md.: Rowman and Littlefield, 1997), 125–47.

33 Wayne A. Cornelius and David Myhre, eds., *The Transformation of Rural Mexico: Reforming the Ejido Sector* (San Diego: University of California, La Jolla, Center for U.S.-Mexican Studies, 1998).

34 Hence, of course, Chiapas.

35 William A. Orme Jr., ed., *A Culture of Collusion: An Inside Look at the*

Mexican Press (Boulder, Colo.: North-South Center, University of Miami, Lynne Rienner, 1997).

36 Notably in 1982–83, 1987, and 1995, the last of which produced the biggest fall in GDP (6.2 percent) since 1932.

37 Such as the EPR. The EZLN, in contrast, have proved to be less quixotic and more successful (despite repression). The closest Porfirian parallel to the EZLN would be the long, arduous regional resistance of the Yaquis of Sonora and the insurgent Maya of Quintana Roo.

38 Raymond Buve, "Un paisaje lunar habitado por bribones y sus víctimas: Mirada retrospectiva al debate sobre las haciendas y los pueblos durante el Porfiriato (1876–1911)," in *Don Porfirio Presidente... nunca omnipotente*, ed. Romana Falcón y Raymond Buve (Mexico City: Universidad Iberoamericana, 1998), 133.

39 Miguel Angel Centeno, *Democracy within Reason* (University Park: Pennsylvania State University Press, 1994), 246.

40 Richard L. Garner with Spiro E. Stefanou, *Economic Growth and Change in Bourbon Mexico* (Gainesville: University Press of Florida, 1993), 28–29, 255.

41 Eric Van Young, *Hacienda and Market in Eighteenth-Century Mexico* (Berkeley: University of California Press, 1981), 249.

42 Claude Morin, *Michoacán en la Nueva España del siglo XVIII* (Mexico City: Fondo de Cultura Económica, 1979), 187–200; D. A. Brading, *Haciendas and Ranchos in the Mexican Bajío* (Cambridge: Cambridge University Press, 1978) 182–83.

43 Florescano, *Precios del maíz*; Garner, *Economic Growth and Change*, 249.

44 Florescano, *Precios del maíz*, 153–54, which is contested, not entirely convincingly, by Richard J. Salvucci, *Textiles and Capitalism in Mexico* (Princeton: Princeton University Press, 1987), 151–52.

45 Van Young, *Hacienda and Market*, 176–82.

46 Garner, *Economic Growth and Change*, 246.

47 I make this point by way of questioning the view, now somewhat in fashion, which attributes the insurgency and independence to entirely exogenous factors and therefore implies, absent Napoleon, a tranquil continuation of Spanish rule in the Americas, perhaps involving "home rule."

48 Tutino, *From Insurrection to Revolution*, chaps. 2–3.

49 On the terminology, see note 12 in this essay. "Decompression" implies reversal of "compression," hence more stable prices, stable or rising real incomes, and greater equality.

50 Margaret Chowning, "Reassessing the Prospects for Profit in Nineteenth-Century Mexican Agriculture," in *How Latin America Fell Behind*, ed. Stephen Haber (Stanford, Calif.: Stanford University Press, 1997), 179–215.

51 Brian R. Hamnett, *Politics and Trade in Southern Mexico, 1750–1821* (Cambridge: Cambridge University Press, 1971), 51.

52 Ibid., 53.

53 Barbara A. Tenenbaum, *The Politics of Penury: Debt and Taxes in Mexico, 1821–56* (Albuquerque: University of New Mexico Press, 1986).

54 For a good résumé of growth scenarios, see Richard J. Salvucci, "Mexican

National Income in the Era of Independence," and for an analysis stressing relative stagnation, Enrique Cárdenas, "A Macroeconomic Interpretation of Nineteenth-Century Mexico," both in Haber, *How Latin America Fell Behind*, chaps. 3, 8.

55 Stephen H. Haber, *Industry and Underdevelopment: The Industrialization of Mexico, 1890–1940* (Stanford, Calif.: Stanford University Press, 1989), 27.

56 For example, in Oaxaca. Hamnett, *Politics and Trade*, 56–59.

57 I base this on random readings of foreign accounts of Mexico in the early national period, which, while stressing, often in Eurocentric fashion, the dirt, poverty, and malodorous rusticity of Mexican life, nevertheless suggest that people ate well enough to survive, did not suffer extreme dearth and mortality (as in 1785), and were resistant to the relentless time and work discipline of modern industrial capitalism.

58 John H. Coatsworth, "Patterns of Rural Rebellion in Latin America: Mexico in Comparative Perspective," in *Riot, Rebellion and Revolution*, ed. Friedrich Katz (Princeton, N.J.: Princeton University Press, 1988), 55.

59 Michael J. Twomey, "Patterns of Foreign Investment in Latin America in the Twentieth Century," in *Latin America and the World Economy since 1800*, ed. John H. Coatsworth and Alan M. Taylor (Cambridge: Harvard University–David Rockefeller Center for Latin American Studies, 1998), 184. Van R. Whiting, *The Political Economy of Foreign Investment in Mexico* (Baltimore: Johns Hopkins University Press, 1992), 31, following David Glass, gives a figure for foreign direct investment of 117 percent.

60 Leopoldo Solís, *La realidad económica mexicana: Retrovisión y perspectivas* (Mexico City: Siglo Veintiuno Editores, 1970), 104–5.

61 Such as 1907. Anderson, *Outcasts in Their Own Land*, 199–200.

62 Thus, in Mexico as in several other developing countries, the 1890s appear to have been a key decade in terms of industrial growth; at the same time, the growth of real wages in Mexico, buoyant during the railway boom of the 1880s, appears to have stalled after the mid-1890s.

63 François-Xavier Guerra, *Le Mexique: De l'ancien régime à la révolution*, vol. 1 (Paris: L'Harmattan, 1985), 274.

64 Moisés González Navarro, *Historia moderna de México: El Porfiriato, la vida social* (Mexico City: Hermes, 1957), 198; Knight, *The Mexican Revolution*, 1.95–96.

65 Simon Miller, *Landlords and Haciendas in Modernizing Mexico: Essays in Radical Reappraisal* (Amsterdam: Center for Latin American Research and Documentation, 1995), 86–87; though I do not think that the conclusion to this cogent essay is such a "radical reappraisal" as the author claims.

66 Anderson, *Outcasts in Their Own Land*, 199–200, 251; Aurora Gómez Galvarriato, "The Evolution of Prices and Real Wages in Mexico from the Porfiriato to the Revolution," in Coatsworth and Taylor, *Latin America and the World Economy*, 351, which sees a sharp fall in real wages at the end of the Porfiriato (1907–10).

67 Anderson, *Outcasts in Their Own Land*, 241; William E. French, "Peaceful and Working People: The Inculcation of the Capitalist Work Ethic in a Mexican Mining District (Hidalgo District, Chihuahua, 1880–1920)" (Ph.D. diss., University of Texas, Austin, 1990), 85.

68 Ibid., 92–93; Haber, *Industry and Underdevelopment*, 28; Anderson, *Outcasts in Their Own Land*, 138, 199–200; Knight, *The Mexican Revolution*, 1.102.

69 Tutino, *From Insurrection to Revolution*, 306–7, 320–21.

70 Knight, *The Mexican Revolution*, 1.309–19, 2.115–29.

71 To refine the model further, we should perhaps imagine a continuum (stretching from free landed peasant through various gradations of independence and empowerment to peon status), along which are ranged—rather like *topes* on a Mexican highway—certain bumpy break points: the shift from landed to landless, from free villager to tenant or sharecropper and ultimately peon.

72 Alan Knight, "Social Revolution: A Latin American Perspective," *Bulletin of Latin American Research* 9, no. 2 (1990).

73 Eyler N. Simpson, *The Ejido: Mexico's Way Out* (Chapel Hill: University of North Carolina Press, 1937), 302, citing Ramón Fernández y Fernández; *La Voz Patronal*, January 31, 1945, 39, cited in Monica Lütke-Entrup, "Business, Labour and the State in Mexican State Development (1938–46): The Political Economy of Unidad Nacional" (Ph.D. diss., Oxford University, 2002), 52.

74 Simpson, *The Ejido*, 313–15; an illustrative recent study is Mary Kay Vaughan, *Cultural Politics in Revolution: Teachers, Peasants, and Schools in Mexico, 1930–40* (Tucson: University of Arizona Press, 1997).

75 It is arguable, of course, that Mexico diverged from the Marshallian norm—whereby civil and political rights precede social ones. Rather, the early democratic promise of the (Maderista) revolution remained unfulfilled, being outflanked by the new social tenets of labor and agrarian reform (e.g., articles 27 and 123 of the 1917 Constitution). Nevertheless, the politics of the revolutionary period—corrupt and illiberal though they often were—did involve a substantial expansion of the "political nation" and, especially during the 1930s, a degree of popular political empowerment, certainly in comparison with the Porfiriato.

76 See the excellent analysis in Enrique Cárdenas, *La industrialización de México durante la gran depresión* (Mexico City: El Colegio de México, 1987).

77 Twomey, "Patterns of Foreign Investment," 184.

78 Stephen R. Niblo, *Mexico in the 1940s: Modernity, Politics and Corruption* (Wilmington, Del.: Scholarly Resources, 1999), is a good recent study.

79 Sylvia Maxfield, *Governing Capital: International Finance and Mexican Politics* (Ithaca: Cornell University Press, 1990), examines the fiscal and financial bases of desarrollo estabilizador; Jeffrey Bortz, *El salario en México* (Mexico City: Ediciones El Caballito, 1986), charts the gradual revival of real wages from the nadir of the 1940s.

80 On the "heated debate" over the causes of inflation, which pitted structuralists against monetarists, see Víctor Bulmer-Thomas, *The Economic History of Latin America since Independence* (Cambridge: Cambridge University Press, 1994), 285–87. Both sides agreed that Latin America was inflation prone; a key factor, especially relevant in the Mexican case, was government reluctance to raise revenues through taxation, especially progressive taxation.

81 J. K. Galbraith, *The World Economy since the Wars: A Personal View* (London: Sinclair-Stevenson, 1994), 204; David Hackett Fischer, *The Great Wave: Price Revolutions and the Rhythm of History* (Oxford: Oxford University Press, 1996), 205–6.

82 Centeno, *Democracy within Reason*, offers a good overview.

83 Mauricio A. González Gómez, "Crisis and Economic Change in México," in *Mexico under Zedillo*, ed. Susan Kaufman Purcell and Luis Rubio (Boulder, Colo.: Lynne Rienner, 1998), 52–53.

84 Ibid., 43, 54.

85 Twomey, "Patterns of Foreign Investment," 184.

86 Fischer, *The Great Wave*, 102–16, 120–42.

87 Anthony McFarlane, *The British in the Americas, 1480–1815* (New York: Longman, 1994), 207–8, 240–41.

88 Barbara Tenenbaum's phrase in "The Emperor Goes to the Tailor," in *Mexico in the Age of the Democratic Revolutions, 1750–1850*, ed. Jaime E. Rodriguez O. (Boulder, Colo.: Lynne Rienner, 1994), 283.

89 John Jay TePaske, "The Financial Disintegration of the Royal Government of Mexico during the Epoch of Independence," in Rodriguez O., *The Independence of Mexico*, 63–84.

90 Fischer, *The Great Wave*, 142–56.

91 Ibid., 156–77.

92 Donald Denoon, *Settler Capitalism: The Dynamics of Dependent Development in the Southern Hemisphere* (Oxford: Clarendon Press, 1983).

93 Steven C. Topik and Allen Wells, "Latin America's Response to International Markets during the Export Silver Boom," introduction to *The Second Conquest of Latin America: Coffee, Henequen and Oil during the Export Boom, 1850–1930*, ed. Steven C. Topik and Allen Wells (Austin: ILAS, University of Texas Press, 1998), 9–18.

94 Nils Jacobsen, *Mirages of Transition: The Peruvian Altiplano, 1780–1930* (Berkeley: University of California Press, 1993), 221–23, 339–43; Erick D. Langer, *Economic Change and Rural Resistance in Southern Bolivia, 1880–1930* (Stanford, Calif.: Stanford University Press, 1989), 79–87.

95 Eric R. Wolf, *Peasant Wars of the Twentieth Century* (New York: Harper and Row, 1969); John Mason Hart, *Revolutionary Mexico: The Coming and Process of the Mexican Revolution* (Berkeley: University of California Press, 1987).

96 As Paul Krugman points out, in the course of a critique of Fischer, "economic downturns before 1800 were the result of 'supply-side' events such as harvest failures and wars. They bore little resemblance to modern recessions, which are the result of slumps in monetary demand." Krugman, *The Accidental Theorist and Other Dispatches from the Dismal Science* (New York: Norton, 1998), 132.

97 Ejidal petitions frequently make play of the petitioners' service to the revolutionary cause, and to particular revolutionary caudillos.

98 I place "populism" in inverted commas because I am not persuaded that it is the best way to describe the phenomenon under discussion; however, it has come to serve as a loose label for the statist, interventionist, socially reformist regimes of the 1930s and 1940s (e.g., the classic triad: Lázaro Cárdenas, Getulio Vargas, Juan Domingo Perón).

99 Fischer, *The Great Wave*, 188.

100 Ibid., 203–4, 211, where the inflationary takeoff is located in the 1960s.

101 The Mexican experience was complicated by the (Mexican) oil boom of the

late 1970s, which boosted consumption and government spending (and hence debt) despite rising inflation. Hence the day of reckoning was postponed but was all the more severe when it came (in 1982).

102 The explanation for these long cycles (whose very existence some might doubt) is a big question that I do not intend to broach (and Fernand Braudel, no less, declared "impossible to solve"); it is enough to show that Mexico has lived through them and has been affected by them. Fischer notes seven macro-models of price cycles ("monetarist, Malthusian, Marxist, agrarian, neoclassical, environmental, and historicist," in *The Great Wave*, 241, where the Braudel quote also appears). Fischer adds an eighth model: "autogenous change," intrinsic to the price cycle itself, and redolent of rational-actor theory. He also discusses, but discards, older cyclical models (Kondratieff, Kuznets, Labrousse, Juglar, etc.) (273–77). I suspect that if long swings—or waves—can be identified, their etiology is likely to vary over time, and no single model is likely to hit the causal jackpot. Malthusian and agrarian explanations clearly carry more weight before 1800 (as Emmanuel Le Roy Ladurie has shown in *Les paysans de Languedoc*, 2 vols. [Paris: Flammarion, 1966]); while Kondratieff, stressing technological innovation and application, wisely did not extend his model back beyond the 1790s.

103 See Eric Van Young's magnum opus on the insurgency *The Other Rebellion: Popular Violence, Ideology, and the Struggle for Mexican Independence, 1810–1821* (Stanford, Calif.: Stanford University Press, 2001).

104 Brading, *Miners and Merchants*, 243–46, 343–44.

105 Guerra, *Le Mexique*, 20, stresses the moderation and even consensuality of the Díaz regime—an interpretation more convincing for the 1880s than the 1900s.

106 See, for example, Teresa M. Van Hoy, "La Marcha Violenta? Railroads and Land in 19th Century Mexico," *Bulletin of Latin American Research* 19 (2000): 33–61, which presents a Porfirian regime more committed to negotiation than coercion; see also Robert H. Holden, "The Priorities of the State in the Survey of Public Lands in Mexico, 1856–1911," *Hispanic American Historical Review* 70, no. 4 (1990): 579–608.

107 Knight, *The Mexican Revolution*, vol. 1, chap. 4.

108 From a strictly determinist perspective, of course, even personal failings and individual errors are thoroughly determined and, a philosopher might say, no less "inevitable" than, say, the building of railways. From a historical point of view, however, structural ("inevitable") and contingent (e.g., individual) factors are of a different order. We can imagine a Mexico in which Díaz does not give the Creelman interview; we cannot imagine a Mexico without railways.

109 John Womack Jr., *Zapata and the Mexican Revolution* (New York: Knopf, 1969), 17; Donald F. Stevens, "Agrarian Policy and Instability in Porfirian Mexico," *Americas* 39 (1982): 153–66.

110 For example, in respect of dress: the aspiring artisans of the Porfiriato are to be seen in suits, wing collars, and ties, not unlike their political masters, while peasants and Indians still wore their baggy white pajamas and huaraches (and were, as a consequence, barred from Mexico City during the centennial celebrations of 1910).

111 Anderson, *Outcasts in Their Own Land*, 148–53, 230–31.

112   Ruth Berins Collier and David Collier, *Shaping the Political Arena* (Princeton, N.J.: Princeton University Press), 1991.

113   Two obvious reasons spring to mind (there are no doubt others): Mexico's integration into the global division of labor was delayed by the endemic wars of the mid-nineteenth century, so that when it got under way, the process was unusually rapid and traumatic; in addition, the proximity of the booming United States further accelerated the process. These trends, of course, affected a dense and ancient agrarian society, especially in central Mexico (contrast the "settler societies" of the Southern Cone).

114   Knight, *The Mexican Revolution*, vol. 1, chap. 2.

115   For example, Vaughan, *Cultural Politics in Revolution.*

116   As already noted, the "populist" counterparts of Cárdenas were to be found in Brazil and Argentina. Societies in which class stratification was reinforced by ethnic ("estamental") barriers—Guatemala, Peru, Ecuador, Bolivia—tended to exemplify a more authoritarian, exclusionary, and racist politics, especially in highland and Indian regions (Guayaquil was therefore an exception), and barring revolutionary upheaval (e.g., Bolivia after 1952).

117   Gabriel A. Almond and Sidney Verba, *The Civic Culture: Political Attitudes and Democracy in Five Nations* (Boston: Little Brown, 1965).

118   A fuller analysis would require a regional and sectoral breakdown, which would take into account important episodes of, for example, syndical dissidence (e.g., the railway workers in 1958–59) and regional protest (e.g., Navismo in San Luis, El Partido do los Pobres in Guerrero). The generalization that appears in the text is, therefore, a broad-brush national observation.

119   Centeno, *Democracy within Reason*, remains the best analysis.

120   Adolfo Gilly, *Cartas a Cuauhtémoc Cárdenas* (Mexico City: Ediciones Era, 1989), 23–24, 85–86, 201, 203, 204, 233, 236.

121   This was written well before the elections of July 2000, which, of course, have exacerbated PRIísta critiques of recent party leadership, culminating in calls for the expulsion from the PRI of Carlos Salinas and Ernesto Zedillo. It remains to be seen whether, chastened by defeat, the PRI makes a serious effort to refurbish its older, more reformist, populist, and statist credentials (perhaps under a Madrazo leadership?), and if so, whether that formula holds out any prospect of success.

122   Another postelectoral update: the PRI has now joined the Communist Parties of Eastern Europe and the Italian Christian Democrats on the long electoral casualty list. Pursuing the speculations raised in note 121, we may wonder whether this is a temporary defeat or a terminal illness.

123   Though some critics might see them as collaborators in a diffuse "informal empire" headed by Washington, Wall Street, the World Bank, and IMF.

124   Future historians will no doubt debate the motivation behind Mexico's long, slow, but generally successful political *apertura*. While early analyses—for example, of the electoral reform of 1977—tended to adopt a "Lampedusan" explanation (reform served to perpetuate the system, including the hegemony of the PRI), this view became increasingly untenable as reform made genuine inroads into that hegemony, culminating in a clutch of opposition governorships, a pluralist congress, and, finally, an opposition victory in the presidential election of July 2000.

Maybe the process acquired a momentum that the early "Lampedusan" PRIístas had never envisioned; maybe some PRIístas—such as Zedillo—came to regard democratization as more important than party interest (whether for reasons of economic calculation, personal image, or genuine democratic commitment).

125 Shakespeare, *Macbeth*, 1.4.7.

126 Roberto Madrazo won the presidential nomination of the PRI, having defeated his chief rival, Arturo Montiel, who withdrew from the contest under dubious circumstances. "La Maestra"—Elba Esther Gordillo—leader of the powerful teachers' union, opposed Madrazo and split from the PRI, forming her own breakaway party, Nueva Alianza, and (allegedly) also giving covert support to the PAN candidate, Felipe Calderón; she thus contributed to Madrazo's poor showing and, perhaps, to Calderón's victory.

127 Jorge Casteñada, *Sorpresas te da la vida: México, 1994* (Mexico City: Aguilar, 1995).

International Wars, Mexico, and U.S. Hegemony

FRIEDRICH KATZ

Most of the studies in this volume focus on political and social crisis internal to Mexico. But a careful reflection on Mexican history and on many of those studies indicates that international wars have been a regular and important factor in the long, complex, and contested history of independent Mexico. Three of those wars, the War of Independence against Spain, the Mexican-American War, and the French invasion, had a direct and decisive impact on Mexican internal developments. Three other wars in which Mexico was not directly involved, the Spanish-American War, World War I, and World War II, had deep though indirect impacts on Mexico.

The War of Independence against Spain, whose outbreak was indirectly affected by the French Revolution and the Napoleonic wars, was similar to the other Latin American wars for independence in ending colonial rule and beginning the long contests of nation building. It was unique, though, in comparison to the other Spanish colonies in that the popular classes played a far more important role in Mexico than elsewhere. In fact, the war for independence began as a popular uprising of the lower classes in the countryside, led first by Miguel Hidalgo y Costilla and then by José María Morelos y Pavón. Although the armies of Hidalgo and Morelos were defeated by a coalition of Spaniards and criollos, the popular uprising had wide-ranging consequences for post-independence Mexico. The defeat of the popular classes was by no means final. Many of their members acquired arms, fighting experience, and above all a consciousness of strength. As a result, Mexico became a unique center of rural movements throughout most of the nineteenth century.

The number of peasant uprisings in Mexico was greater than in any other Latin American country.[1] Many of these uprisings were limited to the lower classes of society, but in other cases, the popular classes aligned themselves with regional caudillos, who were frequently, but by no means exclusively, liberals.[2] In the civil wars that shook Mexico, these caudillos could not have survived without their lower-class allies. In return they protected the landholdings and the autonomy of village communities.[3]

The Mexican-American War, in which Mexico lost half of its territory to the United States, obviously had a tremendous economic impact, since enormously rich areas, highly suitable for settlement, were taken from Mexico. The most immediate impact, though, of that catastrophe was an upsurge of the liberal movement, which blamed the church and the conservatives for Mexico's defeat. The liberals felt that only by eliminating the church as a political and economic—though not a religious—force could Mexico become a modern country. The war between liberals and conservatives began in 1858, lasted three years, ended in a liberal victory, and led directly to the French invasion. Conservatives called on the French to occupy the country and install a monarchy there. The war against the French and their conservative Mexican allies from 1863 to 1867 had wideranging and in some respects contradictory effects on Mexico. It strengthened two highly antagonistic social classes in Mexico. On the one hand, the victorious liberals in their long guerrilla war against France mobilized the popular classes by arming them, giving them new powers. That war led to a new consciousness within these classes of their own strength, as well as a stronger national consciousness. At the same time, the war produced a reconciliation within the landowning class, which had been sharply divided between conservative and liberal hacendados. After the defeat of the church and the French, the two factions united in a common struggle against the popular classes. One result of that unity was the dictatorship of Porfirio Díaz.

After defeating France's army, Mexico's rulers, as well as a large part of the Mexican public, became convinced that the danger of a European invasion had disappeared. Only one foreign threat remained in the eyes of most Mexicans, and that was the United States. The fact that the U.S. government had supported Mexico's struggle against the French after the end of the Civil War and the defeat of the Confederacy did not diminish Mexicans' fears of a possible American intervention. As a result, after only a few years' interval, Mexico sought the support of the same European powers that had either brought Maximilian to Mexico or recognized his regime. Paradoxically, France became one of the most popular countries in Mexico; French fashion, customs, and military equipment became a priority for Mexicans. Finally, it was in France that Porfirio Díaz, who earned his prestige fighting the French invasion, went into exile and died.

The three international wars in which Mexico was directly involved from 1810 to 1867 played an important but not an exclusive role in the limited development of Mexico's economy, leaving the country to fall more and more behind the United States. According to the historian John Coatsworth, at the time of independence, the per capita national income of Mexico was about one-half of that in the United States. By 1877 it had fallen to one-seventh.[4]

Finally, two of these three wars (the Mexican-American War and the war against the French invasion) greatly increased the direct and indirect influence of the United States over Mexico. That tendency would continue at an even greater pace during the wars of 1895 to 1945. These later wars, in which Mexico was not a belligerent, still affected the country in profound ways—some similar to the consequences of the earlier wars, others very different.

The Spanish-American War, World War I, and World War II each had a tremendous impact on Mexico's development. While Mexico did not participate in the first two, and joined only marginally in the third, all three brought enormous increases in U.S. economic and political power in Mexico. All three wartime crises led to increasing integration between the two countries, as well as to Mexican migration to the United States. The combination of increasing U.S. power in Mexico and growing Mexican migration to the United States had deep if indirect political, social, and intellectual implications for Mexico. Mexican resistance to expanding U.S. power had varying degrees of temporary success. In the long run, that resistance never halted the constantly increasing role of the United States in Mexico.

THE SPANISH-AMERICAN WAR

The Spanish-American War was the name given by the United States to its late but transforming 1898 intervention into the Cuban war for independence that had begun in 1868 and reemerged with new intensity in 1895. During those decades of conflict, while many Cubans struggled to abolish slavery and gain independence from Spain, others worked to preserve the sugar plantation system that sustained their wealth. U.S. investors took advantage of the turmoil to buy increasing control of Cuba's land and export production. When the conflict in Cuba appeared locked in a bloody and destructive stalemate and threatened to destroy the plantation economy, in 1898 conservative Cubans collaborated with the U.S. invasion to engineer a rapid victory that brought a proclamation of national independence, the preservation of the plantation economy, and the acceleration of U.S. economic hegemony—under U.S. military occupation and political oversight.

When the Cuban conflict became the Spanish-American War in 1898, opinions in Mexico about the war's consequences divided. A large part of Mexican public opinion identified with the Cuban revolutionary movement; others believed that the United States' entry into the war would finally bring independence to Cuba. A few voiced very strange opinions. One newspaperman with strong Spanish sympathies speculated that Spain would defeat the United States, and as a result the United States would fall apart.[5] This view was not shared by the vast majority of Mexico's newspapers and by the Mexican government.

Mexican newspapers expressed an increasing fear that U.S. expansionism might go beyond Cuba and revive annexationist desires with respect to northern Mexico. "What will happen to Latin America and above all to Mexico if the pearl of the Caribbean were to become part of the coat of arms of the men of the north?" a Mexican newspaper asked.[6] That view strengthened as the United States imposed the Platt Amendment to limit Cuba's political independence, and when dollar diplomacy and the big stick became predominant American policies in the Caribbean.

Mexico's political class reacted in four different ways to what it perceived as an increasing threat from the United States. The first reaction by the Díaz administration was to repeat the policy that Díaz had pursued from 1876 to 1879, when U.S. president Rutherford Hayes had seriously considered another war of annexation against Mexico. Instead of mobilizing troops against the United States, Díaz invited American investors into the country and granted them huge concessions and subsidies, leading the beneficiaries to voice their opposition to war between the two countries. They felt they could obtain economic preeminence without recourse to war, which might devastate Mexico and make profitable investments much more difficult.

In the shadow of the Spanish-American War, Díaz repeated this policy at the turn of the century. In 1916 Francisco Bulnes, a leader of the Científico group that dominated Mexico under Díaz, enumerated some of the enormous concessions that Díaz granted to Americans: "Having sold for next to nothing 3 million hectares of excellent lands in the State of Chihuahua to two favorites of the Mexican government that they might resell them to Mr. Hearst, the celebrated millionaire," and "having permitted the U.S. ambassador, Mr. Thompson, to enter the business field in Mexico, something that would not have been tolerated in any other country, and having granted him personal concessions by means of which he organized a U.S. banking company and the Pan-American railroad."[7]

While such a strategy might appease the United States in the short run, in the long run it threatened to create such American predominance in Mexico that the independence of the country was in real danger. To counter this threat, Mexico's ruling Científico elite hoped to rely on Europe. Both the German minister to Mexico and his French counterpart clearly described the strategy that the Científicos wanted to implement. The German minister reported:

> In their view, the political future of the country depends entirely on the development of the economy. To realize this, however, the country needs help from abroad, including the United States. Mexico is thus increasingly destined to become an area of activity for capitalist firms from all countries. The cosmopolitans, however, paradoxical as this may sound, see precisely in economic dependency the guarantee of political independence, insofar as they assume that the large European interests that have investments here constitute a counterweight to American annexationist appetites, and that they will pave the way for the complete internationalization and neutralization of Mexico. Behind the scenes, but at the head of the cosmopolitan group, stands the Finance Minister, Señor Limantour. His allies are haute finance, as well as the top-level civil servants with interests in the domestic and foreign companies, senators, deputies, and, finally, the local representatives of European capital invested in Mexico.[8]

In an effort to ensure the neutrality and independence of the Mexican "arena," the elite turned with mixed success to France, Germany, Great Britain, and even, after 1905, Japan. On April 28, 1901, the French minister reported a conversation with the president of the Mexican Chamber of Deputies, José López Portillo y Rojas:

> He [López Portillo] spoke at length of the serious efforts made over the last few years by the United States to carry out a general invasion of Mexico with American capital, railways, and industry. "There can be no question that we cannot respond to this invasion in a radical fashion, as the United States has contributed to the development of our country in the past, continues to do so today, and will contribute further in the future. We must keep such a powerful neighbor in a good mood and we must do nothing to antagonize it. On the other hand, we have the right, also the duty to look elsewhere for a counterweight to the constantly growing influence of our powerful neighbor. We must turn to other circles, from which we can draw support under

certain circumstances, in order to preserve our industrial and commercial independence. We can find such a counterweight only in European and particularly in French capital." Señor López Portillo thus summarized the outlook expressed to me by many leaders who are not hypnotized by American power and who are worried about the Americans' attempts at controlling Mexico's economic life.

And the envoy reminded his own foreign minister: "We must support with all our power the efforts of the Mexicans to have important firms financed by French capital, which would be taken over by the Americans without our help."[9]

While the Mexican government never restricted American investment, it did try to favor European over American investments whenever possible. As far as it could, the Mexican government attempted to place all loans in European banks, and when oil became a major factor in Mexico, the Díaz administration favored the British-owned El Aguila Company over its American competitors, including the Waters-Pierce Company affiliated with Standard Oil.[10]

A third response proposed by a part of Mexico's ruling group was to attempt to strengthen the Mexican army in order to discourage American thoughts of invasion. There was talk of replicating the policies of other Latin American countries, which attempted to modernize their armies by inviting German or French officers to train them. Minister of war Bernardo Reyes submitted a proposal to increase the size of the army to seventy-five thousand men; he also proposed a second reserve to strengthen the defensive power of Mexico. None of these projects was realized. Obviously Díaz was convinced that such policies could only boomerang. They would anger the Americans, yet in a real war, the Mexican army would be no match for that of the United States.

The fourth policy espoused by some members of Mexico's elite, such as Enrique Creel, was to flirt with Japan, possibly to offer the Japanese a naval base in Baja California, perhaps to sign some kind of treaty with Japan. While it is not clear how far these offers went, the American government was greatly worried by these rumors and by the fact that the Mexican government had denied a base to the U.S. Navy in Baja California.[11]

Finally, increasingly worried by U.S. expansionism in Central America, Porfirio Díaz expressed sympathy for Nicaraguan president José Santos Zelaya, who had attempted to unify Central America against the United States. The Mexican president risked being seen as a competitor to the United States for hegemony in Central America, hoping to find allies there against the Yankee power so blatantly assertive in the aftermath of the invasion of Cuba.[12]

Thus, while diverse U.S. investors and businesses saw the Díaz regime as favoring their interests, others worried about favors to rivals. The U.S. government saw the regime that had stabilized Mexico, welcomed investment, and promoted export production become an increasingly uncertain and too-independent ally. Meanwhile, the collapse of the Cuban sugar economy caused by the war for independence that became the Spanish-American War brought a short but strong boom in the Mexican sugar industry from the late 1890s into the first decade of the new century. One consequence was the assault on the lands and water of surviving communities by the expansive planters of the Morelos basin, just south of Mexico City. The resulting struggles proved key to setting off the popular agrarian movement that Emiliano Zapata eventually led into Mexico's revolutionary conflagration after 1910.[13]

The results of Díaz's diplomatic policies came to fruition when Francisco Madero led the political opposition that opened the revolution in 1910. There are indications, but no proof, that Madero received support from U.S. oil companies and other business interests.[14] For some time, the U.S. administration refused to enforce the neutrality laws that would have blocked Madero from mobilizing in the United States against Díaz. Meanwhile, since the pro-European and pro-Japanese policies of the Mexican government were carried out surreptitiously, most Mexican public opinion saw Díaz as an agent of the United States at a time when anti-American feelings were strong and rising in Mexico. Thus, when crisis turned toward revolution in 1910, Díaz lacked U.S. backing, while he faced a political opposition backed, perhaps, by U.S. interests. Simultaneously, much of the Mexican populace resented Díaz as a tool of the Yankees, while he faced a rising agrarian mobilization. In such diverse direct and indirect ways, the Spanish-American War contributed to Mexico's early-twentieth-century crisis, and the revolution it spawned in 1910.

WORLD WAR I

The Great War, eventually known as World War I, began in Europe in 1914, with Mexico's revolution under way and approaching its violent peak. While no fighting took place on Latin American soil, and practically no Latin American troops were involved in active combat in Europe or in Asia, World War I profoundly affected all Latin American countries. It strongly influenced commerce with Europe. Trade with Germany collapsed, and Britain and France were less and less capable of sending goods to Latin America. Their investments in the area were drastically curtailed. In contrast, U.S. investments in Latin America greatly increased, as did

U.S. trade with Latin American countries. Many Latin American countries now developed industries of their own to compensate for the absence of goods from Europe. The costs and benefits of these processes were unevenly distributed. For countries, especially in the Southern Cone of South America, where commercial ties had concentrated on Europe, trade with and investments by the United States could not make up for the losses. This was especially true of Argentina. For countries, especially in the Caribbean, whose main trading partner and main source of investment had been the United States, the situation was very different. The loss of European trade was at times more than made up by the increasing prices the Americans were willing to pay for raw materials.

These factors affected Mexico in a very different way from the rest of Latin America. This was due, on the one hand, to the Mexican Revolution, which approached a violent peak as World War I began, and, on the other, to Germany's efforts to use Mexico for its own purposes, attempting to provoke war between Mexico and the United States to prevent U.S. involvement in the European war.[15] When World War I broke out in August 1914, the civil war that would pit the armies of the Convention, led by the northern revolutionary Pancho Villa and the southern agrarian Emiliano Zapata, against the Constitutionalists, loyal to the nationalist Venustiano Carranza and his general Álvaro Obregón, was just beginning.

The early policy of the United States toward the revolutionary factions had been either to force them into a compromise or to play them off against each other. In the face of World War I, U.S. policy reversed course. As Secretary of State Robert Lansing formulated it:

> Looking at the general situation I have come to the following conclusion: Germany desires to keep up the turmoil in Mexico until the United States is forced to intervene; therefore we must not intervene. Germany does not wish to have any one faction dominant in Mexico; therefore we must recognize one faction as dominant in Mexico. When we recognize a faction as the government, Germany will undoubtedly seek to cause a quarrel between that government and ours; therefore we must avoid a quarrel regardless of criticism and complaint in Congress and the press. It comes down to this: Our possible relations with Germany must be our first consideration; and all our intercourse with Mexico must be regulated accordingly.[16]

As a result of these considerations, the United States threw its support in late 1915 to Carranza's Constitutionalist faction, not only by recognizing it and allowing it to have the exclusive right to buy arms in the United States, but also by allowing Carrancista troops to transit American territory to attack Villa's men in Sonora. Villa, incensed at the U.S. abandonment of its

1. Pancho Villa led northern revolutionaries to victory over the remnants of the old regime in 1914—then struggled with less success to shape the new regime. Reprinted by permission of Archivo General de la Nación, Sección Propiedad Artística y Literaria.

policy of neutrality, and convinced that Carranza had transformed Mexico into a colony of the United States, attacked Columbus, New Mexico, on March 7, 1916. That attack led to the punitive expedition sent by Woodrow Wilson to Mexico to try to capture Villa. After attempts to use the expedition to force the equivalent of a Platt Amendment on Mexico failed, the expedition withdrew unilaterally, giving a great victory to Mexico. It is thus not surprising that when the United States entered World War I, Mexico became a hostile neutral. The Carranza government attempted to play the German card, believing that a victorious Germany would create an effective bulwark against the United States.[17]

It is no coincidence that in this atmosphere of increasing tension with the United States, the Mexican Constituent Congress adopted the most radical antiforeign provisions of the Constitution of 1917. None of the measures, however, slowed the rapid American economic expansion into Mexico. This penetration had been accelerated by the progress of the Mexican Revolution before the outbreak of Word War I. Many Mexican land or mine owners, fearing expropriation by the revolutionary armies of Villa or Carranza, sold their properties to Americans at cut-rate prices. American buyers often forged close links to revolutionary leaders, confident that those leaders would respect the sales. They generally did, while also trying to limit them. Villa's measures were most effective, since he confiscated most holdings of wealthy Mexicans and placed them under government control, making it difficult, but not impossible, for Americans to acquire them. Carranza issued decrees prohibiting such sales, to limited effect.

After the outbreak of Word War I, and especially after the United States entered the war, American expansionism found new means. Before 1910 there were no U.S. intelligence agents in Mexico. In fact there was scarcely a military intelligence department in the American army. Intelligence had been provided by the U.S. military attachés, with other information obtained by the State Department, most of whose officials in Mexico were honorary and not permanent appointments. In late 1914, the U.S. War Department appointed the first American intelligence officer assigned to Mexico. Numbers drastically increased upon learning that German intelligence was active in Mexico, and again when the United States entered World War I. A network of American spies proliferated in Mexico.

Some belonged to the Military Intelligence Department, whose funds and membership grew enormously when the United States entered the war. Others were part of the Bureau of Investigation, predecessor of the FBI, which wanted significant input on intelligence activities in Mexico. Not only did this huge array of spies and agents attempt to assassinate Pancho Villa and to penetrate the Mexican army and the German networks in Mexico; it also worked to influence the economic development of the country.

To destroy German influence in Latin America, the United States set up so-called blacklists that included all German companies and companies with German partners. Not only did American businesses and those of countries allied with the United States refuse all relations with German companies, but Latin American companies doing business with Germans were automatically placed on the blacklist. A company wishing to do business with the United States had to submit data on its business partners and its day-to-day operations.

The United States thus obtained a huge amount of confidential data on the economies of the Latin American countries. In the case of Mexico, U.S. censors generated additional information. They opened all correspondence from Mexico destined for the United States or Europe as it passed through the United States. If it was sent by sea to Europe, most ships had to dock either in Cuba or in the West Indies, where the mail was intercepted by American censors in Cuba or British censors in the West Indies. Much of the information thus obtained was released to American businesses.

The most rapid expansion of American economic influence took place in the Mexican petroleum zones along the gulf coast. Manuel Peláez, an independent warlord closely allied with British and American oil interests, ruled most of the region. While Carranza's forces controlled the oil port of Tampico, American warships cruised offshore to ensure that his Constitutionalist government could not prevent the enormous increase in oil production and oil shipments from Mexico. As Carranza received at least limited revenues from petroleum exports, he never attempted to impose limits on production, exports, or U.S. controls.[18]

Amid wartime mobilization, Mexico might have profited from the rising prices for raw materials in the United States. Persistent revolutionary turmoil limited any gains. Revolutionary fighting destroyed much of the rail network and rolling stock essential to internal economic activity and exports to the United States. What remained of the Mexican railways was frequently interrupted by attacks from hostile factions or bandits, and by government appropriation to transport troops, severely restricting exports of minerals, agricultural products, and industrial goods. The only significant increase in exports came from minerals or agricultural products located close to the coast and to ports. Their revenues did have a significant impact on the continuing contests among social and political forces in Mexico. On the one hand, such revenues gave Carranza a means to hold off the factions still fighting him, though not enough to vanquish them. On the other hand, many of his generals used their control of railroads to exact exorbitant prices for both imports and exports, giving the generals the means to create semiautonomous armies loyal to them and to accumulate enormous wealth by cornering exports products. General Obregón all but monopolized the export of garbanzos from Sonora.[19]

In one exceptional case, revenues from the United States helped to carry out a profound social reform. In Yucatán the Carrancista governor Salvador Alvarado created a state monopoly to buy henequen from planters and sell it to the United States, where the price had risen because of a shortage of hemp caused by the end of sisal imports from German East Africa. With the help of export revenues, Alvarado kept the henequen industry productive while freeing long-coerced peons and greatly increasing their wages. Alvarado often reaped enough funds to create new social programs in Yucatán and send a surplus to help the consolidation of the Constitutionalist central government.[20]

A very different yet equally important consequence of the confluence of the Mexican Revolution and World War I was increasing Mexican migration to the United States. As the war economy boomed north of the border, Mexicans fleeing the dangerous disturbances of the revolution, or simply looking for a better life, had no problem finding jobs in the United States. The consequences of such migrations in Mexico are well known. The U.S. government made no attempts to grant protections to these migrants, and many of them returned to Mexico convinced revolutionaries—as in the famous case of Primo Tapia in Michoacán.[21]

While the United States was winning victories in the economic field and in intelligence—American agents penetrated the German intelligence services and cracked the code by which headquarters in Berlin instructed agents in Mexico—it was far less successful in another field that became important during the war: the propaganda war. The Great Powers' propaganda campaigns in Mexico were entirely new. As long as the Díaz dictatorship lasted and guaranteed the safety of foreigners, few cared about what ordinary Mexicans thought. The revolution changed that situation radically; from 1914 onward, no administration and no leader firmly controlled all of Mexico. Even Carranza, who by 1915 led the strongest faction and triumphed in the civil war against the radical forces of the Convention, never had firm hold over his military leaders.

Germany initiated the first great propaganda campaign. Aiming either to drive Mexico into a war with the United States or at least to keep it neutral should the Americans declare war on Germany, the Germans paid large bribes to most Mexican newspapers. One of the most important papers, *El Demócrata*, became dependent on German economic help. The revolution created economic difficulties for Mexican newspapers; desperate for funds, many were open to taking German payments. Currency devaluations brought monetary chaos; many German enterprises in Mexico deposited money with the German legation, which credited accounts in marks redeemable in Germany. It also gave the legation a supply of funds available to purchase press and propaganda support in Mexico.

The German minister to Mexico, Heinrich von Eckardt, was in charge of this campaign:

> Whereas we initially adopted only a defensive posture, countering the lies of the enemy, since the American declaration of war, I have been aggressively attacking the United States and the Allies, especially Great Britain. We could not merely promote the already existing sympathy of the Mexicans for a German policy barely known to them beforehand, nor could we content ourselves with keeping alive a mood that was momentarily favorable, but which could shift all too quickly. No, the policy of neutrality prescribed by Carranza for his government had to be placed on the one solid basis of the "odio de los gringos," of the hatred for the traditional enemy from the North that burns in the heart of every Mexican. The friendship felt for Germany, which even the

rebel leaders communicated to me through couriers in spite of my hostile attitude toward them, could only develop, and did develop, as a secondary result of this hatred. Ruthless attacks on President Wilson in articles we consistently placed in the press, and brochures, of which I should single out for special praise those of legation secretary Freiherr von Schoen, had the desired effect; the Mexican people curses the enemy which robbed it of wealthy provinces 70 years ago, and which to this day will not leave Mexico in peace; it considers every German victory as its own and rejoices at each setback of the "punitivos," that is, members of the "punitive expedition," as it calls the Pershing troops sent to Europe, referring to his Villa expedition of 1916.[22]

It was often skillful propaganda. At times, though, it boomeranged with articles appearing in the Mexican press announcing the destruction of New York, an insurrection in the American army, even the capitulation of England. Still, these exaggerations did not diminish the impact of German propaganda. The head of the U.S. propaganda campaign in Mexico clearly acknowledged German success:

> With the possible exception of Spain, in no other country outside of Mexico did the German propaganda attain such vigor and proportion, and nowhere was it waged with more determination and vicious mendacity. Events and conditions, which it is unnecessary to recapitulate, had caused the people and the government of Mexico to become highly responsive to overt or covert propaganda directed against the United States and in favor of Germany. The people, especially the masses, reacted favorably almost to a unit to the specious and insidious endeavors of the Germans to deceive them into believing that the triumph of the arms of the United States spelled menace and disaster to Mexico, and that a German victory would insure for them and their country every manner of political and economic benefit.[23]

The Americans and their allies attempted to counter German propaganda in several ways. They withheld advertisements by American and allied companies in newspapers that published pro-German articles. With one exception, they were unsuccessful. Carranza's orders encouraging German propaganda, plus German subsidies, kept most newspapers in the German camp. The exception was *El Universal*, which remained a pro-Allies voice—probably also supported by Carranza, who wanted to project an image of neutrality.

For the first time, movies were used as a propaganda tool. The Americans made sure that any theater that did not cooperate was cut off from Hollywood films and rapidly went bankrupt. In this field, the United States achieved limited success:

It goes almost without saying that among a population in which illiterates unfortunately predominate, motion pictures possess an enormous influence. . . . German agents saw to it diligently in the beginning that [our U.S. films] met with an uproariously hostile reception from the audiences to which they were shown. Frequently the police were summoned to restore order. Complaints to the authorities were made by our opponents that our pictures were inciting riots, and that the screening of portraits of the President, Gen. Pershing, and other notable personages, and of the American flag floating at the forefront of marching troops or at the masthead of naval units, constituted an insult to the Mexican government and people and were in violation of Mexico's neutrality. On various occasions our displays were halted until the local authorities could be convinced by tactful explanations, and by private exhibitions given for their benefit, that the pictures might properly be allowed on view. Gradually the demonstrations in the film theaters lessened, and finally ceased. The pictures won their way. The attitude of the public altered until after a few months we were repaid for our persistence by reports from our agents, telling of cheering and applause in place of hoots and yells, and even of "Vivas!" being given for the flag, the President, American war vessels, and American soldiers.[24]

On the whole, though, German propaganda was so effective that when on November 11 news arrived in Mexico that Germany had laid down its arms, even many well-informed Mexican newspaper editors refused to believe the reports. There is little doubt that German propaganda built on a very solid foundation in Mexico. The already strong anti-American feelings that existed on the eve of the revolution were enormously strengthened by the three American interventions that took place between 1913 and 1917: Henry Lane Wilson's active role in the 1913 overthrow of Francisco Madero; the occupation of Veracruz, Mexico's leading port, during key months of conflict in 1914 and 1915; and the punitive expedition that chased Pancho Villa in 1916.

While it is doubtful that American propaganda achieved any great sympathy for the United States, it probably helped communicate to substantial numbers of Mexicans the might and power of their northern neighbor. It would be revealing to examine to what degree the unprecedented propaganda war inspired subsequent Mexican governments in their desires to fuel feelings of nationalism in Mexico—a nationalism that always included important anti-Yankee content.

As in the rest of Latin America, World War I enormously increased the economic power and impact of the United States in Mexico. American oil and mining companies greatly expanded their holdings in Mexico.[25] Large

2. U.S. troops occupied the port of Veracruz in the pivotal summer of 1914; the Mexican revolution was a national and an international conflict. Reprinted by permission of Archivo General de la Nación, Sección Propiedad Artística y Literaria.

American enterprises bought properties at cut-rate prices from Mexican owners who feared expropriation. Small and medium-sized American companies unable to weather the storm of revolution also sold their holdings to more powerful large corporations. Meanwhile, the European countries were so weakened by World War I that none contemplated challenging U.S. predominance in Mexico until 1934, when the Germans once again began an economic offensive. U.S. predominance not only extended mining, landed, and other investments; it grew in banking and trade as well.

It did not include the political realm. In the postrevolutionary period, Mexican governments attempted again and again to curb the power of the United States. They invoked the revolutionary constitution of 1917 to limit the power of American corporations. Some Mexican administrations actively encouraged strikes against American corporations. Many attempted to increase the taxes paid by foreign companies. Again and again, the

United States protested, the U.S. government flexed its muscles, and Mexican administrations retreated, only to renew the offensive a short time later.

The social consequences of World War I for Mexico were complex and contradictory. In Cuba, its export economy earlier fused to the United States by the Spanish-American War and its aftermath, the U.S. wartime economic boom offered great opportunities for profit to the upper classes. Mexican entrepreneurs did not make such gains. Constant civil wars and interruptions of railway traffic created a situation that one of Mexico's most powerful industrial groups, the steel makers of Monterrey, characterized as "the lost opportunity of the First World War."[26]

The only Mexicans who profited substantially from Word War I were the warlords close to Carranza and Obregón. Conversely, perhaps paradoxically, Carranza's tense relations with the United States helped his greatest enemies, the revolutionary factions of Zapata, Villa, and the Cedillo brothers, to survive long after the Constitutionalists wrote the 1917 constitution that aimed to proclaim and consolidate their victory. Carranza never acquired sufficient arms in the United States to defeat his opponents. As a result, the shift from revolutionary civil war to regime consolidation proved a long and contested process that persisted through the 1920s and 1930s.

WORLD WAR II

While the methods used by the Great Powers to influence events in Mexico were in many ways similar to those used in World War I, World War II had a very different impact on Mexico. By the time the war began in the late 1930s, Mexico had finally consolidated a postrevolutionary regime. Notably, during the presidency of Lázaro Cárdenas that began in 1934, key demands for land redistribution and labor rights were met, and the beneficiaries organized in corporate-political organizations tied to the regime. In 1938, Cárdenas made the ultimate nationalist statement by expropriating the foreign companies (mostly U.S. and British) that controlled Mexican petroleum—while promoting a model of national urban and industrial development that created opportunities for diverse investors, Mexican and international. Mexico was more established politically, and more urbanizing and industrializing economically, when the second great war of the twentieth century broke out.

The effects of World War II in Mexico can be divided into three periods, with radically different consequences: a prewar period, lasting from 1936 to 1939, during which the rise of Nazi Germany foreshadowed many tendencies that would emerge once the war began; a second period, from the 1939 outbreak of the European war until the late-1941 Japanese attack on Pearl Harbor, which led a few months later to Mexico's active participation in the war; and a third period including the remainder of the war and the immediate postwar years.

Soon after Hitler took power in Germany, the Nazi regime began to challenge American supremacy in Latin America. It did so in five ways. First it promoted an enormous rise in trade with the Latin American countries through a unique German policy of barter. As a result of the global economic depression, markets for Latin America's raw materials in the industrial countries shrank enormously; Latin American exports fell dramatically. The Nazis, undertaking a tremendous rearmament in Germany, needed great quantities of raw materials from Latin America. Yet Germany, also pummeled by the world depression, did not have convertible currency to pay for Latin American imports. In response, the Germans proposed barter deals with Latin American countries. In exchange for raw materials, Germans would pay with so-called "Aski" marks, only redeemable in Germany for German industrial goods. The barter policy led to a huge increase in German trade with Latin America; in some countries, trade with Germany exceeded trade with the United States.[27]

While German banks and German enterprises did not have massive capital to invest in Latin America, there was one field of key strategic importance where the Germans mounted their second challenge to American supremacy. That was the airline industry. After Word War I, Germans set up a series of airlines in Latin America, notably in Colombia, Brazil, Bolivia, and Argentina. In the Nazi period, an intense battle for air supremacy in Latin America developed between Pan American Airways and German airlines. The U.S. government worried greatly about this German offensive, given the enormous strategic importance of airlines.

The third focus of Nazi Germany led to intense activity among the Germans and the descendants of Germans living in Latin America. On the whole, the Nazis proved successful in controlling most German organizations in Latin America and setting up tight networks to engage Germans and their descendants, culturally, politically, and economically.

The fourth strategy of the Nazis was to attempt to gain the support of right-wing groups in Latin America. They succeeded in gaining great sympathy not only among many right-wing parties but from key Latin American dictators as well. In perhaps the clearest example, until 1937 Brazil's populist dictator Getulio Vargas was well disposed toward the Nazis.[28]

Finally, Nazi Germany sought to revive the ties that imperial Germany had established with many Latin American armies, notably in Argentina,

Chile, and Bolivia. These activities greatly worried the U.S. administration in view of the increasing probability that war would erupt between the United States and Germany.

While trade between Mexico and Germany increased by leaps and bounds, all the other forms of German expansionism had limited effects on Mexico. No German airline established itself there, and Germany never maintained close links with the Mexican army. When the Nazis asserted control of the German residents in Mexico, their number was so small (about six thousand) that they constituted no threat to Mexico. In that respect, Mexico's case was very different from that of Brazil, where hundreds of thousands of Germans and their descendants maintained strong ties to Germany. The Germans did manage to influence the Mexican Right, but often that influence was more indirect than direct. Mexican conservatives might sympathize with the Nazis, but their main allegiance (given their deep Catholicism) was to the Spanish Falange. And the Nazis could count on no sympathy from the Mexican government. President Cárdenas and his supporters strongly opposed the Nazis. Cárdenas, after all, staunchly backed the Spanish republic; his own reformist-socialist ideology contrasted with Nazi visions.

Nevertheless the German threat opened a window of opportunity for the Cárdenas government, an opportunity it used far more effectively than Carranza had during World War I. When the Cárdenas administration began expropriating American-owned landholdings in Mexico and challenged the United States by nationalizing the large American oil properties, the State Department in Washington was incensed: "I have to deal with these communists down there, I have to carry out international law," Secretary of State Cordell Hull wrote to Secretary of the Treasury Robert Morgenthau.[29] Hull complained bitterly that his hands were tied by President Franklin Roosevelt's policies: "We have a lot of problems in Mexico and you know the President and [U.S. ambassador Josephus] Daniels have given the Mexicans the impression that they can go right ahead and flaunt every thing in our face."[30]

Morgenthau did not agree with Hull and supported Roosevelt's policies. Both Roosevelt and Morgenthau realized that in 1938 strategic considerations were far more important than the interests of American companies. Just as Cárdenas nationalized oil, Hitler annexed Austria and threatened Czechoslovakia. Even as Cárdenas nationalized U.S. oil interests, in strategic terms he remained a firm ally of the United States and an outspoken foe of Hitler.

Mexico was the only nation in the world that protested against Germany's annexation of Austria. Roosevelt and Morgenthau realized that if they turned against Cárdenas, the Mexican Right, with strong pro-Axis sympathies, could take power, and the United States would face a direct threat to security along its border. For this reason, the United States continued to support Cárdenas—even when he decided to sell oil to the Axis powers to break the boycott that the U.S. and British oil companies imposed on Mexico.

When war broke out in Europe in September 1939, Mexico once more, as during World War I, became the scene of a major conflict between Germany and its allies, on one hand, and Great Britain, France, and now also the United States, on the other. As they had done in World War I, the Germans sent teams of secret agents to Mexico. They proved as inept as their predecessors thirty years before, as they were rapidly neutralized by Allied intelligence services. New blacklists were set up, and Mexican authorities expropriated German companies. As during World War I, the Germans had more success with propaganda activities. Under their influence, a large number of Mexican newspapers voiced admiration for Hitler, or at least demanded a policy of strict neutrality from the Mexican government.[31]

What differentiated the situation in World War II from that in World War I was that the Mexican government was not neutral. Unlike the fledgling Carranza administration, the established governments of Cárdenas and his successor Manuel Ávila Camacho were clearly and decidedly pro-Allies and pro–United States. One of the most important consequences of the outbreak of World War II was to rapidly reverse the internal political situation of Mexico. In the years before the war, the Left had been the preponderant force in Mexico, though that preponderance began to weaken in 1938 when Cárdenas's reforms led to rising inflation and increasing opposition. Cárdenas responded by favoring a more moderate successor, Ávila Camacho. The Left was further weakened when, after the outbreak of the war in September 1939, the Cardenista left coalition split. While Cárdenas and many others continued to back the allies, the Communist Party and its supporters, influenced by Stalin's nonaggression pact with Hitler, declared the war an imperialist campaign and demanded Mexican neutrality. On this issue, Mexican communists and the Mexican Right coincided. The FBI and other American agencies in Mexico coined the term "Communazis," simultaneously attacking Nazis and the Mexican Left. Once Hitler attacked the Soviet Union, however, the position of Mexican communists and their allies changed dramatically. They became staunch supporters of Mexican involvement in World War II. U.S. opposition to the Mexican Left continued, however. The intelligence services continued their attacks, though more surreptitiously.[32]

Ultimately, one of the most important consequences of World War II was the weakening, nearly the political elimination, of the Mexican Left. The process affected every aspect of Mexican political life. It was notably evident in one area that had been a domain of radicalism during the Cárdenas era: education. Luis Sánchez Pontón, Cárdenas's secretary of education and an advocate of socialist education, gave way under Ávila Camacho to an extreme conservative, Octavio Véjar Vázquez. Véjar Vázquez aimed to expel communist teachers from the ministry and from the schools. Military officers found increasing roles in teaching. And Véjar Vázquez cut funds to the Colegio de México, a distinguished institute of higher learning in which Spanish republicans played key roles.[33]

The most important, successful, and lasting way in which the government limited the influence of the Left was by undermining labor radicalism. Among the national labor organizations, the government threatened and reduced the influence of the radical CTM (Confederacion de Trabajadores Mexicanos) by reviving the CROM (Confederacion Regional de Obreros Mexicanos) and offering new recognition to its longtime leader Luis N. Morones—all to pressure CTM leaders. When the radical Vicente Lombardo Toledano resigned as general secretary of the CTM to become president of the Latin American Federation of Labor (CTAL), his successor, Fidel Velázquez, became the pliant ally of an increasingly conservative Mexican government. For the duration of the war, he signed a no-strike pact with the government and business. Workers who tried to strike when real wages fell because of wartime inflation were fired, sometimes killed.

A similar process of intimidation and repression occurred within the CNC (Confederación Nacional Campesina), the great agrarian federation that organized the beneficiaries of land reform to support Cárdenas. The transformation of the mass popular organizations in turn produced a profound change in the character of the ruling party, the Partido de la Revolución Mexicana (PRM). While president, Cárdenas had played a decisive role within the party; still, it retained strong elements of a genuine coalition of popular forces. Amid the war and the regime's turn to the right, it became a ruling party that controlled popular organizations with an iron fist. At the grassroots level, workers and peasants who resisted might be imprisoned or shot, though the level of repression remained limited.

There is no simple explanation for the profound wartime transformation of Mexican political life. It would be wrong to attribute the changes solely, even primarily, to the personalities of President Manuel Ávila Camacho and his influential, extremely conservative, and extremely corrupt brother, Maximino. The enormous growth of a new bourgeoisie did contribute to the trend toward conservatism. In contrast to the situation during World War I, Mexico's upper classes were in a position to reap genuine profits from the 1940s wartime boom in the United States. As prices of raw materials rose and exports to the United States grew, the profits of these transactions helped to create new Mexican businesses and to strengthen the influence of existing companies. The Mexican steel industry, for instance, greatly increased its capacity and exported more and more products to the United States. Not surprisingly, the new and reinforced bourgeoisie worked to curb the influence of independent labor organizations and to prevent strikes.

A growing influence of the United States in Mexico also contributed decisively to the undermining of the Left. Once the United States entered World War II, the Roosevelt administration did everything in its power to defuse the main source of conflict between Mexico and the United States: the still-contested petroleum nationalization of 1938. The U.S. government brokered an agreement between Mexico and the expropriated American companies in which the companies recognized the nationalization of oil in return for relatively small compensation.

Economic integration between the two countries simultaneously grew by leaps and bounds, as did Mexico's dependence on the United States. Trade increased, along with American investments in Mexico. Another source of Mexican dependence on the United States was the Bracero Program. As during World War I, the United States needed Mexican labor to replace Americans drafted into the army—this time on a far larger scale. In contrast to World War I, the United States instituted a program to guarantee Mexican workers a minimum wage and minimal working conditions. The United States also made sure that a portion of Bracero laborers' wages was remitted to Mexico. Thus Mexican dependence on the United States increased even more. It is thus not surprising that the Mexican government tolerated the presence of American intelligence organizations whose activities worked not only against representatives of Germany, Japan, and Italy but also against the Mexican Left.

Yet it is doubtful that the transition to the right would have been so smooth if significant segments on the Mexican Left had not refused to resist these pressures. Neither the Mexican Communist Party nor Lombardo Toledano and his supporters voiced any strong opposition to government policies. This was largely due to the influence of the Soviet Union, which made it clear to its supporters in Mexico that winning the war should be the main priority and any labor conflict or conflict with the United States should be avoided.

Nor did Lázaro Cárdenas call for any resistance to the conservative policies of his successor. The roots of his attitude were complex. On the one hand, he believed that as a former president he should not be actively involved in politics; after all, he had exiled former president Calles precisely for attempting to influence his policies. Perhaps more important, Cárdenas accepted appointment as secretary of defense in the Ávila Camacho administration. There he had decisive input on what he considered one of the most important problems that Mexico faced: how to retain national independence in spite of the alliance with the United States.

For example, Cárdenas worked to prevent the United States from securing military bases in Mexico. In 1942 the United States asked the Mexican government for permission to establish a U.S. Air Force base at Tehuantepec. The Mexican government replied that it could do so only if the bases were under the command of Mexican officers. U.S. authorities were convinced that they could easily circumvent such a rule: "The actual significance of the word 'command,' as used here, need not concern us for the present, since the entire matter is open to further discussion. Under the most unfavorable circumstances, it can mean no more than that the Mexican flag will fly over the establishment and Mexican authorities will exercise nominal command over the area and its permanent fixtures."[34]

The United States also wanted to build a road in Baja California and set up military bases there. In 1943 these proposals collapsed, largely because of the appointment of Cárdenas as minister of national defense: "The general strategic situation in the Pacific underwent a decided change as a result of our successes in the South Seas. This and other considerations made it appear more and more questionable whether the War Department should proceed further along these lines. Among these considerations was the naming of General Lazaro Cárdenas as Minister of National Defense of Mexico and the full realization by representatives of the War Department that at no time except in dire emergency would units of U.S. air or ground forces be permitted to use such defense facilities as might be constructed in Mexican territory."[35] While Cárdenas thus prevented the United States from acquiring military bases in Mexico, bases that might have become permanent, he could not prevent the rapid shift to the right by the Ávila Camacho administration as the Cold War broke out.

There were great similarities and significant differences between Mexico's situations in the years after World War I and World War II. Álvaro Obregón and Plutarco Elías Calles, the presidents who dominated Mexico from 1920 to 1934, had ideologies similar to those of Manuel Ávila Camacho and his successor Miguel Alemán, who ruled from 1940 to 1952 (with the significant exception of Calles's anticlericalism). None believed in parliamentary democracy, though all, in one way or another, allowed limited opposition. None believed in land reform, and all hoped to domesticate organized labor by supporting official unions: the CROM in the cases of

Obregón and Calles, the CROM and the CTM in the cases of Ávila Camacho and Alemán.

Yet the situations that Mexican rulers faced in the aftermaths of the two world wars were fundamentally different. The state that Obregón claimed in 1920 was weak; essentially, he had to build a regime from scratch. Warlords of limited and uncertain loyalties ruled the army. As a result, Obregón and later Calles had to rely in part on popular organizations to counter constant military coups. Thus, during the 1920s, popular agrarian and labor organizations gained strength, often despite the presidents in power. By contrast, the state that Ávila Camacho inherited in 1940 was far stronger and better organized; in addition, it was linked to a powerful ruling political party. The warlords had disappeared; the government had firm control of a depoliticized military. In the 1920s, Mexico's ruling class had been weakened by revolution and divided between the old upper class and the revolutionary parvenus. After World War II, the ruling class was far more powerful and far more united.

As a result, relations between Mexico and the United States were completely different in 1920 and 1945. In 1920, Mexico was in desperate economic straits. Much of the country's infrastructure had been devastated by the revolutionary wars. Little foreign investment flowed into the country. Meanwhile, foreign powers demanded huge reparations from the Mexican government for damages suffered in the revolution. The one potential source of wealth for Mexico was oil, and it was in the hands of foreign companies that paid minimal taxes on the enormous riches pumped out of the country. When the government attempted to increase these taxes, tensions flared with the United States and other countries.

In contrast, in 1945 the Mexican economy was booming. It had no debts to the United States, and oil had ceased to be a matter of contention. After the end of World War I, the United States dissolved much of its intelligence apparatus; after World War II it remained very active in Mexico. It is not surprising, then, that in contrast to the situation in the aftermath of World War I, the Mexican government offered far less resistance to the growing hegemony of the United States. At times, it appeared that Mexican authorities and U.S. interests worked together to marginalize popular organizations and the political Left. Mexico was increasingly drawn into the Cold War—and despite the persistence of revolutionary nationalist rhetoric, into the orbit of the United States.

International wars have shaped Mexico's history to a degree far greater than has been the case in most Latin American countries. The effects were always paradoxical. The consequences of the three wars in which Mexico was directly involved between 1810 and 1867 were disastrous. As a result of the Mexican-American War, Mexico lost half of its territory, and the foreign wars in general enormously slowed Mexico's economic development. On the other hand, these wars helped to incorporate the popular classes into the political life of the country, giving them an unprecedented degree of power until the latter part of the nineteenth century. As a result, Mexico's village communities were able to keep a large part of the land that they had possessed when Mexico became independent.

At the same time, the international wars that Mexico fought and the participation of the popular classes in these wars created a national consciousness at a time when Mexico lacked the elements that in other countries created such consciousness. The country was not integrated, popular education was little developed, and the weak national governments were incapable of generating the kind of national image that later strong regimes created. One can hypothesize that this early national consciousness contributed to the fact that Mexico did not fragment in the way that other parts of Latin America did. Finally, the second and third international wars that Mexico waged between 1846 and 1867 anticipated the consequences of the three later wars in which Mexico was only indirectly involved: all led to increasing U.S. power and Mexican dependence.

The Spanish-American War, World War I, and World War II all had important consequences for the history of Mexico. On first examination, those consequences seem different: The Spanish-American War warned Mexicans of the rising assertion of U.S. hegemony, economic and military. Even the Díaz regime sought policies that aimed to limit that hegemony. The failure of those policies helped provoke Francisco Madero's political challenge that began the revolution of 1910. The same war helped create the boom of the Morelos sugar economy that helped set off Zapata's agrarian movement—which soon radicalized that revolution.

World War I, begun with Mexico deep in revolution, on the one hand gave Mexico a large degree of autonomy from direct U.S. political and military intrusion (both the occupation of Veracruz and the punitive expedition to capture Pancho Villa ended in quasi-unconditional retreats by the U.S. government). On the other, it brought unprecedented, indirect foreign military, diplomatic, intelligence, and propaganda interventions in Mexican affairs. And despite the deep nationalist goals of the victorious

Constitutionalists, the end of World War I brought the collapse of European power in the Americas, opening the way for U.S. hegemony. The victory of Mexican revolutionary nationalism thus came with the consolidation of U.S. power in North America.

World War II exploded as Mexicans consolidated their regime and a developmentalist economy. Both Mexican politics and global alliances turned Mexico toward cooperation with the United States. During the war, the Mexican economy boomed and became more integrated with, and dependent on, the United States. The Mexican regime turned to the right, worked to control peasants and workers, and joined in the emerging Cold War.

Each wartime conjuncture proved different, yet all contributed to limit the independence of Mexico and draw it into the orbit of the United States. Only in the context of the three wars can we understand how the era of the radical, agrarian, and nationalist Mexican Revolution was also the time of the consolidation of U.S. hegemony in North America. And only in that context can we understand the Mexican Revolution's turn to the right.

NOTES

1 John H. Coatsworth, "Patterns of Rural Rebellion in Latin America: Mexico in Comparative Perspective," in *Riot, Rebellion and Revolution: Rural Social Conflicts in Mexico*, ed. Friedrich Katz (Princeton, N.J.: Princeton University Press, 1988), 21.

2 Friedrich Katz, ed., *Riot, Rebellion and Revolution: Rural Social Conflicts in Mexico* (Princeton, N.J.: Princeton University Press, 1988), 3, 521; John Tutino, *From Insurrection to Revolution in Mexico: Social Bases of Agrarian Violence, 1750–1940* (Princeton, N.J.: Princeton University Press, 1986).

3 Peter F. Guardino, *Peasants, Politics and the Formation of Mexico's Nation State: Guerrero, 1800–1857* (Stanford, Calif.: Stanford University Press, 1996).

4 John H. Coatsworth, "Obstacles to Economic Growth in Nineteenth Century Mexico," *American Historical Review* 1, no. 83 (1978): 80.

5 Andrés Ortega, "España y Estados Unidos," *El Nacional*, April 25, 1898.

6 Tomás Pérez Viejo, "La Guerra Hispano-Estadounidense del 98 en la prensa mexicana," *Historia Mexicana* 50, no. 2 (October–December 2000): 295.

7 Francisco Bulnes, *The Whole Truth about Mexico* (New York: M. Bulnes, 1916), 125–27.

8 Papers of the German Foreign Office Mexico I, vol. 17, Wangenheim to Bülow, January 7, 1907.

9 Archives du Ministère des Archives Ètrangères, Paris Mexique, vol. 17, Blondel to Delcassè, April 28, 1901.

10 Friedrich Katz, *The Secret War in Mexico* (Chicago: Chicago University Press, 1981).

11 Ibid.

12 Daniel Cosío Villegas, *Historia moderna de México: El Porfiriato, política exterior segunda parte* (Mexico City: Editorial Hermes, 1963), 291–94.

13 See John Womack, *Zapata and the Mexican Revolution* (New York: Alfred A. Knopf, 1969).

14 For the two very different points of view on this subject, see Jonathan C. Brown, *Oil and Revolution in Mexico* (Berkeley and Los Angeles: University of California Press, 1993), 97–99, 173–76. Brown is firmly convinced that no oil interests had supported Madero. For a contrary view, see John Skirius, "Railroad, Oil and Other Foreign Interests in the Mexican Revolution," *Journal of Latin American Studies* 35, no. 1 (February 2003): 22.

15 Katz, *The Secret War in Mexico.*

16 Arthur S. Link, *Woodrow Wilson and the Progressive Era, 1910–1917* (New York: Harper and Row, 1954), 134.

17 Katz, *The Secret War in Mexico*, chap. 10.

18 Brown, *Oil and Revolution in Mexico*, chaps. 3–4; Javier Garciadiego, "Revolución constitucionalista y contrarrevolución: Movimientos reaccionarios en México" (Ph.D. diss., El Colegio de México, 1981); Ana María Serna Rodríguez, "Oil Revolution and Agrarian Society in Northern Veracruz: Manuel Peláez and Rural Life in the 'Golden Lane,' 1910–1928" (Ph.D. diss., University of Chicago, 2004).

19 John Tutino, "Revolutionary Confrontation, 1913–1917: Regional Factions, Class Conflicts, and the New National State," in *Provinces of the Revolution: Essays on Regional Mexican History, 1910–1929*, ed. Thomas Benjamin and Mark Wasserman (Albuquerque: University of New Mexico Press, 1990), 41–70.

20 Gilbert Joseph, *Revolution from Without: Yucatán, Mexico and the United States, 1880–1924* (New York: Cambridge University Press, 1982).

21 Paul Friedrich, *Agrarian Revolt in a Mexican Village* (Chicago: Chicago University Press, 1977).

22 Katz, *The Secret War in Mexico*, 450.

23 George Creel, *How We Advertised America: The First Telling of the Amazing Story of the Committee on Public Information That Carried the Gospel of Americanism to Every Corner of the Globe* (New York: Harper and Brothers, 1920), 303.

24 James R. Mock and Cedric Larson, *Words That Won the War: The Story of the Committee on Public Information, 1917–1919* (Princeton, N.J.: Princeton University Press, 1939), 327.

25 Robert Freeman Smith, *The United States and Revolutionary Nationalism in Mexico, 1916–1932* (Chicago: Chicago University Press, 1972).

26 Mario Cerutti, *Propietarios, empresarios y empresas en el norte de México* (Mexico City: Siglo XXI, 2000), 139.

27 Friedrich Katz, *Raíces y razones, ensayos mexicanos: Algunos rasgos esenciales de la política alemana en América Latina, 1898–1941* (Mexico City: Alianza Editorial, 1994), 363–456; Reiner Pomerin, *Das Dritte Reich und Lateinamerika: Die deutsche Politik gegenüber Süd- und Mittelamerika, 1939–1942* (Dusseldorf: Droste Verlag, 1977); Brigida von Mentz, Verena Radkau, Daniela Spenser, and Ricardo Pérez Montfort, *Los empresarios alemanes, el Tercer Reich y la oposición de derecha a Cárdenas* (Mexico City: CIESAS, Ediciones de la Casa Chata, 1988); Friedrich Schuler, *Mexico between Hitler and Roosevelt: Mexican Foreign Relations*

in the Age of Lázaro Cárdenas (Albuquerque: University of New Mexico Press, 1998).

28 Stanley Hilton, *Brazil and the Great Powers, 1930–1939: The Politics of Trade Rivalry* (Austin: University of Texas Press, 1975).

29 Robert Dallek, *Franklin D. Roosevelt and American Foreign Policy, 1939–1945* (New York: Oxford University Press, 1979), 126.

30 Ibid.

31 José Luis Ortiz Garza, *México en guerra: La historia secreta de los negocios entre empresarios mexicanos de la comunicación, los nazis y E.U. Espejo de México* (Mexico City: Planeta, 1989).

32 Stephen R. Niblo, *War, Diplomacy and Development: The United States and Mexico, 1938–1954* (Wilmington, Del.: Scholarly Resources, 1995).

33 Stephen R. Niblo, *Mexico in the 1940s: Modernity, Politics and Corruption* (Wilmington, Del.: Scholarly Resources, 1999).

34 María Emilia Paz, *Strategy, Security, and Spies: Mexico and the U.S. as Allies in World War II* (University Park: Pennsylvania State University Press, 1997), 211–12.

35 Ibid., 219.

✷ The Revolutionary
Capacity of Rural Communities
Ecological Autonomy and Its Demise

JOHN TUTINO ✷

In 1810 and again after 1910, rural communities pressed insurgencies that endured for years to fuel Mexico's two decades of revolution. Elites might offer organization and leadership, along with visions of past problems and future solutions. They led the regimes that were consolidated as insurgencies and revolutions waned. But without the massive, widespread, and enduring insurgencies of rural communities, the conflicts that began in 1810 and 1910 would not have been revolutionary confrontations—societal conflagrations that led to profound economic, political, social, and cultural changes. Insurgent assertions of rural communities made Mexico's revolutions revolutionary.

In *From Insurrection to Revolution in Mexico*, I offered an analytical model and a historical overview of the origins of popular insurgencies from the war for independence that began in 1810, through the regional uprisings that recurred in waves throughout the nineteenth century, to their explosion into national revolution in 1910. That analysis focused on regionally varying and historically changing social relations of production: access to land, the organization of production and labor, and the ways they structured the lives of families and rural communities. A dual emphasis oriented my analysis: grievances rooted in threats to families' material welfare, and to their autonomy, security, and mobility, emerged as root causes of popular insurgencies. Yet for grievances to produce insurgencies, popular communities awaited opportunities: clear signs of elite division, regime breakdown, or other conflicts indicating that power holders were weak or distracted and that insurgency could begin without quick repression. Insurgent communities then entered national conflicts, pressing their own agendas—notably land and community autonomy—into larger struggles.[1]

The analysis of grievances rooted in changing social relations of production, and of opportunities emerging in the domains of power, remains essential to understanding popular assertions and revolutionary confrontations in Mexico and elsewhere. As many scholars have reminded me, such analysis becomes more persuasive when contending cultural visions are seen as essential to the production and defense of power and the perception and understanding of grievances.[2] Recent research has convinced me, too, that autonomy, security, and mobility operated as patriarchal constructs: when solidified, they first benefited peasant patriarchs; when threatened, challenges were often experienced first as assaults on patriarchy. Thus it was mostly men, facing deeply uncertain prospects of life as even poor, dependent patriarchs, who took the risks of insurgency.[3]

Still, the model of grievances and opportunities leading to insurgencies that fueled revolutions requires a more basic revision: recognition and analysis of the historical importance of the revolutionary capacity of rural communities. Revolutionary capacity focuses on the ability of communities to live, work, and fight outside and against established organizations of power and production, sustaining mobilizations long enough to force fundamental changes. An emphasis on capacity becomes essential when analysis shifts from the origins of insurgencies to their processes and outcomes. *From Insurrection to Revolution* focused on grievances and opportunities because the study emphasized the origins of uprisings—and because the revolutionary capacity of Mexican communities persisted through the era from 1750 to 1940.

When I turned my analysis to Mexico in the late twentieth century, the fundamental importance of revolutionary capacity became clear. Grievances rooted in deteriorating social relations of production were as severe, if not worse, than in the run up to Mexico's two historic revolutions. Opportunities rooted in alternating waves of economic collapse and political conflict recurred from 1980 to 2000. Yet Mexico has not seen the massive, multiregional, and long-enduring popular insurgencies that marked the revolutions of 1810 and 1910, many conflicts in between, and the Cristero revolt of the late 1920s. The Chiapas uprising of 1994, fundamentally important to Mexico's recent transition, appears brief and limited in the shadow of Mexico's historical insurgencies. No leader or faction contending for national power has appealed to popular insurgents—as Hidalgo and Morelos did in 1810, and Francisco Madero did in 1910. Instead, a pervasive discourse of democracy—electoral participation—as the inevitable domain of conflict and change now defines Mexican political culture. The promoters of democratization deserve much credit for that shift. But beneath their success lies a fundamental structural transformation: the demise and eventual collapse of the revolutionary capacity of Mexican communities.

Revolutionary capacity, the ability to create and sustain broad and enduring violent opposition to the prevailing order, requires organization, vision, and material sustenance. The importance of organization, of leadership, coordination, and communication, is widely recognized. Too often, analysts construct leaders as the essential force in revolutions. The best studies, notably John Womack Jr.'s *Zapata and the Mexican Revolution*, Felipe Avila Espinosa's *Los orígenes del zapatismo*, and Friedrich Katz's *The Life and Times of Pancho Villa*,[4] examine leaders in their dynamic and changing relationships with the communities they seek to lead and the forces they have to fight.

Visions and ideologies also matter to revolutionary capacity. They may motivate key leaders, recruit popular support, and help cement relations between leaders and bases in diverse communities. Revolutionary visions tend to be utopian—constructions of ideal futures (sometimes rooted in idealized pasts). They ask people to kill and face death, moral and physical risks that few would undertake for promises of modest improvement. Utopian visions help people grappling with real grievances and facing limited opportunities focus on radical gains. One result is the almost inevitable evaluation of revolutions as failures. In Mexico, as elsewhere, revolutions have generated real gains for popular communities. But those gains, negotiated in real and hard-fought worlds of production and power, cannot approach the promises of revolutionary utopias. Revolutions energized by utopian ideologies sooner or later face disillusion, helping elites and their allies assert the absurdity of revolutionary efforts. Still, utopian visions have helped drive many revolutions to their limited outcomes.

In Mexico, leadership and ideological visions played distinctly different roles in the two eras of revolution. During the wars for independence, while debates about monarchical persistence, popular sovereignty, and liberalism energized conflicts about regime power and the right to rule, key regional insurgencies drove popular participations. Yet those insurgencies lacked leaders beyond local contexts, and ideologies beyond the defense of local autonomy, family welfare, and religious traditions.[5] The absence (or invisibility?) of coordinating leaders and defining ideologies helps explain why those insurgencies long escaped historical recognition and analysis. In contrast, during the revolution that began in 1910, insurgent communities generated leadership focused on Emiliano Zapata and Pancho Villa; ideologies of agrarian community rights began in Zapata's Plan de Ayala and marked pivotal debates through years of revolutionary warfare and decades of political consolidation.

Ultimately, leadership, organization, and vision are but part of revolutionary capacity. They cannot sustain revolutionary mobilizations in the absence of material sustenance. Historically, the ecological autonomy of rural communities has been essential to the material bases and eventual outcomes of revolutions in Mexico, as elsewhere.[6] The concept of ecological autonomy, emphasizes the ability of rural communities to sustain themselves and insurgent fighters independently of the structures of power and production they seek to transform. The ability to produce basic subsistence crops along with livestock for food, transportation, and combat, and to turn basic tools of everyday life—machetes, hatchets, rifles—into weapons of guerrilla war, is the essence of ecological autonomy. Such autonomy is never absolute. But for rural communities with control of, or access to, essential natural resources, tools, and the cultural knowledge to generate sustenance and maintain basic weapons, autonomy can be the key to revolutionary participation.

In the regions that became Mexico after 1810, rural communities maintained such autonomy from time immemorial through the middle of the twentieth century. In the face of devastating, disease-driven depopulation, ecological autonomy was reconsolidated in the aftermath of the Spanish conquest. It sustained insurgent communities in revolutionary confrontations from 1810 to 1930. Then, population explosion, urbanization, and the industrialization of agriculture combined to erode that autonomy. Since 1940, Mexican rural communities have lost the capacity to sustain revolutions. That historic watershed is amply documented, but little recognized. While exploitations and injustices deepen and economic and political crises persist, no widespread, enduring popular mobilizations have developed to create a revolutionary confrontation. The end of ecological autonomy is, I believe, the key to understanding why deepening grievances and repeated opportunities have not generated revolutionary mobilizations in the enduring crisis that Mexicans have lived since 1980.

This essay explores the history of ecological autonomy in New Spain and Mexico from the aftermath of the Spanish conquest until the present. It details how that autonomy proved essential to the revolutions of 1810 and 1910—and how its demise restricts the potential for revolution as the twenty-first century begins. It suggests a complex, sometimes paradoxical relationship between ecological autonomy, social stability, and insurgency. Ample ecological autonomy limits grievances that might stimulate conflict. Limited reductions of autonomy often led to stabilizing adaptations.

Rapid, more disruptive threats to autonomies created grievances that stimulated insurgencies. Yet insurgents required at least remnant autonomies, or ample recreations, to sustain mobilizations. Finally, the end of ecological autonomy created deep grievances—and undermined the capacity to sustain revolutionary mobilizations.

My analysis also explores the complex relations between ecological autonomies and political citizenship. They were closely linked yet locally restricted in colonial times, then deeply contested amid the nation building of the nineteenth century. After the twentieth-century revolution, they separated. The new regime granted landed autonomies and limited effective citizenship. Then the late twentieth century brought final separation: ecological autonomies vanished, while promises of electoral citizenship organized political life.

The democratization currently celebrated and debated in Mexico restricts conflict and the possibility of change to the limited domain of periodic balloting. This analysis suggests that electoral democratization is less a utopian gain, and very much an outcome of a historical transformation that has radically reduced the potential for popular power. Is revolution now impossible? We cannot know. But the end of ecological autonomy suggests that if revolution comes to Mexico again, it will differ fundamentally from the conflicts of 1810 and 1910—conflicts in which the ecological autonomy of rural communities allowed them to press popular agendas to important if limited (non-utopian) outcomes.

CONQUEST, DEPOPULATION, AND THE CONSOLIDATION OF ECOLOGICAL AUTONOMY

For all their destruction, the conquest and devastating depopulation that created New Spain in the sixteenth century ultimately reconstituted the ecological autonomies that had sustained cultivating communities across Mesoamerica since time immemorial. That founding paradox of colonial society remains a key to the long, often conflictive, history of New Spain and then Mexico. The reconsolidation of ecological autonomies in surviving communities provided the bases for those communities to contest, often to limit, their colonial subordination—and eventually to participate in the revolutionary conflicts that created and shaped the Mexican nation.

Since the invention of agriculture, families in communities across Mesoamerica raised maize, frijoles, chiles, and other crops and made cloth, pottery, and other basic craft goods, to consume, to trade in local markets, and to pay as tribute goods to local lords and conquering warlords. Families organized in cultivating communities were the foundation of life from the highland basins around the ancient imperial cities of Teotihuacán, Tula, and Tenochtitlan (modern Mexico City), west to Pátzcuaro and beyond, east to Cholula and the Gulf coast, and far to the south through Mixtec and Zapotec zones of Oaxaca to the Maya societies of Yucatán, Chiapas, and Guatemala. In that broad zone of Mesoamerican civilization, as regional states and expansive empires rose and fell, cultivating communities persisted as the bedrock of society.[7]

From the Bajío northward, Europeans encountered a zone of people without states that extended across an arid plateau country. The sparse, mobile, and fiercely independent inhabitants, whom the Mexica (Aztecs) maligned as Chichimecas (sons of dogs), also lived with fundamental ecological autonomies. Some communities knew agriculture, cultivating along rivers and when rains allowed. Others were hunters and gatherers—taking what a dry landscape provided. Many combined limited cultivation with hunting and gathering to sustain hard lives in a challenging environment. But they maintained an often-fierce independence grounded in ecological autonomies—the direct production of sustenance by families and small, often mobile communities. In zones with few lords and fewer states, there was little tradition of producers providing tributes or labor to rulers.[8]

Spaniards came to conquer the states and communities of Mesoamerica. When they discovered vast veins of silver far to the north at Zacatecas in the 1540s, they faced the challenge of extending European power into Chichimeca country. In deeply different processes of conquest and colonization, during the second half of the sixteenth century, two contrasting colonial orders emerged. In Mesoamerica, states were conquered, lords accommodated or faced destruction, everyone faced disease and depopulation—and communities grounded in ecological autonomies survived as the foundation of the colonial order. In the arid zones to the north, Chichimecas faced disease and depopulation, fought long wars of resistance to the European incursion, and in the end faced destruction or survival on the fringes of the colonial order. There the power of silver and the devastation of indigenous peoples led to a new society of immigrants—Europeans, Mesoamericans, and enslaved Africans—who forged an unprecedented commercial civilization.

As a result, New Spain incorporated two fundamentally different colonial orders: Spanish Mesoamerica, built on the conquered ruins of indigenous states, with indigenous communities as its foundation; and Spanish North America, dynamically commercial, Atlantic in its social and cultural composition, and with few independent communities. Ecological autonomy was strengthened in Spanish Mesoamerica, challenged in Spanish North America.[9]

Spaniards conquered Mesoamerican states using European weapons against indigenous states divided by entrenched antagonisms—while smallpox and other Old World diseases devastated indigenous regimes, religions, and communities. The population fell by one-half within decades, by 90 percent or more in a century. Spaniards claimed regime power legitimated by Catholic Christianity, and slowly began commercial production. It took a century to create Spanish Mesoamerica. During that time, Mesoamerican communities shrank, resisted, adapted—and endured with essential ecological autonomies.

From the 1520s to the 1570s, *encomienda* grants regulated relations between Spaniards and Mesoamerican communities. They gave a favored conqueror rights to tribute goods and work services from designated communities. Encomiendas were administered through the brokerage of indigenous lords. They left indigenous families on customary lands, producing for sustenance, trading in local markets, and paying tributes that now sustained local lords and Spanish overlords. Encomienda labor services brought no compensation; exploitation was possible because indigenous families continued to sustain themselves. Amid disease and disruption, the encomiendas that ruled early Spanish Mesoamerica left the ecological autonomies of cultivating communities in place. In important ways, encomiendas were Spanish legal devices that turned the Mesoamerican tribute system to benefit the first conquerors.[10]

The depopulation that devastated Mesoamerican communities undermined that first colonial order and reinforced the underlying autonomy of those who survived. As the population vanished, *encomenderos* faced declining tributes and absent, recalcitrant workers. Mesoamerican tribute exaction could not sustain Spanish wealth and power while the Mesoamerican population disappeared. The entire colonial project was uncertain when the discovery of silver opened new ways to wealth and power. The first and richest mines were at Zacatecas, pivotal to the emergence of Spanish North America. But silver was also found at Taxco and Pachuca in the heartland of Spanish Mesoamerica, neither far from the colonial capital of Mexico City. And the silver of Zacatecas and other northern zones passed through the capital and the Puebla basin on its way to the Atlantic economy. The result was a powerful axis of commercial dynamism, beginning in Spanish North America and energizing the route through the central highlands to the Gulf.

The confluence of depopulation and silver led to a fundamental reconstruction of colonial society of Spanish Mesoamerica.[11] Three intersecting and often contested processes were key: the end of encomiendas, turning tributes to cash taxes mostly paid to the regime; the congregation of indigenous survivors into reconstituted communities given rights to land and local rule as *repúblicas de indios*; and the allocation of the lands thus vacated to favored Spaniards who undertook commercial estate production to support the silver economy and the urban centers it spawned. These processes accelerated where commercial stimulus was strongest—in the Puebla basin and the Valley of Mexico. They slowed where commercial opportunities were weak across the Mesoamerican south. Everywhere they limited the independent power of the conquerors, strengthened the regime, promoted commercial development—and entrenched landed communities at the base of the colonial order. During a long reconstruction from the 1550s to the 1630s, the regime played an active role: challenging encomiendas, congregating communities, granting lands. As the transformation was consolidated—and the first silver boom waned—in the mid-seventeenth century, the regime shifted to a more judicial, mediating role.[12]

In the process, communities rooted in Mesoamerican traditions, grappling with depopulation and facing unprecedented links to a global economy, consolidated ecological autonomies. Congregation and legal incorporation as indigenous republics gave them lands and rights to self-rule. The lands provided subsistence plots to resident commoners, modest farms to local notables, and holdings worked or leased to sustain local councils and religious festivities. Local governance allowed resident notables to select and participate in councils that oversaw community lands, local justice, and links with the colonial regime. Communities reconstituted as republics became hybrids—sustaining Mesoamerican traditions of cultivation, adapting and integrating indigenous and Christian religious visions, and reconstituting political cultures that were both indigenous and republican. To the regime, reconstituted communities were a means to preserve and to rule the surviving indigenous population—still a large majority across Mesoamerica. To that majority, landed republics allowed the local negotiations of power and production, patriarchy and family, missionary religion and local visions within worlds still indigenous—and the institutional means to contest submission to the colonial regime, to press judicial claims, and to negotiate labor relations with the emerging commercial economy. Republics were stratified within, and often in conflict with neighboring communities. They engaged the regime mostly in court—but sporadically and often effectively through assertions ranging from riots to rebellions.[13]

Across Mesoamerica, reconstituted communities with lands and republican rights became the bedrock of colonial society. Along the axis of commercial dynamism around Mexico City and across the Puebla basin, communities not only ruled production for sustenance but were essential reservoirs of labor for the emerging commercial economy. Villagers built cities; they provided seasonal laborers essential to estate cultivation. In the late sixteenth century and the early seventeenth, the labor draft called the *repartimiento* coerced such efforts. Landed autonomy and low population gave cultivators little incentive to work for others. By the early seventeenth century, the need for cash to pay tributes and the urge to buy goods in the commercial economy led many villagers to offer work for wages. Local notables who had implemented labor drafts increasingly organized work gangs and negotiated the terms of their labor. Across Spanish Mesoamerica, the ecological autonomies, self-rule, and judicial mediation grounded in indigenous republics facilitated resistance to coercion, negotiation of opportunities, and every relationship in between.[14]

Life developed differently across Spanish North America. The few landed republics there concentrated along the southern margins, or rewarded transplanted Tlaxcalans and other Mesoamericans with land to strengthen the colonial order in the lands of Chichimecas. Most missions were not republics; they were transitional institutions that aimed to settle and Christianize indigenous peoples, teaching them to live as subordinates in a commercial world. Mission residents rarely gained rights to land or self-rule. Most communities across Spanish North America were mining camps and estate settlements—essentially company towns. With nearly all residents arriving as immigrants, diverse Mesoamericans, Europeans, and Africans mixed to produce growing populations of mestizos and mulattoes, the latter increasingly free. The regime held fast to the ethnic distinctions; it collected tributes from mulattoes, not from mestizos. Still, interaction and fluidity in a commercial world defined society from the Bajío northward.[15]

Long historical traditions of ecological autonomy reconsolidated in colonial indigenous republics did not characterize Spanish North America. There cycles of silver mining drove settlement. When silver boomed—at Zacatecas beginning in the 1550s, at San Luis Potosí in the 1590s, far north at Parral in the 1630s, at Chihuahua after 1700, and at diverse sites around Zacatecas, San Luis Potosí, and especially at Guanajuato throughout the eighteenth century—surges of urban growth stimulated rural estate development. Across a dry plateau, and facing indigenous peoples never eager to relinquish their homelands (and their historical autonomies), commercial development required incentives to those willing to migrate and serve. Men ready to take the risks of laboring underground in the mines or working with mercury in refineries claimed high wages, ore shares, and food rations for their efforts. To populate estate communities, landed entrepreneurs had to offer tenancies and employment, with assurances of security grounded in the provision of food rations. Northern communities lived in legal and economic dependence, compensated by high earnings in the mines and by basic securities at estate settlements.[16]

Still, a latent ecological autonomy—lacking legal sustenance—remained in northern rural settlements. Estate residents ruled everyday crop production where rains or irrigation permitted; they herded livestock everywhere. In times of crisis, they could claim the crops they produced; in times of drought, they could consume the livestock they herded, undermining estate profits while sustaining families and communities.

Across Mesoamerica, with inevitable regional variations (in the Puebla basin there were estates with resident communities like those that defined Spanish North America), the intersection of Mesoamerican traditions, depopulation, and commercial development led to the postconquest consolidation of legally sanctioned ecological autonomies in thousands of indigenous republics. Across Spanish North America, the stimulus of silver and the resistance of Chichimecas led to a colonial society of migrants and commercial dynamism. Republics were scarce, limiting ecological autonomies. But the historical confluence of opportunities for profit in an arid environment required incentives to migration that gave the working majority high earnings, unusual securities—and, in rural communities, latent ecological autonomies.

Neither colonial order lacked conflicts and exploitations. The autonomies that sustained Mesoamerican communities and the population scarcities that favored northerners' earnings and securities led many an entrepreneur or official to resort to coercion. How else to press people who were in everyday control of production, and little subject to economic pressures? But conflicts and exploitations, and inevitable stratifications within patriarchal families and producing communities, should not deflect analysis from the ecological autonomies that sustained families and communities across Mesoamerica and remained latent across Spanish North America.

EIGHTEENTH-CENTURY EXPANSIONS, COLONIAL CRISES, AND INDEPENDENCE-ERA INSURGENCIES

Across New Spain, the eighteenth century brought new dynamism to commercial production and mounting pressures on communities and cultures forged in the aftermath of conquest. Autonomies and securities that had been consolidated amid the confluence of commercial dynamism and population catastrophe during the late sixteenth century faced a second wave of commercial expansion after 1700, this time with population growth. Those pressures stimulated distinct transformations in Spanish Mesoamerica and Spanish North America. In Spanish Mesoamerica, the ecological autonomies that sustained indigenous republics eroded—yet endured to facilitate adaptations that in most regions helped stabilize new and deepening exploitations. In the Bajío, the foundation of Spanish North America, most of the rural population lived as estate dependents, tenants, or employees historically compensated with solid earnings and good securities. There the eighteenth-century combination of commercial acceleration and population growth brought evictions, declining earnings, and widening insecurities. Their patriarchy challenged, men across the Bajío joined the Hidalgo revolt of 1810. It failed to topple the regime. But in its wake, communities across the Bajío claimed the land, asserted the autonomies latent in lives of estate dependence, and drove a decade of regional revolution that would shape the Mexican nation that began in 1821.

By the eighteenth century, Spanish Mesoamerica had three major zones: the Puebla basin, where commercial development came early in the colonial centuries but waned after 1750; the South, where commercial forces were limited throughout the colonial centuries; and the central highlands around Mexico City, where commercial dynamism peaked during the eighteenth century. All faced population growth after 1700; all included diverse geographies and ethnic communities; all grappled with the reforming goals of the Bourbon regime after 1750. And everywhere across Spanish Mesoamerica, enduring indigenous republics mobilized ecological autonomies, rights to self-rule, and access to the colonial judiciary to orchestrate adaptations to new pressures. Few rose in long-term insurgencies after 1810.

In the Puebla basin, both population growth and commercial dynamism slowed after 1750. Why population stopped expanding is not clear. Were epidemics more severe than in other areas of Spanish Mesoamerica? Why commercial expansion slowed is better understood. The region's textile industry faced competition from new producers in the Bajío and accelerating imports from Europe. Markets for commercial cultivation shrank as Louisiana and British North America supplied the Caribbean, and Valley of Mexico estates fed New Spain's capital. The region's early commercial development left some communities encapsulated on estate lands while others survived as landed republics. Conflicts over land and labor marked relations between estates and communities, dependent and independent. Still, a mix of ecologically autonomous republics and estate communities holding subsistence plots sustained patriarchs, families, and communities facing limited growth after 1750. The Puebla basin saw little insurgency after 1810.[17]

In the South, broadly Oaxaca, Chiapas, Yucatán, and Guatemala, gold and silver proved scarce, commercial opportunities rare. The colonial re-

construction of 1550 to 1650 allocated limited lands for estate development and consolidated thousands of indigenous republics. Spanish cities
remained small, sustained by grazing estates and modest cereal properties.
Most land and most production remained in the indigenous republics. The
one dynamic commercial product of the eighteenth-century South was
cochineal. Women in Mixtec households crushed and dried insects common to the Oaxacan uplands to produce the red dye on lands held as
members of indigenous republics. Ecological autonomy even sustained
export production in the South.[18]

Again, enduring autonomies did not prevent conflicts. Families that
controlled the means of sustenance regularly disputed access to lands and
questions of rule within and between villages. Those aiming to profit from
villagers' production repeatedly saw no way but coercion to extract labor,
food to sustain cities, tributes for the state, fees for the clergy, or cochineal
for export. Still, autonomies grounded in indigenous republics and regime
mediation of inevitable conflicts allowed communities to remain the foundation of society across the South—and to absorb eighteenth-century population growth on community lands without extreme deprivations or
threats to community survival. The South, too, generated few enduring
insurgencies after 1810.

It was in the highland basins surrounding Mexico City where eighteenth-century commercial dynamism and population growth intersected
to generate new pressures that eroded the autonomies of indigenous republics. Yet in most, sufficient autonomies persisted to allow adaptations
that stabilized communities and limited insurgencies after 1810. The revival of silver, first at Taxco, then at Real del Monte near Pachuca, accelerated commercial production across the central highlands. The concentration in Mexico City of financial, commercial, and governmental powers for
all of New Spain meant that the stronger expansion of silver across the
North, first at Zacatecas, later at Guanajuato, also generated urban growth
and market expansion in the core of Spanish Mesoamerica.[19]

There the largest city (and market) in the Americas, with over one hundred thousand people, sat at the center of rural basins in which hundreds
of indigenous republics faced dozens of commercial estates. The great
majority of indigenous families lived in republics, producing for sustenance, providing indigenous products to local and Mexico City markets,
and laboring seasonally at nearby estates for the cash to pay tributes and
buy a few manufactured goods. From the late sixteenth century to the early
eighteenth, most estates in the central basins produced Old World products: sugar in the hot Cuernavaca basin to the south, wheat in the valleys of
Mexico and Toluca, and sheep and other livestock in the dry zones north

and east. While population held low, most indigenous families and communities kept solid autonomies. Central basin estates produced a limited array of products for urban markets and negotiated with community leaders to gain the workers essential to plant and harvest commercial crops. Ecological autonomy and republican self-rule facilitated villagers' adaptations within an emerging commercial order.[20]

The eighteenth-century combination of commercial dynamism and population growth brought new opportunities to estates and new pressures to communities in the basins around Mexico City. In the early colonial reconstruction, most republics gained lands just sufficient to sustain small populations, local elites, limited governments, and religious festivals. When populations grew in the eighteenth century, often doubling by 1750, tripling by 1800, pressures mounted. With inevitable local variations, the land available to village families shrank. The regime, which so easily transferred lands from communities to Spanish entrepreneurs as populations fell, rarely shifted lands from estates to communities when village populations grew.

Through the first half of the eighteenth century, villagers increasingly consumed all they produced, cutting surpluses sold in regional markets. Estate operators saw opportunity: in the valleys of Mexico and Toluca, many took up maize as a commercial crop; in the dry country of the Mezquital, Otumba, and Apan, others found profit in commercial pulque (Mesoamericans' preferred fermented drink). For the first time in the central basins, indigenous products became major commercial crops. The great city was served; profits flowed to agricultural entrepreneurs; village autonomies eroded. To sustain growing families in the face of limited resources, men and boys had no choice but to increase their seasonal labor at estates expanding production. Wage labor, historically a supplement to subsistence production, became essential to sustenance. By the late eighteenth century, most village patriarchs across the central highlands sustained families and communities by combining cultivation and seasonal labor, with growing dependence on seasonal labor. Ecological autonomy declined but survived sufficiently to allow most rural men to sustain claims to household patriarchy, and most villagers to remain villagers, living and worshiping within republics, negotiating as communities their growing dependence on estate labor.

Eroding yet enduring ecological autonomies became the basis of symbiotic exploitations. Institutionally, eighteenth-century links between commercial estates and landed republics in the central highlands were symbiotic: estates could not profit without villagers' labor; villagers could not survive (or assert patriarchy) without the wages of that labor. The same relationships were deeply exploitative: landed entrepreneurs profited to enjoy lives of wealth and power; villagers labored longer and harder to survive and to sustain patriarchy. Village notables and estate managers brokered relationships of symbiotic exploitation. When conflicts threatened, the colonial courts mediated to seek stability.[21] Symbiotic exploitation proved, perhaps, the perfect exploitation. The market was served, entrepreneurs claimed profits—and peasant patriarchs remained patriarchs while villagers remained villagers, sustaining themselves when they could, working for wages when they could not, struggling to survive within the indigenous republics.

Symbiotic exploitation, of course, was never planned, never a colonial policy. It evolved out of historical contests between communities rooted in the Mesoamerican past and reconstituted during the early colonial reconstruction, estate developers seeking profits in the dynamic commercial economy of the eighteenth century, and a regime interested first in revenues, thus in stability. Such relationships inevitably differed in zones of diverse geography, indigenous traditions, and market potential. Symbiotic exploitation proved most stabilizing in the cereal zones of the valleys of Mexico and Toluca. There villagers generally held lands amenable to maize and other food crops. There indigenous peasant patriarchs maintained subsistence production, even as it failed to fully provide for growing families. And there commercial wheat and maize production created seasonal labor demand sufficient to provide village men and boys the supplemental earnings essential to sustain patriarchy, family, and community. When insurgencies exploded to the north in 1810, villagers in the cereal zones might mount brief uprisings. They often linked old local conflicts to new debates about sovereignty. They rarely generated enduring insurgencies.[22]

To the south, in the sugar zones of Cuernavaca and Cuautla, the relationship was less balanced. The expansion of sugar was voracious of basin lands and irrigation waters; communities with growing populations faced expansive estates. Sugar was also voracious of labor, demanding more workers for more months than wheat or maize. Across the sugar basins of the central highlands, communities faced greater challenges to their autonomies—and greater demands for their labor. Local conflicts abounded. Yet there, too, no massive regional uprising denied property and challenged the regime after 1810. When in 1812 the siege of Cuautla became pivotal to the war for independence, the forces loyal to José María Morelos found sympathy and sustenance among local villagers. Yet no uprising sufficient to relieve the siege and to sustain Morelos's challenge to the regime developed.[23]

Where relations of symbiotic exploitation negotiated eighteenth-cen-

tury adaptations to population growth and commercial expansion, indigenous republics remained the foundation of everyday life, patriarchal families survived by combinations of cultivation and seasonal labor, and the
courts mediated to sustain that stability. Most refrained from taking the
risks of challenging a regime that sanctioned the limited rights and ecological autonomies that allowed them to negotiate that survival.

Life in the arid zones from the Mezquital through Otumba to Apan
(between the capital and the mines to the northeast at Pachuca and Real
del Monte) proved more difficult, more conflictive, in the eighteenth century—and more conducive to insurgency after 1810. This was the driest
area of the central highlands. Historically home to Otomí peoples sub-
jected to Mexica rule, then "liberated" by Spanish conquest, the region saw
an invasion of sheep after the conquest. Grazing turned a dry country
nearly barren, prejudicing a population already grappling with disease.
Still, surviving villagers gained recognition as republics, using lands and
local rule to sustain themselves—growing maize when rains or rivers allowed, exploiting the ubiquitous maguey cactus to make pulque and to
harvest fibers for rope and rough cloth. While the population hovered near
its nadir, they survived surrounded by grazing properties that sought little
labor. Pressed to work at regional mines, they resisted labor that threatened life and limb.[24]

The eighteenth-century combination of population growth and commercial expansion again left community lands ever less adequate to sustain local
families and provide surpluses to urban and mining markets. Grazing estates responded by sending livestock north and converting pastures to vast
fields of maguey. Selling pulque to Mexico City taverns and nearby mining
camps became a profitable business for leading entrepreneurs. But commercial pulque generated little labor demand. Many villagers were recruited to transplant young maguey in neat rows across old pastures. But
once maguey fields were in place, and after a three- to five-year wait for
maturity, the work of tapping the syrup and fermenting pulque required but
one or two skilled specialists. Sporadically the creation of new fields, or the
replacement of tapped-out zones, generated large labor demands. Most of
the time, great pulque estates claimed markets once filled by villagers, yet
offered little labor to men struggling to sustain families and communities.
Declining autonomies brought desperate poverty and threats to patriarchy—not symbiotic exploitation—across the pulque zones.[25]

The Otomí communities were not the first to rise. But after the Hidalgo
insurgency passed west of the Mezquital in late 1810, villagers took arms and
claimed lands and livestock from neighboring estates, reconstituting autonomies to sustain insurgencies that endured in the Mezquital into 1815, around

Otumba and Apan into 1816. They dealt with nearby leaders seeking political independence, the Villagrán clan north of the Mezquital at Huichapan, Francisco Osorno east of Otumba and Apan in the Sierra Norte de Puebla. Political rebels and community insurgents facilitated each other as they sought separate but compatible agendas—political sovereignty and community autonomy. The insurgent Otomí of the Mezquital held out for years after the defeat of the Villagráns. Osorno and the communities around Otumba and Apan fought parallel wars until 1816. Threats to patriarchy and to family and community autonomies, without compensating symbiotic exploitations, led the pulque zones toward insurgency. Threatened and then reconstituted ecological autonomies sustained a popular war for independence that separated the capital from the key mines, blocked commercial operations, and cut regime revenues.[26]

Spanish North America, the plateau country beginning in the Bajío and reaching far to the north, experienced more rapid population growth and more dynamic commercial expansion during the eighteenth century. Communities there lived those pressures and opportunities in ways fundamentally different from their neighbors to the south in Spanish Mesoamerica. Silver mining flourished at Zacatecas and far to the north at Chihuahua during the first half of the eighteenth century, later at Guanajuato and across San Luis Potosí. Total production increased four times over and held near its peak for four decades after 1770. Migrants flooded in and drove northward; commercial production of crops and livestock accelerated to sustain mining bonanzas. Silver boom fueled Atlantic trade and wars and brought opportunities and challenges to the peoples of Spanish North America.[27]

Three broad regions emerged from the diversity of life in eighteenth-century Spanish North America: the Bajío, the North, and the Frontier. Spanish North America had begun in the Bajío. By the eighteenth century, it mixed mining, irrigated commercial cultivation, and textile and tobacco manufacturing in a uniquely dynamic and diverse regional society. After 1770, the Bajío was the most commercial, densely settled, and socially polarized region of Spanish North America.[28]

The North included the vast plateau country from San Luis Potosí and Zacatecas through Durango, Chihuahua, and Coahuila. Cycles of silver mining had driven settlement since the later sixteenth century. Mining camps rose and fell; a few became small cities that survived. Everywhere vast grazing estates supplied mines and towns. Agriculture developed at oases of irrigation. Bajío crops and cloth sustained communities across the North, integrating the economy of Spanish North America. Vast herds of livestock took over the northern plateau country. They consumed, trampled, or displaced the plants and animals that sustained historical gatherers and hunters. Indigenous peoples responded by hunting and gathering Spanish livestock and crops—setting off conflicts that defined the northward march of Spanish North America, and adaptations that led indigenous survivors through the missions to lives as sedentary dependents or to exile in isolated uplands.[29]

The Frontier extended the North into regions of indigenous independence during the eighteenth century, incorporating the triangle from the Rio Grande to San Antonio and Corpus Christi in Texas and driving up the California coast from San Diego to San Francisco.[30] It also extended northward to incorporate New Mexico. Long an outlier of colonial society, New Mexico was more like Spanish Mesoamerica than North America: a Hispanic minority ruled an indigenous majority organized in cultivating communities granted rights to lands and self-rule as republics. Simultaneously, New Mexico served as a historic point of engagement—of conflict and accommodation—with the independent, often nomadic, peoples of the North American interior. In the eighteenth century, the consolidation of mining and settlement at Chihuahua brought New Mexico into the larger dynamic of Spanish North America.[31]

The historical settlement of Spanish North America threatened and eventually destroyed the ecological autonomies of its indigenous peoples, who resisted, engaged the missions, and fell to onslaughts of disease. In the commercial development that followed, land rights were all but monopolized by estate operators—and secondarily by missions. Indigenous republics were few and scattered. The northward drive of Spanish North America created zones of economic opportunity and sparse population. Those who migrated north—Europeans, Mesoamericans, and Africans who mixed to become mestizos and mulattoes—gained combinations of land and employment that allowed a modest and relatively secure sustenance. Essential to production and the possibilities for profit, they retained latent ecological autonomies—the skills and everyday experience of working the land to produce the crops and livestock that sustained Spanish North America. While conflicts and coercions were everywhere, those who sought fortunes in mines or profits in estate development continued to offer ample remunerations and basic securities to those who migrated to work and produce. North of the Bajío, there were few sustained insurgencies during the wars for independence.

The Bajío proved different. The longest-settled region of Spanish North America, that key basin had passed (sometime after 1760) the invisible but pivotal threshold in which population scarcities favoring producers gave way to demographic pressures that shifted the weight of power to those who aimed to rule and profit. The mining boom and commercial explosion after 1770 prejudiced everyday life across the region. Mineworkers faced the loss of ore shares and declining wages; estate residents faced stagnant wages, lost food rations, rising rents, and evictions. Dependent security gave way to dependent insecurity with deepening poverty—challenges faced as threats to patriarchy in producing households. Men expecting combinations of tenancies, wages, and rations to implement their claims to rule households as patriarchal providers found they could no longer provide—and thus no longer assert patriarchal prerogatives. Across the countryside around San Miguel and Dolores, estate communities of diverse ethnic backgrounds claimed status as *indios* and went to court seeking rights as republics around 1800. They sought land and self-rule—ecological autonomy and local sovereignty. They failed.[32]

Then, after the Napoleonic invasion broke the Spanish monarchy in 1808 and two years of contested sovereignty amid drought and scarcities heightened political debates and social tensions, in 1810 the men of estate communities around Dolores and San Miguel were the first to join the Hidalgo revolt. More important, after the defeat of that massive but chaotic movement, they returned home to generate local insurgencies that persisted to 1820. They denied estate property and divided lands into family ranchos—creating the ecological autonomies until then only latent in lives of dependence, using them to sustain themselves and guerrilla fighters during a decade of popular insurgency. Paradoxically, an insurgency begun by men facing threats to patriarchal prerogatives generated a growing minority of *rancheras*—women who headed producing households. When royalist forces finally pacified the Bajío in a hard campaign from 1818 to 1820, they recognized the ranchos created across the region during years of insurgency. Rural families had to accept estate property and pay rents—and kept their ranchos. They gained and sustained ecological autonomies, subject to a regime of private property. The short run favored family production; in the long run, they would face continued legal dependence on those who retained rights to property. That long run would be contested in the new polity begun by the assertion of Mexican independence in 1821, a year after the pacification of the Bajío.[33]

Two broadly regional, long-enduring rural insurgencies underlay the independence revolution. One persisted to 1816 in the pulque zones from the Mezquital to Apan, the northern and driest regions of Spanish Mesoamerica. The other fought until 1820 in the Bajío, the richest, most dynamic region of Spanish North America. Both occurred in regions key to silver mining and commercial production. Bajío insurgents all but ended mining at Guanajuato; Mezquital insurgents prejudiced production at Real del Monte. Both inhibited the regime's ability to fight more-political rebels. Both made it clear that lurking beneath conflicts about political independence lay popular movements seeking and reconstituting (patriarchal) ecological autonomies.[34]

There were shorter, less widespread popular mobilizations elsewhere, some lasting a few years, others a few months, many a few days. Nearly all were grounded in the ecological autonomies of rural communities. Many framed demands in terms of new debates about political sovereignty, imagining independence through the lens of community and (patriarchal) family interests.[35] Sometimes communities and political leaders forged strong alliances, as in the southern highlands of Mesoamerica mobilized under Juan Álvarez.[36] Sometimes they found mutual reinforcement in parallel conflicts: Mezquital communities helped the Villagráns; Otumba and Apan insurgents strengthened Osorno. And where communities constituted as republics refrained from enduring insurgencies, they still mobilized in local tumults to assert the ecological autonomy, political sovereignty, and cultural independence that defined their worlds.

The years from 1808 to 1821 generated a revolutionary confrontation that resulted in Mexican independence. Mobilized communities, with few evident leaders and no known ideological proclamations, made the wars for independence revolutionary. The most adamant and persistent popular and patriarchal insurgents responded to lost securities (in the Bajío) and vanishing autonomies (in the Mezquital) to mount mobilizations that claimed lands, reconstituted ecological autonomies, and fought for years to make such autonomies the basis of local society. They pressed popular visions of community independence before the achievement of political independence.

FROM CÁDIZ LIBERALISM TO MEXICAN REVOLUTION:
CONTESTING AUTONOMY AND SOVEREIGNTY

While insurgents in the Bajío and the Mezquital fought to reconstitute community autonomies amid wars for independence, liberal governance began as an experiment aimed to challenge Napoleonic rule in Spain—and to sustain Spanish rule in New Spain. Cádiz liberalism offered people across New Spain limited representation in imperial affairs—and new opportunities to exercise local sovereignty in more participatory municipalities. It also challenged traditions of community landholding—the historical basis of indigenous republics' ecological autonomies. Liberals aimed to privatize community lands, shifting property and autonomy to individuals and families. From 1810 to 1814, liberalism offered indigenous republics broader electoral rights, opportunities they used to blunt liberal attacks on community landholding.[37]

Thus began—in defense of colonial rule—the long, contradictory, and often conflictive history of liberalism in Mexico. Throughout the nineteenth century, liberal promises of popular sovereignty were constant, liberal visions of utopian private property everywhere. Liberal electoral politics peaked during and immediately after the wars for independence. Liberal assaults on landed autonomies were legislated early in the states, later by the national regime, and implemented widely only by the late-century regime of Porfirio Díaz, who sharply limited liberal electoral participations. The historic contest between liberal promises of effective electoral sovereignty and liberal challenges to ecological autonomies led in 1910 to a second revolution. Another round of popular insurgencies sustained by ecological autonomies drove a civil conflict that built a new regime that made landholding a right of every rural Mexican (male head of household) in the Constitution of 1917.

Amid wars for independence sustained by popular insurgencies, those fighting to preserve Spanish rule facilitated the implementation of liberalism's promises of municipal sovereignty—and backed away from pressing its challenge to community landholding. Across rural Mexico, liberalism began as a political opening. Old indigenous republics grasped new status as municipalities, broadening electoral participations within. With independence, and especially under the federal republic of 1824, however, several of the new sovereign states legislated against community landholding—often while limiting the number and sovereignty of municipalities. But those who imagined ruling states and a new nation soon learned that legislating was easier than forcing changes in community life.[38]

Independence began unprecedented contests over the location of sovereignty. Historically, the monarchy and the republics—Spanish cities and indigenous communities—had shared unequally in a sovereignty sanctioned by divine right. Suddenly, sovereignty relocated to the people—or the nation. Its exercise was disputed at three levels: a national regime built on the viceroyalty in Mexico City; provincial states erected on the short and shallow histories of intendancies created in the 1780s and expanded by Cádiz liberalism; and municipalities (cities and towns) grounded in Spanish councils and indigenous republics. The nation claimed the remnants of monarchical sovereignty. The municipalities had long participated in sovereignty, which they aimed to strengthen. The states imagined and legislated new sovereignties; many worked to limit the rights of former indigenous republics while allying with Hispanic city councils. After a decade in which revolutionary conflict mixed popular insurgencies pursuing local autonomies with transatlantic liberalism promoted in defense of colonial rule, independence produced a search for a nation in which sovereignty was contested at three levels. It was a recipe for instability.[39]

Proclamations of national, popular, and municipal sovereignty abounded. Yet elites struggling to consolidate rule repeatedly curtailed popular and municipal rights, notably in former indigenous republics. Conflict proliferated. Those seeking power offered plans and pronouncements, sought sanction in Hispanic councils, and mobilized military force to claim power. Yet in the atomized world of post-independence Mexico, raising military forces often meant mobilizing popular communities—who demanded concessions (often confirmations of community lands and municipal sovereignties) and gained experience in political warfare.[40]

Meanwhile, changing social, demographic, and economic realities facilitated post-independence reconsolidations of ecological autonomies. The Bajío revolution began the shift. Insurgents there took control of vast, often irrigated estate lands and turned them to family production, sustaining themselves first—and secondarily supplying local markets. The decade of warfare collapsed silver mining at Guanajuato and limited it elsewhere; textile production shifted from large workshops to family crafters. Before the new states of Querétaro and Guanajuato worked to create provincial sovereignty and join a national polity, insurgents transformed a once-dynamic commercial economy into a region of family production. The Bajío in the 1820s was a place of ample food and scarce profit. Across the countryside, tenant production ruled a new world of family autonomy subject to estate property. For the near term, autonomy ruled.[41]

The combination of political conflicts and regional insurgencies that defined the wars for independence brought parallel—if less dramatic—transformations to broader regions of Mexico. Silver mining declined everywhere, only to revive at Zacatecas in the 1830s, elsewhere in the 1840s or later. Market opportunities declined accordingly. The decade of Bajío insurgency not only undermined commercial production in a key region; it separated the economies of Spanish North America and Spanish Mesoamerica, historically integrated by the financial and commercial powers of Mexico City. The 1820s saw a decline of market production, accompanied by a fragmentation of markets that survived—notably across the North, where new states opened ports and sought direct access to outside markets. As commercial cultivation weakened, producer autonomies surged, strengthening communities in negotiations of land and labor with nearby estates across Mesoamerica, leading northern estates to offer lands to tenants even where insurgency had not forced the change, creating new opportunities for Hispanic migrants to move into isolated uplands and create ranchero societies—zones of family autonomy sustained by private property.[42]

Demographic changes reinforced emerging autonomies. Population growth seems to have slowed, especially in the regions of concentrated Mesoamerican and colonial settlement. Migration accelerated into long peripheral regions along the coasts and to the north. Demographic pressures subsided as commercial stimuli waned. With inevitable variations and exceptions, ecological autonomies solidified after independence.

The conflictive complexities of Mexican life from the 1820s to the 1870s developed at the intersection of two contradictory sets of developments: in the domain of production, commerce declined and fragmented while producer autonomies consolidated; in the domain of politics, liberal visions promoted popular sovereignty and municipal autonomy, while assaulting the rights to community lands that sustained ecological autonomies across Mexican Mesoamerica (and assailing the Catholic Church, which still held the allegiance of most Mexicans).

With leaders seeking to fuse two radically different colonial societies into one nation, with sovereignty disputed at three levels (municipal, provincial, and national), with the commercial economy facing decline and fragmentation while producer autonomies strengthened, and with liberalism rising as the ideology of national development, promising political sovereignties and municipal autonomies while assaulting community lands and deep religious affiliations, the rapid emergence of a stable national polity was impossible. The common post-independence difficulties of emerging nations proved especially intense and enduring in Mexico.[43]

Two pivotal episodes, in which a deeply divided Mexican polity faced international conflicts and the assertions of popular communities, marked key transitions near the middle of the nineteenth century. In the 1840s there were signs of an emerging national consolidation: mining surged at Guanajuato, with production approaching late colonial levels; a mechanized textile industry took hold at Puebla, Querétaro, and elsewhere; family production by tenants, rancheros, and Mesoamerican communities proved capable of sustaining cities and new industries (despite estate operators' complaints of scarce profits); and moderate liberalism offered the prospect of a political center. Might Mexico consolidate a new economy and polity in the third decade of independence?[44]

The opportunity vanished when in 1846 the United States—seven decades a nation, with an industrializing North and an expanding cotton and slave South—provoked war to claim the Mexican North American frontier. In the long term, the war cost Mexico the territories essential to the expansion of its historically dynamic North. In the near term, it deepened the contradictions inherent in its emerging polity. While national leaders called for unity in mobilizing against the aggressors, many states offered rhetorical support but limited contributions of funds and forces. Indigenous communities saw an affair of those who ruled—or an opportunity to reassert local autonomies against state and national powers distracted and weakened the war. Thus the Maya of Yucatán, after decades of trying to use liberal rights to deflect liberal assaults on community lands, and after mobilizing in political conflicts in exchange for promises of autonomy, only to find promises repeatedly broken, took advantage of the opportunity presented by the U.S. invasion to mount a war for Maya independence that came so close to succeeding it was denigrated as a "caste war." Parallel if more limited mobilizations occurred during the war among the Zapotecs of the Isthmus of Tehuantepec in southern Oaxaca, and the peoples of the Sierra Gorda (a rugged upland enclave of indigenous independence northeast of the Bajío). And when U.S. troops occupied Mexico City in September 1847, national rulers fled to Querétaro while the people of the barrios (lacking the ecological autonomies of their rural neighbors) rose in three days of resistance and commitment to a nation still more imagined than real.[45]

The war deepened and prolonged Mexico's crisis of nation building. In an agonizing aftermath, ideologues lamented the absence of national sentiments, especially among the indigenous majority. Entrepreneurs complained of scarce profits and blamed them on indigenous villagers holding too much land, demanding too much for labor, and working only when it suited their purposes. Moderate liberal rule fell to monarchical conservatism, led by the opportunist Antonio López de Santa Anna, which fell to a liberal triumph in 1855. Juan Álvarez led the liberal rise to national power. The last of the popular leaders who fought in the wars for independence, Álvarez was a regional strongman rooted south of Mexico City, where he had learned to accommodate the promises of liberalism and demands for autonomies that included rights to communally held lands.[46]

Once the liberals were in power, ideologues pressed Álvarez out of the regime and back to his rural homeland. They wrote the pivotal Ley Juárez, which ended separate jurisdictions for the military and clergy, and the Ley Lerdo, which denied rights to corporate landholding to the church and to indigenous communities. Both laws were incorporated in the Constitution of 1857. Aiming to break the stalemate that blocked the consolidation of a Mexican nation, liberals in national power took aim at the Catholic Church and Mesoamerican communities. The first result was to provoke deeper conflicts. Conservatives mobilized to defend the church and its properties, fighting a war against reform from 1858 to 1860. The war blocked any general privatization of community lands; most communities stood aside while liberals and conservatives fought over national power. When the liberals won and the conservatives took the desperate step of seeking out French intervention, key indigenous communities in the Sierra de Puebla and elsewhere did mobilize with the liberals to fight the invaders. In no region did indigenous peoples see the invasion as an opportunity to rise for local autonomies while the regime faced another war. Still, French armies and Mexican conservatives placed Maximilian of Habsburg on a throne in Mexico City—and the European emperor proved more liberal than his Mexican conservative allies, more open to negotiating the rights of indigenous communities than his Mexican liberal foes.[47]

When the post–Civil War U.S. government and investors began to support Mexican liberals and French armies left to face Prussian threats in Europe, Maximilian's experiment collapsed. Liberals reclaimed power under Benito Juárez in 1867. The church knew its properties were gone; conservatives were done as a political force, defeated in war, delegitimized by their collaboration with foreign invaders. Thus strengthened, Juárez began to implement the remaining key to the liberal vision—the privatization of community lands.

Juárez and his allies insisted that privatization offered liberation. Communal restrictions on property would end; indigenous families would be independent proprietors, free to use lands as they pleased: for sustenance, for market production, for sale. Villagers knew things were not so simple. While historical ownership was communal, plots for cultivation were held, used, and inherited by families; village uplands provided pastures and woodlands to all. Local elites also held lands by community tenure, often portions large enough to make them market growers. Other community lands funded local government and religious festivals. Communal landholding, a legacy of the colonial indigenous republics, sustained the complex, integrated ecological, social, and cultural autonomy of Mesoamerican communities.

With privatization, individuals would own cultivation plots, large and small. Uplands would be auctioned, denying most villagers access to pastures and woodlands. Holdings dedicated to paying the costs of government and local religion would be sold; new taxes, fees, and services would have to support local government and religious life. Most important, corporate proprietorship had forged shared interests in defending lands. A threat to any plot, large or small, was a threat to all; local notables and the governments they led had an interest in defending corporate lands—and the resources to do so.[48]

Privatization would fragment historically linked interests. No one would have the interest, the right, or the resources to defend lands other than his own. Privatization would limit the resources available to most rural families, break historical unities into individual interests, and set off processes that would concentrate lands in the hands of the most powerful—and steadily impoverish segments of the village poor. Population growth would make everything worse.

Villagers across Mexico saw beyond liberal rhetoric to the probable outcomes of privatization. Where villages lay near cities and potential markets, local notables often led privatization forward, seeking personal commercial gains despite the costs in community integration. In regions where villages had long jostled with commercial estates, where community cohesion was essential to land retention and negotiating labor relations, villagers often united against privatization. In regions of emerging commercial development, communities easily divided within. In the years following the liberal return to power in 1867, a series of regional uprisings challenged local privatizations: at Chalco in the Valley of Mexico, in the Mezquital, in the Puebla basin, in Chiapas, even in Nayarit. The resistance remained fragmented and regional, contained locally by military force. Elsewhere, as in the Sierra de Puebla, where many villagers had fought with liberals against the French, pressures to privatize led to local conflicts and diverse compromises. In sum, the first broad attempt to privatize community lands in the late 1860s led to widespread conflicts, limited implementation, and a general delay of a program sure to destabilize state consolidation if pressed too rapidly. Once again, the defense of community autonomies—in uprisings sustained by ecological autonomies—constrained those who would build a nation in opposition to such autonomies.[49]

Mexico began to consolidate a national regime in 1876. Porfirio Díaz, a general famed for fighting the French, often supported by indigenous communities, took power in the last military coup of the nineteenth century. A dedicated liberal, he maintained the forms of electoral governance, blocked the substance of popular sovereignty, and limited municipal autonomy while pursuing liberal visions of market development and, in time, the privatization of community lands. Díaz's priorities were political stability and export development. He cut deals with regional elites, trading loyalty for economic opportunity. He appointed personal loyalists to balance local interests—and provided opportunities for profit to both. To stimulate the economy and the communications that integrated his regime, he promoted railroad construction, telegraphs, and steamship links to external markets.[50]

The last decades of the nineteenth century brought a new era of commercial expansion. Mining revived, expanded from silver to copper, and after 1900 to petroleum. For the first time in history, agricultural exports sent Mexican crops overseas: henequen from Yucatán provided twine for harvesters across the Mississippi basin; coffee plantations sprang up in the foothills of the Gulf and Pacific coasts, selling to European consumers; vanilla from Papantla in northern Veracruz became coveted in Europe and the United States; cattle were driven north from the borderlands to supply growing U.S. markets. Meanwhile the integration of the national market by railroads built to facilitate export production brought the expansion of Mexican textile industries. Most mills were located along the Gulf escarpment, where water and hydroelectric power were available; cotton came from the Gulf lowlands, and increasingly from the expanding irrigated fields of the Laguna, far to the north.[51]

At the same time, Mexicans faced another surge of population growth, accompanied by migration into rapidly developing zones of Mexican North America. The decades from 1880 to 1910 brought political closure, commercial growth, population pressures—and renewed efforts to privatize community lands. After decades in which fundamental economic and demographic developments favored ecological autonomies, and liberal programs challenged them with limited success, the Díaz era brought a new concentration of demographic, commercial, and political pressures against those autonomies. Villagers, estate residents, and rancheros negotiated those pressures everywhere, sometimes adapting, sometimes resisting. Ecological autonomy might vanish (yet remain latent) on estates that returned to commercial production, diminish in communities facing privatization, and hold strong among rancheros and villagers in marginal zones far from commercial opportunities.

Pressures, negotiations, and adaptations developed differently across the two social orders still struggling to combine into a Mexican nation. Across Mexican North America, aridity, commercial ways, and the scarcity of communities with legally sanctioned land rights historically limited ecological autonomies. In the Bajío, independence-era insurgency had forced a shift toward family autonomies, turning commercial estates into tenant communities. When commercial expansion resumed there after 1880, family production endured and adapted. When estates resumed commercial wheat cultivation, tenants still monopolized maize—and gained wages at the wheat harvests. Mobilizations proved limited after 1910.[52] Across the regions just north of the Bajío, the aftermath of independence brought parallel expansions of tenant production. Commercial dynamism remained limited after 1880. Revolutionary uprisings there, too, proved scattered. Is was in the far north, where the frontier had become the borderlands, that post-independence autonomies faced the most disruptive challenges of Porfirian development—and where revolutionary mobilizations exploded after 1910.

Hispanic colonists who settled along the frontier in the eighteenth century gained land rights in exchange for fighting Apaches and others who challenged commercial expansion. Settlers retained those rights and autonomies into the nineteenth century. Other independent rancheros found ecological and cultural autonomy by settling zones marginal to market opportunities. They forged locally autonomous patriarchal communities—with patriarchy defined by independent production combined with valor against Apaches. After 1880, commercial opportunity set land engrossers against colonists and rancheros no longer needed to fight defeated Apaches. Once again, now far to the north, assaults on ecological autonomies were lived as attacks on patriarchy.[53]

Meanwhile the borderlands saw the rapid development of vast estates. Entrepreneurs accelerated commercial production, raising rents, ousting tenants, pressing patriarchs and their families to lives of laboring dependence. When railroads first linked the Mexican borderlands to markets in central Mexico and the United States, boom prevailed and compensated widespread dislocation. Mines, ranches, new cities, and the irrigated cotton fields of the Laguna drew migrants northward. They gained earnings far above national norms. The same development pressed against older communities, challenging their lands and autonomies. While the boom held, protests were sporadic and contained—sometimes brutally. When the U.S. financial panic of 1907 revealed that the integration of the Mexican North into the U.S. economy could provoke commercial collapse, prosperous dependency became dependent insecurity, even desperation. Across the borderlands, working patriarchs were threatened nearly everywhere. When regime crisis brought opportunities for mobilization in 1910, the borderlands generated the popular armies that Pancho Villa led into the heart of revolutionary confrontations in 1914 and 1915. In part, Villa's supporters reconstituted ecological autonomies; old colonist and ranchero communities in the Chihuahua highlands reasserted local production to sustain the revolutionary fight. In larger part, Villa mobilized the commercial ways of the North to sustain organized armies that toppled the remnants of Mexico's nineteenth-century order.[54]

Porfirian challenges and revolutionary mobilizations proved different across Mexican Mesoamerica. Communities with ecological autonomies rooted in the Mesoamerican past and consolidated in colonial republics had negotiated a post-independence era in which structural developments reinforced autonomies—and liberal programs challenged them. Conflicts escalated, yet autonomies survived—at least until the era of Porfirian development. Urban expansion and export explosion, both facilitated by rail integration, brought commercial acceleration across Mesoamerica. In the central highlands around Mexico City, it reasserted historic pressures. Across the South and the coastal lowlands, commercial dynamism was a Porfirian innovation. Communities faced pressures nearly everywhere: demands for privatization, claims (legal and otherwise) on lands newly coveted for commercial production, pressures to labor in export enterprises, et cetera. But those pressures varied, as did community adaptations—and, eventually, revolutionary mobilizations.

The Mesoamerican South and East experienced little commercial incorporation during the colonial era. Communities remained republics with ample lands, ready to take advantage of nineteenth-century liberal municipal rights to defend those lands from liberal assaults on corporate property. The post-independence decades brought endless skirmishes and sporadic explosions—notably the Maya war for independence. Still, communities grounded in ecological autonomies survived into the Porfirian era, ready to defend lands and rights after decades of challenges.

Commercial expansion in times of population growth proved harder to resist than liberal legislation. Mesoamerican communities faced three broad patterns of commercial engagement after 1880: incorporation as dependent producers, new relations of symbiotic exploitation, and assaults on autonomies that broke historic symbiotic exploitations. The first pattern characterized the henequen economy of Yucatán. Maya communities lived on commercial properties. Families received small plots for subsistence cultivation. Men and boys labored year-round extracting the fibers from century plants. They often received wage advances at key times in the family cycle (marriages, births, deaths), advances that solidified workers' patriarchal claims within Maya households, creating debts that locked them into laboring dependence. Maya communities incorporated into henequen estates faced dependence, compensated with securities of subsistence that reinforced patriarchy. When all else failed, debts became the pretense for coercion. Conflict between estates and communities persisted, often where estates pressed against still-autonomous communities. But while henequen boomed, patriarchal securities compensated lost autonomies. Even as revolutionary politics came to Yucatán, popular insurgencies proved sporadic.[55]

Across the coastal foothills from Chiapas through Oaxaca along the Pacific, and Veracruz and Oaxaca on the Gulf, coffee became the great export crop of Porfirian development. For the first time, coffee linked diverse southern communities to export production. Some communities saw opportunity, privatized community lands, and planted coffee. Village elites could claim large holdings and become commercial growers; commoners could tend a few trees to complement maize production—and earn wages harvesting beans at larger enterprises. Elsewhere, entrepreneurs established coffee enterprises and recruited seasonal workers, men and women, from villages that retained lands—generating in the late nineteenth century ties of symbiotic exploitation parallel to those that had stabilized estate-village relations across the central highlands in the eighteenth century. Again, the potential for conflict was everywhere—but communities in and near the coffee zones generally retained lands and important, if shrinking, ecological autonomies. Men sustained patriarchy by combining limited subsistence production with wage labor at coffee estates. Conflicts remained local and limited; coffee zones generated little popular mobilization after 1910.[56]

It was in the rural heartland of Mexican Mesoamerica, especially the sugar and cereal zones south of Mexico City, that Porfirian boom, land privatizations, and population growth assaulted the ecological autonomies that had defined indigenous republics during the colonial era and sustained stabilizing symbiotic exploitations in the eighteenth century. Regions of limited, localized mobilizations during the wars for independence became zones of adamant agrarian insurrection after 1910.

After 1880, sugar estates in the Morelos basin and cereal properties in the southern Valley of Toluca and at Chalco in the Valley of Mexico expanded production. Wherever possible, they increased irrigation. In Morelos they evicted tenants to plant more sugar. Rail transport eased links to Mexico City and wider national markets. Once built, railroads cut rural labor demands. So did the industrialization of sugar refining at Morelos estates and the introduction of harvesters on wheat fields across the Chalco plains. Meanwhile, population grew and remained in communities, where land privatizations led to new concentrations. Growing majorities lacked land sufficient for family sustenance, and growing minorities had no land—problems worsened by the loss of tenant holdings. Demand for seasonal hands failed to keep pace. Mechanization curtailed the demand for wage labor, just as a new generation faced landlessness, and thus increased dependence on labor to assert patriarchal prerogatives and sustain families. The demand for hands expanded only in the cane harvests of Morelos. That difficult and dangerous work drew men and boys from Morelos villages, and increasingly from communities across Chalco and the Toluca basin. Growing competition for limited work kept wages down; desperate men from diverse communities discovered a common plight.[57]

Across Chalco and the southern state of México, a rising tide of violence among men within communities, and by men against women and infant girls within families, marked the pathology of deepening crisis. Men unable to become even dependent patriarchs because of declining autonomies and the collapse of symbiotic exploitation turned to violence against neighbors and families. When the Porfirian regime collapsed, men from communities across Morelos, Chalco, and the southern Valley of Toluca joined the agrarian insurgencies led by Emiliano Zapata. They turned long-escalating violence outward against officials and estates, claiming lands, reconstituting ecological autonomies, and reasserting patriarchies.[58]

The complex conflicts of the Mexican Revolution cannot be recounted here.[59] The key is to emphasize that the decade of conflict from 1910 to 1920 became a revolution not because of the political conflicts among those who aimed to replace Porfirio Díaz but because of two great popular mobilizations: the borderlands movement led by Pancho Villa and the agrarian insurgency led by Zapata in Morelos and surrounding zones. Their different roles in the revolution reveal much about the importance of ecological autonomies in sustaining popular participation in national conflicts—and about the persistent fundamental differences between Mexican Mesoamerica and Mexican North America.

Emiliano Zapata led a classic, community-based, agrarian insurgency. Threats to ecological autonomies and the breakdown of symbiotic exploitation hit the men of Morelos, Chalco, and southern Toluca communities as threats to patriarchy, to manhood. Zapata led a small rebellion against local state and estate powers before the Díaz regime broke. The political conflicts that began in 1910 allowed his movement to grow and claim a pivotal role in national developments. As his movement began, villagers used remnant ecological autonomies—land for subsistence production—to sustain guerrilla insurgencies that required only horses, machetes, and rifles to threaten nearby powers. Zapatistas, most clearly in the 1911 Plan de Ayala, demanded rights to community lands. As the movement expanded, so did ecological autonomies. Lands taken from estates shifted from sugar to food crops, feeding villagers and supplying ever-larger guerrilla forces. When in 1914 Zapata claimed uncontested control of the state of Morelos, a key decision rewarded mobilized communities. Zapata and his advisors knew that sugar production could provide revenues to support armies and provide arms and munitions. Morelos villagers knew that sugar was the ultimate cause of their vanishing autonomies. They insisted on converting cane fields to community lands, dedicated to maize and primary sustenance. Zapata understood the communities he led—and consented. The result was a movement that could rarely press beyond its homeland. Zapata did not have the strategic power to shape the conflicts that remade the Mexican polity. But he retained the loyalty of the communities he led—because they regained the ecological autonomies that sustained the cultural autonomies they cherished. The communities of Morelos and surrounding regions became defensive bastions. They could not claim the national state, yet state forces could not defeat them for nearly a decade. And from communities newly entrenched in ecological autonomies taken in revolution, Zapatista villagers asserted rights to land and liberty—to ecological and cultural autonomy—for all Mexicans. In the end, Zapata was assassinated; the movement held strong in adamant communities. The demand for agrarian autonomy persisted to help define the postrevolutionary settlement.[60]

The popular mobilization led by Pancho Villa in the northern borderlands proved different—strong in military-political assertions, weak in shaping postrevolutionary society. The limits of ecological autonomies across the North marked the Villista revolution in important ways. Aridity, a deeply commercial society, and the scarcity of historically autonomous communities defined Spanish and Mexican North America. The key exceptions were rancheros settled in marginal zones and the colonists allocated community lands to fight Apache incursions—and both faced assaults on lands and autonomies during the Porfirian boom. They were among the first to join Villa, among the most adamant in sustaining his movement, building on and expanding the ecological autonomies they cherished. But as Villa rose to lead a vast, multiregional northern mobilization, he tapped the commercial ways of the borderlands to sustain it. When he took lands from Porfirian oligarchs, he promised to distribute them among revolutionary veterans and widows—after victory was won. In the interim, he and his generals operated them as state-private enterprises, selling livestock, cotton, and other goods to purchase arms and gain funds to pay troops, to maintain trains for mobility, for supply, and hospitals. Well-armed, paid, and mobile, Villa's armies destroyed the remnants of the Porfirian regime in 1914. But when defeated in the Bajío in 1916 by the armies of the constitutionalist general Álvaro Obregón and forced to retreat into a war of resistance in Chihuahua, Villistas proved less grounded in community autonomies, less capable of fighting on in defense of a vision of a new society.[61]

The oft-noted inability of Zapata and Villa to forge a popular alliance when together their forces ruled most of Mexico in 1914 and 1915 ultimately reflected fundamental and enduring differences between Mexican Mesoamerica and North America.[62] Zapata was the revolutionary personification of Mesoamerican communities (even as many, notably in Morelos, no longer considered themselves Indian). Corporate landholding to

1. In revolution, women broke patriarchal norms to travel and sometimes fight with rebel armies. Reprinted by permission of Archivo General de la Nación, Sección Propiedad Artística y Literaria.

sustain patriarchy, family sustenance, local governance, and community cultures defined the heart of his movement's vision. Land and liberty—ecological autonomy as the basis of cultural independence and local governance—remained the essential, inevitable program. Zapata could act strategically and politically within the parameters set by that tradition and vision.

Villa was equally the revolutionary personification of Mexican North America. Rancheros and colonists demanded lands, with the patriarchal family the preferred unit of landholding (at least among patriarchs). Commercial production was a way of life, international trade a regular route to social mobility. Villa built a revolutionary state and armies by tapping the existing commercial economy, promising lands as private property to those who fought with him and survived. Like the boom and bust cycles that defined northern life since the first colonial mining bonanzas, Villa's mobilization rose to heights of power—and crashed in crisis. The scarce ecological autonomies of Mexican North America limited the revolutionary potential of Villa's revolution.

Thanks to the persistent pressures of the Zapatistas and those with similar demands rooted in communities across Mesoamerican Mexico, agrarian reform became a program of the victorious Constitutionalists, led by Venustiano Carranza and Álvaro Obregón. The result was a national policy that aimed to demobilize agrarian insurgents by reconstituting community ecological autonomies via state-directed land reform. Beginning with wartime legislation of January 1915, while the Zapatista-Villista alliance still ruled most of Mexico, and sanctioned in the Constitution of 1917—with Zapata still in the field—victorious Constitutionalists offered community landholding as a right. They implemented that right only as necessary to consolidate their power.

The political rise of the Constitutionalists seemed the triumph of the commercial society of Mexican North America over the agrarian demands pressed by the communities of Mexican Mesoamerica. From 1915 to 1934, the men who ruled Mexico came from the borderlands. They had defeated Villa and then Zapata. In the 1920s, Presidents Obregón and Calles promoted a vision of agrarian reform that emphasized not the reconstitution of landed communities but rather the construction of irrigation works and the promotion of commercial cultivation. They insisted that they preferred small private property while they protected (and accumulated) large estates. It was a deeply conservative reform—in the tradition of Hispanic North America.[63]

Yet the triumph of the North and the Constitutionalists' conservative reforms proved difficult. Through the 1920s and 1930s, land distributions and *ejido* communities remained pivotal to state consolidation. When Carranza tried to impose a successor in 1920, Obregón rose to oust him— and forged an alliance with surviving Zapatistas. He had to accelerate land distribution in Morelos and other Zapatista zones. Facing political challenge in 1923, and then the uprising of religious rancheros and others seeking their own vision of autonomies in the Cristero revolt of the late 1920s, the Constitutionalists again and again sought the support of rural communities, recruiting fighters with promises of land reform. And when in the aftermath of the Depression, Lázaro Cárdenas worked to oust his predecessor Plutarco Elías Calles from his persistent power, a radical national implementation of land reform gained widespread popular support —and power against those who would limit revolutionary programs while claiming to be "the Revolution."

By 1940, half of Mexico's arable lands were held by ejidos: communities granted lands that were inalienable, backed by the state, and allocated to male heads of household. Through contested, often violent, political processes, revolutionary pressures led to a vast reassertion of ecological autonomies and the patriarchal powers they sustained.[64] Revolutionary land reform brought the diffusion of landed communities across Mexican Meso-america, where ejidos built on enduring if changing traditions, and in Mexican North America, where such communities were radical innova-tions (or impositions). And while ejidos were institutionally the same every-where, allowing statistical compilations that suggested national unifor-mities, realities on the ground inevitably differed in Mexico's ecologically, economically, and socially different regions.

The new ejidos did not re-create colonial republics. The state was a far more active presence in ejido communities, local governance a scarce reality. While colonial republics had combined rights to land and self-rule in powerful if localized autonomies, the revolutionary land reform kept ejido communities legally separate from municipalities—and dependent on the national state. While many who gained ejido lands aimed to recon-solidate subsistence production, the state pressed them toward the market. And the politicization of the land reform process—with regime builders providing lands in search of political support, local leaders pursuing domi-nating advantages, and cultivators seeking land and patriarchal autono-mies—repeatedly provoked local violence. Still, the vast redistribution of lands proved essential to stabilizing the national regime, in part by re-creating limited landed autonomies, in part by shifting violence back to local domains.[65]

A survey of Mexico around 1940 would reveal a broad reemergence of landed communities, a new assertion of ecological autonomies. Yet differ-ences abounded: the new ejidos adapted best to sustain local traditions in the southern highlands of Mesoamerica—across Oaxaca and Chiapas, where communities had defended their lands through the colonial era and decades of Porfirian development, and where revolutionary mobilizations were limited. Across the central highland core, the heartland of Zapatista insurgency, land reform came early—a necessity of pacification. But taking lands from estates to create ejidos gave communities lands for subsistence, without access to the seasonal labor essential to symbiotic exploitation.[66] In Yucatán, the regime turned henequen estates into ejidos, maintaining commercial production, holding Maya producers in dependence now sanctioned as a revolutionary advantage.

Far to the north, the cotton estates of the Laguna became ejidos under Cárdenas in the 1930s. The goal was to gain political support while sustain-ing commercial production in a more cooperative manner. The regime created ejidos elsewhere across the North in the 1920s and 1930s, some-times producing powerful political movements such as that led by Satur-nillo Cedillo in eastern San Luis Potosí, sometimes provoking conflict with former revolutionaries who sought personal tenure as rancheros—not the restrictions and intrusions of state-forged ejidos. Often, northern ejidos gained only arid lands, keeping autonomies and economic prospects limited. When radicals tried to turn great postrevolutionary irrigation projects into ejidos, they gained very limited success. Across Mexican North America, revolutionary ejidos rarely meshed with local traditions. They were innovations in a historically commercial and increasingly capitalist world. (A clear exception developed among the Yaqui, who fought to use ejido rights to re-create autonomies in the rich river valleys of Sonora, among Mexico's most coveted lands. There, too, conflict was inevitable.)[67]

In the postrevolutionary decades, Mesoamerican communities pressed for land reform and ecological autonomies, their preferred basis of cultural autonomy and political participation. The regime responded with land reform to promote political pacification—and imagined as a new way to commercial production. National stability in an inclusive authoritarian regime that allowed participation to sanctioned corporations (including business, labor, and peasants), but reduced electoral citizenship to a legitimating facade, came in the 1930s. Local conflicts proliferated during the reform and long afterward.

Nearly everywhere, especially across Mexican Mesoamerica, the recipients of ejido lands turned to production for sustenance—feeding families, allocating only limited surpluses to urban markets. Policymakers saw the reform as having failed: production of foods and other agricultural goods for cities and industries proved limited and uncertain. The "problem" was that rural families consumed their produce, gaining real improvements in nutrition. The needs of entrepreneurs, the regime, and urban consumers became secondary. To those who aimed to rule and profit, such an outcome was a failure. Revolutionary mobilization followed by pacifying land reform re-created ecological autonomies. Amid political pressures, local conflicts, and pressures to commercial production, many peasant patriarchs, their families, and communities made significant, not utopian, gains.[68]

POPULATION EXPLOSION, URBANIZATION, AND
GREEN REVOLUTION: THE END OF ECOLOGICAL AUTONOMY

Those gains proved short-lived. Some difficulties were rooted in the nature of the reform. Some resulted from its success. And some derived from global developments that came to Mexico as revolutionary reforms reached fruition. If the revolution led through decades of conflict to new ecological autonomies for Mexican communities, by the 1970s the same autonomies were vanishing. When social grievances deepened and political conflicts escalated in Mexico's late-twentieth-century crisis, the revolutionary capacities of Mexican rural communities faced unprecedented limits.

The limits of the agrarian reform were significant. Most ejidos gained lands barely sufficient to feed poor families. Unlike the colonial republics, which received limited lands in times of population decline, the ejidos of twentieth-century Mexico gained minimal lands amid population growth. Part of that growth came from the success of ejido producers in providing better nutrition to their families. Part resulted from smallholders producing large families. With limited lands, one way to increase production or earnings was to put more hands to work on ejido plots—or for supplemental wages. The land reform created incentives for larger families and provided the nutrition to sustain them. Local populations grew. In a generation, they created new pressures on limited holdings.[69]

Then the world economy brought antibiotics to Mexico. From the 1950s, growing generations survived more childhood maladies and adult infections. Life expectancy soared. For decades, incentives to large families mixed with better nutrition and new medicines to fuel a population explosion. Healthy and well-fed families enjoying longer lives must be accounted a success. By the last decades of the twentieth century, Mexicans saw longer, healthier lives as permanent. They began to have smaller families, and population growth slowed. In the interim, everything changed.

The demographic expansion of the twentieth century accelerated growth that had been under way since the postconquest catastrophe. If population tripled in the eighteenth century (from about two million to six million), almost tripled again in the nineteenth (from six million to about sixteen million), it increased more than five times (from sixteen million to nearly one hundred million) during the twentieth century, mostly after 1940. The geographic space available to that population was vast and open to expansion during the colonial centuries, cut in half by U.S. conquest in the 1840s—and constrained ever since. The twentieth century brought unprecedented demographic pressures.

The decades after 1940 also brought unprecedented commercial expansion and global incorporation. Global links were not new. Since the sixteenth century, silver tied the economies of New Spain to an emerging global economy. A second silver boom powered the dynamism of New Spain's eighteenth century—provoking changes that led toward the insurgencies of 1810. But during the colonial centuries, silver operated as a single yet exceptionally dynamic link to the global economy. Across New Spain, most people either fed and clothed themselves (in the autonomous communities of Spanish Mesoamerica) or gained basic necessities in a colonial commercial economy (in cities and across Spanish North America). The early decades after independence brought a sharp decline in mining—and a reconsolidation of autonomies and regional economies. When Mexican textiles industrialized beginning in the 1840s, they industrialized production for Mexican consumption.

After 1880, political stability and railroad integration combined to promote a new surge of commercial expansion. Old global links driven by silver redeveloped, accompanied by copper and later petroleum. For the first time, products of Mexican land and labor sold on world markets in significant and growing amounts. Just when Mexican resources were constrained and Mexican population grew, Mexican agriculture began to supply consumers in Europe and the United States. Also for the first time, foreign capital became pivotal to Mexico's incorporation into the world economy, taking key roles in railroads and mining, and secondary participation in export agriculture (mostly coffee). Still, most Porfirian agricultural exports (with the exception of Yucatecan henequen) came from regions of recent development and sparse settlement.

The revolutionary conflicts of 1910 to 1940 again turned Mexican production inward—but not as radically as after the wars for independence. Silver and petroleum remained important exports into the 1920s; henequen from new revolutionary ejidos still supplied external markets; other exports held strong and provided the emerging Constitutionalist regime with a counterweight to demands for a radical agrarian reconstruction.[70] It was the depression of the early 1930s that broke the external economic links that the revolution had challenged but not severed. And it was in the context of the depression that Cárdenas completed the most extensive distribution of lands to rural communities across Mexico—and especially across Mexican North America. Facing the collapse of global capitalism, ecological autonomy for communities and economic autonomy for Mexico appeared sound, perhaps inevitable, policies. Cárdenas consolidated the postrevolutionary regime by fusing the nationalist capitalism of the Constitutionalists and the demands for autonomies pressed by Zapatistas and other popular insurgents.

The post-independence turn toward autonomies persisted for half a century. The postrevolutionary experiment in nationalism and community autonomies ruled for barely a decade. Everything—except regime rhetoric —changed in the 1940s. As the land reform that re-created community autonomies peaked, it stimulated population growth that eroded family autonomies and local welfare. Soon after President Cárdenas announced the ultimate act of Mexican nationalism, claiming the U.S. and British petroleum companies in 1938, Defense Minister Cárdenas joined in tying Mexico to the United States in support of the Allied war effort in World

War II. U.S. capital was welcomed (outside petroleum) in joint ventures with Mexican entrepreneurs. Nascent industries supported the U.S. war effort. Mexican agriculture, emerging from Cárdenas's land reform, was encouraged to supply U.S. markets. Mexican workers were organized to provide labor in the United States, primarily in agriculture, but in diverse other sectors as well.[71]

Mexicans first went to labor in the United States under the pressures of Porfirian development. They trekked in greater numbers to escape the violence of revolutionary turmoil from 1910 to 1920, and to flee the Cristero revolt of the late 1920s, and the repression at its end. Mexican conflicts made Mexican workers a key part of the development of the U.S. West—once Mexican territory—from the 1890s through the 1920s. The depression reversed the flow. With the collapse of the U.S. economy, Mexicans were pressed back to Mexico—often by denials of welfare and offers of tickets to the border. Children born U.S. citizens were forced "home." Cárdenas's land reform accommodated returning migrants in communities with newly reconstituted autonomies.[72]

When the U.S. economy shifted to wartime mobilization, it drew men into the army, women into factories, and left sharp labor shortages in the fields that sustained the entire edifice. Across the West, Mexicans had been an important solution to agricultural labor scarcities—but after expulsions and returns to communities with new lands, few looked to return north. In a remarkable parallel to the late-sixteenth-century repartimiento (which, amid the reconstitution of the landed republics, sent villagers to work seasonally for wages at nearby estates), the Mexican government joined the United States to organize the Bracero Program. It recruited Mexicans (mostly rural men and boys) to labor in the United States, organizing transportation, overseeing remunerations, and aiming to guarantee "fair" treatment. Collaboration between the Mexican and U.S. governments tied workers rooted in Mexican communities to the booming U.S. wartime economy. The Bracero Program outlived the war, lasting until 1964. Mexican migrants, first seasonal, then increasingly permanent, provided mobile, malleable, and underpaid workers to the U.S. economy long after the draft ended. Mexican workers and communities still subsidize U.S. consumers and corporate profits.[73]

Population growth and rapid reincorporation into a U.S.-centered global capitalist economy created an unprecedented context for communities with recently won, yet limited and already eroding, autonomies. By the 1980s, ecological independence was a memory in all but the most remote regions of Mexico. Two linked processes drove the transformation that ended ecological autonomy: urbanization and the development and pro-liferation of the scientific cultivation celebrated as the green revolution.

In the aftermath of the revolution, Mexico had about twenty million inhabitants, over 75 percent rural. As the twentieth century ended, Mexico approached one hundred million people, at least 75 percent urban. Rural communities grew, thanks in good part to the agrarian reform—but most of the growth migrated to cities that grew at explosively faster rates.[74] Cities do many things. They are centers of power and commerce, industry and labor. They include growing middle classes that enjoy educational and material benefits. Twentieth-century cities, in Mexico and elsewhere, have spawned massive communities of marginal peoples, with little education, without steady work, and desperate to survive, often in underground econ-omies. Yet they do survive, their growing numbers holding down the in-comes of workers and middle sectors (and subsidizing the middle classes with cheap household service).

The promise and challenge of Mexico's future now resides in its cities. And cities, inevitably and structurally, lack ecological autonomies. They live as vast concentrations of population that must be fed by drawing sustenance from outside—whether nearby farmers or distant suppliers. Historically, cities are parasites on agricultural peoples. Structures of com-mercial and political power draw foodstuffs from rural producers, often prejudicing the rural populations to sustain urban life. When relations were reversed to favor rural producers as consumers—as in the aftermaths of Mexico's war for independence and twentieth-century revolution—the powerful and their urban dependents quickly saw crisis. Cities are strat-ified and internally diverse in many ways; inequalities are negotiated in close quarters. But ecological autonomies are not part of those negotia-tions. Dependence on organized powers and commercial means of gaining sustenance define urban society.

Postrevolutionary ejido communities helped pacify the countryside and stabilize the regime; they re-created ecological autonomies—and failed (or refused) to feed burgeoning cities. The regime pressed ejidos toward com-mercial production, but it often failed for lack of means, and knowing that excess pressures could destabilize a still-uncertain polity.

The regime's solution was the green revolution—a government-backed revival and scientific acceleration of the commercial cultivation that histor-ically defined Mexican North America. Since the 1920s, the authorities had built dams and irrigation districts, creating new commercial farming zones. During World War II, backed by the U.S. government and funded by the Rockefeller Foundation, the Mexican government welcomed teams of U.S.

scientists who came to develop new varieties of wheat that proved exceptionally productive. They chose to focus on wheat—the staple of urban and commercial Mexico, of its upper and middle classes, and of Mexican North America. Maize, the staple of communities struggling to survive with newly reconstituted autonomies across Mexican Mesoamerica, was left for later. The scientific solution required irrigated fields, provided by public works at government expense. It required scientifically manufactured hybrid seeds, herbicides, and pesticides that had to be purchased annually. Seed saved from the previous harvest could not produce to green revolution standards. The result was an explosion of wheat production, justly celebrated, subsidized by government irrigation and profitable to commercial growers, and to agribusinesses that sold seeds, fertilizers, pesticides, tractors, and other machinery. But scientific cultivation was the antithesis of ecological autonomy. The green revolution industrialized agriculture; it fed cities, profited agribusiness, and generated unemployment. The Mexican regime, its U.S. allies, and commercial interests across the globe trumpeted the success of the green revolution and called for its diffusion everywhere. Inherently— never explicitly—the call was for a system of cultivation that sustained burgeoning populations in ways that profited agribusiness, ended ecological autonomies, and limited agricultural employment.[75]

What were rural communities to do—especially those rooted in Mesoamerican traditions, recently reconstituted as postrevolutionary ejidos, and by the 1950s facing pressures of growing populations? The historical option of turning to seasonal labor at nearby commercial properties was rarely possible. Taking estate lands to create ejidos had limited commercial production and labor demands, which were further curtailed by widespread mechanization. Classic relations of symbiotic exploitation, tying cultivating communities to wage work at nearby estates—sustaining communities with eroding autonomies—could not redevelop on a large scale.

The regime pressed villagers away from subsistence cultivation toward market crops. Across Mexico, ejido farmers experimented, often by dividing small plots between maize and market crops. They took new seeds, fertilizers, and pesticides on credit—and faced debts to the government agricultural bank when experiments failed to meet promised expectations. They often returned to maize or tried new crops—and took some of the fertilizer provided for tomatoes or broccoli and applied it to maize, with poor results. All the while, populations grew. Villagers pressed cultivation onto ever more marginal lands, shortened or eliminated fallow, leading to erosion and declining yields. In time, cultivation across Mexico became dependent on purchased seeds, chemical fertilizers, and pesticides. It was the only way to continue planting maize or market crops on lands leeched of nutrients by overproduction. Once maize production depended on inputs available only from the government or in the market, the last vestiges of ecological autonomy declined rapidly. Peasant families might still consume their own maize. But to grow that maize, they had to sell growing portions of the crop to buy essential inputs, or find wage earnings to pay the cost of subsistence production. By the 1980s, ecological autonomy was a fading memory for the great majority of Mexican villagers.[76]

As fathers with rights to ejido lands lived longer, sons and daughters migrated to cities. Urbanization and industrialization promised access to employment and material goods. But Mexican industrialization, seeking maximum profit, followed models of labor-saving mechanization developed in societies more prosperous and facing labor shortages. Urban and industrial employment never expanded sufficiently to absorb Mexico's growing population, either during the state-directed development of the 1930s to the 1970s or under neoliberal policies since the 1980s. Before 1970, the Mexican economy lived three decades of growth. Still, that "Mexican Miracle" generated widening unemployment, new marginality, and deepening inequalities—which have persisted and deepened without sustained growth under neoliberalism.

The one option open to Mexicans in communities facing population growth and vanishing autonomies was long-distance seasonal migration. They provided construction labor in growing Mexican cities; they took long treks to harvest fruits and vegetables in northern Mexico and across the U.S. Southwest, West, and Midwest. A new transnational symbiotic exploitation emerged. Mexicans rooted in communities with declining ecological autonomies again migrated to gain the wages of labor at commercial estates, now over long distances, often across international borders in regions first developed as part of Spanish and Mexican North America. The relationship was forged by the Bracero draft—and sustained long afterward by deteriorating conditions in Mexican communities. North American agribusinesses discovered the subsidies inherent in the miserable wages they could pay Mexican migrants—still sustained in important part, however desperately, by home communities. The earnings brought home from years on the road, or sent home by those who stayed longer in the fields, helped sustain communities. They allowed an enterprising few to buy a truck, build a store, or lease neighbors' lands, creating local middle sectors.[77] Like the relations between Mesoamerican communities and neighboring estates in the central highlands in the eighteenth century, agribusiness profited, and villagers struggled to survive. Into the second half of the twentieth century, exploitations organized by long-distance symbiotic exploitation stabilized deepening inequities.

2. Throughout the twentieth century, rural women worked to sustain families and communities in an urbanizing and globalizing world. Photograph by Norma Suárez, San Miguel de Allende, Mexico.

The transnational symbiotic exploitation of the twentieth century, however, came with destabilizing differences. Historically, men rooted in rural communities had engaged in relations of symbiotic exploitation to consolidate patriarchy: they combined cultivation of community lands with labor at nearby estates to sustain families—and roles as patriarchal providers. Early on, when young men spent a few years as migrants, before returning home with cash to help them start up as cultivators, or truckers, or storekeepers, the reinforcement of patriarchy remained a key to transnational symbiotic exploitation. But as community lands became eroded and scarce, and men and boys undertook migratory treks year after year, communities of women and children proliferated across the Mexican countryside. Patriarchal family relations were strained by the long absences of men, and the inevitable participations of women in communities they dominated for most of every year.[78]

As populations grew, lands eroded, and community autonomies vanished, migrations became longer and often permanent. More women and children joined men in El Norte. Other women migrated alone to cities, and especially to border industries, seeking wages and sustenance for families increasingly desperate for earnings. As the twentieth century drew to an end, seasonal and permanent Mexican migrants, men, women, and children, continued to subsidize the capitalist economy of North America. But they faced exploitations increasingly lacking symbiosis. Without remnant autonomies in home communities, transnational symbiotic exploitation gave way to desperately insecure dependency. The mobility to search for labor, and the wages paid when it was found, were constrained by the illegality that marked most Mexicans when they crossed the border. In an integrated North American economy, national citizenship—the liberation offered by nineteenth-century liberals—became a constraint on Mexican workers' lives and incomes. Commercial producers across the continent profit from subsidies grounded in combinations of desperation and illegality. The benefits to men, women, and children on the road, often hiding as illegals, desperate for work in unknown neighborhoods, are few —the ability to continue the search for work and the barest, least-secure sustenance. The few who find entrepreneurial opportunity in El Norte are important exceptional cases for emulation. For the majority, prosperity is unimagined. And autonomy is gone.[79]

The historical relationship between ecological autonomies and political citizenship has entered a new phase. Most obviously, ecological autonomies vanish while those who rule promote citizenship that is national, electoral, and individual. (Proposals to allow Mexicans in the United States, like U.S. citizens abroad, to vote in home elections only confirms that politics remain national.) People without autonomies are offered celebrated rights to vote. But those rights remain insistently national—while Mexicans live and labor in an economy that is North American, and increasingly global. In that context, citizenship provides rights to vote in diverse elections within Mexico. It might provide a route toward political justice. But national citizenship remains a constraint on Mexicans' ability to negotiate work and remunerations in the continental economy that rules their lives. National citizenship is an improbable route toward economic and social justice in a globalizing world.

As the twentieth century ended, Mexicans faced a historic transformation. The ecological autonomies that had sustained communities and their negotiations of everyday life, and periodically enabled them to mount enduring insurgent challenges to those who ruled, were gone. That fundamental change came just as Mexicans endured decades of crisis marked by population pressures, social polarizations, and political crises. In the past, such combinations of grievances and opportunities led to revolutions driven by popular mobilizations grounded in (and re-creating) ecological autonomies. As the twenty-first century begins, the end of those autonomies sharply curtails the option of agrarian insurgencies. Is the option of revolution also gone?

THE END OF MEXICAN REVOLUTIONS?

The last decades of the twentieth century brought a continuous conjuncture of economic dislocations, deepening social exploitations, and political crises. Grievances rooted in material deprivations and blatant injustices were everywhere. Deep divisions among economic elites and political contenders brought situations parallel to those that became opportunities for revolutionary mobilizations in 1810 and 1910. Yet the regime has not broken, widespread and enduring popular insurgencies have not developed, and no contender for national power has sought a sustaining alliance in the limited mobilizations in Chiapas and elsewhere. The era of Mexican revolutions appears over.

Most analysts of recent Mexican development focus on the demise of the authoritarian party state and the development of electoral rule. They lament persistent problems of crime and corruption, and enduring patterns of social and political injustice. They hope—often promise—that a combination of electoral government with neoliberal development within the North American Free Trade Agreement (NAFTA) will bring shared welfare.[80] The achievements and limits of Mexican democratization are important and demand continued analysis. That NAFTA and neoliberal development have continued, even accelerated, patterns of production that promote concentrations of wealth, deepening inequalities, and proliferating lives of marginality demands even more attention.

This exploration of the long course of Mexican history, focused on popular communities, suggests that analyses of the late-twentieth-century crisis, the turn toward democracy, the absence of revolution, and the persistence of deepening inequalities and proliferating injustices must be understood in the context of the end of ecological autonomies and the constraints of national citizenship in an era of global integration.

The crises of recent Mexican history are legion. The student revolt and government massacre of 1968 shook the legitimacy of the postrevolutionary regime. Economic crisis and agrarian demands marked the end of Luis Echeverría's presidency in 1976. The petroleum boom of the late 1970s crashed in unprecedented debt crisis in 1982, leaving Mexicans to face the 1980s as a lost decade of depression. In 1988, Cuauhtémoc Cárdenas, son of the president who consolidated the regime, left it to challenge for the presidency; by all accounts he won the vote—but lost in a count controlled by the regime. Nineteen ninety-four began with the Zapatista uprising in Chiapas, saw the assassination of the regime's chosen presidential candidate, survived another uncertain election with the regime still in power, and ended with a sudden devaluation of the peso that marked another economic collapse. Poverty proliferated, insecurities spread, exploitations deepened. Yet no revolution appeared.

Prevailing visions credit the slow, steady, limited emergence of electoral governance for the transition to democracy that culminated in Vicente Fox's victory in the 2000 presidential elections. They lament the inability of democracy to address Mexico's social inequalities—while imagining that globalizing development might accomplish that. This analysis suggests a different view, historically grounded and less utopian. Mesoamerican communities have long histories of self-rule grounded in ecological autonomies. They fused in colonial indigenous republics. When nineteenth-century liberalism promised new electoral participations while attacking ecological autonomies, it set off enduring conflicts in which communities used elections, sporadic mobilizations, and two eras of revolutionary insurgencies to defend broadly conceived and locally varying visions of land and liberty.

Amid a long and conflictive era of nation building, through the nineteenth century and most of the twentieth, communities asserted their goals. Those who aimed to rule repeatedly withdrew from proclaimed commitments to participatory popular sovereignty. Local republican rule grounded in ecological autonomies had sustained Mesoamerican communities' negotiations of colonial domination for three centuries. They had used liberal rights to local sovereignty to contest liberal challenges to ecological autonomies, struggling to prolong those autonomies through the nineteenth century. In response, liberal elites turned popular sovereignty into a facade masking authoritarian rule, promoting capitalist development, assaulting autonomies—and generating revolution beginning in 1910. Driven by agrarian mobilizations demanding ecological autonomies, it brought a vast, state-controlled land reform and consolidated a regime of authoritarian incorporation that again reduced elections to empty facades while promoting nationalist capitalism—and after 1940 integration into the U.S. world economy.

Since independence, communities have used liberal rights to mobilize in support of ecological autonomies and popular interests. National leaders repeatedly responded with military repression and authoritarian incorporation to impose often-fragile powers. All along, population growth, liberal programs, and capitalist development have worked together to erode ecological autonomies. In key times of crisis, challenges to autonomies led to mobilizations that reconstituted autonomies to sustain enduring insurgencies—eventually forcing land reform onto reticent postrevolutionary regime builders. But the apparent triumph of popular mobilization came just as pressures undermining community autonomies accelerated. By the 1970s, those autonomies were gone—except in the most isolated, marginal zones.

That is the context in which we must understand the decades of crisis without revolution that defined late-twentieth-century Mexico. Grievances were and remain widespread and deepening. Opportunities recurred in crisis after crisis. Missing was revolutionary capacity—the ability of communities in strategic regions to mobilize and sustain opposition long enough to force the powerful to respond. In that historically unprecedented context, those who presumed to rule could reopen the electoral arenas progressively closed since the explosions of popular sovereignty in the era of independence. Without ecological autonomies (and with the regime joining business to assault organized labor), communities urban and rural have no power but the ballot. Voting, of course, occurs on limited occasions selected by the state. Access to the ballot and political campaigns requires financial resources available only to the powerful. Elections, reduced to ritual selections among alternative candidates chosen and funded by the powerful, become "safe" domains for popular participation. Democracy without ecological autonomies is limited. The backers and beneficiaries of neoliberal development promote such democracy (limited to Mexico, while Mexicans struggle to work and live in a North American economy). The powerful seem safe from popular intrusions. Mexico's crises persist.

The 1994 Chiapas uprising illustrates the limited potential for revolutionary mobilizations in the new Mexico. On January 1, rural communities based mostly in isolated lowlands rose up, demanding lands and effective democracy—essentially, ecological autonomy and participation in sovereignty. They claimed the name of Zapatistas, grounding their rights in the vision of the revolutionary leader of Mesoamerican communities. Many rebels came from communities settled by migrants seeking autonomies no longer possible in crowded uplands. But the recent combination of petroleum development along the nearby Gulf coast and commercial expansion into the Chiapas lowlands assaulted those autonomies and built resentments against deepening injustices. Such classic grievances had long challenged Mexican communities and often set them to protest, sometimes to revolutionary insurgencies.[81]

The uprising was planned for January 1, 1994—not a time of maximum opportunity. It was the day that NAFTA took effect—a day of unity and optimism among Mexican elites, a day when the United States was ready to back the Mexican regime to maximum effect. The date of the uprising aimed to challenge NAFTA, the presidency of Carlos Salinas, and his 1992 reforms that reversed the revolutionary right to community lands. It was a date of maximum ideological effect, but minimal strategic opportunity. The choice seems appropriate to leaders focused on national and global politics. But it was a choice radically different from the historical decisions of Mexico's insurgent communities, who repeatedly bore deepening grievances but waited to take arms only when a clear combination of elite division and regime breakdown (or weakness, or distraction) promised an opportunity to establish insurgency without facing immediate and overpowering repression.

What followed in Chiapas reflected the timing of the uprising, the limits of the opportunity, and the isolation of the communities driving the insurgency. A few days of violent assertions led to quick repression, a stalemate, and a cease-fire that led to long negotiations and limited resolutions. Core rebel communities retain independence grounded in local autonomies in isolated zones. Rebel leaders use the Internet and other technologies of globalization to mobilize support for proclamations of indigenous rights. The Mexican government, before and after the electoral transformation of 2000, has preferred endless negotiation to clear resolution—whether concessions to the insurgents or effective repression. The regime sees Chiapas as a problem of legitimacy, national and international—not of effective rule. The insurgency persists, isolated and unable to claim substantial gains.

The Chiapas mobilization did pressure the regime toward democratization. The Zapatistas placed the issues of exploitation and injustice in Mexican communities before the world and urban Mexicans, who had long preferred to ignore them. The uprising accelerated and shaped in important ways the ongoing transition to electoral governance. One of those ways was to demonstrate that agrarian insurgencies could no longer become revolutionary mobilizations. Autonomous communities were too few, too isolated, too caught up in a world of global dependencies. The few rural mobilizations that followed Chiapas remained in similar isolated regions, notably the highlands of Guerrero. They too never challenged the regime.[82]

Equally revealing, no contender for national power took the pivotal role of Miguel Hidalgo in 1810 and Francisco Madero in 1910—turning to rural communities ready to mobilize ecological autonomies to sustain insurgencies that long outlived the leaders who linked them to debates over sovereignties in crisis. Have late-twentieth-century leaders, left, right, and center, simply changed, ruled by commitments to democracy that prevent any turn to popular mobilizations? Or have they recognized, at least implicitly, that in a world overwhelmingly urban, in which surviving rural communities lack autonomies (except in isolated marginal zones), popular mobilizations no longer offer effective bases of revolutionary assertion?

This analysis suggests—for it is impossible to prove why people do not act in certain ways—that the celebrated turn to democracy in turn-of-the-century Mexico resulted in important part from the collapse of the revolutionary capacity of Mexican communities. The ecological autonomies that sustained that capacity in the mobilizations that began in 1810 and 1910 are gone. With rural communities structurally incapable of sustaining mobilizations—they, and urban Mexicans, are allowed to express themselves in limited balloting. Meanwhile, neoliberal economics in the context of NAFTA continue to concentrate wealth, deepen exploitation, and generate marginality. Criminal and familial violence escalates again. In that context, the calls for a more effective democracy matter. If elections remain theatrical rituals, allowing people brief engagements in the selection of leaders while inequities proliferate, crime persists, courts fail, and meaningful responses to deepening popular grievances remain scarce, the moral outrage of lives defined by persistent and worsening deprivations and injustices can only escalate.

An effective national democracy, offering meaningful choices and transparent results at the polls and allowing even poor and marginal people access to courts they view as legitimate (the courts having been a key to centuries of colonial stabilization in New Spain), might enable the desperate majority to choose and sustain leaders who dampen the hard edges of globalization. An effective North American democracy might allow communities across the continent to seek leaders who know that the lowest wages are not always best, that the lack of benefits is rarely a benefit, that insecurity and marginal survival are not sustainable ways of life, that illegality cannot forever organize pivotal labor relations, and that in a world of global integration, desperate poverty anywhere brings deepening poverty everywhere. Such transnational democracy is imaginable, but hard to see developing in the present historical situation. Still, a Mexican national democracy might allow limited gains and keep communities without autonomies in lives of acquiescent subordination. An effective democracy might allow Mexicans, urban and rural, legally at home and illegally abroad, to blunt the exploitations that make them so valuable to globalization.[83] Without revolutionary alternatives, they might carry on indefinitely—to the benefit of Mexican elites, North American integration, and global accumulation.

But what if electoral theatrics (sometimes circuses) of uncertain legitimacy persist as the only means of popular political expression, while exploitations and injustices continue to deepen and proliferate? The old option of agrarian revolution seems gone. History suggests that desperate peoples find ways to assert themselves. Grievances mount; economic breakdowns and political crises recur. As long as insurgencies grounded in the autonomies of rural communities can no longer sustain revolutions, new ways of assertion emerge. Chiapas insurgents use the technologies of global integration to organize and create global networks of support. Other rebels in Latin America have tapped the wealth of the drug economy —the dark side of globalization in the Americas. Revolutionaries to come will find ways to challenge structures of power and production they cannot escape.

Mexicans live a momentous time of transition. The ecological autonomies that sustained their revolutionary traditions are gone. Thanks to NAFTA, they live at the vortex of globalization, providing petroleum, inexpensive foods, and cheap labor (on both sides of the border), subsidizing transnational corporations and North American consumers. They are promised that democracy will solve their problems—a widespread hope at the moment of euphoria when the 2000 elections ended the rule of the old regime. Now it seems that politics have changed, and nearly everything else has stayed the same—or worsened. Will desperate people vote and work for declining wages without benefits, while growing numbers face marginality, migration, and illegality—for generations? Or will they create new assertions (as did the people of the Bajío in 1810), beginning another time of revolutionary contests, unimaginably different in the new world of global integration and desperation?

EPILOGUE: THE END OF THE AGE OF REVOLUTIONS?

This exploration of the long course of Mexican history, its revolutions, and the improbability of a recurrence as the twenty-first century begins suggests a new reading of modern history. From the late eighteenth century through the late twentieth, the world has lived transformations marked by industrial production, commercial integrations, and regimes of popular sovereignty. In the early twentieth century, industrialization and popular sovereignty split into capitalist and socialist variants, but both promoted industrial production and labor dependency, both insisted that they fulfilled the promise of popular sovereignty—and both assaulted ecological autonomies. Socialism concentrated political and economic powers, often in closed regimes. Capitalism separated national states and globalizing corporations. As the twentieth century waned, socialism collapsed, and ecological autonomies approached their end. The last successful revolutions—in China and Vietnam—transformed societies of persistent peasant communities. The last revolutionary mobilizations in the Americas, in Central America, the Peruvian Andes, and Chiapas, came in enclaves of peasant communities, whose autonomies sustained insurgencies that were contained—as were their revolutions. Was Vietnam the turning point, the last successful revolution grounded in peasant autonomies? Subsequent mobilizations based in rural communities have proved too marginal to force fundamental transformations.[84]

The result is a moment of capitalist euphoria. The triumph of global capitalism linked to national democracies seems at hand. History, however, suggests that the moment should be recognized as a moment. And the keys to the moment are the triumph of capitalism, the promise of democracy, and the end of ecological autonomies—nearly everywhere across the globe. Much analysis has focused on the rise of commercialism and its culmination in the Industrial Revolution beginning in the eighteenth century. The end of ecological autonomies marks the completion of global industrialization: nearly everyone now lives in dependency; the industrialization of production in every domain including agriculture allows us to produce in unprecedented quantities—and to consign growing numbers to marginal lives where their work is not needed, their sustenance uncertain. In that emerging world, the powerful promote the genius of global markets, while the sovereignty of peoples is constrained in nationally limited sometimes democratic polities. Disjunctions between accumulations of wealth and power and exploding populations facing desperate marginality, and between globally integrated processes of production and labor and nationally constrained promises of democracy, deepen to define mounting exploitations and limited solutions. Meanwhile, regimes of capitalist power and peoples facing marginal desperation turn to new versions of divine sanctions—some to legitimate power, others to challenge it.

If the world of industrialization, popular sovereignties, and revolutions grounded in the revolutionary capacity of rural communities was modern, the new world of global dependencies, religious visions, and deepening frustrations is offered as postmodern: a world of integrations and dependencies, cultural constructions and debates, and assertions of utopia—some defending the present in service of an imagined future, others challenging the powerful in service of alternative worlds. There is much to learn in the postmodern vision. But it too often neglects the hard material realities of lives without food, desperate for sustenance, lacking futures for children—deprivations engineered by powers that drove industrialization forward and forced the end of ecological autonomies, the material bases of the revolutions that helped shape the modern world by contesting the power of its power holders.

The powers of the postmodern world of globalization are deeply material, as are the dependencies and deprivations lived by people without ecological autonomies. The emerging assertions of postmodern insurgents are equally material. The cultural conversations of competing ideologies matter, as do the material technologies that allow them to compete globally for legitimacy. But most people, powerful and poor, live grounded in material realities—the few concentrating powers, the many struggling to survive. The end of ecological autonomies, the material bases of popular revolutionary capacities during the modern age (in Mexico and elsewhere), suggests that the age of revolutions is over.

Unless the promised benefits of capitalist globalization and democratic nationalism find ways to become real, new popular assertions will develop. They will be different. They may challenge the linkages essential to globalization as much as the institutions of nations. The end of ecological autonomies brings change as momentous as the beginning of the Industrial Revolution. The future remains unimagined. Will it bring effective participations, shared sustenance, and accessible justice, or new assertions by desperate peoples against bastions of power?

NOTES

1 John Tutino, *From Insurrection to Revolution in Mexico: Social Bases of Agrarian Violence, 1750–1940* (Princeton: Princeton University Press, 1986).

2 Eric Van Young has demonstrated this brilliantly and massively in *The Other Rebellion: Popular Violence, Ideology, and the Mexican Struggle for Independence, 1810–1821* (Stanford: Stanford University Press, 2001). For the twentieth-century revolution, see Salvador Rueda Smithers, *El paraíso de la caña: Historia de una construcción imaginaria* (Mexico City: Instituto Nacional de Antropología e Historia, 1998).

3 See John Tutino, "The Revolution in Mexican Independence: Insurgency and the Renegotiation of Property, Production, and Patriarchy in the Bajío, 1800–1855," *Hispanic American Historical Review* 78, no. 3 (1998): 367–418; and Tutino, "El desarrollo liberal, el patriarcado y la involución de la violencia social en el México porfirista: El crimen y la muerte infantile en el altiplano central," in *Don Porfirio Presidente . . . , nunca omnipotente,* ed. Romana Falcón and Ramond Buve (Mexico City: Universidad Iberoamericana, 1998).

4 Womack Jr., *Zapata and the Mexican Revolution* (New York: Knopf, 1969); Avila Espinosa, *Los orígenes del zapatismo* (Mexico City: El Colegio de México, 2001); Katz, *The Life and Times of Pancho Villa* (Stanford: Stanford University Press, 1998).

5 See Tutino, "The Revolution in Mexican Independence."

6 The classic statement of the importance of mobilized peasant communities to

modern revolutions is Eric Wolf, *Peasant Wars of the Twentieth Century* (New York: Harper and Row, 1969).

7 The literature on pre-Hispanic Mesoamerica is vast. The best recent synthesis is Alfredo López Austin and Leopoldo López Luján, *El pasado indígena*, rev. ed. (Mexico City: Fondo de Cultura Económica, 2001).

8 In *El pasado indígena*, López and López offer an especially fine analysis of the regions they call Arid America.

9 I develop the distinction between Spanish Mesoamerica and Spanish North America in my forthcoming book "Making a New World: Forging Atlantic Capitalism in the Bajío and Spanish North America."

10 The literature on encomiendas is also vast. I have been notably influenced by José Miranda, *La función económica del encomendero y los origines del regimen colonial* (Mexico City: UNAM, 1965); Charles Gibson, *The Aztecs under Spanish Rule* (Stanford: Stanford University Press, 1964); Margarita Menegus Bornemann, *Del señorío a la república de indios: El caso de Toluca, 1500–1600* (Madrid: Ministerio de Agricultura, Pesca y Alimentación, 1991); and recently by the brilliant inquiry of René García Castro, *Indios, territorio y poder en la provincia Matlatzinca: La negociación del espacio político en los pueblos otomianos, siglos XV–XVII* (Zinacatepec: El Colegio Mexiquense, 1999).

11 This vision of the colonial transformation reflects John Tutino, "Urban Power and Agrarian Society: Mexico City and Its Hinterland in the Colonial Era," in *La ciudad, el campo, y la frontera en la historia de México*, vol. 2 (Mexico City: UNAM, 1992), 507–22. For more complex perspectives on the first century of change, see García Castro, *Indios, territorio y poder.*

12 Woodrow Borah, *Justice by Insurance* (Berkeley: University of California Press, 1982).

13 Again, the sources are vast. I have been most influenced by Gibson, *Aztecs under Spanish Rule*; William Taylor, *Drinking, Homicide, and Rebellion in Colonial Mexican Villages* (Stanford: Stanford University Press, 1979); Nancy Farriss, *Maya Society under Colonial Rule* (Princeton: Princeton University Press, 1984); James Lockhart, *The Nahuas after the Conquest* (Stanford: Stanford University Press, 1992); Serge Gruzinski, *The Conquest of Mexico: The Incorporation of Indian Societies in the Western World* (Cambridge: Cambridge University Press, 1993); Marcelo Carmagnani, *El regreso de los dioses* (Mexico City: Fondo de Cultura Económica, 1988); and Kevin Terraciano, *The Mixtecs of Colonial Oaxaca* (Stanford: Stanford University Press, 2001). The emphasis on hybridity and on the importance of republican traditions reflects the essay by Antonio Annino in this volume.

14 In *Aztecs under Spanish Rule*, Gibson detailed how congregated communities resisted and finally ended the labor draft.

15 Classic studies of northern development are Francois Chevalier, *La formación de los grandes latifundios en México*, trans. Antonio Alatorre (Mexico City: Problemas Agrícolas e Industriales de México, 1956); Philip Powell, *La guerra chichimeca, 1550–1600*, trans. Juan José Utrilla (Mexico City: Fondo de Cultura Económica, 1994); and P. J. Bakewell, *Silver Mining and Society in Colonial Mexico: Zacatecas, 1546–1700* (Cambridge: Cambridge University Press, 1971). My vision derives from my work on "Making a New World."

16 For mining, see Bakewell, *Silver Mining and Society*; I first developed this vision of estate communities in John Tutino, "Life and Labor on North Mexican Haciendas," in *El trabajo y los trabajadores en la historia de México*, ed. Elsa Cecilia Frost et al. (Mexico City: El Colegio de México, 1979), 339–78.

17 Juan Carlos Garavaglia and Juan Carlos Grosso, *Puebla desde una perspectiva microhistoria* (Puebla: Universidad Autónoma de Puebla, 1994); Juan Carlos Grosso and Juan Carlos Garavaglia, *La region de Puebla en la economía novohispana* (Mexico City: Instituto Mora, 1996); Norma Castillo Palma, *Cholula: Sociedad mestiza en ciudad India* (Mexico City: Universidad Autónoma Metropolitana, Ixtapalapa, 2001); Brian Hamnett, *Roots of Insurgency: Mexican Regions, 1750–1825* (Cambridge: Cambridge University Press, 1986).

18 William Taylor, *Landlord and Peasant in Colonial Oaxaca* (Stanford: Stanford University Press, 1972); Brian Hamnett, *Politics and Trade in Southern Mexico, 1750–1821* (Cambridge: Cambridge University Press, 1971); Rodolfo Pastor, *Campesinos y reformas: La mixteca, 1700–1856* (Mexico City: El Colegio de México, 1987); Jeremy Baskes, *Indians, Merchants, and Markets* (Stanford: Stanford University Press, 2000).

19 D. A. Brading, *Miners and Merchants in Bourbon Mexico, 1763–1810* (Cambridge: Cambridge University Press, 1971); Laura Pérez Rosales, *Minería y sociedad en Taxco durante el siglo XVIII* (Mexico City: Universidad Iberoamericana, 1996); Doris Ladd, *The Making of a Strike: Mexican Silver Workers' Struggles in Real del Monte, 1766–1767* (Lincoln: University of Nebraska Press, 1988).

20 I first developed this vision in John Tutino, "Creole Mexico: Spanish Elites, Haciendas, and Indian Towns, 1750–1810" (Ph.D. diss., University of Texas, Austin, 1976); see also Cheryl Martin, *Rural Society in Colonial Morelos* (Albuquerque: University of New Mexico Press, 1985).

21 Tutino, "Creole Mexico" and *From Insurrection to Revolution*; Martin, *Rural Society*; Taylor, *Drinking, Homicide, and Rebellion*.

22 John Tutino, "Hacienda Social Relations in Mexico: The Chalco Region in the Era of Independence," *Hispanic American Historical Review* 55, no. 3 (1975): 496–528. For an important case study of a brief and local uprising at Amecameca, see Carlos Herrero Bervera, *Revuelta, rebelión y revolución* (Mexico City: Miguel Angel Porrúa, 2001). For a broad demonstration that most uprisings in regions of indigenous republics were brief and local, see Van Young, *The Other Rebellion*.

23 See Martin, *Rural Society*; and especially the careful consideration of this question in William Taylor, *Magistrates of the Sacred* (Stanford: Stanford University Press, 1996), appendix C.

24 On the early colonial history of the Mezquital, see Elinore Melville, *A Plague of Sheep* (Cambridge: Cambridge University Press, 1994); on late colonial mine labor, see Ladd, *Making of a Strike*.

25 John Tutino, "Buscando independencias populares: Conflictos sociales e insurgencies populares en el Mezquital mexicano, 1800–1815," in *El tiempo de las independencias en la América Española*, ed. José Antonio Serrano and Marta Terán (Zamora: El Colegio de Michoacán, 2002).

26 See Tutino, "Buscando independencias populares"; and Virginia Guedea's fine study of the relationship between Osorno and popular rebels in *La insurgencia*

en el Departamento del Norte: Los llanos de Apan y la sierra de Puebla, 1810–1816 (Mexico City: UNAM, 1996). The Villagráns are analyzed in Hamnett, *Roots of Insurgency*; Herrero Bervera, *Revuelta, rebelión y revolución*; and Van Young, *The Other Rebellion*.

27 Brading, *Miners and Merchants*; Carlos Marichal, *La bancarrota del virreinato* (Mexico City: Fondo de Cultura Económica, 1999); Stanley Stein and Barbara Stein, *Apogee of Empire: Spain and New Spain in the Age of Charles III, 1759–1789* (Baltimore: Johns Hopkins University Press, 2003).

28 Tutino, *From Insurrection to Revolution* and "Making a New World."

29 Robert West, *The Mining Community in Northern New Spain: The Parral Mining District* (Berkeley: University of California Press, 1947); Michael Swann, *Tierra Adentro: Settlement and Society in Colonial Durango* (Boulder: Westview Press, 1982); Cheryl Martin, *Governance and Society in Colonial Mexico: Chihuahua in the Eighteenth Century* (Stanford: Stanford University Press, 1996); Susan Deeds, *Defiance and Deference in Mexico's Colonial North* (Austin: University of Texas Press, 2003).

30 On Texas, see Jesus F. de la Teja, *San Antonio de Béjar* (Albuquerque: University of New Mexico Press, 1995); and Robert Ricklis, *The Karankawa Indians of Texas* (Austin: University of Texas Press). On Sonora, see Cynthia Radding, *Wandering Peoples* (Durham: Duke University Press, 1997). And on California, the essential synthesis is Martha Ortega Soto, *Alta California: Una frontera olvidada del noroeste de México* (Mexico City: Universidad Autónoma Metropolitana, Ixtapalapa, 2001).

31 Ramón Gutiérrez, *When Jesus Came the Corn Mothers Went Away* (Stanford: Stanford University Press, 1991); and James Brooks, *Captives and Cousins* (Chapel Hill: University of North Carolina Press, 2002).

32 Tutino, "Life and Labor on North Mexican Haciendas," *From Insurrection to Revolution*, and "Making a New World."

33 Tutino, "The Revolution in Mexican Independence."

34 Tutino, "The Revolution in Mexican Independence" and "Buscando independencias populares."

35 This is the key conclusion of Van Young's *The Other Rebellion*.

36 Peter Guardino, *Peasants, Politics, and the Formation of the Mexican National State: Guerrero, 1800–1855* (Stanford: Stanford University Press, 1996).

37 François-Xavier Guerra, *Modernidades e independencias* (Mexico City: Fondo de Cultura Económica, 1993); Terry Rugeley, *Yucatán's Maya Peasantry and the Origins of the Caste War* (Austin: University of Texas Press, 1996); Alfredo Ávila, *En nombre de la nación* (Mexico City: Taurus, 2002); Claudia Guarisco, *Los indios del valle de México y la construcción de una nueva sociabilidad política, 1770–1835* (Zinacatepec: El Colegio Mexiquense, 2003); and Antonio Annino's essay in this volume.

38 For an overview, see Tutino, *From Insurrection to Revolution*. For case studies, see Rugeley, *Yucatán's Maya Peasantry*; Guarisco, *Indios del valle de México*; and Guardino, *Peasants, Politics*.

39 Fernando Escalante Gonzalbo, *Ciudadanos imaginarios* (Mexico City: El Colegio de México, 1992); Ávila, *En nombre de la nación*; José Antonio Serrano Ortega,

Jerarquía territorial y transición política (Zamora: El Colegio de Michoacán, 2001); Peter Guardino, *In the Time of Liberty: Popular Political Culture in Oaxaca, 1750–1850* (Durham: Duke University Press, 2005); and Annino's essay in this volume.

40 Guardino, *Peasants, Politics*; Rugeley, *Yucatán's Maya Peasantry*; and Annino's essay in this volume.

41 Tutino, "The Revolution in Mexican Independence."

42 Araceli Ibarra Bellón, *El comrecio y el poder en México, 1821–1864* (Mexico City: Fondo de Cultura Económica, 1998); Tutino, *From Insurrection to Revolution*; Luis González, *Pueblo en vilo: Microhistoria de San José de Gracia* (Mexico City: El Colegio de México, 1968).

43 Charles Hale, *Mexican Liberalism in the Age of Mora, 1821–1853* (New Haven: Yale University Press, 1968); Escalante, *Ciudadanos imaginarios.*

44 Michael Costeloe, *The Central Republic in Mexico, 1835–1846* (Cambridge: Cambridge University Press, 1993); Walter Berneker, *De agiotistas a empresarios: En torno a la temprana insdustrialización mexicana, siglo XIX* (Mexico City: Universidad Iberoamericana, 1992); Ibarra Bellon, *El comercio y el poder*; Tutino, "The Revolution in Mexican Independence."

45 Josefina Vázquez, ed., *México al tiempo de su guerra con Estados Unidos* (Mexico City: Fondo de Cultura Económica, 1997); Nelson Reed, *The Caste War of Yucatán* (Stanford: Stanford University Press, 1964); Leticia Reina, "The Sierra Gorda Peasant Rebellion, 1847–1850," in *Riot, Rebellion, and Revolution*, ed. Friedrich Katz (Princeton: Princeton University Press, 1988), 269–94; Luis Granados, *Sueñan las piedras: Alzamiento ocurrido en la ciudad de México, 14, 15, 16 de septiembre de 1847* (Mexico City: Ediciones Era, 2003).

46 Hale, *Mexican Liberalism*; Guardino, *Peasants, Politics.*

47 Richard Sinkin, *The Mexican Reform, 1855–1876* (Austin: University of Texas Press, 1979); Jan Bazant, *The Alienation of Church Wealth in Mexico* (Cambridge: Cambridge University Press, 1971); Silvestre Villegas Revueltas, *El liberalismo moderado en México* (Mexico City: UNAM, 1997); Erika Pani, *Para mexicanizar el segundo imperio* (Mexico City: El Colegio de México, 2001); and Florencia Mallon, *Peasant and Nation: The Making of Postcolonial Mexico and Peru* (Berkeley: University of California Press, 1995).

48 For an overview, see Tutino, *From Insurrection to Revolution*; for the first detailed case history, see Emilio Kourí, *A Pueblo Divided* (Stanford: Stanford University Press, 2004).

49 Again, for an overview, see Tutino, *From Insurrection to Revolution*; for a local history, see Tutino, "Agrarian Social Change and Peasant Rebellion in Nineteenth-Century Mexico: The Example of Chalco," in Katz, *Riot, Rebellion, and Revolution*, 95–140; for the struggles of peasant communities allied with the liberals, see Mallon, *Peasant and Nation.*

50 François-Xavier Guerra, *Del antiguo régimen a la revolución*, 2 vols. (Mexico City: Fondo de Cultura Económica, 1988); Charles Hale, *The Transformation of Liberalism in Late Nineteenth-Century Mexico* (Princeton: Princeton University Press, 1989); Mark Wasserman, *Capitalists, Caciques, and Revolution: The Native Elite and Foreign Enterprise in Chihuahua, Mexico, 1854–1911* (Chapel Hill: University of North Carolina Press, 1984).

51 John Coatsworth, *Growth against Development* (De Kalb: Northern Illinois University Press, 1981); Stephen Haber, Armando Razo, and Noel Maurer, *The Politics of Property Rights* (Cambridge: Cambridge University Press, 2003).

52 Simon Miller, *Landlords and Haciendas in Modernizing Mexico* (Amsterdam: CEDLA, 1995); Marta Eugenia García Ugarte, *Hacendados y rancheros queretanos, 1780–1920* (Mexico City: Conaculta, 1992); María Otilia Olvera Estrada, *Los tiempos del patrón . . . , Danza de mil soles: Los últimos trabajadores de la hacienda en Querétaro* (Querétaro: Gobierno del Estado, 1997); María de la Cruz Labarthé Rios, *León entre dos inundaciones* (Guanajuato: Ediciones de la Rana, 1997).

53 Ana Alonso, *Thread of Blood: Colonialism, Gender, and Revolution on Mexico's Northern Frontier* (Tucson: University of Arizona Press, 1995); Paul Vanderwood, *The Power of God against the Guns of Government* (Stanford: Stanford University Press, 1998).

54 Wasserman, *Capitalists, Caciques, and Revolution*; William Meyer, *Forge of Progress, Crucible of Revolution* (Albuquerque: University of New Mexico Press, 1994); Katz, *Life and Times of Pancho Villa*.

55 Allen Wells and Gilbert Joseph, *Summer of Discontent, Seasons of Upheaval: Elite Politics and Rural Insurgency in Yucatán, 1876–1915* (Stanford: Stanford University Press, 1996).

56 Daniela Spenser, "Soconusco: The Formation of a Coffee Economy in Chiapas," in *Other Mexicos*, ed. Thomas Benjamin and Mark Wasserman (Albuquerque: University of New Mexico Press, 1984), 123–43; Heather Fowler-Salamini, "Gender, Work, and Coffee in Córdoba, Veracruz, 1850–1910," in *Women of the Mexican Countryside*, ed. Heather Fowler-Salamini and Mary Kay Vaughan (Tucson: University of Arizona Press, 1990), 51–73; and Francie Chassen-López, *From Liberal to Revolutionary Oaxaca: The View from the South, Mexico, 1867–1911* (University Park: Pennsylvania State University Press, 2004). For detailed histories of vanilla at Papantla, Veracruz, generating much conflict yet little sustained revolutionary insurgency after 1910, see Kourí, *Pueblo Divided*; and Ramón Ramírez Melgarejo, *La política del estado mexicano y los procesos agrícolas de los totonacos* (Xalapa: Universidad Veracruzana, 2002).

57 Arturo Warman, . . . *Y venimos a contradecir: Los campesinos de Morelos y el estado nacional* (Mexico City: La Casa Chata, 1976); Ávila Espinosa, *Los origines del zapatismo*; Alejandro Tortolero Villaseñor, *De la coa a la maquina de vapor: Actividad agrícola e inovación technológica en las haciendas mexicanas* (Mexico City: Siglo XXI, 1995).

58 Tutino, "El desarrollo liberal, el patriarcado."

59 For that, see Alan Knight, *The Mexican Revolution*, 2 vols. (Cambridge: Cambridge University Press, 1986); and Friedrich Katz, *The Secret War in Mexico: Europe, the United States, and the Mexican Revolution* (Chicago: University of Chicago Press, 1983).

60 Womack, *Zapata*; Ávila Espinosa, *Los orígines del zapatismo*.

61 Katz, *Life and Times of Pancho Villa*.

62 I explore that juncture in John Tutino, "Revolutionary Confrontation, 1913–1917: Regional Factions, Class Conflicts, and the New National State," in *Provinces*

of the Revolution, ed. Thomas Benjamin and Mark Wasserman (Albuquerque: University of New Mexico Press, 1990).

63 Luis Aboites Aguilar, *La irrigación revolucionaria* (Mexico City: Secretaría de Educación Pública, 1988); Manolo Sepúlveda Garza, *Políticas agrarias y luchas sociales: San Diego de la Unión, Guanajuato, 1900–2000* (Mexico City: Instituto Nacional de Antropología e Historia, 2000).

64 Womack, *Zapata*; Jean Meyer, *La cristiada*, 3 vols. (Mexico City: Siglo XXI, 1973–74); María Eugenia Garcia Ugarte, *Génesis del porvenir: Sociedad y politica en Querétaro, 1913–1940* (Mexico City: Fondo de Cultura Económica, 1997); Jennie Purnell, *Popular Movements and State Formation in Revolutionary Mexico* (Durham: Duke University Press, 1999).

65 Eyler Simpson, *The Ejido: Mexico's Way Out* (Chapel Hill: University of North Carolina Press, 1937), is the classic contemporary analysis. Paul Friedrich, *The Princes of Naranja* (Austin: University of Texas Press, 1986), is the most probing analysis of local violence.

66 On land reform in and near the Zapatista heartland, see Warman, . . . *Y venimos a contradecir*; Guillermo de la Peña, *Herederos de promesas: Agricultura, política, y ritual en los altos de Morelos* (Mexico City: La Casa Chata, 1980); Laura Valladares de la Cruz, *Cuando el agua se esfumó* (Mexico City: UNAM, 2003); and Pablo Castro Domingo, *Chayotes, burros y machetes* (Zinacatepec: El Colegio Mexiquense, 2003).

67 On the varieties of northern land reform, see Romana Falcón, *Revolución y caciquismo: San Luis Potosí, 1910–1938* (Mexico City: El Colegio de México, 1984); Luis Aboites Aguilar, *La irrigación revolucionaria*; Daniel Nugent, *Spent Cartridges of Revolution* (Chicago: University of Chicago Press, 1993); María Vargas-Lobsinger, *La comarca lagunera de la revolución a la expropriación de las haciendas* (Mexico City: UNAM, 1999). On cultural contests linked to land reform in Mexican Mesoamerica and North America, see Mary Kay Vaughan, *Cultural Politics in Revolution* (Tucson: University of Arizona Press, 1997).

68 On the Cárdenas consolidation of the 1930s, see Nora Hamilton, *The Limits of State Autonomy: Post-revolutionary Mexico* (Princeton: Princeton University Press, 1982); and Adolfo Gilly, *El cardenismo: Una utopia mexicana* (Mexico City: Cal y Arena, 1994).

69 The best overview of the difficulties faced by ejidos in the twentieth century, including demographic trends and commercial pressures, is Arturo Warman, *El campo mexicano en el siglo XX* (Mexico City: Fondo de Cultura Económica, 2001).

70 Haber et al., *Politics of Property Rights*, outlines the persistence of export production through the 1920s.

71 Rafael Loyola, ed., *Entre la guerra y la estabilidad política: México en los 40* (Mexico City: Editorial Grijalbo, 1990); Luis Medina, *Hacia el nuevo estado* (Mexico: Fondo de Cultura Económica, 1995). See especially the essay by Friedrich Katz in this volume.

72 Mark Reisler, *By the Sweat of Their Brow* (Westport: Greenwood Press, 1976); Francisco Balderrama and Raymond Rodríguez, *Decade of Betrayal* (Albuquerque: University of New Mexico Press, 1995).

73 The classic analysis, written just after the war, is Carey McWilliams, *North from Mexico* (Westport: Greenwood Press, 1968). The full importance of the Bracero Program to the modern histories of Mexico and the United States awaits its historian.

74 Warman, *El campo mexicano*.

75 Cynthia Hewitt de Alcántara, *Modernizing Mexican Agriculture: Socioeconomic Implications of Technical Change* (Geneva: UN Research Institute for Social Development, 1976); Angus Wright, *The Death of Ramón González: The Modern Agricultural Dilemma* (Austin: University of Texas Press, 1990).

76 This fundamental transformation was first described in Warman, . . . *Y venimos a contradecir*, confirmed in numerous regional and local studies, and recently synthesized in Warman, *El campo mexicano*.

77 Douglas Massey et al., *Return to Aztlán* (Berkeley: University of California Press, 1987); Jorge Durand, *Más allá de la linea* (Mexico City: Conaculta, 1994); Michael Kearney, *Reconceptualizing the Peasantry* (Boulder: Westview Press, 1996); Victor Espinosa, *El dilemma del retorno* (Zamora: El Colegio de Michoacán, 1998).

78 Brígida García and Orlandina de Oliveira, *Trabajo femenino y vida familiar en México* (Mexico City: El Colegio de México, 1996).

79 Wright, *Death of Ramón González*; Kearney, *Reconceptualizing the Peasantry*.

80 Among the best analyses are Medina, *Hacia el nuevo estado*; and Nora Lustig, *Mexico: The Remaking of an Economy* (Washington: Brookings Institution, 1998). For perceptive new views, see the four essays in part III of this volume.

81 The literature on the Chiapas rising is immense. A fine place to begin is John Womack Jr., *Rebellion in Chiapas: An Historical Reader* (New York: New Press, 1999). Larger perspectives are offered in Arturo Warman, *Los indios mexicanos en el umbral del milenio* (Mexico City: Fondo de Cultura Económica, 2003); and Lynn Stephen, *Zapata Lives: Histories and Cultural Politics in Southern Mexico* (Berkeley: University of California Press, 2002).

82 Armando Bartra, *Guerrero Bronco* (Mexico City: Ediciones Sinfiltro, 1997). Equally important to understanding the limits of popular mobilizations toward the end of the twentieth century are the protests at Juchitán, Oaxaca. They achieved important local political and cultural gains by pushing against, but remaining within, the limits of the regime. See Howard Campbell, *Zapotec Renaissance* (Albuquerque: University of New Mexico Press, 1994); and Jeffrey Rubin, *Decentering the Regime* (Durham: Duke University Press, 1997).

83 For a brilliant exploration of the promise of Mexican democracy in an urban context, see Matthew Guttman, *The Romance of Democracy* (Berkeley: University of California Press, 2002).

84 On the peasant bases of the key conflicts of the age of revolution, see Barrington Moore Jr., *Social Origins of Dictatorship and Democracy* (Boston: Beacon Press, 1966); Wolf, *Peasant Wars of the Twentieth Century*; and Theda Skocpol, *States and Social Revolutions* (Cambridge: Cambridge University Press, 1979). On Central America, see Carlos Rafael Cabarrús, *Génesis de una revolución* (Mexico City: Ediciones de la Casa Chata, 1983). On the Shining Path, see Steve Stern, ed., *Shining and Other Paths* (Durham: Duke University Press, 1998).

❧ PART III *Contemporary Crisis* ❧

The Second Coming of Mexican Liberalism

A Comparative Perspective

LORENZO MEYER

Since classical antiquity, the political sciences have made fruitful use of comparative analyses. Identifying and analyzing similarities and differences between observed phenomena can deepen our knowledge about causes and focus our search for explanations. Most comparative analyses of Mexico's political processes since independence have focused on the similarities and differences between the dictatorship of Porfirio Díaz (1877–1911) and the regime that emerged from the revolution that began in 1910, emphasizing the authoritarian nature of both regimes (one a personal dictatorship, the other a state party), as well as their institutional differences. In this essay, I take a different approach. I compare the liberal regime that preceded (and led to) Díaz's personalist authoritarian regime, and the last stage of authoritarian rule by the party state that came out of the revolution. At issue are two key moments of political ferment and change, one in the nineteenth century, the other in the twentieth. They shared a political discourse supported by liberal visions. Both were driven by relatively small but homogeneous political groups claiming to hold the key to the country's future—and aiming to consolidate power in times of crisis.

Following decades of conflict, Mexican liberals consolidated power in the restored republic of 1867. They promised to build a nation antithetical to the unstable, often violent, society that had defined the half century after independence. Mexico confronted a disastrous reality: a paralyzed economy and the wounds of long civil wars; the legal and social predominance of the strong; a state that did not respect the law; insecurity on the roads and highways, in fact nearly everywhere. The liberals promised to redeem the nation from the burdens inherited from the long colonial period, especially the domination of corporations over individuals and the preference for corporate interests over the national interest. Under Benito Juárez's leadership, liberals proclaimed a bright national future, a Mexico that would be stable, with a dynamic economy, viable and sovereign. The triumphant liberals of the late 1860s offered a model derived from, and supported internationally by, the United States.

The second coming of liberalism began 120 years later, when the regime that had come out of the Mexican Revolution faced political decay and structural economic crisis. In the 1980s, young technocrats within the ruling party regime, led by Carlos Salinas de Gortari, seized power from the inside and proposed a radical transformation of economy and society based on principles they labeled "social liberalism." They proposed to dismantle the corporatist apparatus that had dominated Mexico throughout the twentieth century and to rebuild it following the ideological tenets of neoliberalism, already prevalent in the international arena. In the second coming, the model again came from North America, as did key international support.

Of course, the first Mexican liberal revolution was more spectacular than the neoliberal revolution of the late twentieth century. Benito Juárez remains a national icon; no leader of the neoliberal movement appears ready to claim such status. Nevertheless, both liberal movements had profound impacts on the Mexican state and political institutions. In both cases, liberals confronted deep-rooted corporate traditions. In important ways, the second coming of liberalism may be interpreted as the completion of the first.

Before going on, some central differences should be clarified. The first liberal wave took power through armed struggle, after a ruthless and prolonged civil war followed by a war against French invasion. The country that Juárez and his supporters inherited had not grown economically for almost half a century, since the outbreak of the independence wars in 1810. In contrast, the country that the neoliberals took over in the 1980s emerged from a long period of political stability and sustained development. Still, the new liberals took power amid feelings of insecurity and deep pessimism about the future—the result of an economy in collapse in 1982. The second liberal wave did not emerge, like the first, directly from destructive political wars. Rather, it came out of uncertainty, insecurity, and general disappointment—with little hope in sight.

In the long run, despite many conflicts and contradictions, the liberals who took power in 1867 institutionalized and managed it via Porfirio

Díaz's "benign and progressive" dictatorship. The new liberals of the late twentieth century, after a mix of political and economic successes and failures, have taken their project toward an institutionalization the opposite of their predecessors' authoritarian solution. The initiators of the neoliberal revolution within the party state lost power in the elections of 2000 to a democratic-rights opposition. Thus ended, relatively peacefully, the seventy-year PRI monopoly over the presidency and most of the Mexican political system. The democratic transition of the twenty-first century aims to institutionalize the neoliberalism that technocrats within the party state began twenty years earlier. The new framework is democratic. Economic success remains to be achieved.

THE CONTEMPORARY QUESTION AND THE HISTORICAL BACKGROUND

My central concern here is to identify and analyze the main political changes that were initiated or took on new dynamics while Mexico's economy faced structural crisis in the 1980s. Nineteenth-century liberalism is a key point of reference and comparison. The liberal reform begun in the 1850s and consolidated in the 1860s was the first great modernization project of the new nation. The theoretical bases of nineteenth- and twentieth-century Mexican liberalisms, though not identical, share many substantial characteristics. The main differences between the two brands of Mexican liberalism reflect a century of historical change and the styles, especially the political ethics, of their leaders.

The first liberals fought with fire and sword against the Catholic Church and its conservative allies to achieve power. None gave quarter. Nineteenth-century liberals sought power to change everything, from judicial structures to economic institutions, from social structure to culture. They especially aimed to change a deeply traditional religious culture. Ultimately their purpose was to broaden political liberty and to open cultural spaces as understood by the men of the Enlightenment.

The new liberals of the twentieth century did not have to fight a war to take power. Their ascension to power was not easy, but their struggle was not on the battlefield but in the labyrinthine corridors of the party state. The new liberals first claimed power from within the political monopoly of the state party, the Partido Revolucionario Institucional (PRI), created in 1929 to manage the triumph of the 1910 revolution. Precisely because they took power through existing authoritarian institutions, the first neoliberals sought change in limited ways. Their goal was to modify a corporatist economic system that was failing and nearly bankrupt, without destroying the political system that sustained it. But that political system was also obsolete and approaching bankruptcy. The PRI regime had lost legitimacy. Yet it had brought the neoliberals to power, and they aimed to prolong it. Thus, in the beginning, Mexican neoliberalism focused little on citizenship. It aimed to create and promote Mexicans with entrepreneurial spirit who would take the risks of abandoning the corporatist security of the past and dive into the uncertain sea of competition within a globalizing market economy.

Neither the first liberalism of the nineteenth century nor the original neoliberalism of the twentieth accomplished all they promised. In the nineteenth century, the heroic civil war for liberal democracy and the struggle that followed to gain national sovereignty against French intervention gave way to Porfirio Díaz's personal dictatorship and an externally dependent development model. Nineteenth-century liberals never fulfilled the promise of democracy. They always awaited a "better time"—when Mexicans were ready for democracy—a time that never arrived. It took a long and bloody revolution (from 1910 to 1920) to unseat the authoritarian heirs to nineteenth-century liberalism. The regime created in the revolution built institutions that were to a large extent antiliberal.

The second coming of liberalism also failed to control the process of change it unleashed. Thanks to the economic transformations that the neoliberals promoted within the party state, large segments of society demanded the liberalization of politics. The PRI's neoliberal faction lost control of the strings of power on July 2, 2000, in the country's first relatively free and equal elections. The ballot gave power to an opposition equally dedicated to the economic principles of liberalism and to the principles of political democracy. The promoters of both waves of Mexican liberalism learned that no one group easily shapes history. Still, nineteenth-century liberalism and twentieth-century neoliberalism irreversibly transformed Mexico.

THE GREAT CRISIS AND THE NEOLIBERAL PROJECT

In 1973, the world economic system crossed a sudden threshold into instability and crisis that lasted for almost two decades and left an indelible mark on the end of the twentieth century.[1] That year brought the Yom Kippur War between Israel and its Arab neighbors and a new assertiveness by the Organization of Petroleum Exporting Countries (OPEC). OPEC used its power to punish Western industrialized countries for supporting Israel and imposed a sharp increase in oil prices. Post-World War II capitalism's "golden age" (to use Eric Hobsbawm's term) ended. A new era began under the framework of neoliberalism. This was a dynamic change driven by the extraordinary opening of national markets. The "golden" benefits of liberalizing development rapidly concentrated in a few rich and powerful countries. The process repeated itself within most countries; the "golden" benefits of the new age concentrated in very few hands.[2] Neoliberalism demanded a decrease in social programs and of the role of the state, the dominance of the market in the distribution of resources, and the globalization of capital flows. The consequence, without surprise, was the concentration of wealth among and within nations. Toward the end of the process, the Soviet Union and its control over Eastern Europe collapsed unexpectedly yet peacefully. "Real socialism" became history. At the end of the twentieth century, capitalism was the only model of development. The United States emerged as the only great military power. After the attacks of September 11, 2001, the United States looked to remodel the world according to its security needs and perceived interests.

Not everyone recognized immediately the nature of the new era. Its effects, however, were soon felt. In Mexico, the end of the "golden age" meant the end of "stabilizing development" and of the "Mexican economic miracle." However, the discovery and exploitation of great oil fields in the country's Southeast, along with the spectacular rise in international oil prices, allowed the political elite to postpone until 1982 (when oil prices collapsed) the admission that the country had crossed the threshold into the turmoil of a great economic crisis with serious political and social consequences. In the crucial year of 1982, the per-barrel price of oil dropped quickly—to hold for over a decade at levels one-third below its former peak. The price had climbed from a bit more than one dollar per barrel to three dollars in 1973; in 1980, the price reached forty dollars per barrel (for Middle Eastern light oil for immediate delivery). To generate its oil bonanza and the supposed "administration of abundance," Mexico incurred a huge debt. In 1970, Mexico's external debt was $6 billion. Twelve years later, it had increased more than fourteen times to reach $86 billion. Among the nations of the third world, only Brazil owed more, and not much more. In 1982, Mexico owed $24 billion in annual interest. When oil prices collapsed, the nation could not pay. Only an emergency loan from the United States allowed the Mexican government to renegotiate and avoid default and bankruptcy. Still, 60 percent of Mexico's income from exports was assigned to pay for foreign liabilities. Investment for growth all but ceased. Thus, after achieving an 8 percent rate of growth in the gross domestic product, the Mexican economy suddenly stopped expanding in 1982. It would stagnate for years as the result of massive flights of capital and the loss of investors' trust. For the rest of the twentieth century, real growth was almost nil. Economic uncertainty and stagnation persisted until the first years of the new century. The end of the twentieth century became the "lost decades" of Mexican history. Almost 50 percent of the population fell to live within the grasp of poverty.[3] Lack of opportunity and despair defined the prospects for growing numbers of Mexicans at the beginning of the twenty-first century.[4]

It was only after four years of economic crisis—inflation, stagnating or declining gross domestic product, growing foreign debt, contracting internal demand, decreasing public spending, and rising social tensions, all persisting as short-term policies failed—that the leaders of the PRI regime accepted the fact that the country was immersed in a process that could not be resolved by attempting to restore dynamism to the existing structure. They concluded that a radical and irreversible process, changing the basic principles and goals of the economic model established after World War II, was essential. By 1985, the goal of industrializing Mexico, using administrative regulation and customs barriers to protect the internal market, was impossible. Another way had to be found, and there were few alternatives. In reality, all the options were variations of one: the neoliberal transformation.

The change that Mexico pursued starting in 1986 had to follow the model encouraged in an international context dominated by the United States, Western Europe, and Japan, as well as organizations such as the International Monetary Fund and the World Bank they ruled. After the election of Margaret Thatcher (1979) in the United Kingdom and Ronald Reagan (1981) in the United States, the dominant goals of the primary capitalist states included the privatization of production and a radical decrease in the role of the state in economic processes, as well as fiscal discipline and the opening of national markets to foreign investment and competition. In short, they sought to transform the welfare states that had emerged from World War II, reducing their welfare components to the minimum possible given political circumstances. Thus began a return to a liberal economy and a global market, justifying the change and its social costs in terms of efficiency, liberty, and growth.

The Mexican reformers of the 1980s, the president and his economic advisors, committed in pronouncement and policy to great economic changes. These changes came at the enormous expense of poor people and of the many entrepreneurs who could not re-create their enterprises amid deep crisis to compete successfully in the global market. The PRI leadership did not press for the liberalization of the political system with equal vigor. There were only vague and limited proposals for "society's moral renovation," a supposed struggle against endemic public corruption, and limited decentralization of the federal administration. They conveyed, implicitly, that the radical neoliberal transformation of the economy would not necessarily lead to a liberal opening in politics. The regime was unwilling to pay any political cost for its responsibility in creating and long failing to resolve crisis. Political power would remain concentrated in institutions established to benefit the political class, which would implement economic transformation in the traditional authoritarian manner. A selective liberalism aimed to impose fundamental economic changes yet isolate their effects from political processes: a kind of perestroika without glasnost, to use the terms popularized in the last stage of the Soviet era. Ultimately, "moral renovation" did not go beyond discourse. The political will of president Miguel de la Madrid (1982–88) could not alter entrenched political interests.[5] The economic equilibrium was quickly and profoundly altered. In politics, however, the new liberals intended—or pretended—to remain the same. That proved an impossible task in the long run.

The subsequent administration of president Carlos Salinas (1988–94) returned to traditional regime practices, even while official discourse abused the term "modern politics." Modern politics implied a vague promise of changes granted from above. Meanwhile, economic transformations deepened as Mexico dismantled its protectionist barriers and what remained of the revolutionary nationalism that had aimed to keep Mexico independent from the United States.[6] The Salinas administration embarked on the historic task of negotiating the North American Free Trade Agreement (NAFTA), despite the obvious disparity in wealth between Mexico and its potential partners, Canada and the United States, nations that had already completed a free-trade agreement.

At this point, the political consequences that the promoters of economic liberalism hoped to avoid began to threaten. As a result of widespread and persistent economic dislocations—and despite the obstacles that the state party and its authoritarian structure placed in its path—a real opposition grew, consolidated itself on both the left and the right, and gathered the strength to press demands for political democracy. Ernesto Zedillo's administration (1994–2000) began with another drop in the gross national product (6 percent), with the continuation of indigenous rebellion in Chiapas, and with divisions among neoliberal reformers, all strengthening the opposition. Although the economy seemed finally to recover near the end of Zedillo's six-year term, political contradictions and conflicts mounted. On July 2, 2000, the PRI, which had dominated Mexican political life since the party's foundation in March 1929, was forced to cede power through elections and to allow, finally, the possibility of combining political opening with the economic change begun fifteen years earlier.[7] It was not just the first peaceful change of the party in power; it was the first peaceful change of government in Mexican history. Authoritarianism gave way to democracy; the neoliberal economic project continued.

The authoritarian liberals of the 1980s aimed to promote radical, liberalizing economic changes while preserving the authoritarian regime that sustained their rule. That contradiction led to a dead end. In the long run, the economic liberals within the regime were forced to yield power to political adversaries who, however, never questioned the essence of the neoliberal economic model adopted fifteen years before. Those who defeated the state party in 2000, Vicente Fox and the Partido de Acción Nacional (PAN), offered a program to continue market-oriented economics and globalization. They did so with unprecedented political legitimacy derived from elections in an environment of relatively equal, open, and free political competition, a real novelty in Mexico. Democratic liberalism defeated authoritarian liberalism. The victors then faced the fundamental challenge of all liberalism: to combine political freedom with a degree of economic equity. They promised a measure of social justice. Yet just as that challenge came to the fore, the North American economy entered a period of recession that imposed immediate negative effects on Mexico. The challenge to democratic liberals became greater. Democratic freedoms were celebrated and consolidated while economic opportunities became scarce. It was not a promising context for consolidating liberal values.

THE NATURE OF LIBERALISMS

The first Mexican liberalism of the nineteenth century began a historic task with a project that was as great and revolutionary as it was generous: to end once and for all the old colonial Mexico. The old Mexico appeared an obstacle to the modern country desired by new elites who had emerged from the small but strategically important middle sectors. Nineteenth-century liberals were full of energy, optimism, and self-confidence. They pursued progress through profound and rapid change—a revolution in the full meaning of the word, redefining economic, political, and cultural life in Mexico. The second coming of liberalism during the late twentieth century sought nothing less. It aimed to end the corporate, authoritarian Mexico that had developed in the shadow of the Mexican Revolution. Yet from the outset its goals were neither generous nor fair-minded.

The regime that emerged from the terrible civil war called the Mexican Revolution (1910–20) created and consolidated one of the most stable and prolonged authoritarian systems of the twentieth century. It incorporated campesinos and the working class into a state corporate party ruled by a powerful president. To limit the appearance of authoritarianism, to allow the renovation of elites within the regime, and to prevent succession crises like the 1910 fiasco that began the revolution, the prohibition of reelection was an unbreakable rule (especially after the assassination of Álvaro Obregón, who tried to transgress it in 1928). The party and its presidents proclaimed a strong nationalism that, as time passed, was more discourse than reality. From the 1982 crisis on, it became an obstacle to the new globalization project and was abandoned without admitting the change. Without the protective shield of nationalism and the social policies of the "intervening state," the impressive yet fossilized political structure built around the state party—the Partido Nacional Revolucionario (1929), later transformed into the Partido de la Revolución Mexicana (1938), to finally remain as the Partido Revolucionario Institucional (1946)—lost much of its traditional legitimacy. The result was rule without adequate social support.[8]

The liberalisms of the nineteenth century and the twentieth were justified to Mexicans and the world as political and intellectual engines necessary to propel an unavoidable process—forcing the country toward cultural and material modernity, defined by paradigms developed by the core countries of the world capitalist system. The first liberalism led to undeniable and impressive economic transformation during the Porfiriato: the creation of railway and banking networks, an oil industry, and substantial development in mining, the textile industry, and export agriculture. Nonetheless, it was framed politically by a regime opposed to its original postulates of democracy and legality: the long personal dictatorship of Porfirio Díaz. The end of nineteenth-century liberalism proved catastrophic. The 1910 revolution brought a new regime that, by identifying economic liberalism with dictatorship, built a political and cultural framework where (despite honoring the heroic figure of Juárez) liberalism itself was delegitimized, identified with an oligarchic reality opposed to the interests of working people and of the nation as a whole—the proclaimed bases of the new regime.

The second coming of liberalism at the end of the twentieth century, seventy-five years after the destruction of Porfirio Díaz's regime, began with a discourse of "social liberalism" constructed within the postrevolutionary authoritarian regime. It maintained the mechanisms of the strong state party and presidency. Despite the enormous effort by the administration of Carlos Salinas to drive economic reforms without modifying the essence of the political regime, the social forces unleashed by Mexico's abrupt entrance into the globalizing world system, as well as the repercussions created by the so-called third wave of world democratization, forced the new liberals slowly and unwillingly to create a real political opening through successive electoral reforms.[9]

As a result, during several presidential elections near the century's end, control over political processes steadily slipped from the hands of the regime's leaders. Then 2000 brought an irreversible electoral triumph by the opposition. The victory went not to the Left, as had seemed possible in 1988. Instead, it went to the center-right democratic opposition, the other liberals of the PAN. Thus, during the second half of the year 2000, Mexico experienced something unprecedented in its history: a noncatastrophic and legal change of political regime. It was nothing like the great political and social revolution that destroyed Díaz's authoritarian liberal regime at the beginning of the century. Rather, the summer of 2000 was a "velvet revolution," a political transformation achieved by elections. The environment of economic stagnation and increasing social contradictions, however, remained to test the efficiency of the new democracy. It could bring the PRI back to the presidency. Should that happen, however, it would be a PRI that could no longer pretend to be a state party. It would have to resign itself to operating within the rules of liberal democracy.

ORIGINS: THE FIRST LIBERALISM

The original Mexican liberalism of the nineteenth century had little to do with the internal processes of Mexican society. It emerged from Mexicans' encounter with the events and ideas of North American and European liberalism during the eighteenth and nineteenth centuries. In 1808, the transatlantic Spanish monarchy experienced a dramatic denouement when Napoleon invaded the Iberian Peninsula. A war for Spanish liberation followed. It led to the writing and implementation of the 1812 liberal constitution of Cádiz, which was short-lived but had a decisive and long-term influence throughout the colonies of the Spanish monarchy.

Mexican independence was initiated in 1810 by radical Creoles. It became, unexpectedly, a ferocious social and racial war consummated in 1821 as a pact for independence between Spaniards and conservative Creoles, on the one hand, and radical mestizos, on the other. During the brief experiment with monarchy under Agustín de Iturbide, supported by conservatives and the Catholic Church, liberal ideals spread among the enlightened Mexican middle classes, who popularized and systematized them in the Republican Constitution of 1824.[10] A nascent liberalism went from theory to practice. Nevertheless, the weight of a society profoundly divided by racial differences and by extreme inequalities of wealth, while molded by corporate, colonial, and absolutist structures, led to deep and perhaps unavoidable divisions among the new ruling elites. With time, the rift deepened and polarized between the Catholic Church and the liberals.

Electoral processes, always difficult in an agrarian country with neither a common language nor widespread literacy, gave way to direct action, usually military, as the most effective method to achieve power. These difficulties became a crisis after the disastrous 1847 war with the United States.

The early divisions between republicans and monarchists, radical masons of the York rite and conservative masons of the Scottish rite, anticlerical liberals and the Catholic Church, and regionalist (federalist) and centralist factions culminated in a destructive civil war (1858–60) between factions defined as liberals and conservatives. The civil war combined in the 1860s with a war for liberation from an opportunistic French invasion that supported the monarchy of the Austrian Archduke Maximilian of Habsburg.

ORIGINS: THE SECOND LIBERALISM

One hundred and twenty years later, neoliberalism also launched in the face of crisis, though nothing remotely like the crisis faced by the original liberals. The crisis of the 1980s began with an economic collapse that led to deep division within the top PRI leadership over economic theory and policy. Top government economic bureaucrats accused traditional politicians of being populist, statist, and incompetent, and of provoking the economic crises that endangered the regime. They added philosophical accusations: state paternalism led to patronage and endemic corruption, blocking individuals from employing their full energy and creativity. Unlike the nineteenth-century launch of liberalism amid civil war, the late-twentieth-century second coming, beginning as a clash of interests and ideology at the top of an entrenched regime, did not destroy stability. The change provoked recriminations and convulsions and went further than those who initiated it wished. It did not lead to catastrophic violent societal conflicts like those typical of all previous regime changes.

Around 1985, a group of men working at the highest levels of the Mexican regime, after secret and ferocious internal struggles, began a radical transformation. They aimed to substitute neoliberalism for the prevailing statist economic model. They worked to solve the crisis of the economy and to renew the material and political bases of their own power. The old model had propelled industrialization through import substitution thanks to a favorable juncture of conditions: the centralization of political power, the export bonanza created by World War II, and rapid urbanization. The decision taken in the 1940s to create an industrial base focused on an internal market that was relatively poor, but protected by a solid barrier of both customs duties and administrative legislation, had high social costs. They were justified in two ways: the theories promoted by the Economic

Commission for Latin America (CEPAL) in the 1950s, and by a new interpretation of revolutionary nationalism that argued that to achieve independence from the United States, Mexico had to create its own industrial base and end its dependence on the export of raw products.[11] The real power and legitimacy of the post-World War II economic policy, however, came less from theories about protective nationalism and development and more from interests emerging among key groups linked to the authoritarian nationalist regime: a new private and public bourgeoisie and the strong unions that organized a "labor aristocracy."[12] Between 1951 and 1980, Mexico's per capita gross national product averaged 3.3 percent growth.[13] That strong performance contrasted favorably with earlier and later periods. It came accompanied by remarkably stable political processes and consumer prices.[14]

Early difficulties in the postwar regime and development model led to student resistance and state repression in 1968, followed by economic stagnation and mounting debts in the early 1970s. The petroleum bonanza at the end of that decade proved promising, disruptive, and brief. When the price of oil plummeted at the beginning of the 1980s, it struck an economy recently reoriented to petroleum exports, facing a structural external deficit and a large and growing foreign debt. Yet the authoritarian party regime remained entrenched. The state controlled petroleum production and exerted great power in diverse other sectors. The crisis struck the regime hard, but it held the power to direct state enterprises and private producers in the search for policies of recovery.[15]

The new economic policies of 1985 and 1986 reversed the direction that had defined Mexican development for almost forty years. Among many consequences, the new policies strengthened the political forces that, since 1968, had opposed the authoritarian political model.[16] For decades, the ruling class had resisted pressures to democratize access to power. Suddenly, the repercussions of the great economic and social crisis destabilized a political equilibrium already suffering a crisis of legitimacy. Despite regime resistance, Mexican political processes were pushed toward change through the only means possible: the third democratic wave that had already affected much of Latin America.[17]

THE FIRST LIBERALISM IN ACTION

It is obvious that Mexican liberalisms did not emerge naturally within long-term processes of political development, as happened in the core countries of the world system. Instead they began in profound crises. In the nineteenth century, the crisis resulted from the dismemberment of the

Spanish empire in the Americas, followed by decades of administrative disaster as the nation experimented with independent government. The crisis deepened with the humiliating loss of Texas and other northern territories. The army had become Mexico's main national political institution. Its total defeat in the face of U.S. invasion led to the loss of lands that, although barely populated, were part of the collective imagination of the elites who promoted the political nation. The failure to mount an effective defense called into question the feasibility of the imagined nation, to use the concept coined by Benedict Anderson.[18] Northern elites, for example, played with the idea of creating a separate Republic of the Sierra Madre. The Yucatán elite sought, doggedly but unsuccessfully, the protection of the United States or some European power as it waged the horrible war (the so-called Caste War) against part of the Maya community.[19]

In the words of Josefina Vázquez, Mexico's defeat by the United States meant "the renunciation of the brilliant destiny that its vast territory and great wealth as the Kingdom of New Spain had promised."[20] The struggle between Mexico City (the center of the center) and distant regions, north and south, dated back to the Bourbon reforms. After independence, that struggle intensified to become a central political issue in the conflict between conservatives and liberals, a conflict that also divided the Catholic Church from liberals, and moderates and radicals among liberals. Out of the ashes of military defeat and Mexico's irreversible collapse in the world system emerged, once again, a conservative monarchical project. It was designed and led in the early 1850s by Lucas Alamán and supported by the ubiquitous general and caudillo don Antonio López de Santa Anna (imagined as an appropriate interim sovereign until a European prince was found). The plan collapsed because of the unexpected death of Alamán, the irreplaceable political and intellectual leader of the Mexican conservative movement. The subsequent military victory of the liberal rebellion of Ayutla in 1854 ended *santanismo* and an entire stage of Mexican political development.

The radical liberal constitution of 1857 led to civil war. Conservatives and the Catholic Church rejected not only the constitution but the liberal model as a whole, insisting on the monarchical alternative. Defeated in 1860, Mexican conservatives entered an uneasy alliance with France. The defeated Mexican faction sought, desperately, support for their clerical, conservative vision of society. France sought a puppet state on the border of the United States—the beginning of a French project to dominate a New World imagined as Latin America. French withdrawal, followed by Juárez's and the liberals' 1867 victory over Maximilian, brought the definitive defeat of the alliance between monarchists and conservatives in Mexico. Thus began a liberal hegemony that lasted, with changes, until 1911.

In the summer of 1867, the triumph of president Benito Juárez's armies on the battlefield swept away the political obstacles that had blocked the great project that Mexican liberal visionaries had long cherished: the modernization of the country through liberal institutions. Yet as time passed, economic transformation became more important than political transformation. To turn Mexico, still indigenous at its social base and shaped by its colonial past, into a liberal democracy proved a difficult, nearly impossible, task. At the end of the nineteenth century, Mexico had few citizens and many subjects, especially in the rural areas, where corporate organizations, especially *pueblos de indios*, were more important than liberal individualism.[21] From 1867 until 1911, Mexico under liberal hegemony had two strong presidents: Benito Juárez until his death in 1872; and General Porfirio Díaz, who dominated from 1877 to 1911.

During this first liberal era, Mexico's economy was transformed. An internal market developed; an industrial revolution began. Yet the political system remained mired in the dictatorship of Porfirio Díaz for more than three decades. It was an oligarchic system in which the authorities controlled an indirect electoral process, allowing participation by favored elites and limited middle sectors, using persuasion, intimidation, and sometimes violence to gain desired results. The campesino majority and the working-class minority were excluded.[22] By the time Justo Sierra, a prescient member of the Porfirian oligarchy, advised that Mexico should make up for lost time and begin political modernization, it was too late.[23] The Mexican Revolution assaulted the excesses and exclusions of nineteenth-century authoritarian liberalism. The regime it created to repair the damage adapted to the social circumstances of corporatism, offering abstract justice to all and participation to rural communities re-created as corporate *ejidos*, and to state-sanctioned trade unions, chambers of commerce and industry, et cetera. All were incorporated into a mass party and ruled by presidents with powers that knew few limits, legal, political, or other.[24]

THE SECOND COMING IN ACTION:
NEOLIBERALISM'S TRIGGER

Let us advance the Mexican historical clock three-quarters of a century to encounter the beginning of the new liberalism. President Luis Echeverría (1970–76) offered "neopopulism" in response to economic stagnation and political challenge, working to incorporate intellectuals and popular groups in a project still statist and authoritarian. He gained mounting debts and worsening illegitimacy. President José López Portillo (1976–82) followed with an "administration of abundance" that was no more than petrolization.

The rapid expansion of oil production and exports brought brief prosperity and then contributed to the collapse of world petroleum prices—and the Mexican model of state party development. The immediate results were massive flight of capital, currency devaluation, the nationalization of commercial banking, and finally a foreign debt of $92.4 billion. In November 1982, a payment of $12.2 billion had to be suspended. The Mexican government was forced to accept conditions imposed by the IMF, dominated by the United States. It was the only way to obtain an emergency loan of $3.7 billion, to gain the political support to renegotiate its foreign debt with international banks, and to obtain new short-term loans. In a "letter of intent," the IMF imposed, and the Mexican government accepted, the general outline of the "neoliberal revolution": decreasing state intervention in the economy, declining tariffs on trade, and freedom of movement for international capital.

At first, from 1983 to 1985, president Miguel de la Madrid's government (1982–88) tried to control the crisis through superficial measures. It stressed renegotiation of the terms of payment of the foreign debt, provisional budget austerity, and stabilization of the national currency. These strategies proved inadequate, and a second phase began in 1985. Government leaders and policy planners concluded that the premises of "revolutionary nationalism" had become impossible. They accepted the new orthodoxy already prevalent in world financial and commercial centers. Mexico joined the General Agreement on Tariffs and Trade (GATT), earlier rejected by López Portillo's government. The reformers demolished the high tariffs that protected 90 percent of the nation's output, one of the bases of the postrevolutionary economy. By the end of Miguel de la Madrid's mandate, only 20 percent of Mexico's production was protected; the rest had to compete under conditions imposed by the world market.[25]

Under the radical presidentialism of Carlos Salinas (1988–94), economic reform deepened. Protection of national output virtually disappeared. In 1990, the banking system, nationalized only eight years before, was reprivatized. Most state corporations and enterprises with state participation were delivered to the private sector. Of 1,155 corporations under government control in 1982, only 280 remained by the end of the decade. Agrarian reform ended, closing out another promise of revolutionary nationalism. New ways to privatize ejido lands were initiated. By the end of the century, only the petroleum and hydroelectric sectors remained public. And they remained public not because the new liberals believed that energy should stay under the state control but because deep legacies of revolutionary nationalism made privatization of these industries politically risky. Reform in the energy sectors was not abandoned; it was left for a more propitious occasion. The petrochemical sector was privatized, and the generation of power by private enterprises was allowed under certain conditions.

In short, the crisis of the postrevolutionary economic model set off a period of profound and accelerated change during the second half of the 1980s. The second coming of liberalism claimed as its first triumph the end of the postrevolutionary, state-ruled, protected national economy. It opened the way for a new economy dominated by the world market. The promise of land and the corporate structures that had long organized the agrarian sector were dismantled. Labor legislation did not change, but the trade union movement as a whole lost strength as a result of the "labor flexibility" demanded by the new economy. Social marginalization sharpened. Elites also faced difficulties. Much of the entrepreneurial class collapsed because of its inability to compete in internal or external markets. In contrast, new export sectors, especially the labor-intensive maquiladoras that produced for U.S. markets and received important flows of foreign capital, prospered. Profits concentrated among the few favored by privatization and the new export production.[26] At the end of the century, during the government of Ernesto Zedillo (1994–2000), an economist totally committed to the new model, the Mexican economy seemed finally to have overcome the "readjustment period," a major surgery without anesthesia, and was starting to show signs of substantial growth. In 2000, the rate was 7 percent. But it fell dramatically the next year, driven down by economic recession in the United States. The first liberalism proved costly for the agrarian majority, but the economy as a whole grew. The second coming imposed equally high social costs. To date it has not produced sustained economic growth.

LIBERAL REJECTIONS OF THE PAST

In both liberalisms, crises led reformers to present sharply negative views of the old regime. The central institutions of the past were presented as obstacles to achieving modernization, efficiency, justice, and an ethical society. A substantial part of inherited tradition—economic policies, political practices, and cultural outlooks—had to be demolished to allow the birth of new and superior stages of development for Mexican society. At the core of the theoretical framework of the first Mexican liberals were Adam Smith's (1723–90) simple and elegant theory of political economy ("the natural system of freedom") and Jeremy Bentham's (1748–1832) utilitarianism. Spanish, French, British, and North American political liberalism also helped shape new ideas.[27]

At the start of the Reform War in 1858, Benito Juárez, a Zapotec lawyer and former governor of Oaxaca who led both democratic and republican liberals, defined his conservative monarchist enemies as "those who wanted the country to, once more, become a ward of the year 1821." The approaching civil war was another example of "the old struggle between light and darkness."[28] Radical liberals did not seek compromise with their opponents; they sought total victory through the annihilation of their adversaries. This was the only way to settle accounts with a past they considered the great obstacle to modernity and progress.

The immediate goal of the political and military struggles of the leaders of the first liberal wave was to prevail as the new ruling class. Only in power could they "repair today our fathers' mistakes."[29] In their view, the pre-Hispanic past, which Creole patriotism had idealized after the separation from Spain, lost all value. Living and often resistant indigenous communities, legacies of that past, were identified as key obstacles to modernity.[30] Turning to the heritage of Spanish colonial rule, liberals insisted that they had no objections to religion or the Catholic Church, but they adamantly rejected the economic, political, and educational role of the church, along with the idea of an official religion. They rejected across the board any corporate organization of state and society, any corporate (non-individual) privileges and rights. For liberals who neither gave nor expected clemency, the existence of corporately organized and privileged "unproductive" classes (the Catholic Church, the inefficient and pillaging army, the guilds, innumerable landed indigenous communities) explained Mexico's material and moral backwardness and its failures in the face of foreign challenges.[31] Liberal individualism, with producers and citizens responsible for their personal destinies, was incompatible with preserving the colonial corporate organization. The democracy that liberals demanded was incompatible with indigenous peoples' cultures and ways of life. Nor could it coexist with the absolutist monarchy that Mexico had abandoned in 1821.[32]

The belief system that inspired the new liberals of the late twentieth century was equally clear. Its moral, political, and economic bases were the same as those of the original liberals, updated by schools of thought in the United States and Western Europe known for their focus on economics and political economy. From the neoliberals' perspective, the vitality and success of their worldview had been proved dramatically and irrefutably by the spectacular collapse of the Soviet Union and "real socialism."[33] Both liberalisms were obsessed with reducing the size and intervention of state bureaucracy, "empleomania," as nineteenth-century liberals said. They demanded productive work, dominated by market competition and a drive for profitable productivity. A private sector defined by entrepreneurial freedom would control the nature and rhythm of the economy.[34]

The Mexican Revolution, ironically, began in 1910 as a liberal call to respect political democracy and civil society. It ended up rejecting key aspects of nineteenth-century liberalism. Porfirian liberalism's practical consequences had forced painful difficulties on the popular classes. After the revolution, the weakness of the bourgeoisie led the state, not private capital, to control the economy. The framers of the 1917 Constitution had no problem incorporating liberal guarantees into its text, reaffirming the legitimacy of representative democracy, the division of powers (though from the outset it stressed the executive,) federalism, and free municipalities. At least in theory, there were few conflicts between the ideas of the revolution and the liberal principles it inherited. Conflict emerged when legislators tried to subordinate private property to the collective interest. This principle, stated in Article 27 of the Constitution, subsequently justified agrarian reform, the nationalization of the oil industry, and eventually the creation of powerful state enterprises in oil, electricity, railroads, communications, development banking, and other sectors.[35] The new legal framework was only partly liberal and very favorable to the expansion of the state. It permitted in practice the concentration of enormous powers in the hands of the government, especially the presidency. It justified state intervention in economic processes as necessary to defending national interests, particularly the interests of poor people facing the greed of international capitalism. This was the heart of "revolutionary nationalism" consolidated under president Lázaro Cárdenas (1934–40).

By the 1960s and 1970s, the growth of the public sector in the economy was the regime's proud indicator that it had fulfilled its historic commitment to its bases. The public sector sustained legitimacy.[36] In 1910, total government spending was just 3 percent of GNP; in 1970, it reached 25 percent; by 1982 it peaked at 46 percent.[37] It was precisely at this point, and for this reason, that the crisis of the nationalist postrevolutionary system, of the "mixed economy" and the state party, erupted. Miguel de la Madrid's incorporation of Mexico in GATT in July 1986 started the rapidly accelerating engine driving the new economic model and making Mexico compatible with processes rapidly integrating the global market system. The new liberals ignored the fact that the new model was not necessarily compatible with the interests of most Mexicans, at least in the short term.[38] To justify the change and to absolve themselves of responsibility for past crises, government officials, as well as many entrepreneurs, analysts, and critics, condemned the "populism" of presidents Luis Echeverría and José López Portillo—a populism extending back to president Lázaro Cárdenas, the true founder of Mexico's activist state. Of course, the condemnation could not be total. The neoliberals worked within the regime they condemned.

They aimed to use authoritarian mechanisms to impose liberal economic visions. Still, they insisted that the country's future depended on their ability to prevail over nationalist-populists in a struggle within the ruling class.[39]

The statism of the past was accused of causing structural crises and blamed for squandering enormous resources and fostering the growth of a state sector as gigantic as it was inefficient. It was also accused of creating a private industrial base incapable of exporting enough to compensate for the foreign currency it consumed, becoming completely dependent on government support to survive. Finally, liberals insisted that this unhealthy arrangement involved a huge tangle of regulations, bureaucracy, and discretionary decisions that led to ubiquitous and institutionalized corruption.[40]

From the perspective of the official party (the PRI), the 1988 elections were a struggle between modernizers (the neoliberals), led by Carlos Salinas de Gortari, and a "populist" opposition, the Frente Democrático Nacional. Cuauhtémoc Cárdenas, son of the once-honored president and a former PRIísta, led the opposition, calling for democracy and fair elections. The neoliberals entrenched within the PRI insisted that Cárdenas remained committed to his father's past of statist revolutionary nationalism, and refused to change.[41] Meanwhile the PAN moved beyond its origins as a party of Catholic resistance to the revolutionary regime to become a full-fledged political party. Still a minority faction, it worked to achieve power by welcoming a large number of dissatisfied entrepreneurs who renounced support for the PRI and their history of indifference to direct political action. They joined the PAN to bolster the ranks of effective opposition.[42] One example was the Sinaloan agricultural entrepreneur Manuel Clouthier, the PAN candidate for president in 1988. Working to force the political system open, he believed that electoral democracy was the only way to ensure that the presidency, long irresponsible and recently unbearable to many entrepreneurs, could become responsible and legitimate. Clouthier and other entrepreneurs who joined the PAN opposition demanded a quick and decisive abandonment of statism for a predominantly market economy.[43]

The campaign of 1988 proved bitter, more so than any since 1952. The PRI awarded itself another victory, the eleventh since 1929. It claimed just over 50 percent of the popular vote, a sharp contrast with past "statistics," in which the PRI routinely claimed 70 to 90 percent of the vote. Assertions of vast electoral majorities had allowed the regime to claim to represent all of society. In its 1988 claim of a minimal majority—in an election that many saw as stolen—the PRI inevitably accepted a lesser mandate. Hardline neoliberalism and Carlos Salinas took power under the shadow of a great electoral fraud.[44]

1. Since 1989 the Partido de la Revolución Democrática has fought for democracy and political rights. Photograph by Francisco Daniel/*Proceso*. Courtesy of *Proceso*.

Salinas was president. He faced systematic and staunch opposition from the center left led by Cuauhtémoc Cárdenas and his recently created Partido de la Revolución Democrática (PRD). The PAN, still recovering from the shock of being overtaken by the Left as the leading opposition and dropping from the second to the third among national political forces, offered only reluctant acquiescence. Salinas's government quickly and skillfully developed the concept of "social liberalism." The seed of this key concept of *salinismo* had been planted by a small, radical group of nineteenth-century liberals led by Ponciano Arriaga, who argued that indigenous peoples should be granted basic lands, seeds, and tools, the minimum requirements to produce in the market.[45] Salinas's social liberalism promised help to those caught between the old "absorbing statism" and the new "possessive neoliberalism." It pledged equilibrium between state and society, liberty and equality, the individual and the community, social rights and individual guarantees.[46]

In practice, Salinas's social liberalism turned out to be less social than advertised. With the income from privatizing Mexican telephones, banks, airlines, and other businesses, the government shaped a national solidarity program (PRONASOL). Its goal was, in theory, to directly but temporarily help the sectors hardest hit by the crisis and the neoliberal transformation

—until the benefits of the market became a reality. In practice, economic power and income were increasingly concentrated. Poverty increased. In the end, PRONASOL aimed to recover the electoral support the state party had lost in 1988. It was not a fundamental effort to fight structural poverty.[47] After the 1994 election, when the PRI won the presidency for the twelfth and last time, PRONASOL disappeared in a shroud of discredit. Still, Salinas's successor kept some programs under different names. During Ernesto Zedillo's six-year presidency, liberalism continued as economic policy. The social program now called PROGRESA claimed to struggle against growing poverty, especially after the GNP fell by 7 percent in 1995. It concentrated its limited resources on families in extreme poverty.[48] Under Vicente Fox (2000–) PROGRESA became Pa'que te Alcance and other similar programs. According to Julio Boltvinik's calculations, by the end of the twentieth century, Mexico's poverty levels had increased so much that 70 percent of the population fell within some of the criteria used to measure poverty.[49] On the other hand, by the end of Zedillo's six-year term, significant economic growth began. The short-term expansion was greater than demographic growth but was linked to the fluctuations of the U.S. economy. In 2001, Mexico followed the U.S. economy into recession, stagnation, and increased unemployment. Social problems continue to be Mexico's main challenge.

LIBERALS AND THE OUTSIDE WORLD

Nineteenth-century Mexican liberals tried to follow the models of the European powers and, above all, of the United States, their successful northern neighbor and the first New World nation. Extreme, but not unique, examples of Mexican admiration for Anglo-American liberalism are Lorenzo de Zavala, a dynamic liberal politician from Yucatán who became vice-president of the Texas Republic, and Miguel Lerdo de Tejada, who saw little, if any, value in Mexico's Hispanic heritage. Mexico's 1847 defeat by the United States did not turn liberals into anti-Yankees; on the contrary, it confirmed the superiority of the Anglo-American model in comparison with the hybrid and disorderly regimes that struggled to organize Mexico. One particularly radical and atypical group was open to the idea of Mexico's disappearance as an independent country and its incorporation into the United States. Annexation would dispose of an army that was useless to defense but consumed huge resources. A dominant Catholic Church would be neutralized by the diverse churches that flourished in the United States. European immigrants would "improve" Mexico's ethnic mix. Ultimately they hoped that strong U.S. democratic and liberal institutions would dominate Mexico's political, economic, and administrative disorder.[50]

When nineteenth-century liberals reclaimed the government and political system in the republican restoration of 1867, they thought the outside world should contribute to Mexican development. International capital was then mostly European. The United States remained a net importer of capital; still, investors there began to seek opportunities in Mexico. Foreign capital enabled Mexico to build railroads, reactivate mines, modernize the textile industry, and revive and diversify agriculture and foreign trade. It shaped a banking system that barely existed. Things moved slowly at first. After 1876, however, Porfirio Díaz created the necessary conditions (authoritarian stability?) for the arrival of capital and technology. By 1940, American investment in Mexico was calculated at $646 million. European investment, primarily French and British, exceeded $1,600 million. This capital funded Mexico's modernized economy during the late nineteenth century, linking it to the international economic system.[51]

At the end of the twentieth century, neoliberals, like their predecessors, followed North American models. As Mexico adapted to the new demands and opportunities of international economic politics in the 1980s, revolutionary nationalism faded in official discourse and all but disappeared in practice. It was silenced by the North American Free Trade Agreement (NAFTA). President Salinas wanted an agreement that linked Mexico's underdeveloped economy with the enormous, powerful, and innovative U.S. economy and its Canadian adjunct. Negotiations began in 1990. Final agreement came in 1993, after overcoming serious resistance by the trade unions and protectionist interests in the United States. NAFTA was Salinas's great victory, key to completing and preserving the "neoliberal revolution." The government argued that Mexico had taken the lead from the rest of Latin America in the game of economic blocs and had placed itself squarely in the process of globalization. As the twentieth century ended, Mexican imports and exports exceeded $200 billion per year. As 80 percent of this trade was with the United States, the Mexican government sought counterbalance by signing a series of free-trade treaties with other countries and economic blocs: the most important was signed in 2000 with the European Union, followed by others with Latin American countries. Despite these agreements, NAFTA dominated. By 2002, over 90 percent of Mexico's external trade was with the United States; over 70 percent of foreign investment came from the United States.

Like original liberalism, neoliberalism gave foreign investment a central role as a source of capital and technology and as a link to international markets. Exports within large international corporations and from *ma-*

quilas using Mexican labor to supply U.S. markets became a significant part of the total. As a result of the new liberal project, the external market replaced internal demand as the motor of Mexican economic growth. The Mexican economy became integrated with the North American economy in unprecedented ways. Both Mexican liberalisms began by asserting the necessity of transformations in the national interest. Both—perhaps the second more than the first—were led by their economic programs toward increasing incorporation into transnational economic systems, where Mexico and Mexicans played subordinate roles.

The issue of migration between Mexico and the rest of the world was not significant to nineteenth-century liberalism, except for the theoretical goal of attracting European immigrants to "whiten" society and perhaps solve the indigenous problem once and for all. In the twentieth century, emigration, the massive expulsion of labor toward Mexico's northern neighbor, became unavoidably important. Unlike the European Union, NAFTA's free trade between Mexico and its northern neighbor liberated the movement of goods and capital. People, often envisioned as labor power, were to remain in their home nations. The United States adopted policies restricting legal immigration. U.S. political culture inflamed opposition toward "illegal" immigration. Yet at the end of the twentieth century, more than nine million Mexican workers were present in the United States. The flow of undocumented people continued to increase by 150,000 to 300,000 each year.[52]

Despite U.S. legislation aiming to punish employers that hire undocumented workers, and despite the Border Patrol's efforts to stop, capture, and repatriate them, Mexican workers continue to find employers quick to hire them as undocumented, and thus cheap, foreign workers.[53] At the beginning of the twenty-first century, about 20 percent of the Mexican workforce worked, with or without documents, in the United States. One of the great tasks proposed by the newly elected government of Vicente Fox was the negotiation of a new treaty to remove the stigma and exploitation of illegality from Mexican workers in the United States. Early on, the Bush administration seemed open to discussions. Since September 11, 2001, U.S. interest in negotiating Mexican labor and migration ceased. Ultimately and often illegally, yet in full agreement with the laws of the market, Mexican integration with the North American economy after NAFTA includes capital, all types of products, including, unfortunately, outlawed drugs, and people.

Many nineteenth-century liberals, such as José María Luis Mora, believed the landowning class monopolized good judgment on public life. It should dominate political affairs.[54] The right to vote, however, could not be restricted to the few. Nonetheless, indirect elections combined with vote manipulation and fraud to keep the few in control of the political process. Restricted access to rule channeled economic benefits to a small group. In the nineteenth century, liberal Mexico reinforced oligarchic Mexico.

Nineteenth-century liberals lived immersed in a society still basically rural and indigenous. That is why they were so insistent on selling the great rural properties of the Catholic Church (as well as urban holdings) and privatizing the communal properties of indigenous peoples. Their project, however, was not simply to privatize property and favor large haciendas, which they considered inefficient. Rather, they promised to promote small and medium property. That was the best way to promote production and form genuine citizens.[55] The writings of the early liberals are full of references to industry as an ideal. Still, the immediate possibilities for Mexican modernity rested on agriculture. When all was said and done, the liberal goal was a nation of *rancheros*, modest Hispanic commercial farmers. Ranchos and rancheros did proliferate. But vast properties, latifundia, dominated the countryside of liberal Mexico to 1910 and beyond. Great estates persisted side by side with "undesirable" indigenous villages, which held communal properties that also survived liberal attacks. Many villagers took up arms during the revolution, attacking surviving estates and demanding agrarian reform from the new, less-than-liberal state. Is there clearer evidence that the limits, contradictions, and failures of nineteenth-century liberalism led to revolution in 1910?

In the second coming of liberal theory in the 1980s, privatization reappeared as a key demand. This time, however, it focused on the ubiquitous public sector created by the postrevolutionary regime. The goal was to return economic activities to the market and individual initiative, leaving the state to concentrate on its role as a leader and not to "waste energy" as a producer. Neoliberal discourse stressed a "strong state" as opposed to the "obese state" of the recent past. Its ideologues claimed to promote not great monopolistic corporations but medium and small business. Such businesses, like agriculture and the retail and service sectors, produced more employment. Yet in the practice of neoliberalism, the tendencies of the original liberalism repeated themselves. The government repeatedly supported large corporations, creating many through rapid privatizations. This was justified by the argument that only such corporations could engage globalization and compete in the Darwinian international market. From the beginning, Mexico's neoliberal administrations favored foreign conglomerates such as great automobile corporations and national groups like Carso, Cemex, Vitro, and the big banks. The giants retained state support even after some committed huge blunders or engaged in seriously corrupt actions, like the highway construction companies and the banks, which had to be rescued from bankruptcy at enormous cost to the Treasury.[56]

Both Mexican liberalisms failed to solve, or even mitigate, the key historical problem of Mexican society: inequality. Rural property concentrated in the nineteenth century as follows: four-fifths of rural communities, half the population of a basically rural country, lived within private latifundia.[57] Income concentration by the end of the twentieth century can be synthesized thus: in 1996, the wealthiest 10 percent of Mexico's households received 43 percent of the nation's total income; the poorest 10 percent survived with only 1 percent.[58]

LIBERALS AND LEGALITY

In principle, the creation and preservation of a "state of law," applicable to all, respected by all, was a liberal banner in the nineteenth-century fight to death with the conservatives. Defense of the 1857 Constitution justified the bloodletting and destruction of the twelve years of civil war that followed. President Juárez insisted repeatedly that adherence to judicial norms preceded all other considerations. Yet once their adversaries were destroyed and the Republican government was in the firm grasp of the liberals, their attachment to the legal and judicial framework proved relative. After Porfirio Díaz consolidated his rule through military victory, the spirit and even the text of the Constitution were set aside to allow the construction of a prolonged personal dictatorship. "State of law" became a meaningless concept.

The neoliberals of the second coming, like their predecessors, repeatedly promised commitment to a state of law. In practice, especially under president Carlos Salinas, they maintained, even strengthened, the presidential dictatorship that defined the postrevolutionary regime. It differed from the dictatorship of Porfirio Díaz mostly by linking power to the office instead of the person. Presidential promises of neoliberal freedom, while presidents promoted the persistence, the entrenchment, of the state party, made the authoritarian nature of the regime ever more blatant. Violation of the legal framework was obvious in the Chihuahua electoral fraud of 1986, and above all in the national electoral deception of 1988. It was precisely the continued maximization of state power that allowed President Salinas and his entourage of technocrats to promote, impose, and sustain economic reforms more quickly and deeply than in any other Latin American country, except under Chile's military dictatorship. The use of authoritarian state power, breaking constitutional and legal norms, to impose change promoted as new freedom was the ultimate contradiction of both Mexican liberalisms—contradiction that led to revolution in 1910, and to electoral transformation in 2000.

LIBERALISMS AND THE INDIGENOUS PROBLEM

Nineteenth-century liberals never found a solution, in theory or in practice, to the "Indian problem." The greatest liberal ideologue, José María Luis Mora, insisted that the indigenous masses could not sustain Mexican nationality.[59] Mora and his followers imagined diverse solutions. Rebellious, often nomadic, groups—defined as barbarous—might face extermination. For the majority organized in communities within the society inherited from New Spain, liberals legislated education for acculturation and the transformation of communal lands into small individual properties. If racial mixing promoted acculturation to liberal norms, fine. In practice, the original liberals could not design nonviolent policies to confront indigenous issues, just as they failed to find effective measures to solve the problem of general poverty. They outlawed corporate indigenous communities and decreed the privatization of their lands in the Ley Lerdo of 1856—and struggled to implement it in the face of a half century of hard resistance. They passed repeated laws outlawing vagrancy and failed to turn the working majority into productive proletarians.[60]

When the new liberalism took center stage at the end of the twentieth century, the "Indian problem" seemed secondary, though still unresolved. Official statistics defined barely 10 percent of the population as indigenous. In reality, the functional heirs of the great indigenous masses of the nineteenth century were the poor and marginalized of the late twentieth century. It was precisely in the remaining patches of indigenous culture and life that the problems of poverty, marginalization, and discrimination became most acute. It is no surprise that the states of Chiapas, Oaxaca, and Guerrero include the largest indigenous populations and report the highest poverty indices.[61]

By the end of the twentieth century, Mexico was officially mestizo, an achievement of the Mexican Revolution and the *indigenista* policies that integrated ethnic groups and assimilated them into the national whole through the distribution of ejido lands and the expansion of public education, health care, and the other services designed to combat poverty. Post-

2. Delegada Mercedes joined the 2001 EZLN march to
Mexico City with insistent anonymity. Photograph by
Norma Suárez, San Miguel de Allende, Mexico.

revolutionary *indigenismo* shared a key goal with nineteenth-century liberalism: the eventual disappearance of indigenous cultures. The process
aimed to be nonviolent. The higher purpose was national homogeneity.
Indigenous traits would dissolve into accelerating and deepening modernity.[62] Yet indigenous difference and indigenous marginality—thus the
"Indian problem"—remained.

Neither political authorities nor national public opinion considered it
important until indigenous peoples forced the issue into the national arena
by the spectacular armed uprising in the Chiapas jungle on January 1, 1994.
The rebellion led by the Ejército Zapatista de Liberación Nacional (EZLN)
never militarily threatened the regime. Yet it proved an enormous political
challenge because of the legitimacy of the insurgents' demands: redress for
historic injustices, respect for indigenous cultures, judicial autonomy to
preserve and protect Indian communities.[63] In February 2001, thanks to
the favorable conditions created by the end of the authoritarian regime and
the electoral victory of Vicente Fox and the PAN in the preceding year, the
EZLN high command organized a mass march to Mexico City. It became
an enormous mobilization in support of indigenous demands. In a dramatic vote in Congress, most deputies agreed to welcome the EZLN and
the National Indigenous Congress representatives to the gallery and to
hear and consider their arguments for a fundamental change of the judicial
system and national policies on indigenous issues. In the end, however, the
so-called Indigenous Law was crafted and passed by opponents of the
indigenous autonomy demanded by the EZLN. Like the first liberalism, the
second coming faced the difficulty (perhaps the impossibility?) of solving
the "Indian problem." Again, the task has been left for the future.

As a matter of principle, liberalism emerged intimately linked to federalism —demands for provincial and local autonomy. From its nineteenth-century beginnings, centrifugal forces helped carry liberalism to the core of Mexican politics. Yet federalism also threatened the integrity of the nation that liberals intended to rule and transform. The result: the constitutions of 1824 and 1857 promised federalism, yet liberal practice in the restored republic and especially the Porfiriato promoted centralization. The issues of political, economic, and cultural relations between the center and the periphery resurfaced sharply, often violently, during the Mexican Revolution. The North revolted against the Center; states demanded autonomy from the national regime; villagers and ranchero communities demanded free townships and protested the rule of political bosses. In theory, the 1917 Constitution again confirmed Mexican federalism. In reality, again following Porfirian precedent, a ferocious centralism won out. Finally, in the 1980s the second coming of liberalism protested centralization: it was an inefficient way to allocate public funds, antithetical to the administrative flexibility demanded by the market. Yet while neoliberals made decentralization the essence of a new federalism, they concentrated decision-making power in the presidency to carry out economic reforms. Neoliberal decentralization remained caught between theory and its own contradiction: how to impose freedom and progress.

Conflict between the liberals and the Catholic Church organized the violent and chaotic political processes of the nineteenth century. The Reform War and Juárez's victory over the French and Maximilian's empire ended with an almost total exclusion of organized religion from the political arena. Díaz's authoritarian liberal regime forged compromises with the weakened church but never legalized its return to public and political life. In pronounced contrast, the new liberalism ended the religious exclusion. It invited churches, especially the Catholic Church, to play active and formal roles in the new political coalition that promoted neoliberal reforms. President Salinas radically modified the Constitution, legalizing the participation of churches and clergy in public and political arenas. He hoped that legalization would strengthen the legitimacy of the plan to transform the economy. Thus whereas the original liberals violently confronted the Catholic Church as a conservative corporation that threatened the state itself (because the Vatican declared itself officially opposed to liberalism), the new liberals of the late twentieth century designed policies to revitalize their old enemy as a political player. They hoped to neutralize political threats from the nationalist Left, which had little sympathy for the economic processes of neoliberalism. The results, as so often, proved contradictory. Many people committed to the church did support the neoliberal transformation. But most ended up in the coalition created by Vicente Fox and the PAN—the old Catholic party—helping oust the PRI in 2000.

CONCLUSION

Once in power, the first Mexican liberals of the nineteenth century gradually abandoned their commitment to democracy and the "state of law" in favor of economic commitments. Their liberalism ended as an oligarchic system framed by the long personal dictatorship of Porfirio Díaz. The difficulty, perhaps the impossibility, of institutionalizing the personal dictatorship led the opposition to rebellion in 1910, the only way to break the closed circle of oligarchic power. The uprising began only wishing to restore the democratic values of liberalism. A violent conservative reaction led the process into social revolution.

In the 1980s, the second coming of Mexican liberalism began within the last phase of Mexican authoritarianism—and soon helped that regime to its grave. In fact, the sudden emergence of neoliberalism and its imposition of a radically new economic model intensified economic, social, and political contradictions that shaped two great opposition parties, the PAN and the PRD, provoked armed uprising in Chiapas, and finally produced a citizens' "electoral revolt," which, after several attempts, peacefully ended the seventy-one-year monopoly of the PRI in the elections of July 2, 2000.

The first liberalism, after evolving and consolidating itself as a dictatorship, ended when a victorious revolution negotiated a statist solution to national problems. The second liberalism of the late twentieth century, as a result of Mexican society's maturity and favorable outside circumstances, ended by unintentionally and reluctantly creating conditions that gave the political class in power no alternative but to accept electoral defeat in July 2000.

The change of political parties was also a regime change. The democracy that began at the end of the twentieth century, led by the center-right party, did not seek to change the market-based economic model that authoritarian neoliberalism had already created. In essence, the newly elected regime consolidated the new model by creating new political stability, changing pivotal rules of the political game to promote legitimacy. Incipient democracy gave Mexican neoliberalism a modern tone it had been lacking. When the PRI and the authoritarian neoliberals lost power, other liberals, with historically unprecedented democratic legitimacy, took charge.

The new regime of the twenty-first century began energized by the polit- ically liberating change to democracy. It has inherited the challenge of all liberalisms: to solve old and enduring social problems. In the century just begun, Mexican political tasks center on three goals: the political consol- idation of liberal democracy, the creation of a state of law, and a response to centuries-old demands for social justice. The new regime's success is not ensured. But it is possible and worthwhile to continue on the road to nonauthoritarian, socially responsible liberalism. It is the essential pursuit, begun at the inception of national life, but not yet achieved: the creation and consolidation of political institutions that promote legality and social solidarity.

NOTES

1 Eric Hobsbawm, *The Age of Extremes: A History of the World, 1914–1991* (New York: Vintage Books, 1996), 404.

2 The rationale behind the concentration of benefits in the world's economic system at the end of the twentieth century is synthesized in Viviane Forrester, *Una extraña dictadura* (Mexico City: Fondo de Cultura Económica, 2000).

3 Poverty statistics are from Enrique Hernández Laos, *Crecimiento económico y pobreza en México* (Mexico City: Universidad Nacional Autónoma de México, 1992).

4 An analysis of the 1980s crisis and the new economic collapse of 1995 can be found in Julio Boltvinik and Enrique Hernández Laos, *Pobreza y distribución del ingreso en México* (Mexico City: Fondo de Cultura Económica, 1999).

5 When attempting to evaluate Miguel de la Madrid's six-year term, the Unidad de la Crónica Presidencial—which was in charge of producing an official history of his term—divided the task into twenty-five items that ranged from the stabilization of public finances and elections to soccer. Nothing was said, though, about democ- ratization. That issue simply did not exist. See Presidencia de la República, *Las razones y las obras: Gobierno de Miguel de la Madrid; Crónica del sexenio 1982– 1988; Sexto año* (Mexico City: Fondo de Cultura Económica, 1988), 16–162.

6 About the nature and main characteristics of Mexican foreign policy before the 1982 crisis, see Mario Ojeda, *Alcances y límites de la política exterior de México* (Mexico City: El Colegio de México, 1976).

7 A general overview of Mexico's political evolution during this economic change can be found in Lorenzo Meyer, *Liberalismo autoritario* (Mexico City: Editorial Océano, 1995), and also in Meyer, *Cambio de régimen y democracia incipiente* (Mexico City: Editorial Océano, 1998).

8 For a summary view of revolutionary nationalism, see the second part of Josefina Vázquez and Lorenzo Meyer, *México frente a Estados Unidos un ensayo histórico, 1776–1988* (Mexico City: Fondo de Cultura Económica, 2001), 148–76. For a similar exercise with regard to the nature and changes of the Mexican state's social policies from the 1970s to the 1990s, see María del Carmen Pardo, "La

administración de la política social: Cuatro estudios; El diseño administrativo de programas de emergencia" (Ph.D. diss., Universidad Iberoamericana, Mexico City, 1998).

9 For the nature of world democratization starting in 1973, see Samuel P. Huntington, *The Third Wave: Democratization in the Late Twentieth Century* (Norman: University of Oklahoma Press, 1991).

10 Jesús Reyes Heroles, *El liberalismo mexicano*, vol. 1: *Los orígenes* (Mexico City: Fondo de Cultura Económica, 1974).

11 For an analysis of the protected industrial growth project, see Blanca Torres, *Historia de la Revolución Mexicana*, vol. 21: *Hacia la utopía industrial* (Mexico City: El Colegio de México, 1984), 15–154.

12 This model's success before the political and entrepreneurial elites is reflected in Frank Brandenburg, *The Making of Modern Mexico* (Englewood Cliffs, N.J.: Prentice-Hall, 1964).

13 Víctor L. Urquidi, "El gran desafío del siglo XXI: El desarrollo sustentable; Alcances y riesgos para México," *El Mercado de Valores*, December 1999, 51.

14 A brief and fair description of the import substitution model in Mexico at its height can be found in Clark W. Reynolds, *La economía mexicana: Su estructura y crecimiento en el siglo XX* (Mexico City: Fondo de Cultura Económica, 1973).

15 An analysis of the development and outburst of the 1982 economic crisis can be found in Enrique Cárdenas, *La política económica en México, 1950–1994* (Mexico City: Fondo de Cultura Económica, 1996), 86–152; and René Villareal, *Industrialización, deuda y desequilibrio externo en México: Un enfoque neoestructuralista (1929–1997)* (Mexico City: Fondo de Cultura Económica, 1997), 391–453.

16 A synthesis of the changes within Mexico's economy starting in the mid-1980s can be found in Cárdenas, *La política económica*, 153–90; and Nora Lustig, *Mexico, the Remaking of an Economy* (Washington: Brookings Institution Press, 1998), 28–213. For a synthesis of the nature of the political system during the same period, see, among others, Héctor Aguilar Camín and Lorenzo Meyer, *A la sombra de la Revolución Mexicana* (Mexico City: Cal y Arena, 1989); and Susan Kaufman Purcell, *The Mexican Profit-Sharing Decision: Politics in an Authoritarian Regime* (Berkeley: University of California Press, 1975).

17 Soledad Loaeza, "Liberalización política e incertidumbre en México," in *Las dimensiones políticas de la reestructuración económica*, ed. Maria Lorena Cook, Kevin J. Middlebrook, and Juan Molinar Horcasitas (Mexico City: Cal y Arena, 1996), 171–94.

18 Benedict R. Anderson, *Imagined Communities: Reflections on the Origins and Spread of Nationalism* (London: Verso, 1983).

19 Vázquez and Meyer, *México frente*, 66–67.

20 *México y el mundo: Historia de sus relaciones exteriores*, vol. 1 (Mexico City: Senado de la República, 1990), 150.

21 Fernando Escalante, *Ciudadanos imaginarios* (Mexico City: El Colegio de México, 1992).

22 For a political view of the Porfiriato, see François-Xavier Guerra, *México: Del antiguo régimen a la revolución*, vol. 1 (Mexico City: Fondo de Cultura Económica, 1988). The nature of elections in Juárez's and Díaz's tenure has been analyzed by

Luis Medina in José Varela Ortega and Luis Medina, *Elecciones, alternancia y democracia: España-México, una reflexión comparativa* (Madrid: Biblioteca Nueva, 2000), 217–26.

23 See the final part of Sierra's interpretation of the Mexican process in his *Evolución política del pueblo mexicano* (Mexico City: La Casa de España en México, 1940).

24 Jorge Carpizo, *El presidencialismo mexicano* (Mexico City: Siglo XXI, 1978); Julio Scherer García, *Los presidentes* (Mexico City: Grijalvo, 1986).

25 Lustig, *Mexico*, 117–22.

26 See the works in Esthela Gutiérrez Garza, Juan Manuel Ramírez, and Jorge Regalado, eds., *El debate nacional*, vol. 4: *Los actores sociales* (Mexico City: Diana, 1997).

27 Charles A. Hale, *El liberalismo mexicano en la época de Mora* (Mexico City: Siglo XXI, 1972), 42–73.

28 Angel Pola, ed., *Benito Juárez: Discursos y manifiestos*, vol. 2 (Mexico City: Instituto Nacional de Estudios de la Revolución, 2000), 211.

29 Luis González y González, *Obras completas*, vol. 4: *El siglo de las luchas* (Mexico City: Clío, 1996), 68.

30 Ibid., 68–69.

31 Hale, *El liberalismo mexicano*, 123–51.

32 Reyes Heroles, *El liberalismo mexicano*, vol. 2: *La sociedad fluctuante* (Mexico City: Fondo de Cultura Económica, 1974), 89–136.

33 An excellent example of neoliberalism's present-day sources is Milton Friedman's work, especially *Capitalism and Freedom* (Chicago: University of Chicago Press, 1962). A triumphant view of Western capitalism's success over Soviet socialism can be found in Francis Fukuyama, *The End of History and the Last Man* (New York: Free Press, 1992).

34 See Gobierno Federal de la República Mexicana, *Plan Nacional de Desarrollo, 1983–1988* (designed at the begining of Miguel de la Madrid's government).

35 Charles C. Cumberland, *Mexican Revolution: The Constitutionalist Years* (Austin: University of Texas Press, 1972), 351–55.

36 Raymond Vernon, *The Dilemma of Mexico's Development: The Roles of the Private and Public Sectors* (Cambridge: Harvard University Press, 1963), 72–87.

37 Statistics from Gabriel Zaid, *La economía presidencial* (Mexico City: Vuelta, 1987), 25.

38 Presidencia de la República, *Las razones y las obras: Gobierno de Miguel de la Madrid; Crónica del sexenio 1982–1988; Cuarto año* (Mexico City: Fondo de Cultura Económica, 1987), 514–28.

39 Roberto Newell G. and Luis Rubio F., *Mexico's Dilemma: The Political Origins of the Economic Crisis* (Boulder: Westview Press, 1984), 260.

40 A good overview of all the charges against the economic policies of the Mexican government during this time can be found in Zaid, *La economía presidencial*, and its sequel, *La nueva economía presidencial* (Mexico City: Grijalvo, 1994).

41 This struggle within the state party and the divisions that it caused make up the core of Luis Javier Garrido's book *La ruptura: La corriente democrática del PRI* (Mexico City: Grijalbo, 1993).

42 Regarding the nature of the PAN and its relationship with neo-Pan entrepreneurs starting with the 1982 crisis, see chapter 5 of Soledad Loaeza, *El Partido Acción Nacional: La larga marcha; Oposición leal y partido de protesta, 1939–1994* (Mexico City: Fondo de Cultura Económica, 1999), 347–98.

43 Enrique Nanti, *El Maquío Clouthier: La biografía* (Mexico City: Editorial Planeta, 1998), 141–92.

44 See Juan Molinar Horcaditas and Jeffrey Weldon, "Elecciones de 1988 en México: Crisis del autoritarismo," *Revista Mexicana de Sociología* 52, no. 4 (October–December 1990): 229–62.

45 Antonio Escobar Ohmstede, "La política agraria y los grupos indígenas, 1856–1857," *Papeles de la Casa Chata* 5, no. 7 (1990): 4.

46 Salinas presented his "social liberalism" in a meeting to celebrate the PRI's fifty-eighth anniversary on March 4, 1992. Presidencia de la República, *Crónica del gobierno de Carlos Salinas de Gortari, Cuarto año* (Mexico City: Fondo de Cultura Económica, 1994), 99–101.

47 Denise Dresser, *Neopopulist Solutions to Neoliberal Problems: Mexico's National Solidarity Program*, Current Issues Brief no. 4 (La Jolla: Center for U.S.-Mexican Studies, University of California, San Diego, 1991).

48 For a panoramic view of the problems of poverty and social polarization in the last decade of the twentieth century, see Esthela Gutiérrez Garza, ed., *El debate nacional*, vol. 5: *La política social* (Mexico City: Editorial Diana, 1997).

49 Boltvinik and Hernández Laos, *Pobreza y distribución*, 22. For a historical examination of poverty as a central element of national debate, see Julieta Campos, *¿Qué hacemos con los pobres? La reiterada querella por la nación* (Mexico City: Aguilar, 1995).

50 Hale, *El liberalismo mexicano*, 193–200.

51 Vázquez and Meyer, *México frente*, 114–17.

52 Consejo Nacional de Población, *La situación demográfica de México, 1999* (Mexico City: CONAPO, 1999), 45.

53 There is an extensive bibliography about Mexican migration to the United States at the end of the twentieth century. See, among others, the work of experts such as Jorge Bustamante in Mexico and Wayne Cornelius and Manuel García y Griego in the United States.

54 José María Luis Mora, *Obras* (Mexico City: Porrúa, 1963), 64.

55 Silvestre Villegas Revueltas, *El liberalismo moderado en México, 1852–1864* (Mexico City: Universidad Nacional Autónoma de México, 1997), 135.

56 The 1995 crisis led many of the banks' debtors into bankruptcy, and many of the banks were also on the brink of bankruptcy. In this case, the government did not allow the famous "market laws" to function and, through the creation of the Fondo de Protección al Ahorro, rescued the banking system. This was done, though, at a cost of 80 billion dollars, which became part of the foreign debt.

57 Alan Knight, *The Mexican Revolution*, vol. 1 (Cambridge: Cambridge University Press, 1986), 96.

58 Consejo Nacional de Población, *La situación demográfica de México*, 153.

59 José María Luis Mora, *México y sus revoluciones*, vol. 1 (Mexico City: Porrúa, 1986), 65–74.

60   Luis González y González, *El indio en la era liberal* (Mexico City: Clío, 1996); Romana Falcón, *Las naciones de una república: La cuestión indígena en las leyes y el congreso mexicanos, 1867–1876* (Mexico City: Enciclopedia Parlamentaria, Congreso de la Unión, 1999).

61   Consejo Nacional de Población, *La situación demográfica de México* (Mexico City: CONAPO, 1997), 58.

62   A radical and critical discussion of these policies and their premises, goals, and achievements can be found in Guillermo Bonfil, *México profundo: Una civilización negada* (Mexico City: Grijalbo, 1989).

63   Héctor Díaz-Polanco, *La rebelión zapatista y la autonomía* (Mexico City: Siglo XXI, 1997).

❧ Civil Society and Popular Resistance
Mexico at the End of the Twentieth Century

GUILLERMO DE LA PEÑA ❧

During the 1990s, three important social processes focused attention on the transformation taking place in Mexico's public sphere. The first was the crisis of the national-populist state and the related rise of a neoliberal model for development within the context of a global economy. The second was the democratization of the electoral system, linked to the strengthening of opposition political parties and public opinion. The third was the proliferation of "civil society" organizations, strategic vehicles for citizens' discourse as well as their collective demands, actions, and resistance in many areas (electoral observers, human rights, ecology, religiosity, multiculturalism, gender politics, education, information, etc.). This essay explores some of the organized forms of popular resistance that appeared at the end of the century, especially as they were connected to these processes.

We must begin, however, by remembering that the groups included in the "popular classes" have changed radically during the second half of the twentieth century. In 1959, only one out of three Mexicans lived in urban settlements of more than fifteen thousand inhabitants. Today almost 70 percent of the population is urban, and 30 percent is overcrowded in the country's largest metropolis.[1] In the countryside, a large number of peasants have gradually become wage earners. The remaining rural families are in deep poverty and survive only by sending half of their members to the United States, where they stay for indefinite periods. Such more permanent emigration contrasts with the more circular migrations of the 1960s, when most migrants to Mexican cities and the United States returned to their villages after limited periods of work.[2] Half a century ago, 60 percent of Mexico's economically active population (EAP) engaged in agricultural and livestock production; today, barely 25 percent are involved in these activities, and many of them must complement their income through non-agricultural activities such as casual employment in rural industries. In the urban-industrialized world, the model of import substitution has been rapidly dismantled: formal blue-collar employment is mainly supplied by the export-focused maquiladora industries and the modern service sector; the diverse and precarious "informal" sector includes nearly 40 percent of the workforce. Women's employment is rapidly increasing and already makes up 30 percent of the EAP.[3]

The family and community values of Mexican popular culture, framed in the past within discourses of traditional Catholicism and official nationalism, are now challenged by Protestant, Pentecostal, and New Age religions; feminist, ethnic, and transnational demands; punk and cholo styles; ethical and aesthetic models derived from telenovelas; and so on. This does not mean that popular culture is or has ever been a mere reflection of dominant institutions or current fashions. Still, expressions of popular culture do incorporate and expropriate the experiences of its adherents; inevitably it is heterogeneous.[4] Politically, popular expressions have overrun the corporatist channels established earlier by the hegemony of the "revolutionary" state and its official political party. Conceptions of politically active people have ceased to presume the primacy of traditional and supposedly homogeneous social classes, such as the "working class" and the "campesino class," as they forge new relationships with the state. Instead, what stand out today are organizations and groups that simultaneously, or alternatively, defend specific economic or political interests, open spaces for new types of collective identities, propose new forms of citizen participation, and demand new democratic definitions not only of the state but of daily life.

I begin with a brief review of the most important popular organizations between 1940 and 1970, marked by state power and participation through vertically integrated corporate structures. I then discuss the process of radicalization that characterized the 1970s. For the years after 1980, my analysis focuses on three forms of organized collective resistance: the mobilization of rural classes, old and new; the emergence of urban players advancing demands concerning their neighborhoods and the quality of daily life; and the rise and assertion of new ethnic associations. By "organized forms of resistance" vis-à-vis the state and the dominant social actors, I refer particularly to the gray area located between open insurgency and mass mobilizations linked, for instance, to political parties or national organizations, and the concept of "everyday resistance" studied by James Scott. I am interested in asking about the options open to local and regional groups who seek to imagine and effectively defend alternative visions of development, global insertion, and "communal modernity."[5]

As the twenty-first century begins, Mexico's popular organizations must be understood primarily in terms of what recent sociological literature has labeled "new social movements." Such movements struggle for "the right to have rights"—social, political, and civil rights, but also the right to cultural and gender differences, the right to an improving quality of life, and the right to complete and truthful information. This struggle to broaden human rights is tied to a new definition of citizenship—not a given, but a goal to achieve, a constructive process that demands the constant participation of dynamic and heterogeneous social sectors. Thus the concept of "civil society," a public space of sociability and cultural communication independent from both the state and the market, becomes key. I will return to these concepts at the end of the essay; their greater or lesser relevance at various times during the period under study will emphasize the depth of the changes experienced by the Mexican nation.

CORPORATE CONTAINMENT, 1940–1970

In the 1940s, the pacification of the Mexican nation appeared a fait accompli. The last great caudillo rebellion of Saturnino Cedillo had been extinguished. All that remained of the insurgency known as the Cristiada were a few local uprisings such as "la bola chiquita" in Morelos, Puebla, and Guerrero, where participants were angered by military conscription. These small outbursts of insurgency were quickly eliminated with fire and sword.[6] In the political arena, the hegemony of the Partido de la Revolución Mexicana (PRM)—renamed Partido Revolucionario Institucional (PRI) in 1946 —seemed unquestionable. The strongest political opposition came from the Unión Nacional Sinarquista (UNS), which could marshal more than five hundred thousand active members, most in the central-western region of the country. The *sinarquistas* protested against religious persecution, corruption in public administration, and the subordination of campesinos in the agrarian reform—all from a traditional Catholic ideological perspective. Nevertheless, the progress of the UNS was stopped by direct repression followed by a legal ban.[7] The other party of Catholic opposition was the Partido Acción Nacional (PAN). It also bitterly criticized official corruption and political manipulation but presented itself as a loyal opposition promoting civilian rule and democratic ideology. At the time, the PAN only attracted limited groups, mostly from the middle sectors.[8]

The political hegemony of the PRM-PRI can be explained by its strategy, begun by president Lázaro Cárdenas in the 1930s, of incorporating urban and rural workers into the official party, making the party a mass organization capable of processing, managing, and controlling social demands through selective responses and patronage mechanisms.[9] In formal and practical terms, this meant that all beneficiaries of the agrarian reform belonged to the party's Confederación Nacional Campesina (CNC), simply because they were beneficiaries; similarly, urban and rural workers who were members of the great labor and popular organizations—the Confederación de Trabajadores Mexicanos (CTM), the Confederación Revolucionaria de Obreros Mexicanos (CROM), and later the Confederación Regional de Obreros y Campesinos (CROC) and the Confederación Nacional de Organizaciones Populares (CNOP)—were tied corporately to the party and the regime. Even private rural smallholders (though we should remember that many holdings were not small) and the owners of urban real estate were linked to the PRI through the Confederación Nacional de la Pequeña Propiedad (CNPP).

Beginning in 1948, however, the corporate organizations that resulted from Cárdenas's negotiations with leftist political and labor organizations became increasingly critical of the PRI's authoritarianism and corruption, as well as its deceleration of social reforms, especially in the countryside.[10] Three great popular opposition movements appeared, institutionalized in three mass organizations: the Unión General de Obreros y Campesinos Mexicanos (UGOCM), the Partido Agrario y Obrero led by Rubén Jaramillo, and the Central Campesina Independiente (CCI). Nevertheless, the demands these movements pressed could be managed without significant alteration of the corporatist regime or its constitutional base (unlike many demands of the organizations that later appeared during the last three decades of the century).

Vicente Lombardo Toledano, one of the founders of the regime's CTM, created the UGOCM in 1949. This union became the labor branch of the Partido Popular (PP), also led by Lombardo, after his exclusion from the official labor central. He claimed to resume and go beyond Cárdenas's radicalism through an alliance between rural and industrial workers (sectors separated by the PRM), using land takeovers, strikes, independent cooperative institutions, and electoral struggles as the union's main weapons. The government decreed all action by the UGOCM illegal, dismantled its credit unions, dissolved its public meetings by force, and ordered jail terms, and sometimes the murder, of its most conspicuous leaders. Yet, in fact, the government agrarian machine responded to the new protests in several rural areas through increased land distributions, contributing to the weakening of Lombardismo at the end of the 1950s, and to its subsequent taming.[11]

The Partido Agrario y Obrero of the former Zapatista Rubén Jaramillo, focused on the states of Morelos and Puebla during the 1950s, protested the slowness of agrarian reform, the corruption in the great state-owned sugar mill of Zacatepec, and the disadvantages faced by *ejido* cane growers in their dealings with both public and private sugar mills.[12] In 1962, Jaramillo and his family were massacred, his followers persecuted; but his demands could be met (as some of them were) through the simple implementation of existing legislation and the recognition of the new organization as a legitimate mediator. Politically, Jaramillismo was linked to the opposition led by Miguel Henríquez Guzmán, who had broken off—like Lombardo's PP—from the official political party and claimed to be the true repository of the legacy of the Mexican Revolution.[13]

The CCI, founded by Alfonso Garzón in 1959, was a dissident wing of the dominant party's CNC, first in Baja California, then in Sonora, Puebla, and the Laguna region. It rejected the CNC leadership's indifference to the ejido problems, its unrepresentative character, and the government's general lack of interest in the less-favored classes. As a result, it became the most active member of the Movimiento de Liberación Nacional (MLN), a coalition sponsored by Lázaro Cárdenas, designed to struggle for a return to revolutionary purity. (Cárdenas himself soon disavowed this coalition, in exchange, it was said, for the Mexican government's recognition of Fidel Castro's government.)[14] In the mid-1960s, the CCI divided into two factions: Garzón's group was co-opted by the PRI, while Ramón Danzós Palomino led an independent communist-influenced branch.

Thus, for thirty years, the Mexican state responded to popular demands in the countryside through co-optation and repression. It conditioned protests so that they were often expressed through the state's own institutions of agrarian reform and corporate control. To the extent that it satisfied demands, the state machine was legitimized and strengthened. Moreover, the leaders of popular resistance often operated like PRI bosses: they concentrated on the personal politics of control and mediation. Their roles might facilitate agreements with the regime at the top levels of the leadership hierarchy (co-optation); alternately, if they resisted negotiation and co-optation, they might be murdered (or otherwise removed), thus beheading the organization and undermining its resistance.[15]

Something very similar took place in the urban labor arena, where trade unions, especially in strategic state industries, struggled and gained better wages and fringe benefits, gains achieved without abandoning the channels of vertical corporatism. In fact, "union conquests" such as closed shops and the inheritance of jobs strengthened corporatism. In 1947, the CTM (still the largest workers' organization) signed the Pacto Obrero Industrial with the chambers of commerce and industry. The elimination of leftist or restless elements began a "cleansing" of official trade unions. There was significant resistance to this new control—for example, the independent railway workers, who were repressed in 1958, and the "white syndicates" of Monterrey who broke away from state corporate control only to fall into domination by management. But the dependence of the Juntas de Conciliación y Arbitraje, the only labor courts, on the government made worker insurgency difficult. President Adolfo López Mateos (1958–64) attempted to create an alternative organization to the CTM in the Central Nacional de Trabajadores, aiming to gain support for his plan to nationalize and unify the hydroelectric industry. Yet after achieving that goal, he virtually dissolved it.[16]

In the 1950s and 1960s, two sectors of middle-class government employees, teachers (1956) and medical doctors (1965), led two of the most important urban mobilizations. The benefits the corporate state had granted no longer satisfied their aspirations for social mobility. The teachers' and doctors' mobilizations, following precedents set by the Unión Cívica de San Luis Potosí (1960–62) in organizing professionals and middle-class employees in the private sector, demanded the democratization of the PRI and respect for the voting process. They all were (literally) hit hard.[17] The student movement that challenged the regime in several cities in 1968, with the greatest force in Mexico City, was also crushed. Yet the "utopian democracy" demanded by the students implicitly denounced the government of President Díaz Ordaz and the authoritarian political model as unconstitutional. Many have recognized the 1968 student mobilizations as the symbolic beginning of the political transition toward democracy.[18]

CAMPESINOS, WORKERS, AND THE STRUGGLE AGAINST PRI CAPITALISM, 1970–1980

Between 1930 and 1960, the land under cultivation in Mexico expanded at a phenomenal rate, increasing from about four to fourteen million hectares. Almost 60 percent of this expansion took place in ejidos, landed communities created by the revolutionary agrarian reform. Some ejidos gained lands taken from large estates; others colonized in new settlements in coastal areas and along the border. Meanwhile, the national mortality rate fell, thanks to better nourishment combined with government health campaigns and institutions.[19] In the countryside, the availability of land allowed the geographic redistribution of a growing rural population, which grew its own food while providing cheap surplus staples for the cities. Those decades of agrarian reform and expansion reinforced and reproduced a model of peasant social organization characterized by extended families that operated as units of production and consumption, embedded in communal relations, usually legitimized through religious symbols, that facilitated interfamilial cooperation.[20] This peasantry was not particularly prosperous: the mechanisms of the agrarian reform had granted only small amounts of land to families; government market regulation kept the prices of agricultural products low, while the costs of industrial products and consumer items rose. Nevertheless, until 1960 rural poverty was not extreme, at least in central and northern regions. The growth of school attendance and urban employment even allowed for a degree of social mobility. Thus, despite conditions in the countryside that were anything but idyllic, the rural situation did not critically threaten the expanding state machine or the economy. The state made its presence felt in the countryside not only through health and education services but also through infrastructure works (roads, electricity, irrigation), credit and insurance institutions, and access to marketing through institutions such as the Compañía Nacional de Subsistencias Populares (CONASUPO).

The 1960s signaled the beginning of the deterioration of this system: the agricultural frontier (the availability of unused arable land) was closing while population continued to grow. The lands that the government continued to distribute were often arid or lacked good market access; some were not new lands at all, but merely official certifications of communal lands already owned by the pueblos. Furthermore, many ejido applications remained unanswered. At the same time, monetization intensified in the rural economy. Thanks to new roads, goods mass-produced in the cities circulated throughout the country and replaced local crafts. The unequal commercial exchange between the city and the countryside became sharper. The "guarantee prices" of basic products such as maize and beans, conceived to protect rural producers, increasingly protected urban consumers. CONASUPO faced mounting accusations of incompetence and corruption. Small farmers had to resort to new commercial crops sustained by industrially produced inputs (hybrid seeds, fertilizers, pesticides, etc.). This required more money, money not always supplied by official credit institutions. Moreover, no insurance covered the risks of cultivating new products for uncertain markets. Thus agricultural innovation and diversification could lead to catastrophic results, ranging from mounting indebtedness to the abandonment of lands.[21] An army of agricultural day laborers without union protection, four million strong by the 1970s, continued to grow. Many, called *golondrinos* (swallows), traveled (and still travel) throughout the country, following the demands of commercial agriculture, facing low salaries and subhuman living conditions.[22] Meanwhile a prosperous modern sector of agricultural entrepreneurs built "neolatifundia" by grabbing the best lands and taking the lion's share of the waters supplied by government irrigation projects.[23] Although these entrepreneurs primarily produced specialized crops for the international market (coffee, cotton, sugar cane, fruits and vegetables) and bred cattle for beef, they increasingly took advantage of government subsidies to produce food for the domestic market.

Hence the loyalty of campesinos to the PRI regime was challenged, and expressions of open rejection began to appear. Many were guided by new leaders who no longer invoked a Mexican Revolution they now considered "bourgeois" or, at best, "interrupted" or "debased." Instead these leaders invoked the (universal) revolution of the proletariat to support their cause. The CCI dissident Ramón Danzós Palomino ran for president in 1964 on the ticket of a reborn Communist Party (PC). He failed to get the full support of the MLN opposition alliance; he was denied official registration as a candidate. After being harassed and jailed, in 1975 he regrouped his rural followers in the Central Independiente de Obreros Agrícolas y Campesinos (CIOAC). The CIOAC was openly linked to the PC and led many protests and land takeovers. It also provided legal advice to support petitions (for land, credit, and market access for small growers; for decent salaries, minimal social benefits, and free trade unions for day laborers) presented to the government by the local organizations mushrooming across the country.[24] Around the same time, president Luis Echeverría (1970–76), confronted by a handful of fleeting yet ominous guerrilla outbreaks, tried to balance the wobbling legitimacy of the PRI in the countryside by creating a more comprehensive corporate organization: the Congreso Permanente Agrario. This organization incorporated the UGOCM, Garzón's CCI, and the Congreso Agrario Mexicano (CAM), an amalgamation of landless peasants that the PRI used as shock troops. In addition, the regime recognized new institutions, such as the Uniones de Ejidos (UE), which were legally registered and allowed to negotiate public and private subsidies and credit. Concomitantly, the state created the Programa Integral de Desarrollo Rural (PIDER), in charge of government projects at the local and regional levels. Still, these measures could not co-opt all independent groups (many of which gained recognition as UEs) or prevent mass movements.

In 1976 the Frente Campesino Independiente de Sonora invaded the irrigated properties of the neolatifundia enterprises in the Yaqui and Mayo valleys. Meanwhile similar mobilizations sprang up in Sinaloa, Veracruz, Chiapas, Durango, and Jalisco. There were also campesino protests against the official banks in Yucatán.[25] Since Echeverría wanted to be remembered by history as a benefactor of the countryside and the restorer of PRI hegemony, he ended his term by confiscating 100,000 hectares from the agricultural entrepreneurs in Sonora, and 500,000 in the rest of the country. Still, he could not achieve the submission of independent organizations. His successor, José López Portillo (1976–82), had no choice but to accept the weakening of the CNC and the other official unions, which ceased to be privileged mediators between the peasantry and the government.

In Sonora, for example, the Coalición de Ejidos Colectivos de los Valles del Yaqui y del Mayo refused from the beginning to be underlings of the PRI and established direct negotiating links with agents of public credit and technical assistance. In 1979 this coalition and about ten UES and independent organizations from the whole country founded the Coordinadora Nacional Plan de Ayala (CNPA). Their goals were ambitious: defend the lands and natural resources of indigenous and peasant communities; increase land distribution ("all the land for campesinos"); gain free unionization for campesinos and day workers; defend women's and indigenous rights; and, eventually, take over the government ("Today we fight for land, tomorrow for power"). The CNPA claimed to be independent from any political party, although some of its organizations had links with the Communist CIOAC. It created its own negotiating agency in Mexico City to deal with the Secretaría de Agricultura y Recursos Hidráulicos and the Secretaría de la Reforma Agraria. To avoid corporatist authoritarianism, the organization promoted a system of community participation, which elected representatives to regional assemblies who, in turn, elected delegates to a national assembly that annually appointed members of the permanent commission in Mexico City. Between 1979 and 1983, CNPA organizations not only led marches, land invasions, and occupations of public buildings at the regional and national levels but also became critical opponents of the government's implementation of the policies of the Sistema Alimentario Mexicano (SAM). The SAM was a program by which López Portillo distributed subsidies to the peasantry—based more on political than technical criteria—and increased "guarantee prices" in an effort to recover national self-sufficiency in basic cereals, lost in 1974.[26]

The innovations brought by many of the organizations and movements that appeared in the 1970s and 1980s must be stressed. In contrast to earlier groups, they displayed a deep skepticism toward the discourse that glorified the Mexican Revolution.[27] They did not see the Mexican state as a potential ally; rather, they considered it an agent of capitalist domination, and therefore they considered negotiations with state institutions to be difficult and provisional agreements (even truces) with the enemy. They rejected decisions imposed from above along with corporate rigidity; they expressed themselves using language cast in Marxist discourse. They maintained regular relations with leftist parties, legalized in 1977 by López Portillo's government; they worked with the radical university-based groups (Marxist and Christian) that, after 1968, started to visit rural communities and act as advisors to campesinos. For example, the Frente Nacional Democrático Popular, founded by Oaxaca university students, attracted many rural organizations from the south and southwest; the Maoist Unión del Pueblo and Línea de Masas, based in Mexico City, worked with groups in the center-north and the southeast. In municipal elections, the new campesino organizations supported leftist parties, helping to install a handful of mayors who officially, if locally, proclaimed the radicalization of agrarian demands.[28]

In the industrializing cities, popular groups also took advantage of the "political opening" that developed as the Echeverría and López Portillo governments tried to rescue the regime's legitimacy. But unofficial labor unions, even after creating two broad political fronts, the Unión Obrera Independiente and the Frente Auténtico del Trabajo, met enormous difficulties in their struggle against official corporatism. Both presidents repressed movements clearly intended to emancipate workers from state corporatism. The remnants of the independent railway workers' and oil workers' movements were dismantled. Perhaps the best known struggle for trade union independence was led by the Tendencia Democrática of the Sindicato Único de Trabajadores Electricistas de la República Mexicana (SUTERM), which sought to create a new hegemony within one of the largest and most strategic labor unions of the country. Despite its prestige, the Tendency was dissolved by force in 1976.[29]

An analysis of why industrial workers were less successful than rural peasants in creating independent organizations, or at least organizations that could maneuver in the face of the state (and challenge the power of the sclerotic leadership of the PRI), lies beyond the scope of this essay. Without doubt, however, the government made a special effort to control and co-opt workers in strategic and visible sectors: electricians, oil workers, and telephone, steel, and railway workers; it deemed many other sectors of the economy to be distant, fragmented, and irrelevant. It is also true that, compared to peasants, industrial workers were, as a class, favored by the regime. To date, the debates about the presence or absence of the organized working class (which in Leninist orthodoxy should be the agents of change) in the process of the country's democratic transformation are not settled.[30]

Urban radical organizations gathered more strength with the advent of the Movimiento Urbano Popular (MUP). It mobilized tenants in the *vecindades* (old buildings in city centers), who protested landlord abuses and inadequate urban services, and especially *paracaidistas* (parachutists), squatters on private, public, or ejido urban properties who demanded basic services and the legalization of their claims. The efforts of the MUP developed in the context of the rural crisis and the extraordinary increase in the flow of migrants toward cities from 1960 to 1980. Urban demands and protests were nothing new, and the PRI had often been able to neutralize them through patronage mechanisms and the co-optation and absorption of their leaders into state-ruled corporate organizations. The regime also used direct repression occasionally, yet effectively. Urban migrants, of course, did not always resort to protests in the presence of uncertainty and scarcity. Family and neighborhood mutual aid networks helped to mitigate the grievances of urban dwellers and facilitated urban survival.[31] Yet the saturation of urban spaces during the 1960s, the politicization of urban inhabitants and their leaders, their contacts with opposition trade unions, and, after 1968, the presence of university advisors in urban neighborhoods led to a striking multiplication of independent and active groups in many cities during the 1970s.[32]

These mobilizations drew support from neighborhood solidarity networks, which were transformed from safety nets to springboards for resistance. Manuel Castells celebrated them as representing a new type of urban organization. In addition to articulating unprecedented demands for "collective consumption" that automatically pitted them against the state, and not simply against "class enemies," the new urban movements stimulated both the language and practical construction of communal cultural identities and the search for a participatory and decentralized government.[33] Castells noted three Mexican cases: the Colonia Rubén Jaramillo (named after the campesino leader murdered in 1962) in Cuernavaca; the Campamento Dos de Octubre (the date of the student massacre of 1968) in Mexico City; and the Frente Popular Tierra y Libertad (the Zapatista motto) in Monterrey. The Colonia Rubén Jaramillo assembled twenty-five thousand paracaidistas who, during six months in 1973, struggled to create an independent urban organization. The army repressed them, but the Morelos state government was forced to create a formal agency to negotiate the petitioners' claims for urban land. The leaders in the colonia influenced later groups.

The Campamento Dos de Octubre appeared in the federal capital in

1975 with the active support of students and professionals. Together they called for a wide Bloque Urbano de Colonias Populares to coordinate urban struggle in the Valley of Mexico. With a great enthusiasm—and, according to Castells, naiveté—the Campamento was proclaimed a "self-governed liberated area." In January 1976 the police violently evicted the squatters. Yet they returned, rebuilt their houses, and started a negotiation process with the government, during which they had to moderate their claims for autonomy.

In Monterrey, where there was also important participation by student groups, the radical experiment lasted longer. The Frente Popular Tierra y Libertad formed in 1971 and eventually united thirty settlements and more than 100,000 squatters. Taking advantage of the conflicts between President Echeverría and Monterrey's business leaders, who were pressuring the municipal governments to destroy the settlements, the Frente successfully gained the president's protection. Yet it skillfully refused to accept legalization proposals that would have tied it to the federal government. Thanks to a very strong neighborhood organization, the Frente successfully established local services and government functions. It also achieved an impressive public presence: when six members died in a confrontation with the police, a huge demonstration paralyzed the city. But federal protection ended in 1977, and the Frente faced internal divisions. Most colonias finally accepted the proposals to regularize landownership and provide services negotiated by an ad hoc trustee. By 1984, little remained of the autonomous neighborhood government in Monterrey.[34]

The creation in 1978 of a federal organization to deal with illegal settlements, the Comisión de Regularización de la Tenencia de la Tierra (CORETT), was a triumph of urban mobilizations—and an attempt to end them through institutional means. The CORETT allowed the return of the PRI's corporate mediation; CTM and CNOP agents often managed the normalization process. Yet the mobilized groups did not disappear easily. Following the "frentista" model of the CNPA, focused on coordinating autonomous subgroups, one hundred thousand families in cities in northern and central Mexico created the Coordinadora Nacional del Movimiento Urbano Popular (CONAMUP) in 1981.[35] Its goals stressed practical issues—access to housing and services—as well as the creation of self-managing communities. Its ultimate objective was a great national alliance that would lead to the destruction of the bourgeois state and full autonomy of the communities. Thus, as in the case of many radical peasant organizations, the search for socialism in urban neighborhoods no longer meant support for a strong, centralized institution that commanded exclusive loyalty and reduced all existing identities to a proletarian consciousness.

From 1970 to 1982, the repression of dissidence did not stop, but the regime made an effort to gain popular support through increased public spending, especially during the brief oil bonanza (1978–81). President López Portillo, besides directing subsidies toward rural areas through the SAM, founded the Coordinación Nacional de Planeación y Apoyo a las Zonas Marginadas (COPLAMAR), which promoted health, education, and road-building projects across the country. In 1982, however, the collapse of public finances (caused by the collapse of world oil prices) forced president Miguel de la Madrid's government (1982–88) to eliminate COPLAMAR and to drastically reduce both public investment and social spending. Between 1981 and 1988, investment in the rural sector fell by 50 percent, credits were reduced by 40 percent, and interest rates soared from 12.5 percent to 96 percent. In 1985, 70 percent of rural producers lived below the subsistence level. The scarcity of credit—both for staple maize and beans and for commercial products like sugar cane, coffee, and cotton—led many to reduce cultivation and turn arable lands over to cattle, cutting employment in agriculture. From the 1980s, the agencies of the PRI's corporate rule were more focused on identifying and containing discontent than on distributing benefits.[36] Public negotiations stopped being about general policies. Instead they emphasized help for specific groups of producers. The CNPA found a new cause: protest against the "austerity policies." It did not prove effective. Divided by party jealousies, the Coordinadora gradually lost strength. In 1985 the Unión Nacional de Organizaciones Campesinas Autónomas (UNORCA) was founded. Its dominant members were the ejido unions of the northwest. They sought fair prices for agricultural products and greater access to official credit and technical support. At the same time, associations of producers (coffee, sugar cane, fruits, and vegetables) advanced particular demands. Meanwhile the northern agricultural and cattle bourgeoisie, reorganized after their standoff with Echeverría's and López Portillo's populist policies, began to appear with new strength in the public arena.[37]

Despite the persistence of agrarian rhetoric, after 1982 agrarian reform —the distribution of "land to those who work it"—ceased to be part of the Mexican government's agenda. The CNPA and other radical organizations denounced the so-called *rezagos* (legal land petitions frozen by the bureaucracy), which had reached record numbers. Many latifundia in disguise also remained.[38] The new rural agenda of President de la Madrid, later capped off by President Salinas (1988–94), could be summarized by two goals: opening the Mexican economy to international markets by ending protectionism and "modernizing" the countryside. The state would provide concrete help to efficient producers that made genuine efforts to increase productivity, as in the deals negotiated with UNORCA. To combat the "irrational pulverization" of production units, the government encouraged associations among ejidos, ejido unions, landowners, and agribusiness enterprises.[39] In fact, the cattle and agricultural bourgeoisie had associated (at least since the 1940s) with private smallholders through Regional Agricultural Unions and Ranchers Unions (CNPP). Yet, in the 1980s, several legal reforms facilitated the incorporation of ejidos into capitalist enterprises, reforms negotiated through agreements between the government and the Consejo Nacional Agropecuario (which private entrepreneurs had created in 1984).[40] Asociaciones Rurales de Interés Colectivo (ARIC), which linked ejido and small and middle landowners' unions with enterprises in charge of financing, insuring, processing, packing, and marketing their produce (coffee, tobacco, fruits, milk), found official favor. The businesses that serviced agro-industrial producers had in the past belonged to the state sector. Now, with very few exceptions, the government gradually sold or dissolved them. The radicalization of some of these new comprehensive organizations—a famous case is the ARIC–Unión de Uniones in Chiapas—makes sense because many small producers were powerless if one link of the chain tying capitalists and small producers broke, as happened too often during repeated financial crises.

The insecurity of marketing rural products without tariff protection became more serious with Mexico's membership in the General Agreement on Trade and Tariffs (GATT) in 1986. GATT increased the importation of many agricultural goods (113 percent between 1986 and 1989 alone) and deregulated industrial prices.[41] The opening of Mexico's market to international production and trade deepened during the presidency of Carlos Salinas de Gortari (1988–94), who successfully sought a privileged deal with the United States and Canada: the North American Free Trade Agreement (NAFTA). Salinas also completed the privatization of state enterprises: in 1989 there were 103; by the end of his presidency, only 20 remained. At the same time, price subsidies fell and credit subsidies disappeared. Moreover, credits could no longer be negotiated collectively through ejidos or other organizations (like UEs and ARICs); instead, they had to be negotiated individually.

Salinas started his term in the midst of a serious legitimacy crisis. Many Mexicans considered his election spurious. In 1988, for the first time, virtually all leftist groups had united in an opposition front and supported Cuauhtémoc Cárdenas, son of the mythical Lázaro Cárdenas. This front later became the Partido de la Revolución Democrática (PRD). To gain legitimacy after his uncertain accession, especially in rural areas, the new president did not trust the old machine of cacique domination within the much-weakened CNC. In his own electoral campaign, he admitted that the PRI's union could not control rural demonstrations.[42] Moreover, the CNC, with its old pretensions of being an intermediary between campesinos who demanded land (and other benefits) and the state, seemed an obstacle to the new modernization project. Thus Salinas created a new version of the Congreso Agrario Permanente (CAP), giving it a mandate different from its role in the Echeverría years. The new CAP was to create a space for dialogue and planning so that old and new campesino organizations (he attracted some UNORCA groups and even parts of the radical CIOAC and CNPA, for example) would break away from "state tutelage" and become more autonomous and competitive. Salinas used the new CAP as a cover for one of his most daring projects: supported by 268 rural organizations and approved by the PRI Congress in 1992, he reformed Article 27 of the Constitution to end land distribution and authorize the privatization of ejidos.[43] Soon, however, the CAP became irrelevant, outshone by another Salinas invention supported by the World Bank: the Programa Nacional de Solidaridad (PRONASOL). This program promoted "solidarity groups," not limited by the ejido structure or of any other association, to receive soft loans to undertake self-managed projects to promote production, consumption, and infrastructure. In rural areas, PRONASOL also administered individual small loans for basic foodstuff production: Crédito a la Palabra. Politically, PRONASOL became a huge, vertically organized institution capable of absorbing dissidents. This created new patronage networks that strengthened the PRI but were largely autonomous from its old corporate power structures—which were thus weakened.[44]

With PRONASOL came glimpses of a new governmental model for dealing with agrarian Mexico, a model that was dichotomous and neocorporate. On the one hand, the business associations that were increasingly tied to foreign capital and sometimes connected with selected ejido groups thrived under the new economic opening. They became both key players and primary beneficiaries of an accelerating process of capital concentration. On the other hand, the many campesinos (ejidos, communities, or private smallholders) who depended on subsidies were not expected to contribute to the economic development of the country. They gained minimal services yet were expected to provide political support.[45]

There were, however, players and mobilizations of different kinds. Beginning in the 1970s, protests against caciques (rural bosses, usually associated with the PRI) and repression had become important. In the 1990s they combined demands for civil and political rights and strengthened thanks to the campaigns of the opposition parties (especially the PRD in the south and southeast, and the PAN in the north and center west). In addition, older independent organizations (notably the CIOAC) kept up their demands for better support for rural production and for implementation of delayed (*rezagadas*) land distributions.[46]

New and more combative organizations also continued to appear. Some, such as the Coordinadora de Centrales Campesinas y Organizaciones Sociales del Sector Agrario (in Chihuahua), the Foro Permanente de Productores Rurales (also in Chihuahua), and the Unión Campesina Democrática (in Jalisco, Nayarit, and Colima), followed the "frentista" model of broad alliances and developed strong regional roles. These groups sponsored protests against neoliberal policies and NAFTA. They also defended members of ejidos and other rural communities from official abuses or omissions (in conflicts over land tenure and the administration of government programs) and against invasions by ranchers and timber entrepreneurs, failures to fulfill contracts, and so on. The rights of day laborers, whose numbers had climbed to around eight million people at the beginning of the 1990s, became the top priority for some independent organizations (such as, again, the CIOAC). Efforts to support day laborers, however, have found little success, mostly because of the geographic dispersal and nomadic lives of the majority of those who plant, cultivate, and harvest crops.

Other organizations have found enormous power to mobilize by confronting, explicitly and directly, the relationship between the countryside and the interventionist state. The most famous case was the Movimiento El Barzón, named after an old *corrido* that described the overwhelming indebtedness faced by peons before the revolution. According to the movement's leaders, eighty years later history was repeating itself: campesinos were again betrayed by the state, now left at the mercy of commercial banks that were as exploitative as the hacendados of bygone days.[47]

The founders of El Barzón were not campesinos but small agricultural entrepreneurs. In the summer of 1993, they organized a tractor blockade in the city of Guadalajara, a tactic soon repeated in other cities. They orchestrated a spectacular takeover of the Ciudad Juárez–El Paso international bridge to denounce the banks' soaring interest rates and harassment of debtors. El Barzón also expressed other grievances: increased prices for consumer goods while agricultural prices stagnated; the reduction of public investment; the destruction of public support institutions; and the disadvantages of domestic producers relative to foreign producers. These critics mobilized in El Barzón were precisely the proclaimed beneficiaries

1. Members of El Barzón mobilized their machines of production against the government and banks across the country. Photograph by Leonardo Garza Treviño/Procesofoto. Courtesy of *Proceso*.

of the new policies: those who had capitalized and mechanized their ranches and smallholdings; those who had improved their herds; those who had looked for new and expanded markets. Their disillusionment resulted not just from economic failure; they felt that the government's response to their problems had been misleading and insufficient, and that decisions that affected the countryside's future were taken, as usual, to protect the government's system of vertical corporate control.[48]

Despite government threats and a negative campaign unleashed by segments of the mass media, by the end of the summer of 1993, the movement had more than ten thousand members and continued to grow, even among ejido and private small landowners' groups traditionally controlled by the CNC and the CNPP. Furthermore, urban debtors, about to lose their homes, cars, or small businesses, began to organize and support the *barzonistas*. Likewise, the independent press, civic organizations, and the Catholic Church criticized the malicious and disproportionate increases in interest rates that maintained the supposed financial health of "the macro sector" at the expense of the majority of Mexicans. To undercut the campesinos' support for El Barzón, Salinas started the Programa de Apoyos Directos al Campo (PROCAMPO), which granted personal subsidies to the poorest farmers. But public protests continued, and displays of solidarity by campesino organizations multiplied.

In 1994, El Barzón divided into two sections: El Barzón Unión, which for a while attempted to became an agrarian-based political party, and El Barzón Nacional, which defined itself as an apolitical organization and promoted multiple and heterogeneous alliances. Although there was acrimony between the split organizations, neither the PRI nor the state nor entrepreneurial institutions were able to capitalize on the divisions and co-opt them. Their structures were not monolithic; instead, they were flexible and decentralized. This allowed them to carry out ad hoc negotiations. Their assemblies were open, and their proclamations stressed democratic participation within the movement and society at large. They demanded respect and dignity for everybody. They insisted on democratic participation that included the right to *barzonear*, or "barzonize": to promote a moral economy—the ethical imperative of defending the welfare of their families.[49] Thus the movement built a public image in which resistance to banks and to state financial policies was justified in defense of human rights, now threatened by the globalized economy. In its peak period (1996–97), El Barzón had three million supporters, including members of all political parties and all kinds of organizations. Its various sections managed to prevent the bankruptcy of many families in both the city and the countryside. At present, El Barzón continues to aid debtors in several states, protecting their claims to legitimate patrimonies.

Although El Barzón Unión eventually gave up the goal of becoming a political party, *barzonismo* demonstrated the possibilities of new forms of citizenship within the context of the state-promoted modernization project. Because of this, it contributed, at least indirectly, to the electoral triumph of opposition parties without demanding a return to the patronage patterns of old. Most barzonistas did not envision political parties as managers of social peace via the distribution of sinecures and handouts. Rather, votes would be gained by convincing voters about political programs. The civic life of El Barzón was seen as independent from the electoral preferences of its membership.[50]

The same could be said about other new movements and organizations that sprouted during the 1980s and 1990s in diverse areas of the country. In the Sierra de Santa Marta (Veracruz), for instance, the Organización de los Pueblos Popolucas Independientes and the Frente Cívico de Pajapan appeared in the mid-1980s. In contrast to the authoritarian and official Uniones de Ejidos of the region and the PRI's CCI (and even to some recent organizations such as the Coordinadora Nacional de Pueblos Indígenas, which was under the protection of the Instituto Nacional Indigenista), both had links with Catholic parishes and left-wing parties. These groups sought participatory mechanisms that would lead to democratic reappraisals of decision making within local communities; through such means, they promoted environmental protection, community and family health, just organization of production and markets as the public sector disappeared, and the defense of voting rights.[51]

In Jalisco an organization called Comercializadora Agropecuaria de Occidente (COMAGRO) was created in 1992. It linked thirty-one *ejidatario* organizations in five states and, with the support of government officials, took advantage of the sale of FERTIMEX (the state corporation to distribute fertilizers) to buy collectively four of the company's regional distribution centers. In other regions, business groups pursuing maximum profits purchased most of these centers. In contrast, COMAGRO decided to keep prices affordable to their producers while maintaining profitability, and encouraged a participatory and transparent management style.[52] The organization thus contributed to the gradual creation of a democratic political culture that avoided directly opposing the government and its modernizing policies while being careful to maintain good relations with the CNC (in practical, not political, terms).

The Ejército Zapatista de Liberación Nacional (EZLN) appeared in Chiapas on January 1, 1994, the date of NAFTA's legal implementation. The sympathy displayed by many popular organizations toward the EZLN sent a clear message that the countryside opposed the program of internationalization advanced by the government. Yet not all independent groups joined that opposition. COMAGRO is a good example: from the outset, it accepted the inevitability of NAFTA and sought, through technical consultations and alliances with other groups from Canada and the United States, the most advantageous position within the emerging situation. It was not alone. UNORCA and some of the CNPA organizations, along with a growing number of regional fronts, pursued communication and solidarity with organizations north of the border.[53]

Nongovernmental organizations (NGOs)—defined as nonprofit organizations that pursue goals of social and community service and are not linked to unions or interest groups—have promoted these efforts. Since the 1970s, NGOs have become essential players in Mexican society. In the last fifteen years, they have filled much of the vacuum left by the withdrawal of government institutions from the cities and the countryside. NGOs are voluntary associations made up mostly of young, university-educated men and women who dedicate anywhere from a few years to their whole lives to service work for reasons ranging from religious convictions, to humanitarian visions, to beliefs in nonparty politics. Usually these volunteers do not become leaders of popular organizations, but they help as advisors and are sometimes key players in the process of consolidation. COMAGRO, again, is a typical case.[54] To help struggling transnational

2. Subcomandante Marcos became a symbol of the new Mexican rebel, leading insurgency in the digital age. Photograph by Norma Suárez, San Miguel de Allende, Mexico.

coalitions defending agrarian interests, NGOs have built important translation and communication bridges. Beyond this, NGOs have helped give popular movements a new language to express their hopes and aspirations, a language very different from the "revolutionary nationalism" many consider outdated. This language articulates concepts such as human rights, personal dignity, gender equality, multiculturalism, interculturalism, participation, transparency, respect for the environment, and, of course, democracy.

URBAN IDENTITIES AND ENGAGEMENT
WITH DIGNITY, 1980–2000

In the cities during the 1970s, NGOs often developed partnerships with the Catholic Church, especially with Comunidades Eclesiales de Base (CEBs, or Christian Base Communities). CEBs had appeared in Brazil under the fervor of pastoral reforms introduced by radical bishops such as Helder Cámara, responding to the reevaluation of lay pastoral work prompted by Vatican II (1961–65).[55] In Mexico, they were welcomed in the working-class parishes of progressive dioceses such as Morelos, San Cristóbal de las Casas, Tehuantepec, Ciudad Juárez, and Chihuahua, with the approval of their bishops: Sergio Méndez Arceo, Samuel Ruiz, Arturo Lona, Manuel

Talamás, and Adalberto Almeida. But they also prospered in cities branded as conservative, such as Guadalajara, Aguascalientes, and Puebla. In addition, they emerged in many rural areas; for instance, they played important roles in the movements in the Sierra de Santa Marta in Veracruz, as well as in the organizations of the Tehuantepec Zapotecs, and in the massive 1985 protests against CONASUPO operations in the Cuauhtémoc (Chihuahua) region.[56] Still, urban density and established interparish links facilitated coordination among CEBs, and between CEBs and other social organizations, in the cities.

A CEB was a self-generated group of neighbors who met to read and discuss the Bible and to search for practical applications of biblical teachings in everyday life. Parish priests oriented their meetings, often assisted by members of male and female religious orders and university NGOs influenced by the nascent Liberation Theology.[57] A new discourse was constructed. The church was not simply the religious hierarchy. Instead, all of God's people were the church, and the struggle for social justice became imperative for all Christians. Rather than reproducing church mechanisms of vertical control, CEBs encouraged the horizontal participation of young and old, men and women, in the struggle against oppression and in expressing solidarity with the needy, regardless of their religion. In the Guadalajara metropolitan area, CEBs were especially successful in immigrant neighborhoods. These neighborhoods lacked urban services; their residents felt cheated by real estate developers and municipal governments. With the biblical groups as a base, campaigns for social and political awareness used neighborhood newspapers, pamphlets, and public festivals to engage residents. They periodically organized large mobilizations of protesters, which were often successful in gaining immediate goals.[58] The concept of *concientización*—personal consciousness based on a reflection on one's experience—taken from the work of the Brazilian Paulo Freire, opposed the traditional impositions of authoritarianism and propaganda manipulation. In Mexico City's metropolitan area—for instance, in Santo Domingo de los Reyes, Ciudad Nezahualcóyotl, and other colonias on the slopes of the Ajusco range—CEBs became a basic part of several movements that successfully demanded services and secure ownership of urban property.[59] In some cases, the government and local bosses repressed parish groups and their ecclesiastical leaders. In 1977, two priests, Rodolfo Aguilar and Rodolfo Escamilla, were murdered in Chihuahua and the DF, respectively, because of their work in neighborhood organizations.[60]

The radical Catholic organizations must be understood within the context of the Urban Popular Movement that also appeared in the 1970s. They were part of a search for community identity and democratic participation in the face of poverty and dislocation. The ideology of CEBs stressed a consciousness of personal dignity and a need for solidarity that went beyond specific issues. Perhaps for this reason, many of their members—even after an issue was solved or exhausted—continued to participate in pan-neighborhood demonstrations and in leftist and centrist political parties that defended the right to vote and rejected patronage and vote manipulation as violations of human rights.

The emergence of this ideology was not confined to CEBs. In 1986, for example, the pioneering multiclass civic demonstrations in Ciudad Juárez and Chihuahua protested electoral fraud in local elections, the manipulation of the media (especially TV), and many other obstacles to independent civic participation. The movement was remarkable for its breadth; demonstrations were joined by radical Christians and the political Left, as well as by moderate Catholic groups such as Acción Católica and the Movimiento Familiar Cristiano, and even by church groups with a reputation for being "quiet" and apolitical, such as the Movimiento de Renovación Carismática.[61]

Protestant and Evangelical churches historically respected the "revolutionary" regime because only under its protection were they able to operate in Mexico and challenge the religious preponderance of the Catholic Church. Yet many members of the so-called historical Protestant sects (Lutherans, Methodists, and Presbyterians) rejected PRI patronage because of an acute sense of personal values. Similarly, some religious groups that are neither Evangelical nor Catholic, such as the Jehovah's Witnesses in Chiapas or the Mormons in Mérida, have repeatedly participated in demonstrations in defense of political and civil rights.[62] Therefore the key to understanding Protestant involvement in political and social mobilizations is not a formal label. Such involvement has developed among religious groups that, whatever their official affiliation, have articulated languages of respect and solidarity and have taken advantage of existing kin and community networks in constructing communal social identities, neighborhood survival activities, and antiauthoritarian political training.

In the last two decades, movements led by victims of urban disasters—natural or otherwise—have provided remarkable examples of how struggles for pragmatic and material goals, and protests against concrete grievances, became movements of unconditional help for others and for the defense of human rights and dignity. The earthquakes that shook Mexico City on September 19 and 20, 1985, had a terrible effect: more than 20,000 deaths, 300,000 displaced people, and uncounted thousands buried by rubble; innumerable buildings damaged or destroyed; places of work unfit for employment; houses no longer habitable. While the state machinery responded slowly and indecisively, volunteer brigades appeared immediately and everywhere. CEBs and other religious groups provided shelters and medical help; NGOs stored and distributed food, clothing, and information; construction workers volunteered their labor and their equipment for rescue operations. Above all, everyday citizens contributed labor, money, food, and medicine. Along with the volunteers, victims' organizations started to sprout, organized by buildings, barrios, and colonias. They soon combined into the Coordinadora Única de Damnificados (CUD). They expressed many grievances: corruption by contractors who had built defective buildings (including some metropolitan subway stations), and by the authorities who had allowed it; the corrupt and clumsy administration of private and public residential buildings by bureaucrats who had tolerated, even encouraged, overpopulation and structural deterioration; the impunity of many slum landlords, especially in the old vecindades, which were highly unsafe; the illegality of hundreds of informal sweatshops where thousands of women sewed in crowded and unsafe conditions; the absence of adequate channels of representation for citizens to report and manage the problems that disaster brought; and, generally, the authorities' incompetence at solving all these problems. Despite the PRI's efforts to co-opt them, most earthquake relief organizations remained autonomous. The CUD was able to persuade President de la Madrid to condemn many damaged buildings and to create a program of renovation, reconstruction, and new housing to benefit the victims.[63]

In the Mexico City earthquake victims' movement, the PRI was irrelevant, as were the opposition parties (even those on the left). Instead, a new self-definition started to circulate among the people: a faith in civil society. Setting aside theoretical debates about the "correct" meaning of the concept, people began to understand civil society as "the community's effort toward self-management and solidarity," a catchphrase that united families, streets, and barrios with networks of wider organizations and the city at large.[64] Several organizations that appeared after the earthquake took up the task of broadcasting the new discourse and sense of unity. Most important was the Asamblea de Barrios with its emblematic Superbarrio, a hero in the costume of popular culture: the mask of wrestling stars, the printed sweatshirts of the superheroes of children's cartoons. Something similar took place among other victims of the same earthquake. In Zapotlán el Grande (Ciudad Guzmán), Jalisco, there were also deaths, injuries, and destroyed houses. Because of the inefficiency and delay of official rescue efforts, CEBs and other neighborhood groups spontaneously built shelters and storage systems, chose representatives to express grievances to the government, and started to create a common language that linked solidarity and autonomy.[65]

On April 22, 1992, the country was shaken by another urban disaster. Sewer explosions caused by accumulated deposits of gasoline, natural gas, and other flammables, and by the poor construction of rain conduits and fuel pipelines, shook the old barrio of Analco (Sector Reforma) in Guadalajara. The explosions rocked thirteen kilometers of streets, left hundreds of people dead, and destroyed hundreds of buildings, leading to the collapse of many small businesses and mid-size factories. State and municipal governments, with the support of the PRONASOL, created a reconstruction foundation and started to build shelters. Despite the government's efforts, civil protest occurred. Independent media reports showed that, despite substantial evidence of imminent danger, authorities had not evacuated the population. Confronted by generalized outrage (and apparently pressure from President Salinas), the mayor, the governor, and several state and municipal civil servants were forced to resign. Meanwhile, the Coordinadora de Ciudadanos y Organismos Civiles 22 de Abril was created. This organization included about twenty NGOS, CEBS, and university groups, as well as victims' representatives. The victims, on the other hand, created the Movimiento Civil de Damnificados and reached an agreement to stand united in their demands, strategies, and negotiations, while remaining independent of political parties.[66] Their demands were only partially met. The Movimiento was profoundly divided by the patronage interventions of the government and PRONASOL. Nevertheless, in Guadalajara, as in Mexico City and Zapotlán, postdisaster processes of dialogue, reorganization, cooperation, and struggle (revitalizing old neighborhood associations and building new ones) created a new consciousness.[67]

Ecological and feminist movements were also important to this new consciousness, especially in the cities, though they were not limited to urban areas. Women's presence in urban social movements was obvious from the outset. Women took on the important tasks of summoning people for meetings, disseminating information, and weaving together social networks, for example, through the CEBS. They were often at the forefront of demonstrations and assemblies. Yet they rarely found general leadership roles or articulated specifically feminist proposals. They primarily supported common demands for services, justice, and popular representation without questioning the role ascribed to women by society: "self-sacrificing wives and mothers."[68] Still, the social phenomena that affected women's lives—migration, labor outside the home, access to education, exposure to the media, and participation in urban struggles—gradually facilitated a critical rethinking of the social construction of gender and its political implications.[69] Although these reflections were present mostly among middle-class professional women, notably after the 1975 celebration of the

International Women's Year in Mexico, political parties gradually became arenas for expressing feminist issues. Women members demanded more female presence in party leadership and more female candidates in elections. In the 1980s, women's groups from Mexico City became linked through networks such as the Regional de Mujeres (related to barrio movements) and the Movimiento Amplio de Mujeres. The Movimiento Amplio de Mujeres began as a mostly symbolic union but mobilized to advance Cuauhtémoc Cárdenas's candidacy during the 1988 presidential elections. Later, its participation in the 1991 legislative elections in the Federal District led to the Convención Nacional de Mujeres por la Democracia.

New concepts and ideas—including the essential equality between men and women, the democratization of daily life, and the redefinition of the boundaries between the public sphere and the private sphere—emerged from these multiclass networks and through the ever-present NGOs. Gradually, popular organizations started to incorporate these ideas into their discourses and strategies.[70] The environmental movement also developed within the NGO sphere. Rather than an "ecological movement" defined by massive demonstrations, we should understand the movement (as with feminism) as the creation of networks and languages that fostered awareness among the most active organizations about the right to a certain quality of life—inherent to the dignity of every individual—and the disasters that threaten present and future generations. As with gender demands, the ecological movement led to unprecedented political participations, moving attention beyond demands to change the state and its apparatus to visions of change in all areas of social life.[71]

ETHNIC RESURGENCE

Ethnic resistance cannot be considered a new social movement. It has been present throughout Mexican history. It has peacefully negotiated daily life within indigenous communities for centuries, often by promoting visions of a moral economy. It has asserted itself violently in the "caste wars" of the liberal era, during the Mexican Revolution, and in the many rural mobilizations of modern Mexico. Still, only in recent decades has an indigenous movement become truly national in scope and responded specifically to ethnic issues within the context of demands for citizenship and democratic participation. Perhaps it began at the conference that met in 1974 in San Cristóbal de las Casas, Chiapas, to commemorate the anniversary of Fray Bartolomé de las Casas, the apostle to the Indians. Indigenous participants came from all over the country and converted the conference into a stage to castigate the Mexican state and the Catholic Church, which had spon-

sored the event through the Chiapas state government and the San Cristóbal Diocese.

As is well known, the "revolutionary" regime, particularly after the founding of the Instituto Nacional Indigenista (INI) in 1948, had developed a
policy of acculturation that aimed to convert Indians into "Mexicans like
everyone else." By the teaching of the Spanish language, general schooling
in the national culture, and agrarian reform, highway construction, and
public health campaigns, the state aimed to turn Indians into individuals
equal before the law and sharing a homogeneous mestizo culture. Cultural
promoters and bilingual teachers, recruited among promising young Indians, would play an essential role in this task. Similarly, the Catholic
Church made its presence felt in indigenous zones through evangelization
and "de-paganizing" programs. The church trained native catechists, carefully selected for their piety, intelligence, and leadership qualities. Despite
their training, these young indigenous promoters and catechists became
leaders in criticizing state and church institutions. A significant number
had university training and were pursuing successful careers in the liberal
arts or the civil service (even within the INI) but remained in touch with
their communities. Their restlessness was a reaction to authoritarian paternalism, to assaults against indigenous cultures, to the lack of democratic
representation, and particularly, in the INI's case, to the failure to end the
extreme poverty and social and political exclusion of indigenous peoples.
The new ethnic leaders used language that NGOs had broadcast internationally. They included militant formulations—the struggle against eth-
nocide and neocolonialism, reassertions of indigenous values, demands for
collective rights—proclaimed in a series of documents known as the Bar-
bados Declarations (1971 and 1977), visions produced by meetings among
representatives of ethnic organizations from across the Western Hemisphere, academics, writers, and left political activists.[72]

The Catholic Church, at least part of it, responded to this condemnation
through self-criticism expressed in the tenets of Vatican II. Vatican II had
recognized a need to "embody" the gospel through and within cultural
diversity. Some dioceses with large indigenous populations (San Cristóbal,
Tehuantepec, Tarahumara) implemented substantial reforms that went so
far as to incorporate indigenous languages and symbolism in worship, as
well as an acceptance of local religious forms.[73] The Mexican government
developed three strategies: to commit more funding to indigenous policies; to include terms such as "participatory *indigenismo*" and "ethno-
development" in their discourses; and to create, within the CNC, new ways
to incorporate indigenous groups and co-opt their leaders. Thus, during
the 1970s, even the CNC organized several congresses to voice the new

demands and encouraged the creation of "Consejos Supremos" within Mexico's ethnic zones. The Consejos, in turn, were linked to the National Indigenous Congress. In fact, a Tarahumara Consejo Supremo had existed since the 1940s, founded by indigenous teachers and local authorities. Yet it never gained official recognition; the INI considered it an annoyance.[74] The Consejos Supremos were neither new forms of representation nor new political authorities; they could not officially mediate between communities and municipal and state governments. Rather, they were part and parcel of the PRI's machinery of patronage. Nevertheless, ethnic groups and their leaders often appropriated them and their congresses not only as venues in which to assert demands but also as spaces in which to form incipient organizations at the regional level and as platforms for proclamations about participation, democracy, and ethnic autonomy.[75]

Independent ethnic organizations mushroomed along with official ones. At the outset, their demands were basically agrarian—the defense of common lands—and often linked with those of the CIOAC and the CNPA. Afterward, step by step, they developed a complex discourse that was both political and ethnic.[76] For instance, the Unión de Comuneros Emiliano Zapata (UCEZ) was created in 1979 when the members of the community of Santa Fe de la Laguna, Michoacán, reclaimed pasturelands that mestizo ranchers from Quiroga, a neighboring village, had appropriated. The operation was led by young Purhépechas who had been influenced by Marxist ideology while studying at the Universidad Michoacana de San Nicolás Hidalgo, in Morelia, or in rural teacher-training colleges. Thanks to the networks that these young people established linking several communities, the struggle for land spread to the area around lake Pátzcuaro and throughout the Tarascan Meseta. Efrén Capiz, a Morelia lawyer and native speaker of Purhépecha, led the union. It pressed material demands, an insistence on cultural and linguistic autonomy, and the rights of communal indigenous governments against mestizo *ayuntamientos*. During the UCEZ assembly at Tingambato on October 7, 1979, ethnic culture received emphasis equal to agrarian and political programs. Then, as a member of the CNPA from 1980 to 1984, the UCEZ promoted ethnic discourse within the national rural protest movement. Between 1980 and 1986, Cuauhtémoc Cárdenas, still a member of the PRI at the time, was governor of Michoacán. During his governorship, the UCEZ consolidated itself. Its membership included not only most Purhépecha communities but also many Otomí villages. Leaders from these communities became advisors to the state secretary of culture. Yet, after 1986, with Cárdenas out of office, they began to experience repression. Leaders and militants were murdered. Still, the UCEZ continued to be Michoacán's most important independent social force, broadcasting its ideas through publications and radio programs in the Purhépecha language. Despite its members' sympathy toward Cárdenas, the UCEZ did not support the opposition front that launched him as a presidential candidate in 1988, nor did it later support the PRD. Similarly, despite its affinity with the radical Left, the UCEZ refused to establish a formal alliance with the Maoist and Communist university groups that appeared in the area, as happened in other rural areas of the country in the 1980s and 1990s.[77] Over the years, many other Purhépecha organizations have appeared, often formed by old UCEZ militants. The UCEZ, however, remains the leading organization. The most important outcome of all of this is that, despite fragmentation and factionalism, the issue of ethnicity, with land and community as its core, cannot be avoided by any political program in the state of Michoacán.

Unlike the UCEZ, the Coalición Obrero-Campesino-Estudiantil del Istmo (COCEI) did formally link with left political parties (first with the Partido Comunista Mexicano [PCM], then with its successor the PRD) in its struggle to gain municipal power. That did not mean it lost the ability to develop independent programs and strategies. COCEI was born in 1974 in the city of Juchitán, Oaxaca, prompted by the dissemination of Liberation Theology by left-wing teachers and student activists educated at the Universidad Autónoma Benito Juárez in the city of Oaxaca. An election to select Juchitán's Communal Lands Commission was the coalition's first battle. The point of contention was the illegal privatization of recently irrigated communal lands. Also at issue was how to struggle against widespread corruption and to defy PRI power, locally in crisis after the death of General Charis, the caudillo who had dominated the region since the revolution. In 1976 COCEI, despite violent harassment by PRI local bosses, won the elections for the Communal Lands Commission. In 1981, running under the aegis of the legalized PCM, COCEI carried the municipal elections. It formed the first leftist municipal government in the county. From the beginning, the movement used ethnic language to present its political program and justify its demands. After taking city hall, it initiated an intense program of cultural revitalization based on the Casa de la Cultura Juchiteca, led by two indigenous intellectuals: the painter Francisco Toledo and the writer and historian Víctor de la Cruz. The program included the reinvention of Zapotec artistic symbols adapted to modern sculpture and painting techniques, the promotion and publication of literature in the Isthmus variety of the Zapotec language, and the writing of local, regional, and national history from an indigenous perspective. In 1983, with the support of the state police, the PRI took over city hall. But COCEI regained it through elections in 1989, making COCEI the hegemonic political force in the Isthmus.[78]

A third example of an independent ethnic organization is the Consejo de Pueblos Nahuas del Alto Balsas (CPNAB), formed in 1990 to block the construction of a large dam in Tetelcingo, Guerrero. The dam would flood fifteen settlements and displace about forty thousand people from their houses, lands, and ceremonial sites. The project had been shrouded in secrecy by the government but was discovered by chance by some university students from the area who were living in Mexico City. The CPNAB was created to oppose the project with the support of traditional and municipal authorities (one of the municipalities to be flooded had a leftist government), and with links to CEBs, human rights groups, and environmental NGOs. After attracting the media's attention and organizing marches, sit-ins, and press conferences, leaders gained meetings with often ambivalent INI officials, the governor of Guerrero, and even President Salinas. Ultimately, the Nahuas from Alto Balsas won the indefinite suspension of the project in 1992, amid the massive commemoration of the five hundredth anniversary of Columbus's arrival in the Americas. From the beginning of the struggle, the CPNAB used the ethnic identity of the communities threatened by flooding as its symbol and justification. These Nahuas are famous for paintings done on *amate* bark, paintings that became the CPNAB's emblem and propaganda medium. In an open letter to the president, paintings were presented as a testimony of the vitality of indigenous culture ("Mexico's pride"), culture that would disappear if their communities were flooded.[79]

The three ethnic organizations I have briefly described gained the national spotlight. There are many other more modest organizations, usually focused on production or agrarian goals. These groups do not operate in isolation; they communicate with each other through meetings, congresses, and computerized networks, linked to larger networks of similar organizations throughout the Americas. We find urban ethnic organizations such as the Zapotecs in Mexico City, and transnational ones, like those in California and Baja California. The latter defend the rights of migrants against the authorities on both sides of the border and provide support for those seeking jobs, housing, or other services. Others promote Mixtec culture through radio broadcasts and artistic activities.[80]

Among these wide and varied groups, common characteristics stand out. At root there is always the demand for the recognition of the indigenous universe as valid and worthy. These groups denounce racism and exclusion within Mexican society, a racism long hidden under the myth of *mestizaje*—the pretense that Indians will be included within the nation inevitably by becoming mestizo. Essential to demands for ethnic recognition are a respect for indigenous life rhythms and modes of development and change, the protection of traditions and forms of expression, and the preservation of territorial units that will allow the reproduction and evolution of indigenous cultures without becoming marginal to modernity and the modern comforts of life. The process of conserving and using their own natural resources in an appropriate manner implies full participation in decentralized local government, as well as the representation of their specific interests before the state and national society.[81]

Thus developed a basic concept of ethnic autonomy that gradually became the formula that synthesizes the demands of indigenous organizations and movements. To a great extent, the creation of the Atlantic Autonomous Region in Nicaragua in 1987 disseminated the concept and showed that its implementation was not a mere utopian illusion. Autonomy might be organized regionally, as in Nicaragua, or promoted as a community right, as in Oaxaca. In 1991 the Mexican government signed Agreement 169 of the International Labor Organization and then modified Article 4 of the Constitution, responding to the national indigenous movement's emerging agenda by making ethnic autonomy a legal option. President Salinas accepted Agreement 169 as part of his strategy to obtain international legitimacy. The agreement introduced indigenous peoples as judicial subjects and granted them relative rights over their territory along with political self-determination. The new Article 4 of the Constitution recognized that the multicultural nature of the Mexican nation was "sustained by its original peoples," and asserted the government's obligation to grant these peoples "access to jurisdiction" and to protect their culture, practices, and customs. Both texts, especially Article 4, were ambiguous and limited. Still, they opened the way for interpretations that, in practice, might allow the gradual implementation of indigenous autonomy and other forms of citizen participation. The INI, suddenly an enthusiastic defender of multicultural policies, announced a new round of consultations with ethnic organizations, seeking a consensual and reasoned proposal to implement Article 4. Nevertheless, officials proved slow to begin the consultations. In fact, they never took place because the armed uprising of the EZLN rendered them impossible and redundant.[82]

CONCLUSION

President Ernesto Zedillo led the federal executive from 1994 and 2000. Vicente Fox, candidate of the opposition PAN, succeeded him. For the first time in seventy-one years, there was a democratic change of government at the federal level in Mexico. During the previous decade, this change had already taken place in the governments of ten states. These events were the result of changes in electoral legislation, especially those proposed and approved in the months that followed the sudden appearance of the EZLN. By virtue of these changes, the institutions in charge of elections at the federal and state levels became independent from their respective governments. Furthermore, new spaces were created to facilitate the institutional development of political parties, while rigorous control mechanisms aimed to guarantee the transparency of the vote. These changes in government and the general transition toward democracy cannot be understood without considering the broadening of the scope and content of citizenship. This came, in turn, from a general blossoming of civil society.

I have attempted here to show that among the fundamental causes of the changing rules governing formal politics in Mexico is a varied set of new popular organizations and forms of resistance. The dominant form of popular organization between 1940 and 1970 had the following characteristics: the leadership of state agents through the networks and institutions of the official party; the subordination of local groups within mass organizations, and of local identities within class identities, both defined in corporate terms; and the ability of corporate groups to become vehicles for limited welfare and development policies while controlling grassroots demands through patronage mechanisms. This dominant form facilitated a *sui generis* definition of citizenship where civil and political rights were minimized and social rights were granted on the condition that they were incorporated within the official system.[83] Most options presented as alternatives during this time did not really question corporatist principles. Instead, they questioned the lack of response from the party in power to demands for social benefits.

In the 1970s and 1980s, criticism of this lack of response deepened. Furthermore, the state corporate model began to collapse amid a prolonged crisis of public finances. From 1977, the government itself pushed the fragmentation of popular organizations and the establishment of new styles of negotiation easier to manage. In practice, many new organizations took advantage of the weakening of the corporatist model to define their goals more independently. Many also sought to overcome fragmentation, not through an alternative recorporativization (or "remassification") but through flexible alliances in popular fronts and *coordinadoras*. As the 1980s began, the alternative to authoritarianism was still expressed in terms of class opposition.

Gradually, however, political language changed to focus grievances on respect for the dignity of the individual and demands about citizenship, the latter understood as a continuous enlargement of civic, social, and political rights. The basic cause of this change was the growing heterogeneity of the popular sectors and their rapprochement with the middle classes, which had been hit hard by economic crises and government authoritarianism. There was also the perception, notable in the urban movements for disaster victims, but evident in rural mobilizations that protested producers' help-lessness, that the public authorities were the direct cause of most griev-ances. Meanwhile, public authorities responded to these grievances with a mixture of indifference, manipulation, and repression, which ironically contributed to an increased awareness of the importance of political and civil rights in addition to social rights. Also, the development of an in-creasingly responsible and independent media, the renewed concern of the Catholic Church (and Protestant organizations such as the World Council of Churches) about social justice, the mushrooming of NGOs, and the international dissemination of a discourse of human rights (which is ex-tremely important and merits another essay) all combined with general social unrest to define a new set of criteria to evaluate the state's legitimacy. Ultimately, the state has gradually come to be viewed less as a dark force that "does" things that are either "good" or "bad," and has started to be seen as a participatory sphere that must be monitored to ensure public well-being.

All of this has led to a new culture of citizenship and the strengthening of what we today call civil society: a space that is organized neither by state cor-poratism, nor by the market, but where forms of association are negotiated and created. Although we cannot understand this space without relating it to the blossoming of civil and political rights, it should not be understood only in terms of a return to the individualist vision of nineteenth-century liberalism. Civil society is not only a healthy reaction against authoritarianism; it is also a reaction against the type of modernization that destroys the possibility of community life and thus threatens the sociabilities that are capable of inte-grating the historical and emotional dimensions of human beings. Because of this, recent mobilizations look beyond the old patterns of union or class identities to recover or reinvent communal identities in which personal dignity is not an abstract idea but a concrete set of relationships. Similarly, the new mobilizations do not abandon material demands in their struggle for social rights: inequality is as antagonistic to human sociability as authoritarianism.[84]

Of course, history is not linear. The dismantling of the corporatist state brought more than the appearance of democratizing groups. In some states, old governors and politicians took advantage of the vacuum to create new patronage networks and to reproduce authoritarian ways. President Salinas's PRONASOL, dissolved in 1995, reproduced some traits of the old patronage system. Such traits also continued within President Zedillo's Programa de Educación y Salud (PROGRESA), which the Fox government is revitalizing. Nor has the democratic change of government coincided with the arrival of social justice and the weakening of raw capitalism. Still, the popular resistance of the last thirty years has created a new sense of community and new ways of bringing attention to communal demands that do not exclude anybody and are, at the same time, compatible with modernity.

At the time of this writing (2001), the EZLN, whose story has been told repeatedly, though it is perhaps just beginning, occupies the center of the nation's attention. I do not know if the EZLN, along with the National Indigenous Congress that supports it, represents a good synthesis of the social demands of recent times (rights to dignity, participation, justice, identity, cultural difference, community). I will not try to elucidate the accomplishments, limits, and prospects of the EZLN in this essay. Yet its enormous power to summon the attention of Mexicans must be a symptom of the reality of a transformation that is grounded in dialogue and democracy and explores the feasibility of a society where the expansion of human rights is the best guarantee of living together.

NOTES

1 INEGI, *Anuario estadístico de los Estados Unidos Mexicanos: Edición 1998* (Mexico City: Instituto Nacional de Estadística, Geografía e Informática, 1999), 30.

2 Douglas S. Massey, Rafael Alarcón, Jorge Durand, and Humberto González, *Return to Aztlán* (Berkeley: University of California Press, 1987); Jorge Durand, *Más allá de la línea: Patrones migratorios entre México y Estados Unidos* (Mexico City: Consejo Nacional para la Cultura y las Artes, 1994); Jorge Durand, Douglas S. Massey, and Emilio A. Prado, "The New Era of Mexican Migration to the United States," *Journal of American History*, September 1999, 518–36.

3 Orlandina de Oliveira and Bryan Roberts, "Urban Growth and Urban Social Structure in Latin America, 1930–1990," in *The Cambridge History of Latin America*, ed. Leslie Bethell, vol. 6, pt. 1 (Cambridge: Cambridge University Press, 1994); Orlandina de Oliveira, Marina Ariza, and Marcela Eternod, "La fuerza de trabajo en México: Un siglo de cambios," Documento de Trabajo, Proyecto, Cien Años de Demografía en México, El Colegio de México, 1998.

4 John Calagione, Doris Francis, and Daniel Nugent, eds., *Workers' Expressions: Beyond Accommodation and Resistance* (New York: State University of New York Press, 1992); Néstor García Canclini, *Culturas híbridas: Estrategias para entrar y salir de la modernidad* (Mexico City: Grijalbo, 1989).

5 James C. Scott, *Weapons of the Weak: Everyday Forms of Peasant Resistance* (New Haven: Yale University Press, 1985); Arturo Escobar, *Encountering Develop-*

ment: *The Making and Unmaking of the Third World* (Princeton: Princeton University Press, 1995); Guillermo de la Peña, "La modernidad comunitaria," *Desacatos* 3 (2000): 51–62.

6 Ramón Ramírez Melgarejo, "La bola chiquita," in *Los campesinos de la tierra de Zapata*, vol. 1, ed. Arturo Warman et al. (Mexico City: Centro de Investigaciones Superiores del INAH, 1973).

7 Jean Meyer, *El sinarquismo, ¿un fascismo mexicano?* (Mexico City: Joaquín Mortiz, 1979); Rubén Aguilar and Guillermo Zermeño, "De movimiento social a partido político: De la UNS al PDM," in *El PDM, movimiento regional*, ed. Jorge Alonso (Guadalajara: Universidad de Guadalajara, 1989).

8 Soledad Loaeza, *El Partido Acción Nacional: La larga marcha, 1939–1988* (Mexico City: Fondo de Cultura Económica, 1999). Unlike the UNS, the PAN never operated as a social movement.

9 Arnaldo Córdova, *La política de masas del cardenismo* (Mexico City: Ediciones Era, 1974). The classical thesis is that mechanisms of political control also had the effect of increasing the autonomy of the state in economic matters. See, for example, Nora Hamilton, *México: Los límites de la autonomía del Estado* (Mexico City: Ediciones Era, 1983).

10 Ilán Semo, invoking Max Weber, has mentioned the drastic change that Alemanismo experienced as the movement shifted from a "social corporativism toward an oligarchic corporativism": the PRM protected the social interests of different sectors within the context of a market economy, and the PRI manipulated these sectors "in order to privatize accumulation forms." Semo, "El cardenismo: Gramática del sobreviviente," *Historia y grafía*, no. 3 (1994): 92–94.

11 Fernando I. Salmerón, *Los límites del agrarismo: Proceso político y estructuras de poder en Taretan, Michoacán* (Zamora: El Colegio de Michoacán, 1989); Víctor Manuel Durand Ponte, "La descomposición política del lombardismo," in *Entre la guerra y la estabilidad política: El México de los 40*, ed. Rafael Loyola (Mexico City: Grijalbo, 1986).

12 Rubén Jaramillo, "Autobiografía," and Froylán Manjarrez, "La matanza de Xochicalco," both in *Rubén Jaramillo: Autobiografía y asesinato* (Mexico City: Editorial Nuestro Tiempo, 1967); Raúl Macín, *Rubén Jaramillo, profeta olvidado* (Mexico City: Editorial Diógenes, 1984).

13 Elisa Servín, *Ruptura y oposición: El movimiento henriquista, 1945–1954* (Mexico City: Cal y Arena, 2001).

14 Ilán Semo, "El cardenismo," 93–94.

15 For an overview of campesino movements, see Armando Bartra, *Los herederos de Zapata: Movimientos campesinos posrevolucionarios en México* (Mexico City: Editorial Era, 1985), esp. chaps. 6–7; also Guillermo de la Peña, "Rural Mobilizations in Latin America since c. 1920," in *The Cambridge History of Latin America*, vol. 6, pt. 2, ed. Leslie Bethell (Cambridge: Cambridge University Press, 1994), esp. 409–15. About rural leadership patterns, see Guillermo de la Peña, "Poder local, poder regional: Perspectivas socioantropológicas," in *Poder local, poder regional*, ed. Jorge Padua and Alain Vanneph (Mexico City: El Colegio de México, 1986).

16 Not only did the government decide which trade unions and leaders should be considered legitimate; it also determined salaries, wages, and dismissal conditions

in every company. See Javier Aguilar García, "El Estado mexicano, la modernización y los obreros," in *El nuevo Estado mexicano*, vol. 3, *Estado, actores y movimientos sociales*, ed. Jorge Alonso, Alberto Aziz, and Jaime Tamayo (Mexico City: Nueva Imagen, 1992), 46. About workers' organizations during this period, see José Luis Reyna and Marcelo Miquet, "Introducción a la historia de las organizaciones obreras en México, 1912–1966," in *Tres estudios sobre el movimiento obrero en México*, ed. José Luis Reyna et al. (Mexico City: El Colegio de México, 1976), esp. 52–71. The huge movement of railway workers demanded, besides autonomy, a significant expansion of the rights of organized labor. See Antonio Alonso, *El movimiento ferrocarrilero en México, 1958–1959* (Mexico City: Editorial Era), 1972.

17 Aurora Loyo Brambila, *El movimiento magisterial de 1958 en México* (Mexico City: Editorial Era, 1979); Ricardo Pozas Horcasitas, *La democracia en blanco: El movimiento médico en México, 1964–1965* (Mexico City: Siglo Veintiuno Editores, 1993); Tomás Calvillo, "A Case of Opposition Unity: The San Luis Potosí Democratic Coalition of 1991," in *Subnational Politics and Democratization in Mexico*, ed. Wayne A. Cornelius, Todd Eisenstadt, and Jane Hindley (La Jolla: Center for U.S.-Mexican Studies, University of California, San Diego, 1999).

18 Sergio Zermeño, *México: Una democracia utópica* (Mexico City: Siglo Veintiuno Editores, 1978).

19 The total birth rate increased from 5.8 per thousand in 1940 to 6.7 per thousand in 1970; the gross death rate during the same time period went from 23 per thousand to 11 per thousand. Francisco Alba and Joseph Potter, "Population and Development in Mexico since 1940: An Interpretation," *Population and Development Review* 12, no. 1 (March 1986): table 1.

20 About campesino organization models, see Arturo Warman, '... y venimos a contradecir': Los campesinos de Morelos y el Estado nacional* (Mexico City: Ediciones de la Casa Chata, 1976); Guillermo de la Peña, *Herederos de promesas: Agricultura, política y ritual en los Altos de Morelos* (Mexico City: Ediciones de la Casa Chata, 1980); and Kirsten Appendini, Marielle P. L. Martínez, Teresa Rendón, and Vania Salles, *El campesinado en México: Dos perspectivas de análisis* (Mexico City: El Colegio de México, 1983).

21 See de la Peña, *Herederos de promesas*, chap. 6.

22 Arturo Bonilla, "Un problema que se agrava: La subocupación rural," in *Neolatifundismo y explotación: De Emiliano Zapata a Anderson Clayton & Co.*, ed. Rodolfo Stavenhagen et al. (Mexico City: Editorial Nuestro Tiempo, 1968); Enrique Astorga Lira, *Mercado de trabajo rural en México: La mercancía humana* (Mexico City: Editorial Era, 1985).

23 There is a complete history of agriculture and agrarian issues up to the 1960s, as well as a diagnosis of the acute problems that were starting to surface at the time; see Centro de Investigaciones Agrarias, *Estructura agraria y desarrollo agrícola en México* (Mexico City: Fondo de Cultura Económica, 1974); also Sergio Reyes Osorio and Salomón Eckstein, "El desarrollo polarizado de la agricultura mexicana," in *La sociedad mexicana: Presente y futuro*, ed. Miguel Wionczek (Mexico City: Fondo de Cultura Económica, 1974). The term "neolatifundio" was used by authors like Arturo Warman to describe a new dominant class in the countryside whose main resource was not monopoly over land but monopoly over

credit, irrigation, and technology. Warman, "El neolatifundio mexicano: Expansión y crisis de una forma de dominio," *Comercio Exterior* 25, no. 12 (1975): 1368–74. Warman also wrote a useful synthesis of the 1970s agrarian collapse, "El problema del campo," in *México hoy*, ed. Pablo González Casanova and Enrique Florescano (Mexico City: Siglo Veintiuno Editores, 1980).

24 Luisa Paré, "Movimiento campesino y política agraria en México, 1976–1982," *Revista Mexicana de Sociología* 46, no. 4 (1985): 85–111; Neil Harvey, *The Chiapas Rebellion: The Struggle for Land and Democracy* (Durham: Duke University Press, 1998), 94.

25 Steven E. Sanderson, *Agrarian Populism and the Mexican State: The Struggle for Land in Sonora* (Berkeley and Los Angeles: University of California Press, 1981); Gustavo Gordillo, *Campesinos al asalto del cielo: De la expropiación estatal a la apropiación campesina* (Mexico City: Siglo Veintiuno Editores, 1988); Eric Villanueva, *Crisis henequenera y movimientos campesinos en Yucatán, 1966–1983* (Mexico City: Instituto Nacional de Antropología e Historia, 1985).

26 About the process that led to the creation of the CNPA (and its subsequent division), see Bartra, *Los herederos de Zapata* 147–54; also Graciela Flores Lúa, Luisa Paré, and Sergio Sarmiento, *Las voces del campo: Movimiento campesino y política agraria, 1976–1984* (Mexico City: Siglo Veintiuno Editores, 1988). The food crisis linked to the attempt to substitute basic staples with export produce (sorghum, fruits, vegetables) is documented in David Barkin and Blanca Suárez, *El fin de la autosuficiencia alimentaria* (Mexico City: Editorial Océano, 1985).

27 In historiographic terms, during the 1970s and 1980s there was a revisionist current about the meaning of the revolution. For a critical discussion, see Alan Knight, "The Mexican Revolution: Bourgeois? Nationalist? Or Just a 'Great Rebellion'?" *Bulletin of Latin American Research* 4, no. 2 (1985): 1–37.

28 Adriana López Monjardín, *La lucha por los ayuntamientos: Una utopía viable* (Mexico City: Siglo Veintiuno Editores, 1986).

29 Silvia Gómez Tagle and Marcelo Miquet, "Integración o democracia sindical: El caso de los electricistas," in Reyna et al., *Tres estudios*; Enrique de la Garza et al., *Historia de la industria eléctrica en México*, vol. 2 (Mexico City: Universidad Autónoma Metropolitana, 1994), esp. 80–97.

30 For relatively optimistic views of the workers' movement, see Francisco Zapata, *Trabajadores y sindicatos en América Latina* (Mexico City: Secretaría de Educación Pública, 1987); and Victoria Novelo, ed., *Democracia y sindicatos* (Mexico City: CIESAS, 1989). A wider discussion can be found in Kevin J. Middlebrook, *The Paradox of Revolution: Labor, the State, and Authoritarianism in Mexico* (Baltimore: Johns Hopkins University Press, 1995).

31 About the PRI's control over the settlers, see Susan Eckstein, *The Poverty of Revolution: The State and the Urban Poor in Mexico* (Princeton: Princeton University Press, 1977); on neighborhood networks, see Larissa A. Lomnitz, *Cómo sobreviven los marginados* (Mexico City: Siglo Veintiuno Editores, 1975).

32 See the overview of these groups in Juan Manuel Ramírez Saiz, *El movimiento urbano popular en México* (Mexico City: Siglo Veintiuno Editores, 1986); and Jorge Alonso, *Lucha urbana y acumulación de capital* (Mexico City: Ediciones de la Casa Chata, 1980).

33 Manuel Castells, *The City and the Grassroots: A Cross-Cultural Theory of Urban Social Movements* (Berkeley and Los Angeles: University of California Press, 1983), 194–99, 319–20.

34 Diana Villarreal and Víctor Castañeda, *Urbanización y autoconstrucción de vivienda en Monterrey* (Mexico City: Centro de Ecodesarrollo, 1986).

35 Ramírez Saiz, *El movimiento*, 172–95.

36 About the crisis of the 1980s, see Jorge Zepeda, ed., *Las sociedades rurales hoy* (Zamora: El Colegio de Michoacán, 1988); Mercedes González de la Rocha and Agustín Escobar Latapí, eds., *Social Responses to Mexico's Economic Crisis of the 1980s* (La Jolla: Center for U.S.-Mexican Studies, University of California, San Diego, 1991); Jean-François Prud'homme, ed., *El impacto social de las políticas de ajuste en el campo mexicano* (Mexico City: Plaza y Valdés, 1995).

37 Merilee Grindle, *State and Countryside: Development Policies and Agrarian Politics in Latin America* (Baltimore: Johns Hopkins University Press, 1986), esp. 66–67, 101–4, 178–79.

38 Michael W. Foley, "Agenda for Mobilization: The Agrarian Question and Popular Mobilization in Contemporary Mexico," *Latin American Research Review* 26, no. 2 (1991): 39–74.

39 In the *Plan Nacional de Desarrollo, 1983–1988* (Mexico City: Poder Ejecutivo Federal, 1983), 273–94, these measures were called "integral rural development" and "integral agrarian reform."

40 Hubert Carton de Grammont, "Los empresarios agrícolas, un grupo en consolidación," in *Las sociedades rurales hoy*, ed. Jorge Zepeda Patterson (Zamora: El Colegio de Michoacán, 1988), 400–406.

41 Emilio Caballero, "El Tratado de Libre Comercio y la agricultura," in *La disputa por los mercados: El TLC y el sector agropecuario*, ed. Alejandro Encinas et al. (Mexico City: Editorial Diana, 1994), 30–32.

42 In his electoral campaign in the Laguna region, for example, Salinas and his entourage hastily had to leave a meeting intended to gain support from the peasants followed by loud boos and even some projectiles. See Adriana López Monjardin, "La cultura política y los campesinos: La deferencia y el desafío," *Coyuntura*, nos. 42–43 (1993): 3–8.

43 María de los Ángeles Guzmán, "Organizaciones campesinas y sistemas de representación," *Estudios Agrarios: Revista de la Procuraduría Agraria*, no. 15 (2000): 211–12. Yet even the CAP complained that the implementation of the reform was too hasty and did not allow time for a reasoned discussion. See Hubert Carton de Grammont, "Nuevos actores y formas de representación política en el campo," in J.-F. Prud'homme, *El impacto social*, 112–13n7.

44 About rural areas during the Salinas years, see Foley, "Agenda for Mobilization," 60–65; Wayne Cornelius and David Myhre, eds., *The Transformation of Rural Mexico: Reforming the Ejido Sector* (La Jolla: Center for U.S.-Mexican Studies, University of California, San Diego, 1998); and Kirsten Appendini, "La transformación de la vida económica del campo mexicano," in J.-F. Prud'homme, *El impacto social*. A "you have never had it so good" view (from the government's perspective) can be found in Luis Téllez Kuenzler, *La modernización del sector agropecuario y forestal* (Mexico City: Fondo de Cultura Económica, 1994).

45 Carton de Grammont, "Nuevos actores," 108–17.

46 Blanca Rubio, *Resistencia campesina y explotación rural en México* (Mexico City: Ediciones Era, 1987).

47 A *barzón* is the belt that links the traditional plow to the yoke of oxen; in the song, the *peón* must go on plowing to pay his debts even if his barzón is as broken as he is.

48 Gabriel Torres, "El Barzón: Por la dignidad de los agricultores," *Coyuntura*, nos. 42–43 (1993): esp. 58–59; Humberto González, "Movimiento 'El Barzón': Una contrapropuesta al neoliberalismo autoritario del Estado mexicano," in *Ajustes y desajustes regionales: El caso de Jalisco a fines del sexenio salinista*, ed. Jesús Arroyo Alejandre and David E. Lorey (Guadalajara: Universidad de Guadalajara–UCLA Program on Mexico), 1995.

49 Gabriel Torres, "The El Barzón Debtors' Movement: From the Local to the National in Protest Politics," in *Subnational Politics and Democratization in Mexico*, ed. Wayne A. Cornelius, Todd A. Eisenstadt, and Jane Hindley (La Jolla: Center for U.S.-Mexican Studies, University of California, San Diego, 1999), 147–48. The term "moral economy" refers to the fact that, in subaltern struggles, the defense of economic interests takes on an ethical dimension, since it implies an immediate compromise to protect family and community. See E. P. Thompson, "La 'economía moral' de la multitud en la Inglaterra del siglo XVIII," in *Tradición, revuelta y conciencia de clase: Estudios sobre la crisis de la sociedad preindustrial* (Barcelona: Editorial Crítica, 1984); also Scott, *Weapons of the Weak*.

50 Some of the barzonista leaders went so far as to take a federal sinecure through the PRD, but this did not mean that the movement was co-opted.

51 Emilia Velázquez and Luisa Paré, "Centralismo y autoritarismo: Dos obstáculos político-culturales para el desarrollo rural," in *El estudio de la cultura política en México: Perspectivas disciplinarias y actores políticos*, ed. Esteban Krotz (Mexico City: Consejo Nacional para la Cultura y las Artes, 1996), 345–48.

52 Gabriel Torres, "El discurso de la modernización agropecuaria y la estrategia de las organizaciones campesinas emergentes," in *Las disputas por el México rural*, vol. 1, ed. Sergio Zendejas and Pieter de Vries (Zamora: El Colegio de Michoacán, 1998). El Barzón itself has been viewed not as a rejection of globalized modernization but as an attempt to appropriate and redefine the process. Guadalupe Rodríguez Gómez, "El Barzón y la construcción popular de una nación globalizada al cierre del siglo," in *La antropología sociocultural en el México del milenio*, ed. Guillermo de la Peña and Luis Vázquez León (Mexico City: CONACULTA, Fondo de Cultura Económica, 2002).

53 Luis Hernández, "Globalización y coaliciones transnacionales en el sector rural," in Zendejas and de Vries, *Las disputas*.

54 It was accompanied from its creation by Educación y Desarrollo de Occidente (EDOC).

55 About the emergence of CEBs, see Daniel H. Levine, ed., *Religion and Political Conflict in Latin America* (Chapel Hill: University of North Carolina Press, 1986); David Lehmann, *Struggle for the Spirit: Religious Transformations and Popular Culture in Brazil and Latin America* (Cambridge: Polity Press, 1996); and William Swatos Jr., ed., *Religion and Democracy in Latin America* (New Brunswick: Transaction Publishers, 1995).

56 Víctor Gabriel Muro, *Iglesia y movimientos sociales, 1972–1987* (Mexico City: Red Nacional de Investigación Urbana, 1994).

57 See Luis G. del Valle, "Teología de la Liberación en México," in *El pensamiento social de los católicos mexicanos*, ed. Roberto Blancarte (Mexico City: Fondo de Cultura Económica, 1996). After the Latin American Bishops' Conference of Medellín, Colombia, in 1968, where the Catholic hierarchy proclaimed its "preferential option for poor people," many religious orders and churches opened their doors in the depressed urban periphery.

58 Guillermo de la Peña and Renée de la Torre, "Religión y política en los barrios populares de Guadalajara," *Estudios Sociológicos* (El Colegio de México) 24 (1990): esp. 582–87.

59 Enriqueta Curiel and Elvira Enríquez, "Experiencia de lucha del Movimiento de Pueblos y Colonias del Sur," in *Los movimientos sociales en el Valle de México*, vol. 2, ed. Jorge Alonso (Mexico City: CIESAS, 1988); José A. Alonso, "La Iglesia y los movimientos urbano-populares: Un estudio de caso en Ciudad Nezahualcóyotl," in Jorge Alonso, *Los movimientos sociales*; and Jorge Alonso, *Lucha urbana*.

60 Penny Lernoux, *Cry of the People: The Struggle for Human Rights in Latin America; The Catholic Church in Conflict with U.S. Policy* (Harmondsworth: Penguin Books, 1982), 357–59.

61 Muro, *Iglesia y movimientos sociales*, 175–78.

62 Patricia Fortuny Loret de Mola, "Cultura política entre los protestantes en México," in *Cultura política y educación cívica*, ed. Jorge Alonso (Mexico City: Miguel Angel Porrúa, 1994), 406–7, 409–10. The same author remarks that the tendency of most so-called Pentecostal churches was to be allied with the PRI. About this, also see Renée de la Torre, *Los hijos de la luz: Discurso, identidad y poder en La Luz del Mundo* (Guadalajara: CIESAS, 1997).

63 Carlos Monsiváis, *Entrada libre: Crónicas de la sociedad que se organiza* (Mexico City: Editorial Era, 1987); Ligia Tavera-Fenollosa, "The Movimiento de Damnificados: Democratic Transformation of Citizenry and Government in Mexico City," in *Subnational Politics and Democratization in Mexico*, ed. Wayne A. Cornelius, Todd Eisenstadt, and Jane Hindley (La Jolla: Center for U.S.-Mexican Studies, University of California, San Diego, 1999).

64 Monsiváis, *Entrada libre*, 78–81, 110–12; Ann Reid and Miguel Angel Aguilar Díaz, "Barrio y vida cotidiana: Una experiencia de trabajo en la reconstrucción de la vivienda," in *Procesos rurales y urbanos en el México actual*, ed. Alejandra Massolo et al. (Mexico City: Universidad Autónoma Metropolitana–Iztapalapa, 1991).

65 Guillermo de la Peña and Renée de la Torre, "Pastoral social y organización popular en Jalisco: Dos estudios de caso," in Jorge Alonso, *Cultura política y educación cívica*.

66 There were five fundamental demands: (1) the reconstruction of buildings in the same location and with the democratic participation of the interested parties in planning the process; (2) temporary grants of decent housing while reconstruction was taking place; (3) compensation for human and material losses, including the salaries and profits that had been lost and damages that followed the disaster; (4) an exhaustive investigation of the facts and a stern application of the law toward the

responsible parties; and (5) the removal of industrial facilities that created high-risk situations like, for example, the PEMEX storage tanks and warehouses.

67 About the Guadalajara disaster and its sequel, see Cristina Padilla and Rossana Reguillo, eds., *Quién nos hubiera dicho: Guadalajara, 22 de abril* (Guadalajara: ITESO, 1993); and Rossana Reguillo, *La construcción simbólica de la ciudad: Sociedad, desastre y comunicación* (Guadalajara: ITESO, 1996).

68 Alejandra Massolo, "Las mujeres en los movimientos sociales urbanos en la ciudad de México," *Iztapalapa* 9 (1983): 152–67.

69 Teresita de Barbieri and Orlandina de Oliveira, "Nuevos sujetos sociales: La presencia política de las mujeres en América Latina," *Nueva Antropología* 30 (1986): 5–29.

70 Esperanza Tuñón, "El quehacer político del movimiento amplio de mujeres en México," Documento ILET, 1992, cited in J.-F. Prudhomme, "Acción colectiva y lucha por la democracia en México y Chile," in *Transformaciones sociales y acciones colectivas: América Latina en el contexto internacional de los noventa*, ed. María Luisa Tarrés et al. (Mexico City: El Colegio de México, 1994); Amparo Sevilla, "Participación política problemática: Mujeres dirigentes en el movimiento urbano popular," in *El estudio de la cultura política en México*, ed. Esteban Krotz (Mexico City: CIESAS-CONACULTA, 1996). In the rural areas, the organized presence of women can be seen, for example, in the appropriation of the Unidades Agrícola-Industriales de la Mujer (UAIM), which had been sponsored by the government, in the ejidos; see Magdalena Villarreal, "Power, Gender, and Intervention from an Actor-Oriented Perspective," in *Battlefields of Knowledge*, ed. Norman Long and Ann Long (London: Routledge, 1992).

71 Jorge E. Aceves, "Del ecologismo e historias personales," in *Historia oral: Ensayos y aportes de investigación*, ed. Jorge E. Aceves (Mexico City: CIESAS, 1996).

72 Alicia Iwanska, *The Truths of Others: An Essay on Nativist Intellectuals in Mexico* (Cambridge: Schenkman, 1977); Jesús Morales Bermúdez, "El Congreso Indígena de Chiapas: Un testimonio," in *Anuario 1991* (Tuxtla Gutiérrez: Instituto Chiapaneco de Cultura, 1992), 242–370; Guillermo Bonfil Batalla, *Utopía y revolución: El pensamiento político de los indios de América Latina* (Mexico City: Nueva Imagen, 1992).

73 See Manuel Marzal, ed., *El rostro indio de Dios* (Mexico City: Centro de Reflexión Teológica, 1994).

74 Gonzalo Aguirre Beltrán, *Formas de gobierno indígena* (Mexico City: Imprenta Universitaria, 1953), 86–93.

75 Lourdes Arizpe, *El reto del pluralismo cultural* (Mexico City: Instituto Nacional Indigenista, 1978); Félix Báez-Jorge, "¿Líderes indios o intermediarios indigenistas?" Documento, Escuela Nacional de Antropología e Historia, 1984.

76 See my article "La ciudadanía étnica y la construcción de 'los indios' en el México contemporáneo," *Revista Internacional de Filosofía Política* 6 (1975): 116–40.

77 About the UCEZ, see Jorge Zepeda Patterson, "No es lo mismo agrario que agrio, ni comunero que comunista; pero se parecen: La UCEZ en Michoacán," in *Perspectivas de los movimientos sociales en la región centro-occidente*, ed. Jaime

Tamayo (Mexico City: Editorial Línea, 1986); Luis Vázquez León, *Ser indio otra vez: La purhepechización de los tarascos de la sierra* (Mexico City: CONACULTA, 1992); José Eduardo Zárate, "Faccionalismo y movimiento indígena: La UCEZ entre los otomíes de Zitácuaro, Micoacán," in *Intermediación social y procesos políticos en Michoacán,* ed. Jesús Tapia (Zamora: El Colegio de Michoacán, 1992); José Eduardo Zárate, *Los señores de la utopía: Etnicidad política en una comunidad purhépecha* (Zamora: El Colegio de Michoacán, 1993); and Margarita Zárate, "The Creation of Community and Identity in a Rural Social Movement: The UCEZ of Michoacán, Mexico" (Ph.D. diss., University College, London, 1996).

78 About the COCEI, see Hélène Rivière d'Arc and Marie-France Prevôt-Schapira, "L'état mexicain 'modernisateur' face à la voie zapoteque de développement," Document de Recherche 30 (Paris: CREDAL, 1985); Monsiváis, *Entrada libre,* 151–66; Muro, *Iglesia y movimientos sociales,* chap. 4; Howard Campbell, *Zapotec Renaissance: Ethnic Politics and Cultural Revivalism in Southern Mexico* (Albuquerque: University of New Mexico Press, 1994); Jeffrey Rubin, *Decentering the Regime: Ethnicity, Radicalism and Democracy in Juchitán, Mexico* (Durham: Duke University Press, 1997).

79 About the CPNAB, see Jonathan Amith, ed., *La tradición del amate: Innovación y protesta en el arte mexicano* [The Amate Tradition: Innovation and Dissent in Mexican Art] (Mexico City: La Casa de las Imágenes; Chicago: Mexican Fine Arts Center Museum, 1995); and Jane Hindley, "Indigenous Mobilization, Development, and Democratization in Guerrero: The Nahua People versus the Tetelcingo Dam," in *Subnational Politics and Democratization in Mexico,* ed. Wayne A. Cornelius, Todd Eisenstadt, and Jane Hindley (La Jolla: Center for U.S.-Mexican Studies, University of California, San Diego, 1999).

80 Carol Nagengast and Michael Kearney, "Mixtec Ethnicity: Social Identity, Political Consciousness, and Political Activism," *Latin American Research Review* 25, no. 2 (1990): 61–92.

81 Luis Hernández Navarro, "Ciudadanos iguales, ciudadanos diferentes: La nueva lucha india," *Este País,* February 1997, 30–40.

82 The importance of ethnic mobilizations around the five hundredth anniversary of Columbus's arrival in the Americas, which led to the creation of the Frente Nacional de Pueblos Indígenas and to the campaign "500 Años de Resistencia," where independent groups and groups linked with the government came together, should be mentioned. See Joaquín Flores Félix, "Los pueblos indios en la búsqueda de espacios," *Cuadernos Agrarios,* Nueva Epoca, 11–12 (1995): 148–58.

83 I use T. H. Marshall's well-known terminology where civil rights refer to individual freedoms, political rights to representation in the decision-making process, and social rights to the general enjoyment of a minimum standard of living. See Marshall, *Class, Citizenship, and Social Development* (New York: Doubleday, 1964).

84 Regarding social public spirit and its manifestation and possibilities, see Alberto Olvera, ed., *La sociedad civil: De la teoría y a la realidad* (Mexico City: El Colegio de México, 1999).

❊ The Left in the Neoliberal Era

ENRIQUE SEMO ❊

The Left is an inevitable position within political systems. Historically, the Left evolves and transforms in response to changes in the system. We can understand the evolving goals and roles of the Left only in the context of those larger changes. During the last quarter of the twentieth century, the world and Mexico faced important transformations. The Mexican Left responded, participated, and changed.

For the Mexican Left, the unfolding twenty-first century is a time of paradox. It is difficult to know whether it is gaining or losing strength, whether it is transforming or dissolving. One sector has turned to legal participation, yet has lost its compass; it unleashes its energy more effectively, but it is not certain to what end. The other, more radical wing of the Mexican Left became the center of world attention by reducing its agenda to one issue: the indigenous problem. The new focus solidifies its ethical foundation; the same perspective limits its ability to engage the vast economic and technological changes of our times.[1]

The larger world now lives an era of counterrevolution, or perhaps a conservative revolution from above. Under the force of globalization, the European and North American welfare states weakened; powerful conservative trends coalesced around President Ronald Reagan and Prime Minister Margaret Thatcher. In the Soviet Union and Eastern Europe, state socialism collapsed to make way for a savage capitalism linked to the awakening of political democracy. In China and Vietnam, socialist systems moved toward mixed economies, without modifying their political systems. In Latin America, the 1980s saw the cycle of dictatorships and guerrilla movements end while the continent was swept by neoliberal reforms linked to political democracy. As the Cold War ended, the United States became more tolerant of those Latin American left movements willing to join this process, while it continued to blockade Cuba. In Mexico as late as 1976, the one-party system that excluded most of the Left from legal participation remained in place without substantial changes. Since the sixties, the regime had become more repressive, while the attacks against its hegemony became more frequent and massive.[2] In the 1970s, the post–World War II economic boom ended, and the economy began a period of instability, stagnation, indebtedness, and dependency that has not ended.

In 1977 and 1978, the government of President José López Portillo began a reform that opened, in limited ways, the option of elections for the independent Left.[3] Five years later, in 1982, a devastating economic crisis struck, enabling technocrats promoting an orthodox neoliberal project to take power within the regime. The Left's reaction was vigorous but ineffective. Still, the great protest movements of the early eighties laid the groundwork for the 1988 electoral mobilization—when Cuauhtémoc Cárdenas, candidate of a left coalition, won the vote but lost the count.[4]

The fall of the Berlin Wall and of the socialist system, combined with the nearly simultaneous candidacy of Cuauhtémoc Cárdenas for Mexico's presidency, brought pathbreaking changes in the Left. Most important was the rise of neo-Cardenismo and the creation of the PRD (Partido de la Revolución Democrática, the Democratic Revolutionary Party). In 1988, in elections marked by massive fraud, Carlos Salinas de Gortari became president and quickly carried out a series of neoliberal reforms. The key emphases were the privatization of state industries and agencies, the end and reversal of agrarian reform, the weakening of social welfare institutions, economic deregulation, and the signing of the NAFTA treaty that locked the nation in a disadvantaged role within a North American economic bloc. The Left turned to the electoral arena. Its most prominent goals were to defend local electoral victories and to oppose Salinas's economic policies in the Congress.[5]

The next presidential election year, 1994, generated an unprecedented crisis within the ruling elite. The murder of the PRI presidential candidate Luis Donoldo Colosio, Manuel Camacho's rebellious refusal to follow the rules of PRI succession, followed by more political murders, were symptoms of an irreversible political breakdown. The PRI's replacement candidate, Ernesto Zedillo, won a closely contested presidential victory; a disastrous economic crisis punctuated his December inauguration. PRI rule continued; the PRI system faced irreversible breakdown.

On January 1 of the same year, the EZLN emerged as a new expression of the Left. From the depths of Chiapas, a guerrilla movement with a strong indigenous base declared war on the system. A few days later, the war became an armed peace that began a prolonged process of negotiation that has not ended. The Zapatistas gained vast international attention but faced insurmountable obstacles within Mexico.[6] From 1994 on, the Left had two poles, a moderate PRD and a radical EZLN.

Facing a serious deterioration of the standard of living of the majority of the population, Zedillo's government pressed draconian policies of economic austerity while reversing the government's repressive policies against the PRD. In the mid-term elections of 1997, the party of the electoral Left achieved important municipal, congressional, and gubernatorial victories. The system gradually opened and moved toward electoral pluralism. Finally, in 2000, with the economy recovering, July presidential elections finally produced the opposition victory that ended the one-party state. The hopes and expectations derived from Vicente Fox's victorious appeal for change created a new political situation. Subsequently, however, an acute economic recession, a government without a plan, and the attacks of September 11, 2001, and their aftermath created conditions of general disillusionment—with unpredictable consequences.

The Mexican Left is a political current characterized by defined ideas, ethical values, and patterns of action. It resists the privileges that mark a society structured by great inequalities and deep social conflicts; it embraces workers, the poor, and the excluded. It struggles for the redistribution of income, the deepening and widening of democracy, and the strengthening of civil society. It defends the rights of women, of indigenous people, and of migrants in the United States. It demands economic and political sovereignty for Mexico, along with state services in education, health care, and social security. It identifies with the secular state, rational philosophy, and scientific advancement.

No single leader or political party defines the Left. A person or party may be on the left on one issue, on the right concerning another. No political party or movement is totally left. Thus the Left always pursues self-criticism and imagines utopias. It cannot exist without constantly redefining the boundaries that separate it from the Right—while the Right works to erase those boundaries.

In a context of accelerating change, political and ideological positions inevitably face profound transformations. For example, before 1979 the concept of democracy focused on reclaiming citizenship rights. After that year, it revolved around reforming the electoral system.[7] After NAFTA, the notions of sovereignty associated with policies of import substitution (production for Mexican markets with Mexican workers) had to be reassessed amid accelerating globalization and a regional integration in which Mexicans were to serve as inexpensive laborers producing for consumers in the United States and Canada.

In 1976, Marxism and socialism held enormous influence in the Left. Books by Marxist authors, European and Mexican, sold widely—sometimes tens of thousands of copies. A few Marxist texts sold hundreds of thousands of copies. In the social sciences faculties of many universities, Marxism and socialism displaced other schools of thought. Every form of Marxism had its supporters; debates among the proponents of Lenin, Gramsci, Mao, and Althusser led to a vibrant theoretical life.[8] In the interpretation of Latin American history, supporters of dependency theory and the defenders of theories of modes of production waged battles that generated a vast literature. After 1968, European communism shook established communist theories by challenging the policies and programs that structured the "really existing socialist countries" of the Soviet Union and Eastern Europe. Thus began the differentiation and then dispersion that broke the monolithic intellectual atmosphere of a Marxism fading into the past. Supporters of vanguard parties faced new demands for adaptability. Militants of new social movements denounced the ideological rigidity and bureaucracy of old communist parties.[9]

Still, this flourishing development of Marxist theory did not engage the masses. In Mexico, socialism developed historically among intellectuals and urban youth. This explains its rapid eclipse after 1989. Instead, a persistent revolutionary nationalism predominated among the popular sectors that responded to the Left. Deep into the 1970s, this ideological current remained vigorous, as evidenced by the movement for labor independence led by Rafael Galván.[10]

Throughout the 1970s and 1980s, large numbers of intellectuals also supported revolutionary nationalism. They sympathized with the ideals of the Mexican Revolution, with social democracy, and with the development programs promoted by the United Nations Economic Commission for Latin America. Some used Marxist concepts without citing their sources. Their ideas about Mexico's national reality were often critical and open to the new expressions of popular culture. In political practice, however, they actively cooperated with the PRI regime and especially with the presidents who came and went. Many revolutionary nationalists held important posts

1. Heberto Castillo, Valentín Campa, and Rosario Ibarra de Piedra, leaders of the Mexican Left, joined the fight against *los desaparecidos*—the disappeared. Photograph from Archivo *Proceso*. Courtesy of *Proceso*.

in the academic and cultural bureaucracies. At critical moments, they lent governments their prestigious seals of approval; the government, in turn, rewarded their cooperation, often generously.

Their power and influence in the academic and cultural worlds were substantial. They controlled important journals, publishing houses, and newspapers; their presence in the mass media was obvious. Though they displayed important differences in their ideologies and personal careers, the intellectual revolutionary nationalists formed a strong faction united by common interests and mutual support networks. The PRI regime's sudden neoliberal turn and the emergence of a democratic tendency within the party, however, proved to be tests that most could not pass: the revolutionary nationalists' allegiance to power proved stronger than their principles.

In a system in which the PRI government ruled or permeated every political space, independence was the symbol of the dignity of the socialist Left. Revolutionary nationalists stayed within the ruling party, with sporadic sorties that allowed them to keep in touch with struggling popular sectors and radical intellectuals.[11] Until the mid-eighties, socialists were revolutionaries, while nationalists remained reformers. Socialists believed that the Left could achieve its goals only by revolution; nationalists worked to achieve the ideals of the Mexican Revolution without breaking with the regime. Socialists stayed outside the political system; independence from the state gave clarity to their vision. Revolutionary nationalists remained critical fellow travelers of the PRI system.

Beginning in 1988 and 1989, however, left political culture experienced a profound transformation. Basic goals remained, but socialist ideology and organizations collapsed and disappeared from the political scene. The fall of the Berlin Wall had devastating effects in Mexico. In the PRD, ideas of revolution and independence from the regime gave way to visions of reform and a fusion of one sector of the PRI with the socialist Left—under the leadership of the former PRIístas. Dogmatism, long the scourge of left programs, gave way to opportunism—without even the anchor of populism. Revolutionary nationalism and *caudillismo* (political personalism) dominated. Utopias gave way to crass pragmatism without a vision for the future.

In the face of the onslaught of a neoliberal revolution set on dismantling the gains of the people during the previous half century, the Left took positions suddenly conservative: defense of agrarian rights and of state social programs, opposition to the indiscriminate opening of the economy, and defense of the state's role in regulating the market. The Right appeared to replace the Left as the proponent of change. To many, the Left only defended a preferred past; it lacked a vision of a better future. The result was that after the 2000 presidential elections, the PRD's political stance looked dangerously like that of the PRI, which had lost presidential power and joined the opposition.

In contrast, the EZLN allied with intellectuals who had remained on the left and led a flight toward the future. Their direct opposition to neoliberalism and their demands for revolutionary dignity, direct democracy, a vibrant civil society, and human rights without doubt offer a premonition of a better future. The singular global utopia of socialism is giving way to an open and experimental utopia.[12] However, the EZLN message did not take hold among the majority of Mexicans, who insist on gradual change and oscillate between the defense of a past rooted in revolutionary nationalism and the attractions of a future shaped by the neoliberalism promoted by national and international centers of power. While the Zapatista vision spread spectacularly across the world and created a global network of solidarity, its appeal in Mexico declined. In matters of vision and ideology, the Left now faces a time of uncertain expectation as it seeks to synthesize yet move beyond democratic liberalism, revolutionary nationalism, and Marxist socialism—all in the context of Mexico's rapidly changing history.

In 1976 the Left made its last unsanctioned (by regime registration) attempt to participate in Mexican presidential elections. The PAN (Partido

Acción Nacional, on the right) declined to participate; the PRI candidate, José López Portillo, faced no legally recognized opposition. As a result, the PRI attitude toward Valentín Campa, an old labor leader and a member of the Mexican Communist Party (PCM), was unusually tolerant. He did not face the usual harassment and repression. A left coalition formed by the Communist Party, the Socialist League, and the Movimiento de Organización Socialista (the last two with Trotskyite tendencies), backed Campa. The campaign was called "The March for Democracy." Its main slogan was "Campa, Candidate of the Workers' Struggle," inspired by intensifying labor conflicts. Its discourse emphasized democracy in general, and labor democracy in particular. Within this framework, the campaign also supported demands for priests' political rights, academic freedom, and democracy within the army.[13]

Campa's march, run without access to the media, proved modest. It lasted three months and included ninety-seven political meetings attended, according to organizers, by about one hundred thousand people. The main events took place in Puebla and Guadalajara, with more than ten thousand people at the closing meeting at the Arena México in the national capital. The regime never officially recorded or reported the vote for Campa. Still, the campaign of the old labor leader showed both the will of the Left to participate in the electoral system, and the limits of its influence in the repressive conditions of the time. (The regime's unacknowledged but well-known "dirty war" against rural and urban guerrilla movements began in 1971 and remained vehement in 1976.) Three years later, the Left registered officially and participated within the system for the first time in national elections for congressional representatives.[14]

Meanwhile, popular movements remained active. They were reluctant to join with the parties with left programs; they often agreed on immediate demands but differed on tactics. In 1975, Rafael Galván organized the Democratic Tendency within the SUTERM (a national electrical workers' alliance), which led to a series of large mobilizations that spread across the country. Although the leaders of official labor organizations tried to divide the movement and harass it, on May 1 forty thousand electricians joined a march demanding labor independence. Democracy within the unions was the key goal. On November 15, another demonstration assembled more than one hundred thousand people, including the labor unions of the National University (UNAM). In the months that followed, thugs sent by PRI-backed "official" union leaders took over union halls and accused Galván of being a "red fascist." Rather than concede, in October 1976, many independent unions and organizations joined to create the Frente

2. Rafael Galván and the electrical workers of SUTERM led the strongest mobilization for trade union independence in the 1970s. Photograph from Archivo *Proceso*. Courtesy of *Proceso*.

Nacional de Acción Popular. Two years later, however, the movement dissolved in the face of repression.[15]

Amid continued attempts at independent organization on the left, and in the context of continuing repression, in 1977 the PRI regime issued the Federal Law for Political Reform. It did not offer effective political pluralism; instead, it aimed to grant a limited expression to what the government called "minorities." It provided limited seats in Congress to parties that gained consistent minority votes at the polls—but could not win a majority anywhere against the PRI's hegemonic power. The Left, fearing a new means of co-optation, approached the new law with caution. Yet during the next six years, every important political party became legal. Attracted by the new law's possibilities, the Left began a series of movements toward unity. In 1981, on the eve of the presidential elections, the PCM led the creation of a new political party, the Partido Socialista Unificado de México (PSUM), uniting four organizations.[16] Yet the new party was far from fully unified. Many important organizations had misgivings and kept a distance. In 1986 a new merger took place. It united the PSUM with two other organizations to form the Partido Mexicano Socialista (PMS).[17] Despite these efforts, success at the polls was limited. The total vote reported for the independent Left never exceeded 6 percent, and from 1982 onward there were always multiple left slates dividing that small vote. While the data are not trustworthy (there was no independent electoral institute), they reflect a clear trend toward the fringe. The mergers, attempts to unify dispersed groups, had little effect on voters who saw little attraction in left parties with ever-changing initials and incomprehensible differences. The left vote stagnated while PAN votes increased, eventually placing the party of the Catholic and business Right in a clear second place. The ghost of a bipartisan system began to appear.

The PMS was a last effort to create a great electoral socialist party. On May 19, 1989, it dissolved to form the Partido de la Revolución Democrática (PRD), dominated during the next decade by neo-Cardenistas (followers of Cuauhtémoc Cárdenas, emerging from the Democratic Current that broke from within the PRI). The passage from semilegality to legal electoral life brought enduring changes. The Left became less dogmatic and more concerned about public opinion. "Organic" intellectuals lost influence, and campaign managers became more important. Militants promoting an ethical pathos yielded to Mexican-style professional politicians. Corruption cases began to appear; internal struggles became less ideological and more linked to questions of power. Still, the Left's identity remained unmistakable.

Seventy years of PRI rule had stimulated an endless succession of massive protests, public expressions of grievances that looked beyond Congresses that served only the PRI regime. Many citizens considered such mobilizations normal political life. From the 1970s into the 1980s, social movements pressing specific popular demands and challenging the corporate pact (by which the PRI regime gave limited services and other benefits only to loyal subordinate organizations) experienced an unprecedented boom.

Unlike legal parties, social movements preferred demonstrations, strikes, civil disobedience, and, as a last resort, guerrilla warfare. Such movements inevitably collided with the monopoly PRI and its mass organizations. Some movements emphasized class, status, or ethnic traits and defined themselves as campesino, worker, indigenous, or student movements. Others had regional, civic, or urban-popular identities. Generally, their leaders belonged to, or emerged from, left parties. In 1979 the Coordinadora Nacional de Trabajadores de la Educación appeared; its main goal was union democracy. During the next three years, it mobilized more than 150,000 teachers in sit-ins and demonstrations.[18] An example of a regional movement with strong indigenous content was the Coalición Obrero Campesino Estudiantil del Istmo. This group became a powerful anti-PRI force at Juchitán on the Isthmus of Tehuantepec. It struggled for community autonomy and citizens' rights and pressed the demands of the region's workers: land and an end to bureaucratic corruption and arbitrary rule by local PRI bosses. COCEI became a local political force and gained national prestige.[19]

The leading social movements in the major cities differed in their goals and composition. They resisted efforts by elites to mold city life in strict accordance with their own interests. Movements appeared in the mid-1970s demanding popular housing and cheap and efficient transportation, along with water, electricity, and schools for the popular barrios. They opposed relentless demands to promote commercial use of land. Starting in 1980, the Coordinadora Nacional del Movimiento Urbano Popular organized national meetings that attracted representatives of hundreds of popular urban organizations. After 1982, demands became more general and more linked to issues of national politics.

That year saw an unprecedented political and economic crisis caused by the collapse of world oil prices. Suddenly Mexico faced an insurmountable debt, owed mostly to New York banks. The neoliberal turn of Mexican policies followed quickly and set off a wave of nationwide social movements that maintained intensity for over two years. October saw the creation of two *coordinadoras*, one moderate, one radical. They included hundreds of national and local organizations. In November they began a series of strikes that mobilized the Mexican Electricians Union (SME) and dozens of smaller organizations. By July 1983, strike participants totaled over three hundred thousand. The movement, however, was defeated, and the strikes ended without achieving their goals. October 1983 brought a successful general strike, at least in terms of vast participation; June 1984 brought another—a failure.[20] From then on, social and workers' movements entered a lull, interrupted only by the mobilizations during the 1987–88 presidential campaign of Cuauhtémoc Cárdenas. None of the movements, by themselves, could limit the implementation of neoliberal policies or modify the political system.

The appearance of the Democratic Current within the PRI began a radical change. It was a rebellion within the dominant party against President Miguel de la Madrid, who amid debt crisis had turned against the development model sustained by the PRI during the previous forty years. From the outset, Cuauhtémoc Cárdenas, recently governor of Michoacán, and Porfirio Muñoz Ledo, formerly Mexico's representative to the United Nations, led the internal resistance. Cárdenas's challenge caused a deep rift within the ruling elite and the PRI and attracted broad sectors of Mexican society struggling with economic crisis and upset by the painful social costs driven by the imposed shift to neoliberalism.[21] In 1988, without a unified organization or access to the mass media, Cárdenas, in 120 days of political campaigning as candidate of the Frente Democrático Nacional, managed to gain 40 percent of the vote. He drove the system to the wall. Thus was born the myth of Cuauhtémoc Cárdenas's invincibility.

Cárdenas's 1988 candidacy gave the parties of the ideological Left and the diverse social movements a chance to jump into the political arena after five years of intense mobilizations that had brought only defeat after defeat. Most of Mexico's vast and diverse Left supported his candidacy. For the first time in decades, the Left was united.

Cárdenas proved to be the ideal candidate for the historic moment of 1988. As the son and political heir of President Lázaro Cárdenas (who had consolidated the postrevolutionary regime in the 1930s), Cuauhtémoc galvanized regime supporters who opposed the rise of neoliberalism, promising to protect them against its radical excesses. Many voters fed up with official demagogy welcomed his firm yet sober style. His untiring *pueblear* (going among the people) and his willingness to listen brought hope to forgotten sectors. His skill at tying *amarres* (knots, or deals, with local leaders) linked apparently incompatible political forces.

His electoral success shook the national conscience to its roots. He showed irrefutably that even in the confines of the prevailing system, the PRI could be defeated in elections, strengthening the credibility of voting in the popular imagination as a way toward change and to express discontent. Cárdenas's campaign (despite its much-questioned "defeat") proved an important contribution to legitimating the democratic way in a country of strong authoritarian traditions.

A year later, the Democratic Current, the parties of the ideological Left, and most social movements combined to create the PRD—the Democratic Revolutionary Party. The new party arose from the ideological shipwreck of the old Left produced by the fall of the Berlin Wall and the social movements' renunciation of their long and stubborn nonparticipation in electoral and congressional life, which had kept them anchored in civil society. A revised vision of revolutionary nationalism and a political pragmatism reminiscent of the PRI quickly filled the ideological gaps.[22]

Perhaps the most revealing phenomenon of the time was the strength of neo-Cardenismo. For a decade, the Left united around the illusion that the name Cárdenas would bring victory. The unifying slogan was simple and electrifying: Cárdenas for President! With that, the Left emerged from the fringes and found legitimacy in public opinion. Moreover, the Democratic Current's split from the PRI created an open wound through which, for a decade, thousands of the old party's cadres and many associated groups flowed toward the new party. For the first time, members of the PRI learned to be members of an opposition. Cárdenas's three failed presidential bids and one successful campaign to become regent of the Federal District (including Mexico City) instilled new life in Cardenismo, one of Mexico's great political traditions. Neo-Cardenismo is a populism of the Left. It began as a reform project within the PRI, promoting the founding vision of Lázaro Cárdenas. It became a way to resist the neoliberal policies of those in power after 1982, with some nostalgia for the benefits, however unequal, of the welfare state of the 1940s to the 1980s. It was simultaneously a traditional caudillo (strongman) movement, organized around the charismatic figure of the leader (Cuauhtémoc) and the experience of his four campaigns. The strength of the leader displaced the power of ideology and of political organization. It also revived and reformed a style of politics that linked political elites and the disadvantaged, pressing for reforms and concessions that did not threaten the system. Neo-Cardenismo is radical in opposition, reasonable in Congress, and moderate when governing.

The victory of Vicente Fox and the PAN in July 2000 was the first defeat of the PRI and its power as monopoly state party. It was also a defeat of neo-Cardenismo, which lost its leading role in the Left. No coherent alternative has emerged. Victory by Lázaro Cárdenas Batel (grandson of Lázaro, son of Cuauhtémoc) in the election for Michoacán's governorship may bring new political vigor. National primacy, however, came from unique circumstances, unlikely to redevelop. Neo-Cardenismo and the PRD were key catalysts of the transformation of the Left into an electoral force, and its inclusion as an influential participant in the process of democratic transformation. As neo-Cardenismo wanes, the Left retains full legitimacy within the new pluralistic system still under construction.

The Achilles' heel of the new party is its internal organization. From the beginning, the PRD has been a loose federation of diverse forces, groups, and personalities. That heterogeneity led to statutes that legitimize the existence of diverse currents and imposed secret, direct, and universal elections to select leaders and representatives. On the one hand, this has allowed the new party to adapt to existing popular organization and to take root quickly in diverse sectors. On the other, it has created among the new leadership an "instrumental" vision in which the party is not an end in itself but a means to achieve their factions' goals. Thus the PRD has moved slowly toward institutionalization and the creation of party loyalties.[23]

Today the PRD is composed of professional politicians, or at least of politicians who want to be professionals. There is little room in the party's ranks for members, however committed and active, who do not seek positions of leadership and do not respond to patronage relationships. The new party is not an ideological community, open to every effort to promote a common ideal. There is little room for militants promoting land and labor rights, environmental issues, women's rights, or intellectual and artistic communities. Party activists focus on electoral campaigns, congressional activity, and state and municipal governments; their political vision is limited to these activities.

Electoral struggles and common experiences have shaped loyalties that unite thousands of people who consider themselves members of the PRD and respond willingly to their party's appeals, yet their participation in the internal decisions of the institution is negligible. Moreover, PRD leaders do not promote political education within or outside the party—a major obstacle to generating support in the most politically aware sectors of society, especially in the most prosperous cities and regions.

Still, the PRD currently occupies the Left of Mexico's political spectrum. This is most evident in its congressional work, nationally and in the states. From the beginning, it has struggled for a profound democratization of the Mexican regime. During the era of PRI domination, it denounced the authoritarian nature of the presidential corporatist system; it defended principles of pluralism, the division of powers, and electoral transparency. With other opposition parties, the PRD contributed decisively to dismantling the PRI authoritarian regime that for decades checked the development of electoral democracy.

What makes the PRD different from the other two major Mexican political parties is its continuing struggle for change in social and economic policies. PRD members of Congress denounce the alarming increase of poverty and the growing difficulties of access to basic public services. They have opposed the privatization of the Mexican Social Security Institute and cutbacks in eligibility for food assistance programs. They defend the social benefits promised to all citizens by the 1917 Constitution. The PRD also opposed Salinas de Gortari's termination and reversal of the revolutionary agrarian reform. The party actively works to protect Mexican migrants in the United States. Its representatives insist that if NAFTA guarantees the mobility of capital, it must also facilitate the mobility of labor.

PRD representatives demanded basic changes in the 1998 and 1999 federal budgets, seeking to increase social spending. When they failed, they voted against the final plans—forcing approval by an alliance of the PRI and the PAN. In 2000, the pivotal election year, the PRD was more successful. In alliance with other opposition parties, it substantially modified the last budget negotiated under PRI hegemony. The PRD similarly influenced the budget in 2001, the first year of the PAN government.

In addition, the PRD has been active in turning the defense of the en-

vironment into a constitutional right of all Mexicans and opposing privileges that favored great private corporations such as FOBAPROA. The
clarity and coherence of the PRD's political project is most obvious in
legislative chambers. Rather than in projects and ideological documents,
the real orientation of the new party emerges from positions taken by its
senators and congressmen. There are currents within the party that would
like to align the PRD more securely within the establishment. Others
would rather use congressional powers to consolidate the party's ties with
society's most rebellious sectors and construct an alternative force, perhaps smaller, yet more radical and closer to the least advantaged sectors of
society.[24]

The other pole of the Left, Zapatismo, offers different proposals. The
first and best known is cultural and political autonomy for indigenous
communities. Its originality lies precisely in transforming a previously
secondary demand into the core of its struggle. The congressional nul-
lification of the law on indigenous rights has postponed indefinitely any
decisive progress in this area. The Zapatistas' second emphasis is the creation of a social movement outside the party and congressional system,
which will struggle to fulfill its "Thirteen Demands" independent of the
legislative arena. Facing a left political party that works to conquer a majority in both legislative chambers and eventually to claim the executive
branch in order to advance its project within the state, the EZLN seeks to
create a great popular movement. It would conquer the streets, the countryside, and the factories and from there struggle through legal and peaceful means to achieve the objectives of the poor. The "capture of power," the
traditional goal of Marxist parties, has been abandoned in favor of direct
popular action. The Zapatista approach argues that the congressional system puts insurmountable obstacles in the way of any transformation favoring the people, and that only a movement "from the bottom up," creating
social and political awareness and mobilizing popular action, can decisively change existing power relations.[25]

To date, the initiatives aimed to create efficient and enduring centers of
popular organization have not proved fruitful. The idea of a political force
that does not struggle to take power, does not apply old methods, but
instead works to strengthen the citizens' movements, has a long tradition
within social movements. Without such work, the recent changes would
have been impossible. The effect of such movements, however important,
is limited, as history has shown. A political system with enough legitimacy
can absorb, co-opt, or neutralize such extraparliamentary actions without
endangering its own existence.

There are, obviously, points of agreement and of contention between the

PRD and the EZLN. A left electoral party cannot behave as a social movement, and the movements cannot participate effectively in elections. Each thus follows a different trajectory and serves different functions; each has its culture, its democracy, its capacity to change, its followers—and its limitations. In the coming years, Mexico will see much of the PRD and the EZLN. Neither can successfully substitute for the other; the persistence of both may allow for complementary efforts at key moments.

During 2004 the candidacy of Andrés Manuel López Obrador, then PRD mayor of Mexico City and the Federal District, gained strength, creating a strong possibility for the left in the presidential election of 2006. In that contest, the left found new strength, becoming the second strongest political force in the nation. Everything indicated that López Obrador won the election but was the victim of an electoral fraud that gave the victory to the candidate of the right, Felipe Calderón of the PAN—by the minimal margin of .58 percent. López Obrador has refused to accept the fraud and has called for a movement of peaceful resistance against the imposition of Calderón and the politics of the right in general.

There remains the problem of the left utopia. The Left cannot move from resistance to participation in search of social change without engaging the challenge of forging a unifying vision. The future will be contested and won in the domain of ideas. The Left's answer must reconcile immediate goals with a vision of the future.

There are two kinds of utopias. The first constructs new worlds, paradises on earth. They will, they insist, fully achieve harmony, equality, solidarity, and freedom. After the experience of the twentieth century, we know that such absolute utopias are impossible to achieve and dangerous to attempt. The idea of a "new society" or a "new man" that will resolve all human contradictions once and for all must face Goya's dictum "The dreams of reason create monsters." Imperfection is the unavoidable condition of civilizations. Systems may seek perfection; they cannot be perfect. The inevitable contradiction between values and interests will persist. In pursuit of perfection, the proponents of absolute utopias have demanded prolonged sacrifices of fundamental rights. Inevitably, they have produced tyrannies.

The second type of utopia claims the possibility not of a perfect world but of a better one, a different future. They may resolve contradictions now prevailing, but they cannot abolish the conflicts, tragedies, and pains of the human condition. They pursue goals impossible under present conditions (otherwise they would not be utopias), but they do not imagine universal harmony. As alternatives to closed utopias, they propose open futures.[26] Adolfo Sánchez Vázquez says, "Utopias point toward the possible, unrealizable today, but perhaps achievable tomorrow, if the possible has roots in reality."[27]

The alternatives to exclusionary tyrannical utopias are pluralistic utopias. The great lesson of the twentieth century is that, instead of following a predetermined project, a utopia should offer mobilizing proposals. Utopia must remain unfinished and ever changing. Future possibilities are neither singular nor inflexible. Utopia must be constructed with liberty and inevitably open to many variations. It must be defined by the awareness that every great victory of human civilization is at once an achievement and a beginning that brings new problems.

The two great models that dominated the imagination of humankind in the twentieth century, state socialism and free-market capitalism, failed because both were absolute and exclusionary. The new utopia must be secular, critical, pluralistic, and radically opposed to any fundamentalist philosophy. These are some of the conditions necessary to the great task of reconstructing ideas for the future. The task will require deep humility and enduring patience.

NOTES

1 Manuel Vázquez Montalbán, *Marcos: El señor de los espejos* (Mexico City: Aguilar, 1999), 74–78.

2 Enrique Semo, *La búsqueda. 1. La izquierda mexicana en los albores del siglo XXI* (Mexico City: Océano, 2003), 72–74.

3 Kathleen Bruhn, *Taking On Goliath: The Emergence of a New Left Party and the Struggle for Democracy in Mexico* (University Park: Pennsylvania State University Press, 1997), 59; and Barry Carr, *La izquierda mexicana a través del siglo XX* (Mexico City: Era, 1996), 59.

4 Jorge I. Domínguez and James McCann, *Democratizing Mexico: Public Opinion and Electoral Choices* (Baltimore: Johns Hopkins University Press, 1996), 18–20, 81.

5 See Carlos Acosta Córdova's articles in *Proceso* 634 (December 26, 1988): 20–22; and Gerardo Galarza in *Proceso* 662 (June 12, 1989): 8–9.

6 Neil Harvey, *The Chiapas Rebellion: The Struggle for Land and Democracy* (Durham: Duke University Press, 1998), 249–54.

7 Julio Moguel, *Los caminos de la izquierda* (Mexico City: Juan Pablos Editor, 1987), 26–33.

8 Carr, *La izquierda mexicana*, 244–46.

9 See Juan Luis Concheiro and Eduardo Montes Manzano, chapters 8 and 9 in *Historia del comunismo en México*, ed. Arnoldo Martínez Verdugo (Mexico City: Editorial Grijalbo, 1983), 321–405.

10 Raúl Trejo Delarbre, "El movimiento de los electricistas democráticos, 1972–1978," *Cuadernos Políticos* 18 (October–December 1978): 47–69.

11 Miguel Angel Villegas, "El MLN: Historia de un recorrido hacia la unidad, Mexico, 1957–67, (Ph.D. diss., UNAM, Mexico, 2000) 123–52.

12 EZLN, documentos y comunicados, no. 3 (Mexico City: Ediciones Era, 1997), 79–89, 125–27.

13 See *Socialismo* 1, no. 2 (segundo trimestre, 1975): 14–29; *Oposición* 144 (July 10, 1976): 1; and *Oposición* 145 (July 17, 1976): 3–5.

14 Verdugo, *Historia del comunismo*, 474.

15 Jorge Basurto, *La clase obrera en la historia de México* (Mexico City: Siglo XXI, 1984): 245–79.

16 Carr, *La izquierda mexicana*, 290–94.

17 Massimo Modonesi, *La crisis histórica de la izquierda socialista mexicana* (Mexico City: UCM–Casa Juan Pablos, 2003), 49–52.

18 Luis Hernández, "The SNT and the Labor Movement," in *The Mexican Left: The Popular Movements and the Politics of Austerity*, ed. Barry Carr and Ricardo Anzaldua (San Diego: Center for U.S.-Mexican Studies, 1986), 56–60.

19 Jeffrey W. Rubin, "Ambiguity and Contradiction in Radical Popular Movements: The Peasant-Worker-Student Coalition in Juchitan, Mexico, 1973–1992," in *Culture of Politics/Politics of Cultures: Revisioning Latin American Social Movements*, ed. Arturo Escobar, Sonia Alvarez, and Evelina Dagnino (Boulder: Westview Press, 1998).

20 Moguel, *Los caminos de la izquierda*, 56.

21 For a history of the Corriente Democrática, see Luis Javier Garrido, *La ruptura: La Corriente Democrática del PRI* (Mexico City: Editorial Grijalbo, 1993); and Jorge Laso de la Vega, *La Corriente Democrática: Hablan los protagonistas* (Mexico City: Editorial Posada, 1987).

22 Bruhn, *Taking on Goliath*, chaps. 3 and 4, pp. 67–164, and Modonesi, *La crisis histórica*, 69–113.

23 Enrique Semo, César Cancino, and Marco Aurelio Sánchez, *El cuaderno blanco de la reforma del PRD* (Mexico City: PRD, 2000).

24 Semo, *La búsqueda*, 115–25.

25 See "Zapatismo: Recomposition of Labour, Radical Democracy and Revolutionary Project," in *Zapatista! Reinventing Revolution in Mexico*, ed. John Holloway and Eloína Peláez (Sterling, Va.: Pluto Press, 1998), 126–58.

26 Fernando Ainsa, *La reconstrucción de la Utopía* (Mexico City: INESCO, 1997), 62–70.

27 Adolfo Sánchez Vázquez, *De Marx al marxismo en América Latina* (Mexico City: Ítaca, Universidad Autónoma de Puebla, 1999), 36.

❧ Another Turn of the Screw
Toward a New Political Order

ELISA SERVÍN ❧

The end of the twentieth century found Mexico immersed in a complex process of political transformation. In a peculiar coincidence with developments around 1800 and 1900, when the colonial Bourbon monarchy and the regime of Porfirio Díaz faced challenges in which they had to transform themselves or collapse, the end of the twentieth century brought a complex political transition provoked both by the exhaustion of the regime built after the revolution of 1910 and by the growing demands emerging from a mobilized society. That regime reached its limits in 2000, the turning point of an apparent transition to democracy. The fundamental political crises of the Bourbon and Porfirian regimes led to the ruptures of 1810 and 1910. Can Mexico's contemporary struggles—the fundamental crisis of the PRI regime—break with precedent and lead to broadening and deepening processes of democratic reform? Or is there a real possibility that the mounting demands of an exasperated society will lead, once again, to an outbreak of revolutionary violence?

A historical perspective on the present must emphasize the importance of the presidential election of 2000. Voting, not violence, brought opposition victory and the end of the PRI monopoly on the presidency. Those events culminated a long process of transformation that profoundly altered a political regime based on presidential power (*presidencialismo*), the symbiotic link between the presidency and the official party, and the mechanisms they used to control presidential succession.

The political machinery built within the legal and institutional framework of the state generated by the 1910 revolution revolved around two fundamental axes. The first was the authority of the presidency, an authority in part constitutional and in part supraconstitutional. The ability to appoint his successor was the president's most important informal power, since control of succession balanced the entire political system. The second axis was the official party. In practice, the party functioned as a state apparatus, using a powerful corporate structure and a thickly woven network of interests and relationships to operate as a privileged space for mediation and negotiation between state and society.

Throughout the second half of the twentieth century, the system allowed the practice of power and the transfer of the presidency in a stable environment. The combination of presidential power and party mediation regulated the process through which power was transferred, allowed for the inclusion and circulation of political groups, and guaranteed control of the means to rule. The system negotiated and sustained basic compromises in relations between state and society, allowing the regime a basic legitimacy. As for opposition groups, they either struggled to participate in limited ways within the bounds of the system or were subject to the use of force whenever the weight of "revolutionary" authority had to be displayed.

In the final decades of the twentieth century, however, the political machinery of the postrevolutionary regime experienced dislocations and challenges that first loosened and then took apart nuts, bolts, and gears, reversing the process that led to its construction. During the 1920s and 1930s, the engineers of the revolutionary regime drove an intense and complex process of centralization, searching for political stability by building institutions of mediation and control to deal with social demands and to contain mobilizations. In contrast, during the last two decades of the twentieth century, the gradual constriction of presidential power, the redefinition of the PRI's social and political role, the limited opening of the mechanism of succession, and the growing role of electoral alternation set new limits on regime power and modified traditional forms of political life. Those changes, in part engineered from within the regime, in part provoked by mounting opposition, forced those who aimed to rule the system to change—or be changed.

Without doubt, the possibility of regime transformation through peaceful and democratic means was unprecedented, especially in light of the political crises that became revolutions in the early nineteenth and twentieth centuries. For the first time in Mexico's history, elections became the way to transform the political order. Yet, as in any process of renewal, the unknowns exceed the certainties about Mexico's future. Dismantling the political apparatus built during the postrevolutionary years brought new and enduring questions and political challenges.

The regime created by the Mexican Revolution guaranteed a level of political stability that facilitated economic development and allowed the construction of an infrastructure of basic public services. It regulated conflicts between centralized authority and the diverse local and regional powers that had reappeared during the revolutionary struggle. Additionally, it strengthened a national and civil conscience by reaffirming a nationalist discourse and maintaining democratic formalities. Political stability and economic development, however, did not resolve the enduring problems of social inequality and poverty that afflict a majority of the population. As the twenty-first century begins, it is clear that the resolution of social grievances and a response to demands for a more equal distribution of national wealth are tasks that cannot be postponed with the excuse that the nation is embarking on a new political order.

THE REGIME OF THE MEXICAN REVOLUTION

The year 1910 began the fall of a regime. The political crisis that surrounded Porfirio Díaz's orchestrated election to a seventh term culminated a year later with the fall of his government to forces mobilized by Francisco Madero. Madero and his allies—elite and popular, urban and rural—came from the northern borderlands, the central highlands, and even Yucatán to initiate an era of profound change that defined the history of Mexico's twentieth century.

The collapse of the Porfirian order radicalized the diverse political and social demands that had emerged to challenge the regime during the first decade of the twentieth century, demands that were not met during Madero's brief and contested period of government. Yet when Victoriano Huerta led a military coup at the head of reactionary groups threatened by Madero's opening to democracy, the difficulties of renewing the old regime became clear. Armed mobilizations across the country and the organization of a Constitutionalist army under Venustiano Carranza set the stage for a long and violent struggle that eventually culminated in the new regime and the achievement of important, if limited, social goals: agrarian reform and basic labor rights.

The fall of Porfirio Díaz's regime and its centralized political authority led to an explosion of social demands and a deep regionalization of political power. As had happened in the decades following the independence revolution that began in 1810, after 1910 the regions claimed autonomy while a wide range of local and state powers pressed specific interests and issues. During the 1920s, complex contests between regional power holders and those who would eventually win central authority—Álvaro Obregón and Plutarco Elías Calles—marked political life, especially affecting relations between presidents and congresses.

The multiplication of political and social forces produced an explosion of organizations—workers' fronts, agrarian leagues, political clubs, and local, regional, and national political parties—many controlled by governors, military bosses, and "strongmen." Many who first built bases in armed movements now aimed to convert the legislative arena into a space for political struggle, seeking a counterweight to the centralizing goals of presidents Venustiano Carranza, Álvaro Obregón, and Plutarco Elías Calles. Diverse political parties coming from local and regional domains expressed their interests through parliamentary life, making Congress a place where governors and strongmen struggled against the center. The first attempts to construct a new and centralized executive power proved very difficult.[1]

Revolutionary forces created political clubs and parties throughout the 1920s. That proliferation was facilitated by the 1911 decree that established political parties as judicial entities, the 1917 Constitution, and the 1918 Electoral Law. The laws that emerged after the revolution authorized direct elections for all representative posts and broadened local municipalities' powers to organize and define electoral procedures.[2] As Luis Medina emphasizes, the demands for power and the modus operandi that had driven revolutionary violence increasingly transferred to the electoral sphere. Elections became another venue for confrontations between revolutionary groups.[3]

The new importance of municipal governments in elections, the explosion of social and political demands, and the intense mobilizations stimulated by the revolution and its promises gave new meaning to electoral contests, especially at the municipal and state levels. They became arenas for confrontation, negotiation, and—perhaps—resolution of conflicts between different political factions and between them and mobilized social interests.[4] Still, electoral practices inherited from the Porfiriato—patronage and behind-the-scenes arrangements among key players—remained. New local caciques and strongmen, often the allies of revolutionary military chiefs and governors, replaced Díaz's political bosses in making these arrangements. According to Jean Meyer, parties, clubs, and local organizations acted as electoral machines organized by new political leaders, *ejido* commissariats (representatives of communities that received lands in the agrarian reform), or union leaders to win elections, not to compete democratically.[5] Elections became a source of legitimacy for local and regional authorities in struggles against the center. They continued to strengthen the local and regional autonomies asserted amid revolutionary armed conflicts.[6]

Throughout the 1920s, then, the country remained fragmented by the assertive power of diverse local, regional, and national interests. Violence and armed struggle remained the primary mechanisms to resolve contests for presidential power. Thus the creation of an institutional order became a primary concern of the military-political group (the "Sonora dynasty" of Obregón and Calles) that had gained and maintained power through force after 1920. The country could not be stabilized unless continuing conflicts for power were resolved—or at least contained by institutional mechanisms.

From its 1929 creation, the Partido Nacional Revolucionario (PNR) was designed to be the institution to resolve disputes peacefully, as well as the source of legitimacy for the political class that emerged after the revolution. The party became an extraordinary electoral agency, steadily taking control of the selection of political candidates, guaranteeing their victories with the resources and machinery of the state. The 1929 elections tested the incipient state party's strength. Under Plutarco Elías Calles, "Jefe Máximo de la Revolución," the PNR managed to impose its presidential candidate, Pascual Ortiz Rubio, on all "revolutionary" forces and to defeat the opposition united around José Vasconcelos. The existence of the PNR and its new electoral and political legitimacy also contributed to limiting the revolt led that year by José Gonzalo Escobar, which failed to elicit support sufficient to threaten the regime.[7]

During its first stage, the PNR was more a front than a true party—an alliance of regional and local political parties and organizations working together without ceding their relative autonomy. Gradually but steadily, they began to see the party as an important environment for resolving political conflicts. Despite early resistance to a party that many saw as Calles's instrument for political control, in a few years the PNR managed to impose its authority over most important regional organizations.

Despite rivalries rooted in twenty years of armed struggle and initial resistance to "revolutionary unification," within a few years the revolution's party became the main instrument of a gradual process of political centralization. It also became a tool to control the legislature: the diverse interests expressed in the congresses of the 1920s were steadily substituted by voices committed to PNR hegemony.[8] Meanwhile the PNR saw electoral procedures as a key to centralization. By limiting and controlling candidacies and guaranteeing that PNR candidates would win elections, the party took away the autonomy that had sustained regional and local parties. Elections became a legitimizing mechanism, finalizing representation already determined by negotiations and agreements among political groups—François-Xavier Guerra's "democratic fiction." Electoral control defined the revolutionary party. Internal negotiations followed by controlled elections became, in a short period of time, the privileged mechanism to resolve disputes and limit conflicts over access to power.[9]

In 1934, Lázaro Cárdenas reached the presidency, backed by Calles and the campesino organizations that were the most important popular force, yet not full members of the party.[10] During his first year in office, Cárdenas consolidated his ascendancy within the agrarian movement and collaborated to gain support from the leading labor organizations. Combined with his authority over the army, within a few months the support of these groups allowed Cárdenas to displace Calles from the political scene and, most of all, to become both head of state and party leader. From 1935 onward there would be no challengers to the enormous power of the presidency.

During the first half of his mandate, Cárdenas focused on organizing and unifying the regime's social bases. He incorporated the leading campesino and worker organizations into the PNR, transforming it from a party of political elites into an organization with an encompassing social foundation. In exchange for a vast program of social reforms—land distribution for rural communities, support for workers in conflicts with business—the country's most important campesino and labor organizations accepted membership in the Party of the Revolution. The creation and incorporation of the Confederación Nacional Campesina (CNC) and the Confederación de Trabajadores de México (CTM) as party sectors consolidated the task of expanding the party to include Mexico's strongest social organizations. Cárdenas thus extended the process of party formation initiated by Calles, which initially included only political groups.

In 1938, after three years in power, Cárdenas transformed the PNR into the Partido de la Revolución Mexicana (PRM). The new party incorporated the four main social groups in the country: agrarian communities, industrial workers, civil servants and the middle class, and the military. Ejido communities (favored with regime-sanctioned grants of lands) and trade unions became—through their state-backed organizations—key actors in postrevolutionary corporatism. As representatives of collective units, they could press social demands and political grievances within the regime. They claimed early successes in exchange for support of the centralizing state. Quickly, however, the bureaucratization of the CNC and CTM leaderships, their influence on party structures, and the centralized allocation of political candidacies for elections combined to diminish the roles of the CNC and CTM as defenders of agrarian and industrial workers' interests.

The way was open for the institutionalization of the party as a disciplined organization promoting presidential power—often asserted in calls for the "unity of the revolution."

The president led the new corporate scheme. He became the unquestioned head of the party and, through the party, ruler of the political apparatus. Mexico took a giant step toward centralization when the power of the presidency fused with the encompassing strength of the party. By organizing the political class, sustaining governmental legitimacy, orchestrating elections, managing social control, and mediating conflicts in all those domains, the party and its corporate structure became the essential foundation for the presidencialismo that characterized the Mexican political system.

Still, the subordination of political and social forces to presidential power and party discipline did not prevent public expressions of political struggles. Into the 1940s, in the Congress, within the party's institutions, and especially in the presidential successions that began in 1939 and 1945, power and office remained contested. Blocks of senators and deputies on the left and right of the political spectrum, combined with the CTM's strength within the party, led to confrontations and power struggles with other political players, especially with governors who had to operate both as the PRM's provincial representatives and as leaders of regions still seeking autonomy.[11] Conflicts between provincial elites and CTM leaders persisted during Manuel Ávila Camacho's administration (1940–46), leading to new party reform in 1946. The result was a more centralized internal structure (and the elimination of the military as a formal sector) in the reformed and renamed Partido Revolucionario Institucional (PRI).[12]

Presidential control over the party and party control over candidacies and elections brought submission of the Congress to the executive. In the 1920s and 1930s, Congress was a fundamental space for political life, where different groups, interests, and proposals confronted each other. However, as presidential control tightened over the PRM and then the PRI, legislative autonomy decayed. The Congress became an extension of presidential power. Cárdenas and Ávila Camacho consolidated power while dealing with a Congress open to political discussion and debate. Miguel Alemán began his six-year term (1946–52) ready to impose "discipline" and prevent displays of legislative dissent.[13]

Once the president ruled the primary networks of power and made the fundamental political decisions, presidential succession became central to the stability and permanence of the system. Lázaro Cárdenas, Manuel Ávila Camacho, and Miguel Alemán implemented changes that strengthened presidential and party powers and their ability to appoint a successor.

They also tested the party's ability to reconcile the ambitions of political factions and forge majorities in support of its candidate. In all three cases, the outgoing president faced dissent within the political class—the so-called "revolutionary family." The elections of 1940, 1946, and 1952 saw powerful groups, denied succession within the party, break away and turn internal dissent into electoral opposition. The presidency and its party machinery combined to defeat all three oppositions. Each victory consolidated the power of the presidency, facilitating subsequent president's ability to choose a successor "in secret" and without interference. The power to designate a successor became the most important nonconstitutional power of Mexican presidents.

From the beginning, the founders of the postrevolutionary regime faced electoral opposition. The most challenging opponents emerged from within the ranks of the regime. Despite regime control of electoral results and the organizational disadvantages encountered by those who attempted opposition, resistance persisted through the long process of constructing and consolidating the revolutionary regime. Opposition was strongest during presidential campaigns. In 1929, José Vasconcelos found support among those who believed that Madero's democratic promise had been sacrificed for power and political stability.[14] Ten years later, in the election of 1939–40, General Juan Andreu Almazán coordinated a growing opposition. His supporters included multiple social groups opposed to Cárdenas's reforms and those who resented the powers the president increasingly exercised over the social groups incorporated into the regime. The result was an intense, sometimes violent, campaign.[15]

The Partido Acción Nacional (PAN) was founded in the political crucible of 1939, capturing the interests of diverse groups of intellectuals, Catholics, and members of the middle and upper class. Following the example of Vasconcelos, they proclaimed democratic and civic ideals to criticize the corporate regime that had come out of the revolution. From the beginning, the PAN debated whether to join in elections, hoping for an eventual triumph and exercise of power, or instead to refrain and promote education and ideological opposition outside the obviously controlled electoral arena. As Soledad Loaeza argues, the "dilemma of participation" was not resolved until the 1980s.[16] In the interim, the PAN entered many campaigns, asserting demands for effective representative democracy. The PAN's democratic stance coexisted with the notion of elections as negotiation that persisted within the dominant PRI.

Opposition from within the ranks of the "revolutionary" political class emerged again in 1946, led by Ezequiel Padilla. Like Almazán, Padilla united the discontent of diverse political groups and social constituencies.

Though not as popular as Almazán, Padilla gained (according to the official recount) a higher percentage of votes than would any opposition candidate in the following four decades.[17] In 1952, the regime again faced opposition from within, led by General Miguel Henríquez Guzmán. After failing to pressure the PRI to support his candidacy, Henríquez managed to build an opposition movement by mobilizing widespread discontent against Miguel Alemán's increasingly closed government, a government more obviously oriented to favor business and political allies and to control peasants and workers than its more circumspect predecessors.

Henriquista leaders began with a will to open the succession process within the PRI. As the campaign progressed, they proclaimed themselves heirs to the "true project of the Mexican Revolution." A broad group of former governors and military commanders from different regions joined the movement, emphasizing Henriquista resistance to unconditional submission to the president and political centralism.[18] The 1952 campaign proved intense. The PRI, the PAN, the Federación de Partidos del Pueblo Mexicano (FPPM), and the recently created Partido Popular (PP) presented candidates for the presidency and the Congress. That competition and the democratic discourse of Alemán's government combined to create expectations that at least local and legislative opposition triumphs might be recognized. Instead—and in the face of well-documented reports of fraud presented by every opposition party— official statistics reported an overwhelming victory for the PRI at all levels of government. The campaign and controlled outcome of 1952 consolidated the *carro completo* (full load) approach that arrested Mexico's political development for decades.

The crushing defeat of the opposition asserted by the official tally and the violent repression the government unleashed against Henriquista grassroots supporters after the election contributed to silencing expressions of opposition to presidential power, especially regarding the designation of a successor. Skepticism about the feasibility of democratic participation became widespread. In subsequent years, a sense of electoral impotence permeated the ranks of those who remained outside the PRI. Even the PAN, which from 1943 continued to present candidates in local and federal elections, repeatedly debated the possibility of nonparticipation (it finally abstained from offering a presidential candidate in 1976).[19] The demonstrated dominance of the PRI in federal contests reduced elections as a means to participate in political struggle to the local, often municipal, level.[20]

In the 1950s and 1960s, Mexicans harvested the fruits of economic developments that began in the 1920s and accelerated in the 1940s. In exchange for political stability and the benefits of economic growth, the social groups favored by "stabilizing development"—business leaders and much of the middle class—kept distant from politics and elections. Important social mobilizations developed during these decades among the railway workers, teachers, campesinos, doctors, and students—even among middle-class Catholics during the early 1960s. All sought means other than elections to engage and challenge the regime.[21] The governments of Adolfo Ruiz Cortines (1952–58), Adolfo López Mateos (1958–64), and Gustavo Díaz Ordaz (1964–70) offered uniform responses to these diverse mobilizations: authoritarianism and repression of varying intensity. The cycle of nonelectoral mobilization followed by violent repression culminated in the 1968 student movement, crushed by Díaz Ordaz's troops in the blood bath at Tlatelolco. That cataclysm, in turn, created an atmosphere favorable to a return to armed struggle by those who felt excluded from political participation within the PRI institutional framework. The loyal opposition (PAN, PP, and the Partido Auténtico de la Revolución Mexicana [PARM], created in 1954) continued to offer fruitless campaigns that helped to legitimate democratic formality more than they truly competed for power. Only in the 1980s did elections again become a way to express discontent—and then a means to struggle for political change.

NEOLIBERAL ADJUSTMENTS

The 1970s brought new challenges and mobilizations, along with attempts at reform. The economic model of "stabilizing development" came to be seen as *agotado*—exhausted or sold out. The promise of popular welfare remained unfulfilled. Inflation, currency devaluation, and the threat of massive capital flight brought daily challenges to political and economic stability.[22] The 1968 student movement and repression became a highly symbolic end to one phase of social mobilization and politicization—and the beginning of another. Spurred by economic crisis, an independent workers' movement gathered strength. Demands for democratization of the labor movement built on long-standing claims for higher wages. Meanwhile, rural and urban guerrillas proliferated. Amid widening difficulties of everyday life, driven by discontent and disillusionment with the absence of real political options outside the PRI, they radicalized political and social struggles.

The need to find new and more open avenues of political participation became urgent. President José López Portillo (1976–82) proposed changes that became the 1977 electoral reform, directed by secretary of government Jesús Reyes Heroles. The reform aimed to recover the regime's legitimacy, uncertain at best since 1968, by opening electoral procedures. Electoral nonparticipation was widespread and increasing. The rigidity of a system in which loyal opponents (including the PAN) offered candidates that expected to lose—and lose gracefully—had become transparent. The need for change was unmistakable, even within the entrenched political class. The regime had to open space to institutionalize, in the form of new political parties, organizations that had emerged in the first half of the decade under Luis Echeverría's contested rule. The state and the party also had to make the terms of electoral participation more flexible.[23]

The first fruit of the new legislation was the strengthening of the political and electoral presence of the Left, harshly punished by PRI governments beginning with Miguel Alemán's term during the early Cold War. For the first time since 1946, the Mexican Communist Party participated legally in elections. In 1981 its members joined other political forces to create the Partido Socialista Unificado de México (PSUM).[24] The reform opened the floodgates of institutional political participation as diverse parties and organizations joined the system of democratic competition. Elections recovered their role as the main venue for opposition political participation. The opposition's percentage of the vote increased rapidly.

The political opening began during the brief but intense oil boom of the late 1970s. It widened as boom collapsed into debt crisis in 1981, followed by the presidential elections of 1982. The 1982 succession unfolded amid an intense debate that the economists Rolando Cordera and Carlos Tello detail in the book *México: La disputa por la nación* (Mexico: The Struggle for the Nation).[25] Cordera and Tello defined and contrasted two possible roads to Mexico's future. One would continue and deepen the nationalist project that came from the revolution. Implemented during Lázaro Cárdenas's government, the nationalist project advocated inclusive development, seeking to benefit the majority of the population and to achieve national integration through economic independence. The second model was the neoliberal project. It proclaimed that the way to modernization was to yield development to market forces, allowing a greater integration with the U.S. economy. Public opinion captured this debate as a confrontation between "politicians" and "technocrats." In the struggle for designation as the PRI candidate to the presidency, secretary of planning and budget Miguel de la Madrid represented the neoliberal technocrats, while PRI national president Javier García Paniagua proclaimed the need for nationalist development.

During 1981, the press reported escalating confrontations between political factions and social sectors, especially between leaders of private enterprise and the unions. They understood that the national future was at stake. The active political participation of the business sector, provoked by growing government participation in the economy, attempts to reform tax laws, and Luis Echeverría's populist discourse, was unprecedented—and harshly criticized by the CTM's leadership.[26] The nationalization of the banks in September 1982 accelerated the move of entrepreneurs into politics. Most joined with the PAN, beginning the trend toward political participation by entrepreneurs that culminated with Vicente Fox's victory in 2000.

At the same time, the labor leadership of the CTM became disenchanted with López Portillo's "administration of abundance" during the oil boom. After years of restricted wage gains, the boom had brought few benefits to workers—and those vanished with the collapse and debt crisis. The CTM decided to concentrate its strategy for the elections on a nationalist platform that aimed to satisfy the needs of the popular classes. The CTM insisted that economic power should remain in the hands of the state, and that the state should serve labor and other social sectors.

Javier García Paniagua, PRI president since March 1981 and a strong internal contender for nomination to the presidency, championed the CTM vision. He knew the corridors of politics and attempted to balance the power of private enterprise and the bureaucratic elite with that of the PRI and, above all, with the CTM. Ultimately, his backers demanded a nationalist politician—a "true revolutionary" candidate.

On September 25, 1981, however, Miguel de la Madrid gained the public endorsement of the three sections of the PRI—formally including the CTM—as the presidential candidate, following the will of López Portillo. Presidential power imposed itself on the party structure. Party leaders not only had to accept defeat; they had to announce and promote a candidate who was anything but the "true revolutionary" they sought. Presidency and party no longer worked in symbiosis. The two key axes of the postrevolutionary regime were out of alignment.

García Paniagua's refusal to join in the *destape*—the unveiling—of the chosen successor, his resignation as PRI president on the day the electoral campaign began, and the CTM's absence from the early events of the campaign signaled the growing difficulty of maintaining party discipline and the public unity of political forces within the official party. Such discontent and indiscipline had not been expressed since 1952, when the last *ruptura* had occurred.[27] Though García Paniagua did not break with the system, he made his disagreement public. He set a precedent that culminated when the Corriente Democrática led by Cuauhtémoc Cárdenas and Porfirio Muñoz Ledo broke away from the PRI six years later.

Miguel de la Madrid was the candidate of technocracy. His selection ratified the marginalization of the traditional political class, especially those from the CTM who defended the corporate power of the PRI's labor

sector. His candidacy also ratified the political preeminence of the bureaucratic elite (not all members of the PRI) in charge of economic and financial matters within the administration, which had begun with the nomination of López Portillo back in 1976. In 1982, amid a deepening economic
crisis, the selection—and inevitably the election—of de la Madrid announced the triumph of the neoliberal project, which would transform the
state apparatus and government discourse in the following years. Once
again, economic modernization defined the paradigm that drove the Mexican governments. But during the last decades of the century, the way to
modernization was no longer state-directed "revolutionary" nationalism.
With the presidency of de la Madrid, neoliberalism brought an ever less
fettered global market to the task of bringing economic growth and popular welfare to Mexico.[28]

Liberalism in the economic sphere, however, was not accompanied by
political liberalization. Although de la Madrid's administration announced
its early commitment to political change and flirted with the possibility of
strengthening a bipartisan scheme in local elections—acknowledging the
PAN's 1983 surprise electoral victories in Guanajuato, Chihuahua, San Luis
Potosí, and Durango—the initiative stalled. It was blocked by de la Madrid's need to compromise with the traditional groups within the PRI. In
particular, the CTM refused to yield ground to the opposition. In the 1985
local and federal elections, it became evident that the regime was in political reverse. Instead of acknowledging opposition electoral victories, the
PRI announced its own electoral recovery. Accusations of fraud escalated
across the country, as did intense postelectoral protests.[29] Despite close
scrutiny by national and international media, and amid more accusations
of fraud at the polls, in 1986 the PRI machine retook in Chihuahua what it
had lost—and ceded—in 1983.[30]

Despite the obstinacy of PRI hard-liners and the government's resistance
to political democratization, the opposition increased its participation in
elections from 1979 on. The elections of the first half of the 1980s showed
that in the urban areas—with more middle-class voters, more media cover-
age, and proliferating civic organizations—the PRI could no longer guarantee electoral victory and legitimacy. In the North and in important cities,
the PAN became an alternative for real democratic change. The option of
the PAN attracted those who had benefited most from economic development and were most critical of the government's management of the economy and its political authoritarianism. "Neopanismo," the incorporation of
entrepreneurs and their growing ascendancy over the PAN's traditional (as-
sertively Catholic) membership, resolved the party's founding dilemma. It
would now pursue power, without hesitation, by participating in elections.[31]

1. In the state of Chihuahua, the contested gubernatorial elections of 1986 led to an active popular protest against electoral fraud. Photograph by Dolores Leony, Mexico.

Meanwhile, another phenomenon begun in the early 1970s also matured. This was the so-called "municipal insurgency" through which local elections again became spaces for politicization and social mobilization. Especially in the central and southern parts of the country, the Left won elections and thus control of many municipal governments. Municipalities became the first enclaves of political alternation, confirming their historical importance as privileged sites for political and social participation. Municipalities reemerged as crossroads where demands for political modernization fused with the defense of local and communal interests, especially in rural areas.[32] The regionalization of opposition, fully developed in the following decade, started to take shape.[33]

López Portillo had abandoned established mechanisms of political conciliation when he turned against the CTM and named de la Madrid his successor. De la Madrid became president, yet he quickly faced electoral losses that revealed a weakening of the PRI's political machinery amid deepening economic deterioration.[34] During the first months of his administration, Miguel de la Madrid engaged in a remarkable public confrontation with Fidel Velázquez, the long-entrenched head of the CTM. The president asserted his refusal to be pressured to accept the "old styles of negotiation and distribution of power" demanded by "irresponsible and demagogic minorities."[35] Yet despite the president's public efforts to confront the corporate power of the labor sector, which he and the technocrats regarded as an obstacle to economic reform, de la Madrid's efforts were limited by the PRI's and the CTM's continuing usefulness as machines that generated votes for the regime. The fundamental paradox of the Mexican transition became clear. Modernization promised an opening of the economy and of the political system. But to achieve the neoliberal opening of the economy in a time of crisis, the regime needed the power of the closed machine of the PRI regime. The technocrats could not rule without the politicians they aimed to displace. Globalizing economic neoliberalism would run far ahead of political liberalization.

Still, the wearing down of the PRI as a hegemonic political party, its difficulties maintaining discipline and reconciling its constituent interests, and the authoritarianism that it imposed on its corporate sectors, especially rural villagers and urban workers, inevitably impinged on the other axis of the political system: the president's management of succession. Without the strong and publicly unified party that gave previous presidents the autonomy to appoint their successors without questioning, Miguel de la Madrid faced a deteriorating political apparatus and the weakening of presidential control when it came time to choose a successor.

The approach of the 1988 presidential elections again brought disagreements within a divided political class, as political nationalists faced off against neoliberals. In 1987, in a process that evoked the origins of Henriquismo in 1950, Cuauhtémoc Cárdenas (son of the president who consolidated the regime in the 1930s) and Porfirio Muñoz Ledo (former labor secretary and PRI president) led a dissident movement within the PRI, the so-called Corriente Democrática. It demanded an opening of the process of presidential succession and a return to the patrimonial state that honored the legacy of the Mexican Revolution in commitments to nationalism and popular welfare. De la Madrid's government had abandoned even the rhetoric of revolution, leaving the legacy of the regime's founding promise to the dissidents.[36]

Far removed from the discipline that defined the relationship between the president and the PRI during previous decades, the Corriente Democrática challenged de la Madrid's authority to choose his successor and publicly criticized the continuation of technocratic rule implied by the emergence of Carlos Salinas de Gortari as the most likely candidate. Facing the possibility of Cuauhtémoc Cárdenas as a precandidate of the Democratic Current and deepening divisions within the PRI, de la Madrid refused all negotiation and closed the PRI to dissent (as Miguel Alemán had done), contradicting the promises of political modernization so prominent at the beginning of his term. Meanwhile the president orchestrated a public presentation of possible candidates, the *pasarela*, or promenade, hoping to mitigate the tension of dissidence. De la Madrid attempted to use a formal procedure to diffuse a fundamental problem: the rising demands inside and outside the PRI to democratize access to power.

The process culminated when the Corriente Democrática broke from the PRI and later became the Frente Democrático Nacional (FDN). The Frente advanced Cuauhtémoc Cárdenas's candidacy for the presidency, in alliance with the older PARM.[37] Throughout the campaign, a vibrant social movement labeled neo-Cardenismo questioned the economics of neo-liberalism and their social effects. With the inclusion of the recently created Partido Mexicano Socialista (PMS) in the center-left front, a move encouraged by Cárdenas's gradual turn toward the left (helping him overcome the misgivings of those who saw him as an untrustworthy PRIísta), the FDN became the main opposition in the 1988 elections. The renewed alliance between Cardenismo and the Left evoked memories of the 1930s, when the common enemy was fascism, then spreading dangerously across Europe.

In the most contested presidential election since 1952, the PAN offered Manuel J. Clouthier, a militant representative of neopanismo. The campaign was intense, the turnout at polls large. Expectations of a Cárdenas victory were high—and seemed confirmed by early reports from the provinces. Suddenly the opposition faced unprecedented cybernetic fraud: a "system crash" stopped the tabulation. When counting resumed, the regime reported the electoral victory of Carlos Salinas de Gortari. Yet even the official figures showed a decrease in the PRI's vote. The party claimed only 48.74 percent of presidential ballots.[38] Salinas could claim victory, but not a majority. The defeat of many PRI congressional candidates demonstrated that the official party no longer guaranteed electoral victory. Losses suffered by several well-known labor leaders showed the breakdown of the party's once-dominant corporate structure.

Still, the party was not dead. The PAN and the FDN won 240 seats against the PRI's 260, slightly more than half of the Chamber of Deputies. The PRI retained a slim majority, but it was no longer a hegemonic force in the legislature. Despite the apparent frauds that gave the regime and its party a victory, the 1988 elections showed that the polls could be a venue for participation and political change.[39] The opposition was gaining ground, seriously threatening to obtain power. While the PRI retained the presidency and a legislative majority after 1988, "undisciplined" factions of the party explored alternative spaces for political activities, particularly after 1989, when the Partido de la Revolución Democrática (PRD), heir to the FDN, was founded. In processes that were mutually complementary, while the two main opposition parties grew and strengthened, they allowed and nourished political affiliations and possibilities for patronage that became more fluid and uncertain.

The man who eventually became the most conspicuous supporter of modernization through neoliberalism began his term amid severe challenges to his legitimacy. Carlos Salinas de Gortari responded by working to rebuild the presidential powers weakened by de la Madrid. Yet while restoring power to the presidency, Salinas pushed to end the nationalist patrimonial state and the corporate regime. Using resources concentrated in the presidency, Salinas imposed authority over the old political class and the PRI. He "modernized" the old system of *clientelismo*, or party patronage. He established a useful alliance with the PAN that included the negotiation of key elections. He skillfully handled the media to construct a grandiose image of his presidency and eventually brought his political enemies to submission through unrestrained corruption and a "heavy hand."[40]

Early in his administration, Salinas struck against the PRI's corporate power. He arrested the long-entrenched boss of the petroleum workers' union, Joaquín Hernández Galicia, who had refused to support Salinas's candidacy. The violent arrest demonstrated Salinas's will to assert his authority by whatever means necessary against the most powerful, corrupt representatives of "revolutionary nationalism." The conflict strengthened the new president's public image. Salinas also aimed to undermine the old party corporatism by creating the Programa Nacional de Solidaridad (PRONASOL), a separate state program that de facto stole from the PRI the key role of dominant intermediary with the disadvantaged classes. PRONASOL used the early gains of the economic recovery that began in 1990, World Bank financing, and the proceeds of the sale of state enterprises to create a vast network of social support agencies. The goal was to finish off the corporatist web of "the old PRI" and to reconstruct a patronage machine tied directly to the presidency.[41] Salinas's insistence on the virtues of the program prompted rumors that a new reform might replace the decaying PRI with a Solidarity Party.[42]

The replacement did not occur. A complex process to reform the PRI did. The reform was promoted as the re-creation of the party, the establishment of a "new PRI." The goal was to replace the old sectors (agrarian, labor, and popular) with "movements" and territorial structures closer to the Programa Nacional de Solidaridad. Sharpening conflict with the old political class was inevitable. Leaders of the CTM adamantly blocked Salinas's proposal to re-create the party. Still, Luis Donaldo Colosio, Salinas's appointee as PRI president, managed to displace the leaders of the old labor and agrarian sectors from the general party leadership. State governors gained strength in the Consejo Político Nacional, emerging as the most powerful group within the new PRI.[43]

The shift in power and leadership within the PRI came with political reform and offers of democratization intended to strengthen the relationship between President Salinas and the PAN. In 1989 Salinas recognized the PAN victory in state elections in Baja California. Ernesto Ruffo became the first opposition governor in the twentieth century.[44] The discretionary handling of elections to maintain the appearance of democratization led to the negotiations that made Carlos Medina Plascencia the PAN governor of the state of Guanajuato.[45] But when the opposition united around Cuauhtémoc Cárdenas and reconstituted a center-left coalition in the Partido de la Revolución Democrática (PRD), openings and negotiations disappeared: during Salinas's six-year term, more than five hundred PRD members were assassinated across Mexico. PRD electoral victories were not recognized. Salinas appeared open to limited competition from the PAN-business alliance on the center-right, which shared much of his vision of politics, ideology, and modernization. He remained closed to the challenge from the left that had almost cost him the presidency and left him with tarnished legitimacy.

Like his predecessor, Salinas de Gortari favored economic opening over deep political reforms. Unlike de la Madrid, however, Salinas managed to build a mirage of consensus around his modernizing project, bolstered by the apparent success of economic policies (including the promise of NAFTA), the reshaping of patronage links, and the use of the media (a new and crucial component in the political life at the end of the century). But as presidential elections again raised the question of succession, the mirage broke into a thousand pieces.

DISMANTLING THE SYSTEM

The illusory triumph of Salinas's project shattered on January 1, 1994, with the Chiapas insurgency of the Ejército Zapatista de Liberación Nacional (EZLN). The EZLN embodied in opposition the paradox that had become the fundamental contradiction of the late-century model of modernizing development. Indigenous insurgency exploded from the depths of "México profundo" to challenge the neoliberal project, demanding effective democracy along with economic and social justice. The poorest, most marginal of Mexicans refused to wait while free markets generated wealth for some—and promised prosperity to the majority in a distant and uncertain future.

The violent challenge that began with insurgency from outside the regime soon struck within. In the months after the Chiapas uprising, the murders of PRI presidential candidate Luis Donaldo Colosio and party general secretary José Francisco Ruiz Massieu demonstrated new and growing difficulties establishing engineered agreements among political elites—one of the consequences of Salinas's efforts to finish off "the old PRI." The official party collapsed as an arena for negotiation. The institutional mechanism to ensure an orderly presidential succession was broken. Even as the president overcame obstacles and imposed his chosen candidate, Ernesto Zedillo, to replace Colosio as the PRI nominee, Salinas could not prevent months of open talk about the influence of drug traffickers at the highest levels of power and about scandalous corruption within his family and administration. All of this led to a rapid devaluation of the political figure of the president, much of it driven from within the office of the presidency.

Ernesto Zedillo became the PRI presidential candidate in a time of unrest, political uncertainty, and economic deterioration. Facing the emergency, the PRI reconsolidated the forces of official power. No leader or faction broke party discipline to publicly question Zedillo's designation. Regime survival became first priority; PRI leaders and membership closed ranks around President Salinas and his new presidential candidate.

The uncertainties and insecurities proliferating across a society alarmed by insurgency, instability, and a perceived risk of political breakdown produced what was called a "vote of fear" that gave the PRI the presidential victory in 1994. Still, only 48.7 percent of the total vote supported the PRI, confirming the trend toward stagnation evident in previous elections.[46] A few days after the inauguration, the country suffered a devastating economic crisis that brought it to the brink of political and financial bankruptcy. The so-called "December mistake," a sudden devaluation of the peso (in response to an overvaluation sustained during the political season), revealed the fragility of the Mexican economy. The crisis proved long and deep. Promoters of neoliberalism called it an unfortunate but necessary adjustment. Opponents saw the predicted outcome of market-driven globalization. Conflict escalated among political factions.

Facing economic debacle and political illegitimacy, President Zedillo, like his predecessors, began his term promising to accelerate political modernization. Pressured by the neo-Zapatista mobilization and the 1995 economic crisis, Zedillo's government did not interfere in the electoral reform of 1996, the last of the twentieth century. For the first time, the organization of elections was placed in the hands of political parties, the Congress, and citizens through the Instituto Federal Electoral. The Federal Electoral Tribunal became the final authority in electoral disagreements.[47] The new independent electoral institutions passed their first test the following year by recognizing opposition victories. That recognition, necessary and unavoidable, both strengthened electoral processes and worked as a safety valve for growing social tensions.

The 1997 federal elections again discredited the PRI regime and confirmed elections as the privileged way for wide-ranging social groups to engage in politics. For the first time, the PRI lost several governorships and the newly created government of the Federal District (Mexico City). It also lost its majority in the Chamber of Deputies, consolidating the opposition presence in the legislature.[48] Trapped as a state party in a new scenario of national, state, and municipal politics defined by three parties in competition, the PRI had to redefine itself as a true political party for the first time. In key places, it had to become an opposition party.

The fragility of the political system was obvious. If the official party historically supported the presidential system, the party's widening defeats, loss of legitimacy, and political weakness inevitably undermined the president's autonomy and his ability to exercise power. In a scenario curiously similar to the twenties, the Congress recovered its role as an independent branch of government, a counterweight—not a subordinate—to the executive branch. At the same time, opposition electoral victories gave the country a multiparty system instead of the one-party monotony that had been the norm for decades. The resurgent importance and independence of regional powers created additional counterweights to presidential centralism.[49]

During the last years of the twentieth century, Congress reclaimed its role as the privileged forum for discussion and confrontation among political factions, reviving memories of stormy sessions during the postrevolutionary decades. Yet unlike its predecessors in the twenties, the end-of-the-century Congress, constituted by members of diverse party affiliations, no longer responded to strongman interests, regional or local. Nor did it divide into "the official right and the official left," as in the thirties and early forties. And in contrast with the legislatures that after 1946 canceled all dissonance with the presidency (except for a few colorful "appeals" against Miguel de la Madrid's and Carlos Salinas's state-of-the-union messages), Zedillo at least twice endured serious opposition challenges to his government in congressional debates. The Chamber of Deputies repeatedly rejected his proposed federal budgets, forcing intense and complicated negotiations between the secretary of the treasury, the PRI, the PAN, and the PRD.[50] In an extreme act of defiance, the legislature refused Zedillo the authorization (required by the Constitution) to travel to meet with the president of the United States.

As the weight of the presidency, the pivot of the system of centralized power, declined, regional powers strengthened. Lacking the powers of discipline that had sustained earlier presidents, Ernesto Zedillo suffered the defiance of Roberto Madrazo, who refused a presidential request to resign as governor of Tabasco.[51] Manuel Bartlett, governor of Puebla, refused to implement a federal law on the distribution of fiscal funds. Zedillo also failed in several attempts to impose his selections of PRI candidates for state governorships.[52]

As 2000 and another presidential succession approached, the crisis of presidentialism—a key axis of the political system—again became acute. From within the PRI came new threats of internal divisions and demands for real participatory competition. From the beginning of his term, Zedillo had tried to keep a "healthy distance" from his party, establishing an ambiguous relationship with the PRI, using it or fighting it at his convenience. He paid the political cost when in 1996 the PRI's National Assembly approved the so-called "padlocks"—unbreakable requirements of ten years of proven active PRI membership, a leadership position, and prior election to office—as prerequisites to selection as a presidential candidate.[53] As the succession approached, the limits on Zedillo's ability to impose his choice of candidate on a resentful and militant PRI became public knowledge. For the first time in decades, a president—himself the product of presidential designation—was forced to open the selection of a presidential candidate to primary elections. The primary campaign of 1999 fueled public airings of disagreements, creating opportunities for factions, groups, and tendencies—particularly those headed by Governors Madrazo and Bartlett—to organize and gradually take over the party and practice politics beyond the president's authority.

The opposition victory in the presidential elections of July 2000 completed the dismantling of the political machinery that sustained the regime that claimed to be the revolution. The PRI ceased to exist as a state party symbiotically linked to the presidency. A new and unprecedented relationship between the executive and the legislature emerged—a president elected from the opposition faced a Congress in which no party held an absolute majority. No group faced discipline—power that could not be debated or negotiated. As the twenty-first century opened, there reappeared in full view and proud voice the diverse national, regional, and local interests and powers that for decades had struggled, hidden and contained within the suffocating spaces of the "institutionalized revolution."

TOWARD A NEW POLITICAL ORDER

The electoral defeat of the regime forged by the revolution opened questions that must be resolved as a new political order emerges. The reorientation of presidential powers and of the relationships between the president and his political party, the Congress, and the opposition will not be easy. The effects of the end of PRI political control will be debated intensely. New relationships must develop between the different levels of government: federal, state, and municipal. Will a new political class take hold? Or will participation in government be more fluid? How will the government engage diverse social sectors? How will strengthened regional powers deal with a changing national regime?

The symbiotic relationship between the president and the party, the foundation of the political system since the thirties, belongs to the past. In the time of the PRI, conflicts within governments and among political cliques developed and were resolved in secrecy, reinforcing the image and reality of unified presidential-party power. Now, open disputes between "Foxismo" and the PAN revealed to all the limited political-institutional support available to the elected president. Furthermore, the 2000 elections ratified the new relationship between the executive and the legislature that began in 1997 when the PRI lost its majority in Congress, and thus the president lost control of the legislature. From then through the midterm elections of 2003, voters have demonstrated a preference for a legislature that works as a counterweight to executive power, dividing their votes to ensure that the president's party lacks an absolute majority. That clear demonstration of the new electoral openness also reveals a fundamental challenge to political stability and governmental efficacy: a continuing new difficulty in forging agreements between the executive and the Congress.

Could that difficulty, if it continues, eventually undermine the government's ability to rule, as happened in the years after the revolution? It seems clear that a new structural reform must redefine the powers and domains of action of the executive and legislative powers. Still, the Federal Congress has become a key negotiating space between the president and the political and social interests and groups that elected legislators represent. It could also become a privileged arena available for the final mediation and resolution of conflicts that cannot be resolved in other government offices. Demonstrations that begin in the streets—and historically would have marched to the presidential palace or PRI headquarters—now turn to the Congress as the chosen target of discontent and demands.

The disintegration of the PRI as a state party broke the structure of central political control over municipal and local governments, strengthening their autonomy. In addition, the new diversity of the party affiliations of governors and mayors has contributed to a new relationship between the several levels of regime power. It has also created a new domain of conflict where opposition governors heading regional cliques could challenge executive power. All of this contributes to the growing political weight of all governors, not only in their dealings with the president, but also as key actors in the internal affairs of all parties and in their relations with legislatures, state and national.

The PRI's new role as an opposition party also raises questions: With the political discipline long imposed by the president and the party leadership gone, how will the party's diverse sectors and members negotiate with each other, with other parties in Congress, and with the opposition executive? Can the PRI redefine itself as one of multiple parties, adhere to electoral rules, increase its presence, and eventually reclaim power? Can it remain a unified organization, or will it disintegrate, perhaps breaking into regional political blocs, linked to one or more new national parties? The experience of the Fox government points toward a PRI divided between those who try conciliation, seeking immediate roles of importance, and others who assert adamant opposition, looking for an electoral road to reclaim the presidency.

The redefinition of the PRI also forced change in the links between the regime and a society of diverse sectors. It has forced a reconstruction of the means of mediation and negotiation between the government and popular organizations. With the corporate links that long tied many groups to the PRI now weakened, and without the network of protection offered by mechanisms such as PRONASOL, how will the state engage and respond to social demands? Will militants from the old base of the PRI found new organizations, perhaps outside the party, to fight for their demands? Will social organizations find new strength in the regions, perhaps becoming bases for regional and local political forces, like those historically important during the 1920s?

The PRI is not the only institution struggling to redefine itself. The fall of the PRI regime and the new political conditions produced by the 2000 elections have combined to force the PAN and the PRD to rethink their fundamental political positions. All three parties now govern. All must also operate as oppositions. It is a new political world for all. Unfortunately, party leaderships have not risen to these challenges. The political class seems caught in the romance of power, daily more removed from a society with rising expectations and new mobilizations.

The defeat of the regime that emerged from the 1910 revolution did resolve the political opposition's principal demand of the twentieth century: Mexico has opened the door to representative democracy. The results of the July 2000 and 2006 elections also confirm that to broad and diverse social groups, the electoral option is the principal means of political participation. Unfortunately, after years of struggle for trustworthy electoral machinery and believable results, the midterm elections of 2003 and the presidential election of 2006 revealed an electorate uncertain, at times fed up, in the face of the excesses of a system that appears increasingly to be an electoral circus designed to favor the political parties and their leaders. Even worse, the presidential election of 2006 should have consolidated the foundations of a nascent Mexican democracy; instead it produced a crisis of legitimacy based on widespread doubts about whether the count was clean. That disenchantment is an unmistakable alarm signal, confirming the difficulty and uncertainty of a political transformation that, after six years of non-PRI rule, appears to have stagnated.

The complicated process of political opening and change that accelerated during the last years of the twentieth century was part of a great social mobilization in which new forces and leaders, outside the party structure, carried banners of social unrest. As with the export-driven liberalism of the late Porfiriato, globalizing neoliberalism—the paradigm of modernization at the end of the twentieth century—has proved immensely unjust and exclusionary for vast unprotected social sectors. The unequal distribution of the benefits of development and of economic and technological modernization creates social frustration and unrest. Inequity and exclusion drove the indigenous insurgency of the Zapatistas and other rural and indigenous organizations, the fight for debtors' rights of El Barzón, and the mobilizations of schoolteachers, university students, and diverse labor unions, among others.[54]

Behind these challenges lie the social disjunctions and general unrest left by successive economic adjustments followed by repeated crises. Poverty, unemployment, limited opportunity, and the absence of social mobility combine to create widening insecurities accompanied by escalating violence throughout the country, especially in the large cities. The spread of organized crime, notably the drug trade, cannot be concealed, especially since it has infiltrated the institutions of national and regional public security. The judicial system cannot implement clear and equal justice. Powerful lawbreakers carry on with shocking impunity. The institutional incapacity to punish corruption fuels additional discontent.

Paradoxically, while negotiating the opening of the presidential succession, the new independence of the legislature, and the advancing electoral gains of the opposition, the administrations of de la Madrid, Salinas, and Zedillo clung to the "old" authoritarianism when dealing with social challenges. As the formal political system became more democratic, there was a growing use of selective repression. The indigenous zones of Chiapas, Guerrero, Oaxaca, Chihuahua, and the Huasteca were militarized. Governments that engaged in unprecedented political openings faced risks of political and social breakdown—and responded by reinforcing the national

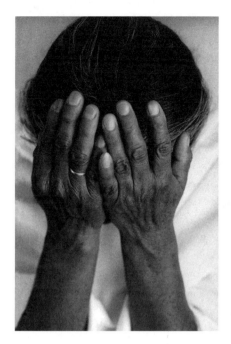

2. The democratic transition of 2000 has not ended violence and repression against indigenous communities and their leaders. Photograph by Norma Suárez, San Miguel de Allende, Mexico.

security system. Accusations of human rights violations, in national and international forums, grew to alarming levels. Despite its democratic origins, the government of Vicente Fox acted like its predecessors when in its last year it turned to repression in response to social demands.

Political alternation has not resolved the most urgent social demands. As a result, the last decades of the twentieth century brought resurgent campesino and indigenous violence. The poorest, most marginal, most excluded peoples did not find a means to resolve social demands and conflicts in the new institutions of electoral democracy. The EZLN, the Ejército Popular Revolucionario (EPR), and other armed groups remain mobilized in different regions of the country. The Fox government, facing an economy in recession with limited political strength, continued the neoliberal policies of its predecessors, generating even greater social discontent.

As in the first years of the 1800s and 1900s, Mexico today grapples with the difficulties of economic transnationalization while an impoverished majority feels increasingly distant from the few who lead the nation, caught halfway between the exhaustion of the "revolutionary" regime constructed in the first decades of the twentieth century and the difficulties of establishing an imagined new political order. The institutions that regulated the negotiation of political conflict, the transmission of presidential power, and the management of social demands are caught in a complex process of transformation. Amid the uncertainties of a newly participatory effort to construct a new regime and a new relationship between the state and society, a vast array of social expectations has emerged, challenging the political process and the economic model.

As in other key moments of Mexico's history, a time of change has revealed the fundamental diversity of a nation that includes enclaves of modernity, enduring sectors clinging to old powers and corporate ways, and emerging groups creating hybrid forms of "communal modernity"— each with different goals, expectations, and demands.[55] There is a shared certainty that Mexico changed on July 2, 2000, although the direction of change remains uncertain. The imagined possibility of a more just and equal path for all Mexicans demands attention, discussion, and debate. Is Mexico now grappling with its definitive transition to democratic modernization? Or is it lurching once again toward breakdown into violent reconstruction? The answers to these historic questions depend on how Mexicans engage the challenges of democracy and social justice in a changing world.

NOTES

1 Jean Meyer, "Estado y sociedad con Calles," in *Historia de la Revolución Mexicana, 1924–1928* (Mexico City: El Colegio de México, 1977).

2 José Varela Ortega and Luis Medina Peña, *Elecciones, alternancia y democracia: España-México, una reflexión comparativa* (Madrid: Editorial Biblioteca Nueva, 2000), 232, 238.

3 Ibid., 243–45.

4 See, for example, Guerrero's case in Armando Bartra, *Guerrero Bronco: Campesinos, ciudadanos y guerrilleros en la Costa Grande* (Mexico City: Ediciones sinfiltro, 1996), chap. 3.

5 Jean Meyer, "Estado y sociedad," 97.

6 Ibid., 175–98. For a concrete example, see Luis Miguel Rionda, "Las elecciones locales guanajuatenses de 1927: La confrontación entre el obregonismo y el callismo en los albores de la institucionalización revolucionaria," paper presented at the XII Congreso Nacional de Estudios Electorales, Mexico City, December 4–8, 2000.

7 The best work on the PNR-PRM is still Luis Javier Garrido's *El partido de la revolución institucionalizada: La formación del nuevo Estado en México, 1928–1945* (Mexico City: SEP–Siglo Veintiuno Editores, 1986). See also Lorenzo Meyer (with Rafael Segovia and Alejandra Lajous), "Los inicios de la institucionalización: La política del Maximato," in *Historia de la Revolución Mexicana, 1928–1934* (Mexico City: El Colegio de México, 1978); and Arnaldo Córdova, *La revolución en crisis: La aventura del maximato* (Mexico City: Cal y Arena, 1995).

8 Benito Nacif, *El impacto del PNR en las relaciones entre el ejecutivo y el legislativo, 1928–1934*, working paper 82 (Mexico City: CIDE, 1998).

9 François-Xavier Guerra, *México: Del Antiguo Régimen a la Revolución*, vol. 1 (Mexico City: Fondo de Cultura Económica, 1988). See also his essay in this volume.

10 Lorenzo Meyer, "Los inicios de la institucionalización," 273–92.

11 For an outline of the PRM's territorial and sectorial (or "direct and indirect") structures, see Luis Javier Garrido, *El partido de la revolución*, 320.

12 Luis Medina, "Del cardenismo al avilacamachismo," in *Historia de la Revolución Mexicana, 1940–1952* (Mexico City: El Colegio de México, 1978); Ma. del Carmen Nava, "Las elecciones federales de 1946," in *Revolución y contrarrevolución en México: IX jornadas de historia de Occidente* (Mexico City: Centro de Estudios de la Revolución Mexicana Lázaro Cárdenas, 1986), 206–8; Rogelio Hernández Rodríguez, "La historia moderna del PRI: Entre la autonomía y el sometimiento," *Foro Internacional* 40, no. 160 (April–June 2000): 281–83.

13 A revealing case was the appointment of the senator and colonel Carlos I. Serrano as chair of the Congress's Permanent Commission at the beginning of the six-year term as chief of the political control of the Chambers. Besides his duties as a legislator, Col. Serrano organized and controlled the Federal Security Directorate during Alemán's government. Elisa Servín, *Ruptura y oposición: El movimiento henriquista, 1945–1954* (Mexico City: Cal y Arena, 2001), 99.

14 John Skirius, *José Vasconcelos y la cruzada de 1929* (Mexico City: Siglo Veintiuno Editores, 1978); Córdova, *La revolución en crisis*.

15 Albert Michaels, *The Mexican Election of 1940* (Buffalo: State University of New York Press, 1971); Ariel José Contreras, *México 1940: Industrialización y crisis política* (Mexico City: Siglo Veintiuno Editores, 1977); Leticia González del Rivero, "La oposición almazanista y las elecciones de 1940," *Historia y Grafía* 3 (1994): 11–33.

16 Soledad Loaeza, *El Partido Acción Nacional: La larga marcha, 1939–1994* (Mexico City: Fondo de Cultura Económica, 1999), 170–81.

17 Rafael Loyola Díaz, "Ezequiel Padilla: Un camaleón revolucionario," *Historia y Grafía* 3 (1994): 35–60; Nava, "Las elecciones federales," 221–35; Juan Molinar Horcasitas, *El tiempo de la legitimidad* (Mexico City: Cal y Arena, 1991), 45.

18 Servín, *Ruptura y oposición*.

19 Loaeza, *El Partido Acción Nacional*, 308–13.

20 A typical case involved the municipal elections of San Luis Potosí in 1958 won by Salvador Nava, the candidate of the Unión Cívica Potosina. In 1967 other conflicts appeared in Mérida and Hermosillo and in 1968 in Tijuana and Mexicali. Adriana López Monjardín, *La lucha por los ayuntamientos: Una utopía viable* (Mexico City: Siglo Veintiuno Editores, 1986), 50–62. In 1962 the state of Guerrero also experienced an intense electoral conflict. Bartra, *Guerrero Bronco*, 118.

21 A narration of these mobilizations can be found in Ilán Semo, "El ocaso de los mitos (1958–1968)," in *México, un pueblo en la historia*, vol. 6, ed. Enrique Semo (Mexico City: Alianza Editorial Mexicana, 1989).

22 See Lorenzo Meyer's essay in this book.

23 Regarding the political reform, see Octavio Rodríguez Araujo, *La reforma política y los partidos en México* (Mexico City: Siglo Veintiuno Editores, 1980); Alberto Aziz and Jorge Alonso, *Reforma política y deformaciones electorales* (Mex-

ico City: CIESAS, 1984); Molinar, *El tiempo de la legitimidad*, 95; Varela and Medina, *Elecciones, alternancia y democracia*, 268.

24 Barry Carr, *La izquierda mexicana a través del siglo XX* (Mexico City: Ediciones Era, 1996), 281–304.

25 Rolando Cordera and Carlos Tello, *México: La disputa por la nación; Perspectivas y opciones del desarrollo* (Mexico City: Siglo Veintiuno Editores, 1981).

26 Carlos Arriola Woog, *Los empresarios y el Estado 1970–1982* (Mexico City: UNAM–Miguel Angel Porrúa, 1988); Rogelio Hernández Rodríguez, *Empresarios, banca y Estado: El conflicto durante el gobierno de José López Portillo, 1976–1982* (Mexico, FLACSO–Miguel Angel Porrúa, 1988).

27 In July 1969 Carlos A. Madrazo, the PRI's former president, lost his life in an airplane accident near the city of Monterrey. His death applied the brakes to the creation of a new political organization that, under the possible name of Partido de la Patria Nueva, would certainly have caused a new PRI split surrounding the succession of Gustavo Díaz Ordaz. Raúl Cruz Zapata, *Carlos A. Madrazo: Biografía política* (Mexico City: Editorial Diana, 1988).

28 See Lorenzo Meyer's essay in this book.

29 Molinar, *El tiempo de la legitimidad*, 123–33; Loaeza, *El Partido Acción Nacional*, 366; César Cansino, *La transición mexicana, 1977–2000* (Mexico City: Centro de Estudios de Política Comparada, 2000), 163–72.

30 Alberto Aziz Nassif, *Chihuahua: Historia de una alternativa* (Mexico City: CIESAS–La Jornada Ediciones, 1994).

31 Loaeza, *El Partido Acción Nacional*, chap. 5.

32 Adriana López Monjardín, *La lucha*; Alvaro Arreola Ayala, "Elecciones municipales," in *Las elecciones en México: Evolución y perspectivas*, ed. Pablo González Casanova (Mexico City: Siglo Veintiuno Editores, 1985), 329–47. See also Antonio Annino's essay in this volume.

33 Alberto Aziz Nassif, "Regional Dimensions of Democratization," in *Mexico's Alternative Political Futures*, ed. Wayne A. Cornelius, Judith Gentleman, and Peter H. Smith (San Diego: Center for U.S.-Mexican Studies, University of California, 1989), 87–108.

34 Kevin Middlebrook, "The CTM and the Future of State-Labor Relations," in Cornelius, Gentleman, and Smith, *Mexico's Alternative Political Futures*, 291–305; Ilán Bizberg, "La crisis del corporativismo mexicano," *Foro Internacional* 30, no. 120 (1990): 695–735.

35 Héctor Aguilar Camín, *Después del milagro* (Mexico City: Cal y Arena, 1988), 71.

36 Elisa Servín, "Perspectivas de medio siglo: Dos disputas por la revolución," in *El siglo de la Revolución Mexicana*, ed. Jaime Bailón Corres, Carlos Martínez Assad, and Pablo Serrano Alvarez, vol. 1 (Mexico City: INEHRM, 2000), 287–96.

37 The process from the origins of the Corriente Democrática until its split from the PRI is analyzed in Luis Javier Garrido, *La Ruptura: La Corriente Democrática del PRI* (Mexico City: Editorial Grijalbo, 1993).

38 This percentage is based on the total of issued votes, including void votes and votes for unregistered candidates. Molinar, *El tiempo de la legitimidad*, 218.

39 For an analysis of the election's results, see Molinar, *El tiempo de la legit-

imidad, chap. 5; and Loaeza, *El Partido Acción Nacional*, 450–75. The 1988 elections are fully analyzed in Jaime González Graf, ed., *Las elecciones de 1988 y la crisis del sistema político* (Mexico City: Editorial Diana, 1989).

40 Miguel Ángel Centeno, *Democracy within Reason: Technocratic Revolution in Mexico* (University Park: Pennsylvania State University Press, 1994); Wayne A. Cornelius, Ann L. Craig, and Jonathan Fox, eds., *Transforming State-Society Relations in Mexico: The National Solidarity Strategy* (San Diego: Center for U.S.-Mexican Studies, University of California, La Jolla, 1994); Lorenzo Meyer, *La segunda muerte de la Revolución Mexicana* (Mexico City: Cal y Arena, 1992), chaps. 3–4; Loaeza, *El Partido Acción Nacional*, chap. 7.

41 Denise Dresser, *Neopopulist Solutions to Neoliberal Problems: Mexico's National Solidarity Program*, Current Issues Brief 4, University of California, San Diego, Center for U.S.-Mexican Studies, 1991. See also Guillermo de la Peña's essay in this volume.

42 Centeno, *Democracy within Reason*, 65; Wayne A. Cornelius, Ann L. Craig, and Jonathan Fox, "Mexico's National Solidarity Program: An Overview," in Cornelius, Craig, and Fox, *Transforming State-Society Relations in Mexico*, 19.

43 Rogelio Hernández, "La historia moderna del PRI," 293–97.

44 Irma Campuzano Montoya, *Baja California en tiempos del PAN* (Mexico City: La Jornada Ediciones, 1995).

45 Loaeza, *El Partido Acción Nacional*, 498–504.

46 Cansino, *La transición mexicana*, 306.

47 Varela and Medina, *Elecciones, alternancia y democracia*, 298–99.

48 Cancino, *La transición mexicana*, 305.

49 Wayne A. Cornelius, Todd A. Eisenstadt, and Jane Hindley, *Subnational Politics and Democratization in Mexico* (San Diego: Center for U.S.-Mexican Studies, University of California, La Jolla, 1999); Peter M. Ward and Victoria E. Rodríguez with Enrique Cabrero Mendoza, *New Federalism and State Government in Mexico: Bringing the States Back In*, U.S.-Mexican Policy Report no. 9, Lyndon B. Johnson School of Public Affairs, University of Texas, Austin, 1999; Rogelio Hernández Rodríguez, "Las gubernaturas como nuevos factores de gobernabilidad," and Peter M. Ward, "De clientelismo a tecnocracia: Cambios recientes y nuevos retos en la gobernabilidad municipal en México," in Bailón, Martínez Assad, and Serrano, *El siglo*, 113–21, 27–44.

50 María Amparo Casar, "Las relaciones entre el poder ejecutivo y el legislativo: El caso de México," *Política y Gobierno* 6, no. 1 (1999): 83–128.

51 Todd A. Eisenstadt, "Electoral Federalism or Abdication of Presidential Authority? Gubernatorial Elections in Tabasco," in Cornelius, Eisenstadt and Hindley, *Subnational Politics*, 269–93.

52 María Amparo Casar, "Las relaciones," 116.

53 Rogelio Hernández, "La historia moderna del PRI," 298–305.

54 See Guillermo de la Peña's essay in this volume.

55 Guillermo de la Peña, "La modernidad comunitaria," *Desacatos* 3 (2000).

CONTRIBUTORS ✹

ANTONIO ANNINO is a professor of Latin American history and institutions at the University of Florence. He has authored *Dall'insurrezione al regime: Strategie instituzionali e politiche di massa a Cuba, 1952–1965* (1984). He has edited *Historia de las elecciones en Iberoamérica, siglo XIX: De la formación del espacio político nacional* (1995) and coedited, with François-Xavier Guerra, *Inventando la nación: Iberoamérica, siglos XVIII y XIX* (2003).

GUILLERMO DE LA PEÑA is a research professor of anthropology at the Centro de Investigaciones y Estudios Superiores en Antropología Social, in Guadalajara, Mexico. He is author of *A Legacy of Promises: Agriculture, Politics, and Ritual in the Morelos Highlands of Mexico* (1981) and coeditor, with Luis Vázquez de León, of *La antropología sociocultural en el México del milenio: Búsquedas, encuentros y transiciones* (2002).

FRANÇOIS-XAVIER GUERRA was a professor at the University of Paris I, the Sorbonne, until his death in 2002. Among the key works of his rich legacy are *Le Mexique: De l'Ancien Régime al la Revolution* (2 vols., 1985) and *Modernidad e independencias: Ensayos sobre las revoluciones hispánicas* (1992).

FRIEDRICH KATZ is the Morton D. Hull Distinguished Service Professor Emeritus in History at the University of Chicago. He is author of *The Secret War in Mexico: Europe, the United States, and the Mexican Revolution* (1982) and *The Life and Times of Pancho Villa* (1998), and editor of *Riot, Rebellion, and Revolution: Rural Social Conflict in Mexico* (1988).

ALAN KNIGHT is a professor of the history of Latin America, Oxford University. He has published *The Mexican Revolution* (2 vols., 1986), *Mexico: From the Beginning to the Spanish Conquest* (2002), *Mexico: The Colonial Era* (2002), and *Mexico: The Nineteenth and Twentieth Centuries* (2006).

LORENZO MEYER is a professor at the Colegio de México. Among his many works are *México y los Estados Unidos en el conflicto petrolero, 1917–1942* (1981), *El cactus y el olivo: Las relaciones de México y España en el siglo XX* (2001), and *El estado en busca del ciudadano* (2005). He is coeditor, with Ilán Bizberg, of *Una historia contemporánea de México* (4 vols., 2003, 2005).

LETICIA REINA is a research professor at the Dirección de Estudios Historicos of the Instituto Nacional de Antropología e Historia in Mexico City. She has authored *Rebeliones campesinas en México, 1819–1916* (1980) and *Caminos de luz y sombra: Historia de los pueblos indios de Oaxaca, siglo XIX* (2004), and edited *La reindianización de América, siglo XIX* (1997) and *Los retos de la etnicidad en los estados-nacion del siglo XXI* (2000).

ENRIQUE SEMO is a research professor on the Faculty of Economics of the Universidad Nacional Autónoma de México. He has written *The History of Capitalism in Mexico: Its Origins, 1521–1763* (1993), *La búsqueda* (2 vols., 2003–4), and *De los cazadores y recolectores a las sociedades tributarias en Mesoamérica* (2006).

ELISA SERVÍN is a research professor at the Dirección de Estudios Historicos of the Instituto Nacional de Antropología e Historia in Mexico City. She is author of *Ruptura y oposición: El movimiento henriquista, 1945–1954* (2001), and of *La oposición política: Otra cara de siglo XX mexicano* (2006). With Leticia Reina, she coedited *Crisis, reforma y revolución: México, historias de fin de siglo* (2002).

JOHN TUTINO serves as chair of the history department at Georgetown University. He is author of *From Insurrection to Revolution in Mexico: Social Bases of Agrarian Violence, 1750–1940* (1986) and the forthcoming *Making a New World: Forging Atlantic Capitalism in the Bajío and Spanish North America*.

ERIC VAN YOUNG is a professor of history at the University of California, San Diego. Among his publications are *Hacienda and Market in Eighteenth-Century Mexico: The Rural Economy of the Guadalajara Region, 1675–1810* (1981), *La crisis del orden colonial: Estructura agraria y rebeliones populares de la Nueva España* (1992), and *The Other Rebellion: Popular Violence, Ideology, and the Struggle for Mexican Independence* (2001).

Liberation Army), 114, 120, 212, 255, 256–57, 297, 323, 348, 380: National Indigenous Congress and, 337; Mexican Left and, 351, 359; PRD and, 359–361. *See also* Indigenous movements

Ejidos, 7; as corporate landholding, 149; and state consolidation, 243–44, 249; privatization, 285, 310–11

Election: during nineteenth century, 135–36, 140; during late twentieth century, 91–92; *of 1988*, 114, 254–55, 289, 295, 318–19, 347, 355–57; *of 1994*, 347–48, 381; *of 1995–2000*, 113–120; *of 1997*, 382; *of 2000*, 13, 119, 259, 273, 274, 277–78, 280, 296, 299, 357, 363, 383, 385–86; *of 2006*, ix, 173–74, 385–86. *See also* Cádiz: Cortes and Constitution; Democratic transition

Encomiendas, 217

Environmental movement, 329

Escobar, José Gonzalo, revolt by, 367

Exploitation. *See* Symbiotic exploitation

Federación de Partidos del Pueblo Mexicano, FPPM (Federation of Parties of the Mexican People). *See* Henríquez Guzmán, Miguel

Federalists, 135; conflict with centralists, 138

Ferdinand VII, 6, 57 n. 47

Fertilizantes Mexicanos, FERTIMEX (Mexican Fertilizers), 323

Fondo Bancario de Protección al Ahorro, FOBAPROA (Bank to Protect Savings Funds). *See also* Crisis: of 1995

Fox, Vicente, 13, 17; 2000 victory, 113, 172, 255, 278, 297, 299, 334–35, 348, 357; Pa' que te alcance and, 291; guest workers treaty, 293; authoritarianism, 386–87. *See also*

Democratic transition; Partido Acción Nacional

French intervention, 3, 139, 185–86, 272, 281, 283, 298

French Revolution, 23–24, 63; influences, 130

Frente Democrático Nacional, FDN (National Democratic Front), 289, 378

Frente Nacional Democrático Popular (National Popular Democratic Front), 314

Frente Nacional de Pueblos Indígenas, 345 n. 82

Galván, Rafael, 352

García Paniagua, Javier, 373–74

Garzón, Alfonso, 309

General Agreement on Tariffs and Trade (GATT), 285, 288, 318

Germany: propaganda campaign in Mexico, 195–97; trade with Mexico, 201. *See also* Hitler, Adolf

Globalization, 1, 15, 258–61, 279, 292, 346; neoliberalism and, vii, x, 114, 386; NAFTA and, 5; democracy and, 16; businesses and, 294–95; El Barzón and, 342 n. 52

Goethe, Johann Wolfgang von, 24

Gómez Pedraza, Manuel, letter to Iturbide, 88. *See also* Iturbide, Agustín de

Gordillo, Elba Esther, 183

Green Revolution, 249–51. *See also* Ecological autonomy

Grito de Dolores. *See* Hidalgo y Costilla, Miguel

Guadalajara explosions (1992), 328. *See also* Movimiento Civil de Damnificados

Henequen, Yucatán and, 236, 238, 244

Henríquez Guzmán, Miguel, 309; Federación de Partidos del Pueblo Mexicano, 371

Lombardo Toledano, Vicente, 203, 204; Unión General de Obreros y Campesinos Mexicanos and, 308. *See also* Confederación de Trabajadores de México

López Mateos, Adolfo, 310, 372

López Obrador, Andrés Manuel, 360

López Portillo, José, 284–85, 288, 313, 317, 374, 376; political opening, 314; electoral reform, 347, 372–73

Macehuales, 95; macehualization of power, 96–97. *See also* Communities: indigenous; Pueblos

Madero, Francisco I.: project, 144–45; insurrection, 146–47, 365; presidency, 147–48

Madrazo, Carlos A., Partido de la Patria Nueva and, 390 n. 27

Madrazo, Roberto, 183, 383

Madrid, Miguel de la, 277, 285; General Agreement on Tariffs and Trade and, 288; rural agenda, 317–18; earthquake and, 327; rebellion against, 355; presidential candidacy, 374–75; confrontation with PRI hard-liners, 376–77; authoritarianism, 386–87

Maistre, Joseph de, 24

Maquilas, 293

Maximilian of Habsburg, 185–86, 234, 281, 283, 298. *See also* French intervention

Maya rebellion, 233

Meixueiro, Guillermo, 109–10

Mendieta, Jerónimo de, 80

Mestizaje, 26, 296–97

Mexican-American War, 3–4, 6, 51, 185, 232–33, 281, 283, 291

Mexican independence, 8, 10, 26, 50, 65, 153, 229, 280. *See also* Wars for independence

Mexican Left. *See* Left, Mexican

Mexican Mesoamerica, 237–40. *See also* Spanish Mesoamerica

"Mexican Miracle," ix, 4, 251, 275

Mexican North America, 236–37. *See also* Spanish North America

Mexican Revolution, 129, 150, 288, 296–97; consolidation, 51; World War I and, 194–95; turn to the right, 208; regime of, 365–72. *See also* Revolution: of 1910

Mexico City, 4, 40, 217; earthquake, 326–27

Middle class: expansion during Porfiriato, 142; urbanization and, 249; liberals and, 278, 284; Partido Acción Nacional and, 307; urban mobilizations and, 310, 336

Migrations, ix, 204, 236, 293; neoliberalism and, 5; demographic changes and, 232; golondrino workers, 311–12

Monarquía Indiana (Torquemada), 79

Montiel, Arturo, 183

Mora, José María, 294

Moral economy, 322, 342 n. 49. *See also* Barzón, El

Morelos y Pavón, José María, 50, 69, 72, 184

Motolinía, Toribio de, 80

Movimiento Civil de Damnificados, 328; demands, 343–44 n. 66

Movimiento de Liberación Nacional, MLN (National Liberation Movement); Cárdenas, Lázaro and, 309

Movimiento Urbano Popular, MUP (Urban Popular Movement), 315

Muñoz Ledo, Porfirio, 355, 377

NAFTA (North American Free Trade Agreement), 1, 5, 9, 18, 120, 254, 293; Ejército Zapatista de Liberación Nacional and, 257; neoliberalism and, 258; Salinas administration and, 277, 292, 318

Napoleon Bonaparte. *See* Bonaparte, Napoleon

Nation-state, 95, 137

Natural law. *See* Jesuits

Nazis. *See* Hitler, Adolf

Neo-cardenismo, PRD and, 354, 356–57. *See also* Cárdenas, Cuauhtémoc

Neolatifundia, 312, 339–40 n. 23

Neoliberalism, viii, 5, 14, 15, 170, 172, 254, 272–73, 274, 275–76, 281, 287, 288–89, 292–96, 355, 372–80; globalization and, vii, 114, 386; populist parties' conversion to, 165; positivism and, 170; NAFTA and, 258; North American models, 292; indigenous people and, 296; Catholic Church and, 298–99; the Left and, 98–299; peasant organizations and, 320; Salinas and, 347; de la Madrid and, 375

New Spain, 5–6

Nongovernmental organizations (NGOs), 323–24

Obregón, Álvaro, 7, 149, 205–6, 24, 243, 279; Calles and, 366. *See also* Constitutionalists

Oil: boom, 4, 180–81 n. 101; shocks, 165; Díaz and, 189; nationalization, 201–2, 204, 247–48; bonanza and crisis, 282, 284–85

Organization of Petroleum Exporting Countries (OPEC), 274

Pa' que te alcance. *See* Fox, Vicente; Programa de Educación y Salud

Padilla, Ezequiel, 370–71

Partido Acción Nacional, PAN (National Action Party), 278, 280, 289, 297, 299, 307, 370, 385; entrepreneurs and, 374–75; "Foxismo" and, 384

Partido Agrario y Obrero. *See* Jaramillo, Rubén

Partido Comunista Mexicano, PCM (Mexican Communist Party), 204, 352, 383

Partido de la Revolución Democrática, PRD (Party of the Democratic Revolution), 16, 116, 119, 173, 290, 319, 347–48, 354, 357–59, 378–80, 385; Ejército Zapatista de Liberación Nacional and, 359–61

Partido de la Revolución Mexicana, PRM, 279, 368. *See also* Partido Revolucionario Institucional

Partido Liberal Mexicano, PLM (Liberal Mexican Party), 175

Partido Mexicano Socialista, PMS (Mexican Socialist Party), 353–54

Partido Nacional Revolucionario, PNR, 279, 367. *See also* Partido Nacional Institutional

Partido Popular, PP (Popular Party), 308, 371. *See also* Lombardo Toledano, Vicente

Partido Revolucionario Institutional, PRI (Institutional Revolutionary Party), 169, 171–72, 182–83, 273–74, 276–77, 280, 289–91, 307–8, 312, 363–65, 375; regime crisis and defeat in 2000, 113, 115–18, 299, 357, 363; casualty of 2006, 173–74; Partido Nacional Revolucionario (PNR), 279, 367; Partido de la Revolución Mexicana (PRM), 279, 368; new role as opposition party, 384–85

Partido Socialista Unificado de México, PSUM (Socialist Unified Party of Mexico), 353, 373

Patronato, 138

Petroleum. *See* Oil

Plan de Ayala, 214. *See also* Zapata, Emiliano

Plan de Iguala, 70, 71. *See also* Iturbide, Agustín de

Plan of Veracruz, 73

Political culture, 95

Political rights, 345 n. 83

Populism, 165, 180 n. 98; decompression and, 168–69; in Latin America, 182 n. 116; neopopulism, 284, 288

Porfiriato. *See* Díaz, Porfirio

Positivism, 170

Postliminium right, 78, 90 n. 13

Postmodernism, globalization and, 260–61

Presidentialism, 369–70, 382–83

Privatization of lands, under liberals, 234–35

Programa de Apoyos Directos al Campo, PROCAMPO (Program for Direct Support to Rural Areas), 321

Programa de Educación y Salud, PROGRESA (Health and Education Program), 291, 337

Programa Integral para el Desarrollo, PIDER (Integral Rural Development Program), 312

Programa Nacional de Solidaridad, PRONASOL (National Solidarity Program), 290–91, 319, 336–37, 379. *See also* Salinas de Gortari, Carlos

Pronunciamiento, 136

Pueblos, 66, 77, 85–87, 115, 122, 131–32, 134–35; liberalism and, 67, 75, 84; Reforma and, 87–88; political culture, 95–99, 103–6; participation in elections, 99; electoral conflicts during Porfiriato, 108–12. *See also* Communities: indigenous; Macehuales

Pulque, 223, 225

Quiroga, Vasco de, 78–79

Railroads, 8, 194, 237. *See also* Díaz, Porfirio

Reagan, Ronald, 276

Reforma: Laws of, 87–88; war of, 139, 233–34, 283, 286–87. *See also* Church, Catholic; Conservatives; Constitution: of 1857; Liberals

Repartimiento, 219

Representation, 136

Republics: indigenous (Repúblicas de indios), 5, 6, 8, 59 n.59, 66–67, 92, 218, 222, 225; and Cádiz liberalism, 229–230. *See also* Communities; Liberalism; Pueblos

Revolution, 2, 15; of 1810 and 1910, ix, x, xii, 2, 211; of 1910, vii, 4, 13, 153, 159–61, 168–69, 278–79, 299, 365–67; period of 1910–1940, 15, 247–48; period of 1910–1970, 161–62; politics of, 179 n. 75. *See also* Mexican Revolution

Rights of peoples (*jus gentium*), 78, 79, 90 n. 17

Rockefeller Foundation, 249

Ruiz Cortines, Adolfo, repression of, 372

Ruiz Massieu, José Francisco, murder of, 381

Salinas de Gortari, Carlos, 120, 176, 182 n. 121, 272, 290, 295–96, 319, 341 n. 42; parallels with Porfiriato, 170; Ejército Zapatista de Liberación Nacional and, 257; North American Free Trade Agreement and, 277, 292, 318; economic reforms, 279, 285, 380; 1988 election and, 289; Catholic Church and, 298; neoliberalism and, 347, 379; authoritarianism, 386–87. *See also* Programa Nacional de Solidaridad

Santa Anna, Antonio López de, 283

Santos Zelaya, José, 189

September 11, 2000, 275; impact on Mexico, 173, 293, 348

Sierra, Justo, 284

Silver, 217, 219–20

Urbanization, 249, 251; industrialization and, 251. *See also* Ecological autonomy

Urban movements, 315–16, 325–29; women and, 328–29

Vasconcelos, José, 370

Vecinos (citizens), 33, 63–64, 89 n. 1

Velázquez, Fidel, 203; confrontation with Miguel de la Madrid, 376. *See also* Confederación de Trabajadores de México

Veracruz, Plan of, 73

Victory of 2000. *See* Democratic transition.

Villa, Pancho (Francisco), 7, 213, 237; attack on Columbus, N.M., 192; expropriations, 192–93; Zapata and, 240–43; ecological autonomy and, 242

Virgin of Guadalupe, 26, 27, 80–81

Virgin of Immaculate Conception (Cuautitlán), 33–36

Vitoria, Francisco de, 77

Wars for independence, vii, 1, 6, 8, 10, 51, 81, 184, 213, 230. *See also* Mexican independence

Women: migration, 252–53; employment, 306; urban social movements and, 328–29; in rural areas, 344 n. 70

World Bank, 276

World War I, 13, 164, 186; Mexico and, 190–99, 207–8

World War II, ix, 4, 13, 14, 186, 247–48; Mexico and, 199–205, 207–8

Yaqui war, 245

Zapata, Emiliano, 7, 16, 159, 213–14; Villa and, 240–43; ecological autonomy and, 240–41

Zapatistas uprising (1994). *See* Ejército Zapatista de Liberación Nacional

Zavala, Lorenzo de, 291

Zavaleta Pact, 73

Zedillo, Ernesto, 182 n. 121, 277, 286, 291, 334–35, 348, 381; authoritarianism, 386–87

ELISA SERVÍN

is a research professor at the Dirección de
Estudios Historicos of the Instituto Nacional de
Antropología e Historia in Mexico City.

LETICIA REINA

is a research professor at the Dirección de
Estudios Historicos of the Instituto Nacional de
Antropología e Historia in Mexico City.

JOHN TUTINO

serves as the chair of the Department of History
at Georgetown University.

Library of Congress Cataloging-in-Publication Data

Crisis, reforma y revolución. English
Cycles of conflict, centuries of change : crisis, reform,
and revolution in Mexico / edited by Elisa Servín, Leticia
Reina, and John Tutino.
p. cm.
Includes bibliographical references and index.
Rev. and expanded Spanish text translated into English.
ISBN-13: 978-0-8223-3985-4 (cloth : alk. paper)
ISBN-13: 978-0-8223-4002-7 (pbk. : alk. paper)
1. Mexico—History—19th century. 2. Mexico—Economic
conditions—19th century. 3. Mexico—Social conditions—
19th century. 4. Mexico—History—20th century.
5. Mexico—Economic conditions—20th century. 6. Mexico—
Social conditions—20th century. I. Servín, Elisa II. Reina,
Leticia. III. Tutino, John. IV. Title.
F1231.5.C8513 2007
972'.04—dc22   2007007935